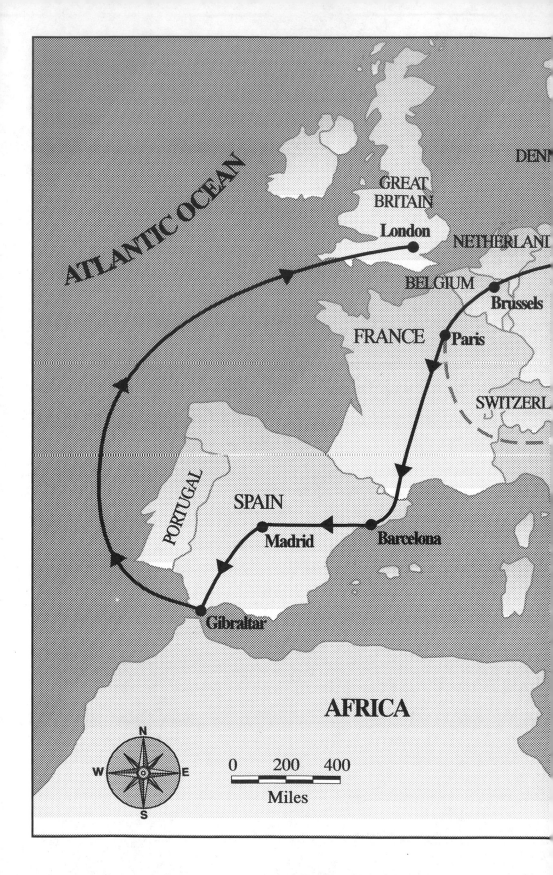

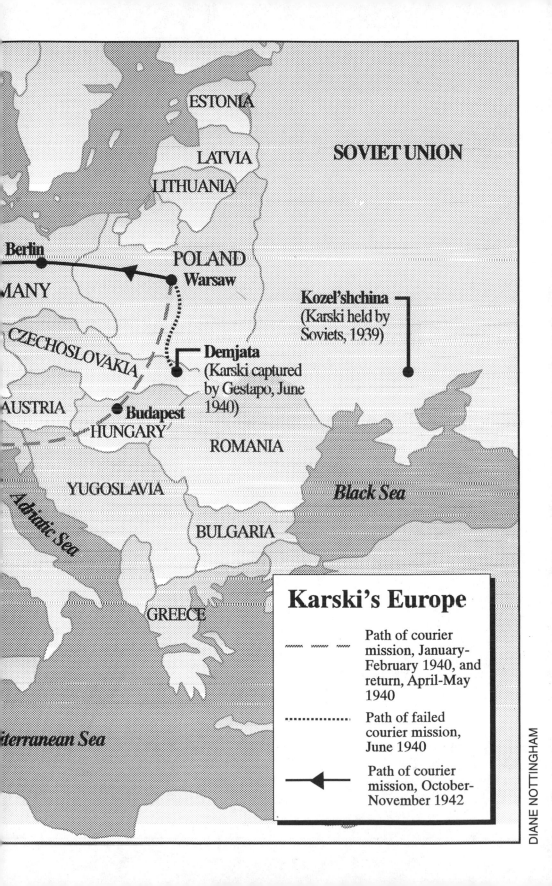

ESTONIA

LATVIA

LITHUANIA

SOVIET UNION

Berlin

POLAND

Warsaw

...MANY

Kozel'shchina
(Karski held by
Soviets, 1939)

CZECHOSLOVAKIA

Demjata
(Karski captured
by Gestapo, June
1940)

AUSTRIA

Budapest

HUNGARY

ROMANIA

YUGOSLAVIA

Black Sea

Adriatic Sea

BULGARIA

GREECE

Karski's Europe

— · — · —   Path of courier
mission, January-
February 1940, and
return, April-May
1940

....   Path of failed
courier mission,
June 1940

◀——   Path of courier
mission, October-
November 1942

...iterranean Sea

DIANE NOTTINGHAM

KARSKI

How One Man Tried to Stop the Holocaust

E. Thomas Wood
Stanisław M. Jankowski

Foreword by Elie Wiesel

John Wiley & Sons, Inc.

New York • Chichester • Brisbane • Toronto • Singapore

Copyright © 1994 by E. Thomas Wood and Stanisław M. Jankowski
Published by John Wiley & Sons, Inc.

Library of Congress Cataloging-in-Publication Data:
Wood, E. Thomas.
    Code name—Karski / E. Thomas Wood and Stanisław M. Jankowski.
        p.   cm.
    Includes bibliographical references and index.
    ISBN 0–471–01856–2
    1. Karski, Jan, 1914–   . 2. World War, 1939–1945—Underground
movements—Poland—Biography. 3. Holocaust, Jewish (1939–1945)—
Poland. 4. Poland—History—Occupation, 1939–1945. 5. Jews—Poland—
Persecutions. 6. Poland—Ethnic relations. I. Jankowski, Stanisław M.,
1945–   . II. Title.
D802.P6W65   1994
940.53'37–dc20   94–9435

Printed in the United States of America

10 9 8 7 6 5 4 3 2 1

To Jan Karski
and to the memory of
Pola Nirenska Karski

Contents

Foreword   vii

Preface   ix

Rites of Initiation: August 1939—June 1940
1. Autumn of Flight   3
2. Apprentice to the Underground   26
3. Off to the Phony War   44

Life on the Edge: June 1940—September 1942
4. Sacrifice   69
5. A Routine Existence   91
6. Witness   111

Terrible Secrets: October 1942—September 1943
7. Carrying the Message   135
8. In Official Circles   157
9. Defeat in Victory   181

Hearts and Minds: September 1943—July 1945
10. Unmasked   205
11. Fame in Vain   223

Epilogue
Silence Vowed, Silence Broken   243

Glossary of Names   260
Sources and Notes   268
Index   309

Foreword

I owe my meeting with Jan Karski to an idea that came to me in Moscow.

An explanation may be in order.

It was August of 1979. In my capacity as Chairman of the President's Commission on the Holocaust, I found myself in the Soviet Union at the head of an official delegation. Among the personalities to whom the government officials introduced me was the colonel who liberated Auschwitz. We exchanged impressions and memories of the last night we spent there, each in his own world separated by the front line. I was struck by the fact that the person to whom I was speaking had been the first free man to view the abyss. That was how the idea of organizing an international conference of camp liberators was born. Let them bear witness for us. Someone suggested Karski's name: Hadn't he seen, with his own eyes, the implementation of the "Final Solution"? Hadn't he, better and more than others, tried to stop it? The idea tempted me, but . . . where did he reside? What was he doing? Was he still alive? I wasn't the only one who believed him dead.

They introduced him to me during the conference. It was urgent that he see me for a specific reason: so that I would permit him to speak more than the twenty or thirty minutes allotted the different speakers. I asked him how many minutes he needed. His answer was brief: thirty-two. How could he be certain? He was.

His poignant testimony was among the best of the conference.

~

I am more than pleased to have helped him rediscover the support of a large following in this way. What he has to say is important; one must listen. He deserves to be better known, better appreciated.

I'm familiar with his adventure, having read his autobiographical *Story of a Secret State*, published in 1944 in Boston and, unfortunately, no longer available. In it he tells of his life in Poland before and during the war, his imprisonment first by the Soviets and then by the Germans, his activities in the Polish resistance which fought with undeniable bravery but found itself confronted with internal divisions, his secret missions in France, Great Britain, and the

United States. Was his life a great story? It was more than that; it is a masterpiece of courage, integrity, and humanism.

How can one fail to admire this great Pole—great in every sense of the word—who dared to reveal and condemn the anti-Semitism that prevailed in various chauvinistic groups of the Polish underground—this fervent Catholic who risked his life to protect millions of Jews destined to perish in the death camps that the Germans had established in his country? Obsessed by their tragedy, he became unable to think of anything else. He spoke of it to everyone he was able to meet—statesmen, politicians, journalists, diplomats—on his travels. Some refused to listen to him, others to believe him. From General Sikorski to Anthony Eden, from President Roosevelt to Justice Frankfurter, he recounted to each the life and death of the Warsaw Ghetto, the death trucks, the sealed freight cars going to Auschwitz, the fear and hunger, the loneliness and agony of men, women, and children whom the so-called civilized world had abandoned and forgotten. Then he stopped. He realized that his words were of no avail. People were busy with other things, leaders had other priorities. I believe that this was the most depressing time for Jan Karski. He must have felt useless.

But his testimony remains fruitful. Thanks to him, we know that the individual, if he so desires, is capable of having an effect on history. When the Allies raised their voices on behalf of the Jews of Budapest, late, very late, in the summer of 1944, it was because men like Jan Karski knew how to penetrate their consciences.

Jan Karski's human and humanistic message had a significance that neither the flow of time nor the forces of evil could erase or mitigate.

Thanks to him, more than one generation continues to believe in humanity.

ELIE WIESEL

Preface

We have tried to tell the story of Jan Karski's experiences in World War II in a manner that will do justice to all facets of this extraordinary man's life. Our goal has been to convey all the excitement and moral force of Jan Karski's wartime activities while simultaneously presenting a clear and well-documented record of those experiences.

Much of this book is based on the recollections of Jan Karski, as recorded separately, in Polish and English, by each of the authors. Professor Karski allowed each of us to stay in his home and to question him at exhaustive length on many occasions. We supplemented these in-person interviews with telephone interviews. The taped reminiscences we have accumulated, well over forty hours total, constitute a valuable oral history resource in themselves. The prodigious mnemonic talents Karski displayed during the war—often to the amazement of those who received his lengthy oral reports—were tremendously beneficial to us as well.

Although we enjoyed Jan Karski's full cooperation, we devoted great effort to locating other sources of information about Karski's wartime career. We tracked down as many people as possible who could corroborate or expand upon what Karski remembered. The witnesses to Karski's adventures whom we have interviewed include officials of the U.S. State Department and British Foreign Office who met with Karski in 1943, Polish underground members who helped him escape from Gestapo custody, and a Jewish underground fighter, David John Landau, who escorted him into the Warsaw Ghetto—and whom we discovered by sheer chance in Melbourne, Australia, when Karski was invited to speak there in 1993.

In addition to these sources, we visited libraries and archives in the United States, England, and Poland in search of documents related to Karski's activities. We also sought documents by mail from the collections of the Yad Vashem Martyrs' and Heroes' Remembrance Authority in Jerusalem. Nearly everywhere we looked, we found more than we imagined possible. Karski interacted with and left profound impressions upon so many people from so many organizations and governments that references to him appear in even the most unlikely locations.

To the extent we have included verbatim conversations in our text, we relied either on what Professor Karski and others recalled in interviews or on quotations from contemporary documents. There is no manufactured dialogue in this book. One can never be entirely sure after fifty years, but we believe we have faithfully represented what was said in each conversation portrayed here.

Professor Karski bears little of the blame for the many legends that have sprung up about him over the years. It is not his fault that a historian claimed he met with the Pope in 1944, nor that a German playwright portrayed him as having an affair with Churchill's secretary, nor that a 1982 biography of writer Arthur Koestler reported that "Karsky [sic], driven to despair by his inability to arouse world opinion . . . committed suicide."

Professor Karski reviewed the manuscript of this book. The authors have benefited immensely from the wisdom of this man, who views his own experiences through the prism of four decades of scholarly engagement with Polish history. He made many suggestions about minor corrections and clarifications, saving us from several gaffes and broadening our perspectives on historical issues related to his wartime activities. On the other hand, Professor Karski never once sought to steer us toward rosy interpretations of his motives and efforts. He never pressed us to omit or tone down any aspect of our work on the grounds that it might tarnish his image. He looks back on his past with a distant and ironic perspective, displaying no insecurity whatsoever about his place in history.

~

A book like this one cannot avoid the explosive subject of Polish-Jewish relations during World War II. We have necessarily touched on aspects of those relations, knowing full well the extraordinary degree of bitterness that has often tainted the historical dialogue between Poles and Jews.

It would be useless for us to claim that we approach our work with absolute objectivity. History is and should be judgmental. No perceptive human being can learn about this era without drawing some conclusions about relative guilt and innocence, dishonor and nobility, right and wrong. We cannot tell Karski's story without addressing certain difficult issues. Still, though, our purpose is to tell that story, not to cast blame or create controversy.

As Walter Laqueur pointed out in his 1981 study *The Terrible Secret*, neither the "apologetic literature" of some postwar writers—

who would defend the honor of Poland by exaggerating Polish wartime aid to the Jews—nor the "indiscriminate accusations of neglect" leveled by some Jews at Poles can bring about a more complete understanding of the Final Solution. "In a search for scapegoats," commented Laqueur, "few are likely to emerge unscathed."

To write about a time of such unparalleled horror is to take on a special responsibility for sensitivity—toward Jews, Poles, and all who suffered. We hope we have adequately shouldered that responsibility. Jan Karski has devoted much of his life to the cause of fostering understanding between Jews and Poles. We hope that this account of his life will further that cause.

~

A few notes about names:

We should explain at the outset that the subject of our book went by many different names during the war. Born Jan Kozielewski, he took various pseudonyms in the underground. To his fellow conspirators, he was known as Witold. When he traveled to the West as an emissary of the underground, he used a variety of false identities. Under one of these names, Jan Karski, he applied for a visa to the United States in 1943. After the war, when he chose to remain in the U.S., he became concerned about the possible implications of having given false information to his host government. He kept his adopted name and eventually became an American citizen under it.

For readers unfamiliar with the pronunciation of the Polish language, some of the names of people and places mentioned in this book may be difficult to remember phonetically. Without delving too deeply into linguistics, readers may want to keep in mind just a few tips about Polish pronunciation:

The Polish *j* is pronounced like the English *y*. Thus, *Jan* sounds like *Yann*.

The Polish *w* is pronounced like the English *v*. The Polish *c* is pronounced as though it were a combination of the letters *t* and *s* in English—unless it is followed by an *i* or *z*, in which case it is identical to the English *ch* sound: Thus the name *Cyrankiewicz* (the Kraków socialist leader who collaborated with Karski) sounds something like *tseerunkeevich* to the English ear. The name of the Home Army commander, General Rowecki, sounds like *rovetski*.

Ch in Polish is an aspirated sound unfamiliar in English, sort of a hard *h*. The name of Karski's Washington mentor, Jan Cie-chanowski, sounds like *chehanovski* to an English speaker.

The Polish language includes unique alphabetical characters that tend to baffle English speakers. After some deliberation, we have decided to include these characters and explain their pronunciation instead of omitting them.

The name of Interior Minister and later Prime Minister Stan-isław Mikołajczyk demonstrates one such character. The little slash through each "l" in his name means that it is pronounced like the English *w*: *Staniswav Miko-why-chik*.

Nowy Sącz, the town where Karski escaped from the Gestapo, displays another unique Polish character. The diminutive hook under its *a* adds a nasal *n* sound to the letter: *Novee Saunch* (rhymes with *haunch*). The same goes for Kąty, the rural village where Karski was quarantined after his escape: *Kaunty* (more or less rhymes with *Auntie*). Many readers may be familiar with the similar effect the little hook has on the letter *e* in the name of Poland's President, Lech Wałęsa.

Other Polish characters include *ś* (like the English *sh*), *ć* (like *ch*), *ż* and *ź* (both akin to the soft *g* sound in the French word *rouge*) and *ó* (a shortened *oo*, as in *book*. There is also *ń*, pronounced like the *ni* sound in *onion*.

The names of a few Slovakian towns that are mentioned in the text also contain a character unfamiliar to most English speakers: *š*, as in *Prešov*. The *š* is pronounced like the English *sh*.

Traditionally, women's names in Polish differ from those of men in the same family; the names take on feminine endings. Thus the wife of Karski's brother Marian Kozielewski called herself Jad-wiga Kozielewska. Not all women now follow this practice, however. Two of the people who rescued Karski from German captivity, for instance, were Zbigniew Ryś and his sister, Zofia Rysiówna, who later took the name Zofia Ryś.

Variant spellings exist for the names of some of the Jewish leaders mentioned in our text. Ignacy Schwarzbart, for instance, sometimes went by the names Yitshak and Szwarcbart; the name of his colleague on the Polish National Council, Szmul Zygielbojm, is spelled Szmuel and Shmuel in various histories. In such cases, we have used the spelling by which the person appears to be best known for his wartime work, judging from other historical accounts.

In the interest of reader-friendliness, we have borrowed the idea of a glossary of important names from Professor David Engel's excellent study *Facing a Holocaust: The Polish Government-in-Exile and the Jews, 1943–1945* (Chapel Hill: University of North Carolina Press, 1993). We trust that this appendix will make it easier for readers to keep track of the myriad personalities with whom Karski came into contact.

~

Many people helped to make this book possible. We received an extraordinary amount of assistance from scholars, archivists, interview subjects, friends, and family in seven nations. At the substantial risk of leaving someone out, we would like to acknowledge as many of those helpful souls as possible. Of course, inclusion in these lists does not necessarily imply endorsement of our interpretations by any of these parties.

We must first take note of our debt to certain scholars whose work on the Polish and Jewish experience during World War II was invaluable to us. The writings of Martin Gilbert, David Engel, Lucjan Dobroszycki, and Walter Laqueur were especially influential in shaping our interpretations of Karski's time and place. Stefan Korboński's detailed accounts of life in the Polish underground movement were equally helpful. The work of Richard Breitman, Władysław Bartoszewski, Reuben Ainsztein, Israel Gutman, Bernard Wasserstein, Raul Hilberg, Will Brownell, and Richard N. Billings broadened our understanding in important ways. And we must include the scholarly work of Professor Jan Karski in our acknowledgments. Independently of his status as the subject of our research, Professor Karski provided a valuable secondary source with his grand-scale study *The Great Powers and Poland, 1919–1945: From Versailles to Yalta* (Bethesda: University Press of America, 1985).

For research assistance, expert advice, constructive criticism, or some combination of these services, we are indebted to many people, including some of the scholars listed above. We gratefully acknowledge the assistance of Professors Bill Brands of Texas A&M University, Richard Breitman of the American University in Washington, D.C., Lucjan Dobroszycki of the Yivo Institute for Jewish Research, David Engel of New York University, Louis Gerson of the University of Connecticut, Martin Gilbert of Oxford University, Susan Pedersen of Harvard University, Joachim Rusek of Jagiellonian University, Michael Scammell of Cornell University, and Piotr Wandycz of Yale University, as well as Dr. Zbigniew Brzeziński, Janusz

Cisek of the Józef Piłsudski Institute of America, Nicholas Coney of the Public Record Office, Bill Carey, William Carnell of the National Security Archive, Whit Forehand, Oberstaatsanwältin Helga Grabitz of the Hamburg State Attorney's Office, Leo Greenbaum of the Yivo Institute for Jewish Research, Dr. Abraham Peck of the American Jewish Archives, Harry Porter, Kirk Porter, Wendell Smith, Andrzej Suchcitz of the Polish Institute, Derek Tangye, John E. Taylor of the National Archives, and Michael Tregenza.

Archivist Zbigniew Stańczyk of the Hoover Institution went far beyond the call of duty in assisting our research. We are exceptionally thankful for his help.

The American author was the beneficiary of generous Polish hospitality and valuable assistance from Ela and Andrzej Mrowiec, Ździsław Spaczyński, Professors Tadeusz Radzik, Zygmunt Mańkowski and Jozef Marszałek of Curie-Skłodowska University in Lublin, and the family of his co-author, Stanisław M. Jankowski.

During other travels, the same author took advantage of couches, cabins, or computers graciously made available by Steve Altemeier, George and Lavenia Carpenter, Audrey Duff, Sean Gentry, Frank and Micki Pendleton, Matthew and Rosalind Porter, Richard Quest, Lenka and Karel Varhanik, David Wood, and Don and Mary Jo Wright.

The Polish author is most grateful to his friends Zbigniew Wojnar and Walter Poznański of New York, who provided him with all the assistance he could ask for as he conducted research for this book in the United States.

We gleaned valuable advice about the mysteries of the publishing world from Madison Smartt Bell, Kevin Drury, Barbara Enkema, Morgan Entrekin, Charles Flowers, Kath Hansen, Polly Law, Ann Shayne, Steve Wood, Jr. (who furnished many billable hours of free legal and fraternal counsel), and our literary agent, Henry Dunow of Harold Ober Associates. We would also like to express our gratitude to editor Hana Umlauf Lane of John Wiley & Sons, Inc., without whose faith this book might never have seen the light of day.

We are especially grateful to Gay Block for permission to reprint the distinctive photograph of Professor Karski that she took for the book she co-authored with Malka Drucker, *Rescuers: Portraits of Moral Courage in the Holocaust* (New York: Holmes & Meier, 1992). Our thanks also go out to artist Stanisław Westwalewicz of Tarnów, Poland, who has graciously allowed us to reproduce his sketch of a scene in the Kozel'shchina prison camp, where he and Karski were held in 1939 after their capture by the Red Army. We acknowledge the assistance of photographer Jan Zych, who reproduced this sketch for us. And we thank graphic designer Diane Nottingham, who produced the maps included in this book.

We note with deep appreciation the translation assistance we received from Dina Abramowicz of the Yivo Institute for Jewish Research, Krzysztof Krakowiak, Aleksander Kuśnierz, Jan Piekło, Piotr Pieńkowski, and Brigitte Porter.

We are thankful as well to those who allowed us to interview them for this book: Humphrey Burton, Elbridge Durbrow, Dean Peter F. Krogh, David John Landau, Józef Laskowik, Jan Morawski, Dr. Janina Prot, Sir Frank Roberts, Zbigniew Ryś, Zofia Ryś, Dr. Jan Słowikowski, and Wanda Załuska.

Finally, a few personal notes. The Polish author offers his most tender thanks to his wife Krystyna for her support and patience. Likewise, the American author is indebted beyond all expression to his parents, Nancy and Steve Wood, Sr., and to his wife, Nicki Pendleton Wood, who have encouraged his efforts from the inception of this project.

The patient cooperation of Professor Jan Karski and his wife, Pola Nirenska, made this book possible. Not only did Professor Karski open his personal archive to us, endure many full days of questioning, and painstakingly review the manuscript for accuracy, but he and his wife also offered bed and board to both authors on numerous occasions. We profoundly regret that Mrs. Karski did not live to see this book. The authors dedicate their work to Professor Jan Karski, and to the memory of Pola Nirenska Karski, with heartfelt gratitude and admiration.

E. Thomas Wood
Stanisław M. Jankowski

Nashville and Kraków
January 1994

RITES OF INITIATION
August 1939–June 1940

1
Autumn of Flight

In a crisp khaki uniform, his breeches tucked at calf level into immaculate patent leather boots, Lieutenant Jan Kozielewski sat and waited for his boss. By his side, dangling from a polished leather belt, hung a silver-handled sword, awarded by Polish President Ignacy Mościcki in honor of his *primus* ranking as a Horse Artillery cadet. Atop a fine army horse, he would carry that prized weapon into action—or into battle, in the unlikely event that Poland and Nazi Germany actually went to war against each other.

The secret mobilization order had come early that morning, August 23, 1939. Jan and thousands of other reservists were allotted only two hours to settle their civilian affairs, pack up, and join their units for deployment. The order put Jan in a bind. One wing of Poland's government, the Polish Army, was demanding his presence. But he also had obligations to another wing, the Ministry of Foreign Affairs. Early in 1939, he had landed a job as the administrative assistant to the foreign ministry's director of personnel, Tomir Drymmer. The position normally required considerable seniority in the foreign service, but Jan had secured this plum appointment at the age of twenty-five.

"You're not here to be my friend," Drymmer had told Jan when he hired him. "You're here to be my secretary." The personnel director knew that Kozielewski had struck up a friendship with his previous boss in the diplomatic corps. There would be none of that in the personnel office. Drymmer was all business, and Jan was always mindful of the importance of making a good impression on him so as to further his ambition of becoming a professional diplomat—and, eventually, an ambassador.

The mobilization order, delivered at 5:00 A.M., had instructed him to report to the train station at 7:00 A.M. for the trip south to join his unit. But Jan feared the consequences of abandoning his work at the foreign ministry without advising Drymmer about the status of certain pending matters and returning the keys to the personnel department's safes. His diplomatic duties came first. He would just have to be late for the war.

So, after packing his bags and leaving the apartment of his older brother Marian, who boarded him in Warsaw, Jan made his way to the ministry office and waited for Drymmer. The personnel chief arrived midmorning, halted at the sight of Jan in his uniform, and emitted a condescending chuckle. "You look like a clown," he said.

Jan stammered an apology for his sudden impending departure.

Drymmer shrugged dismissively. "Don't worry about it," he said. "You will be back here in a couple of weeks. All this stuff with Hitler will take care of itself. We just need to show him that we are not Czechs."

Jan was inclined to agree. Having previously served as an apprentice diplomat in Romania, Germany, Switzerland, and England, he considered himself an able observer of his nation's foreign policy. His proximity to Foreign Minister Józef Beck had given him a ringside seat for the diplomatic skirmishes of recent months between Poland and Germany.

Like all Poles, Jan had heard Hitler's bluster about the Danzig Corridor, the disputed area in the north that served as Poland's only outlet to the sea. He had watched with disquiet as German troops marched into Czechoslovakia in 1938, seizing Poland's southern neighbor without firing a shot. But he also knew Beck's confident answer to the German threat: Poland had become a powerful, sovereign state in the two decades since it gained independence. The discipline and gallantry of its military forces were admired around the world. For the past six years, almost half the national budget had gone to defense. And Poland had powerful friends in Britain and France. Its treaties of mutual assistance with those nations would guarantee swift retribution if the Nazis attacked Poland. Hitler would never be so foolish.

"You've been looking a little pale anyway," Drymmer said almost jovially. "Go on and join your unit. Get out in the fresh air, ride some horses, pick up some sun. It'll be good for your constitution."

In the August heat, Jan boarded a train to catch up with his unit at its deployment site in southern Poland, his duffel bag weighed down by the winter clothes his sister-in-law Jadwiga had convinced him to carry—"Just in case," she said. More likely to be of use, he thought, was the new Leica camera he had brought along. Perhaps, he joked to himself, he would have an opportunity to snap pictures of defeated German generals as the Polish army paraded them down the Unter den Linden in Berlin.

As the train inched south, however, what Jan saw belied the blithe cockiness of Warsaw's elites. As more conscripts packed into the carriage at each station—responding to a mobilization that was clearly secret in name only—Jan could not help but pay heed to the ashen expressions on the faces of the peasant soldiers and the hordes of mothers and wives weeping into handkerchiefs on the platforms. It was as though they had some premonition of disaster.

As Lieutenant Kozielewski joined his military unit, he found that more reassuring views prevailed. His fellow officers shared Drymmer's optimistic assessment. They were sure the deployment was merely a signal to Hitler, a saber-rattling display to show him that the Poles meant business.

The Fifth Horse Artillery Battery—an elite unit attached to a cavalry brigade—was part of Poland's first line of defense, stationed only a few miles from the German border in the southwestern corner of the country. Its surroundings were not very inviting. The barracks and stables, inherited from the Austro-Hungarian army after the last war, were the worse for wear. And there was nothing of interest in the nearby settlement, a sleepy factory town called Oświęcim.

Still, Jan had no complaints. After the frantic mobilization, the reservists settled into a placid routine. For part of the day there were guns to be cleaned, horses to be groomed, and maneuvers to be carried out, but much of Jan's time was his own. The light workload and warm weather allowed him to indulge in leisurely equestrian jaunts in the countryside surrounding Oświęcim. He and other officers were even permitted to spend a couple of evenings on the town in nearby Kraków. In this relaxed manner Jan and his comrades-in-arms passed the first week of their deployment.

~

The first day of September dawned clear and balmy over the rolling fields of southern Poland. This was riding weather. Arching his lanky frame over the bathroom sink and squinting into the mirror,

Jan ran a razor gingerly over a face still marked by acne. Aside from the diversion of another horseback outing, this Friday looked to be one more day of tedium.

At 5:05, Jan's meditations over the sink came to an abrupt end. Two massive explosions in quick succession shook the camp. Jan ran outside the barracks in time to hear German bombers fading into the distance. For the moment, no further attacks came. But in the camp, chaos already reigned. The horses, spooked by the explosions, had broken out of their stables and were running wildly through the camp. Attempts to corral the animals proved futile. Without horses to haul the artillery, the battery's gunners would be unable to mount any effective defense against the invader. The German Luftwaffe soon reappeared, raining incendiary bombs on the camp. As the barracks blazed, Jan could hear the sound of heavy fighting at the front, where other artillery batteries were being decimated by the German Fourteenth Army. Only later would Jan learn the full significance of the morning's chaotic events. In the opening moments of the Second World War, Poland's horse-drawn artillery had been eliminated as a fighting force by the tactics of a new era in warfare. The Blitzkrieg had begun.

Desperately trying to maintain military order, Jan and his fellow officers organized the surviving men in their battery into ranks and attempted a disciplined withdrawal toward the local railroad line. As the soldiers marched through the streets of Oświęcim, villagers began firing upon them from houses and buildings. They were what would later come to be called *Volksdeutsche*, Polish citizens of German descent—the Nazi "Fifth Column" in the soon-to-be-conquered nation. The officers had to restrain some of their men from setting fire to the town as punishment for its treason.

After waiting for hours on the outskirts of town while the train tracks were patched, the sullen troops clambered into a long line of boxcars. The train pulled out, retreating toward Kraków. Jan took one last glance at "the treacherous windows of Oświęcim." He would never return to the little town where fate had placed him on the morning of the Blitzkrieg. In years to come, however, many of his friends and millions of others would pass by the village on the same rail line to the same campsite, by then refurbished by the Nazis. Oświęcim would soon have a new, German name: Auschwitz.

～

The train crawled through the night, frequently halting for long periods. It still had not covered the short distance to Kraków by the next morning when a group of German Heinkel 111 bombers spotted it and closed in for the kill. For over an hour, the warplanes swarmed in a clear sky, strafing and bombing the defenseless troops. Finally, as hundreds of men lay dead and dying amid the smoking wreckage of the boxcars, the Heinkels moved on to a more challenging target.

Jan's boxcar was not hit. Abandoning the last vestiges of military discipline, he and the other survivors stumbled away from the carnage, walking east. Along every thoroughfare, these troops encountered other military personnel who had endured similar traumas. Some, including Jan, looked for an opportunity to join a detachment that was still fighting. Among these soldiers, rumors spread: A fighting force was being organized: Soldiers could join at the railroad station of this town or that. The men made their way to one hamlet after another, day after day. Every time they arrived at the designated station, they found it in ruins.

Jan and other soldiers, amid an endless, shell-shocked horde of civilians, kept shuffling eastward in an effort to stay ahead of the rapidly advancing Germans. Sleeping in barns, trampling the ungathered harvests of one field after another, the Poles wandered on toward an unknown objective. When Jan's military provisions ran low after the first few days, he had no trouble bartering his stylish new Leica camera for a bag full of bread and cured meats.

Jan's most cherished possession, his silver-handled sword, still swung from his belt. After more than a week, convinced he would have to trade this unwieldy burden for more supplies, Jan approached the owner of a country store. "It's quite valuable," he insisted. "It may have historical significance." Surely it was worth something in cheese and sausage, he told himself.

The store owner's eyes were a hard squint. "You're crazy," he muttered. "Get that piece of shit out of here, before it brings misfortune on both of us." The peasant sensed more acutely than the young diplomat that ownership of this particular relic would confer few benefits in the Poland of the future. The occupiers would have special plans for anyone who displayed trappings of the country's former ruling class.

Jan stalked out of the store, strode a few steps, hurled his sword into a field, and walked on.

Lt. Jan Kozielewski was now little more than a refugee, leaving behind his career, his belongings, and the people and places he knew. In due course he would lose even his name, taking on one false identity after another in the coming years of struggle.

~

The rude shock of defeat struck Jan all the more deeply for having instantly reversed the boundless aspirations of his life before September 1939. Though born in 1914, during the waning years of tsarist rule, Jan was a child of the reborn Poland that emerged after the First World War. The youngest of eight children, he carried the hopes of an earlier generation that had struggled and sacrificed to revive the long-repressed Polish state.

Those who met him later often described Jan's manners as "aristocratic," but in truth his family had little in common with Poland's landed gentry. Jan grew up not on an elegant estate, nor in one of his nation's grand and ancient cities like Warsaw and Kraków, but in Łódź—a new city less than two hundred years old, and a product of the Industrial Revolution. Of the limited manufacturing capacity that existed in a country whose economy was dominated by peasant farmers, much was located in Łódź. A few large textile-producing enterprises gave Łódź a reputation as Poland's clothing capital, but smaller-scale manufacturers also abounded in the city. Typical of these industries was the small tannery and leather-goods factory, really no more than an overblown craft shop, owned by Stefan Kozielewski. Jan barely remembered his father, who had died when Jan was a young child.

The two great influences on Jan's childhood were his eldest brother Marian and his mother, Walentyna Kozielewska. Marian, eighteen years older than Jan, became a surrogate father and played a major role in directing Jan's education and career path. Walentyna Kozielewska, living in a modest apartment with her youngest child, inculcated in him a set of almost contradictory principles that indelibly shaped his being.

Jan's mother adhered stringently to the cult of personality that developed around Marshal Józef Piłsudski, the revolutionary leader who came to power in Poland after a 1926 coup d'état. Piłsudski had no taste for democracy, but his earlier sacrifices in the nation's struggle for independence, his reputation for incorruptibility, and his evident devotion to the welfare of the Polish people won the Marshal widespread public support. His rule was to some extent a benevolent dictatorship. Walentyna Kozielewska never referred to Piłsudski by name; he was simply "the father of our country." Along with Marian, who had been one of the Marshal's trusted Legionnaires in the struggle for Polish independence, Walentyna imbued Jan with this fanatical awe.

She also drilled into her son a passion for Christian belief that was unusual even in intensely Roman Catholic Poland. Walentyna's ability to embrace both the church and the agnostic Marshal Piłsudski, who was often in conflict with the Polish clergy, presaged a similar tolerance for paradox that Jan would later display.

In a similar manner, Jan's mother impressed on the young boy an abiding sense of social tolerance—notwithstanding her fervent support of Piłsudski's authoritarian regime. In particular, Jan was raised to respect and maintain friendly relations with the Jewish community in Łódź, which accounted for nearly forty percent of the city's population. His mother apparently took to heart Piłsudski's lofty pronouncements about equality and interethnic harmony in Poland, words that the Marshal himself did not always back up with deeds. Within a few years of Walentyna's death in 1935, the goodwill toward Jews that she had passed on to her son was destined to have consequences she could never have imagined.

By the age of six, little Jan Kozielewski not only had learned to read, but was already delighting his elders by reciting long passages from the poetry of such venerated Polish bards as Adam Mickiewicz. He started school a year earlier than most children, consistently excelling in history and literature while struggling with mathematics and sciences.

At the same time, spurred by his mother and by the Jesuit fathers of his elementary school, Jan displayed near-fanatical devotion to his Catholic faith. Convinced that hard work and piety would get him to heaven, he joined a semisecret boys' society, Sodalicja Mariańska, dedicated to the veneration of the Virgin Mary. The boys spent hours under the tutelage of an excitable priest, studying artists' portrayals of the Blessed Virgin, Adam and Eve, and other biblical figures. The priest lectured over and over about the contrast between Mary's purity and Eve's wickedness, interpolating stern warnings to the boys to avoid evil women like Eve.

One summer, early in Jan's teenage years, his grandmother gave him a bicycle. She told him it was time for him to become better acquainted with his homeland. Jan loaded the bike on to a train, traveled to the far eastern portion of Poland, and set out to ride back home. As he pedaled from east to west, he was amused by the contrast between the bleak shabbiness of villages in formerly Russian-held areas and the Prussian tidiness of towns that had been under German rule prior to World War I. But wherever he went, he met peasants who lived a life quite foreign to his own. In their coarse but heartfelt way, they offered him food, shelter, and hospitality. Jan returned to Łódź with a new understanding of his society.

Before Jan graduated from high school in 1931, he had resolved to pursue a diplomatic career. Marian Kozielewski, who was funding Jan's education, encouraged this ambition and exploited his excellent contacts in government circles to open doors for his brother at the Ministry of Foreign Affairs. At Jan Kazimierz University in the eastern city of Lwów, Jan pursued a dual track of studies in law and diplomacy. In 1933, he obtained a summer internship at the Polish consulate in Cernauti, Romania.

Out of deference to his fatherly older brother, Jan became active in the Youth Legion, a pro-Piłsudski movement, but his heart was not entirely in it. The problem was not that his support of Piłsudski had cooled; Jan simply had no taste for politics and felt that he had no talent for leadership. Moreover, he became concerned that his position in the movement might someday compromise his standing as an impartial diplomat. Nevertheless, he found himself elected commandant his second year at Lwów. His tenure was, by his own account, disastrous. Convinced that he was not cut out to be a leader of men, he left the legion.

Jan had more success in another collegiate endeavor. In December 1934, during his final year at Lwów, he took part in a time-honored rhetorical competition on campus. Before an auditorium full of students, faculty members, and townspeople, one young orator after another stepped to the podium to present arguments on subjects of their own choosing. Jan Kozielewski, the last speaker, took as his theme the justice, or injustice, of the punishment meted out to King Louis XVI of France, guillotined during the Revolution. Arguing one side of the question, Jan made the case that the king, or at least his reputation, deserved a new trial. Then, skillfully presenting a wealth of evidence against the toppled monarch, Jan launched into closing arguments as a prosecutor. Finally, he exhorted the "jury" in the auditorium to convict the memory of the king, to convict Louis XVI once more by a show of hands.

The professor chairing the event was momentarily taken aback by Jan's audience-participation stunt but, after a moment of chin stroking, said he saw nothing improper in it. "Please vote," the professor told the crowd. "Who agrees with Jan Kozielewski?" Hands flew into the air all over the room. Jubilant shouts of "Liberté! Fraternité! Egalité!" and "Mort au Roi!" echoed through the hall. Almost unanimously, Kozielewski was awarded the *Adeptus Eloquentissimus* certificate as the most talented rhetorician at Jan Kazimierz University.

Jan took up another internship with the Ministry of Foreign Affairs after graduation, spending several months in Germany. Relations between the Polish and German governments were warm at the time. As a representative of Polish youth, Jan was invited to attend the Nazis' Parteitag (Party Day) celebration in July 1935. The event took place in Nuremberg and served as the backdrop for the announcement of the Nuremberg Laws, some of the earliest restrictions on the freedom of Jews in Germany. Oblivious to the implications of his visit, Jan attended a youth rally in the company of young men and women from France, Belgium, and other European nations, all of which had been only too happy to endorse Hitler's regime by sending delegations. On the way to the auditorium, Jan marveled at the Hitlerjugend (Hitler Youth) formations that goosestepped down a boulevard, trampling flower petals strewn at their feet by the adoring masses.

At the rally location, Jan and the other foreigners stood in the back of the enclosed amphitheater, near the huge speakers that surrounded its perimeter. Before them lay a bare, darkened stage. The young people in attendance milled about festively. In the darkness, some of the boys tried to strike up extracurricular activities with the Fräuleins among the Party faithful. After a few minutes, a booming baritone suddenly erupted through the speakers: "Achtung!" When nothing happened after a moment of anticipatory silence, the gleeful hubbub arose once more in the hall and the mating rites resumed. Then again came the disembodied voice: "Achtung!"— again followed by silence and then the rising hum of the crowd. At last, suddenly, a trio of spotlights, brighter than any Jan had ever seen before, flashed onto the stage. When his eyes adjusted to the glare, Jan recognized at center stage the distinctive profile of Adolf Hitler's right-hand man, Reichsmarshal Hermann Göring.

"Sieg Heil!" bellowed Göring, extending his arm in the Nazi salute. His voice thundered through the speakers, followed by a deafening answer of salutes and applause (much of which, Jan later learned, originated not from the crowd on hand but from recordings played through the speakers). Göring, a World War I fighter ace, was nearing the peak of his power. A few months earlier, he had brazenly announced to the world the formation of the Luftwaffe, a German air force built up secretly, in violation of the Versailles treaties. Standing before the Hitlerjugend, his elaborate self-designed uniform festooned with medals, Göring worked the youths into a nationalistic frenzy. "You, the youth of Germany, must take responsibility for the human race, because you belong to the superior race!" the Nazi leader roared. "We are destined to govern, to bring order to the world, to create a lasting peace! And only the honest, decent youth of Germany can make this peace," continued Göring. The Hitler Youth interrupted him with one ovation after another.

Jan and the other foreigners looked at each other a little sheepishly. To Jan, ruling the world did not sound like such a bad proposition. Swept up in the emotion of the moment, he asked himself: "Why couldn't I be born German, so I can be superior, too?"

Like all able-bodied young men in Poland, Jan was required to prepare for military service. Enrolling at artillery training school in 1935, he excelled in all categories of equestrian and military technique. The better he performed, however, the more attention he received from the drill instructor, Captain Rankowicz. During horseback maneuvers, Rankowicz watched Cadet Kozielewski like a hawk. "Hey, Kozielewski, what exactly are you doing?" the drill instructor would yell across the field when he made a mistake. "I swear, if you were as tall as you are stupid, you'd be able to kiss the moon's ass on your knees!"

"Yes sir!" Jan would answer from his mount.

In the summer of 1936, after scoring highest among the seventy-eight men in his cadet class (and earning the coveted sword), Jan moved on to Geneva. There, again funded by Marian and taking advantage of his brother's government ties, Jan worked on his French and held a position with the Polish mission to an international trade-union organization. In 1937, the foreign ministry transferred him to London, where he learned English while attached to the Polish embassy in a low-level position. Whether because of his family contacts or because he was making a good impression on his own, Jan was recalled from England in February 1938 and admitted to an advanced foreign-service training program in Warsaw, despite having much less experience than was ordinarily required.

The meteoric rise of Jan's diplomatic career continued in Poland. He took top honors on the examination administered to his class of trainees. From that moment forward, his career in the foreign service would be secure. Given time, he could work his way up the ladder and attain his lifelong goal of becoming an ambassador. Nothing could stand in his way.

~

Hobbling down the dusty road in the unseasonable heat, wincing with every step as the blister on his heel rubbed itself raw, Jan trudged through another day of flight from the Germans. It was September 17.

Jan was approaching Tarnopol—now the city of Ternopil, Ukraine, but then located in the southeast corner of Poland. Thousands of Polish soldiers and civilians were rushing southward through Tarnopol toward the relative safety of neutral Romania. The only other place to run was the Soviet Union, whose border lay nineteen miles to the east. But few Poles would willingly cross that border.

Polish antipathy toward Russia was rooted in centuries of conflict. Western-oriented, Roman Catholic Poland had been a dominant power in central Europe until the eighteenth century, while Orthodox Russia remained backward and isolated. But partitions by Russian, Austrian, and Prussian forces reduced the territory of a weakened Poland in 1772 and again in 1792. In 1794, Tadeusz Kosciuszko led a rebellion against Russian hegemony in what was left of Poland; when the revolt failed, Prussia and Austria joined Russia in stamping out the last vestiges of Polish independence with a third and complete partition. The Polish nation remained under the control of foreign powers until the end of World War I.

Insurrections against Russian rule in 1830 and 1863, as well as more limited unrest in 1905, stoked the flames of Polish nationalism but provoked savage repression from the Tsar's forces. Following World War I and the 1917 Bolshevik revolution in Russia, an independent Poland finally reemerged after two years of fighting between Poles and Red Army troops. Against such a background of ingrained hostility between the two nations, Poles generally harbored deep suspicions about their neighbors to the east.

Despite the record of aggression between the two countries, the men walking toward Tarnopol were stunned by the news that filtered through their ranks: The Red Army had entered Poland. Jan puzzled over the possible meaning of this development with a nearby group of medical officers. Concerned, but not immediately assuming that the Soviets had hostile intentions, Jan and the medics resolved to continue toward Tarnopol, where more information might be available. Two miles outside the city, however, the pedestrian traffic came to a halt. Under the September sun, thousands of Poles stood and strained to hear a voice emanating from a barely visible vehicle down the road. The address was in Polish, but the accent was Russian. The voice coming over the loudspeaker, which was mounted on a military truck, was asking the Poles to join with Russia in a fraternal alliance. As he stepped closer, Jan could see a line of Soviet T-26 tanks, emblazoned with red stars.

The crowd buzzed with suspicious murmurs. After some deliberation among the ranking Polish officers present, a captain emerged from the troops, waving a white handkerchief over his head as he approached the tanks. A Soviet officer greeted him with a salute, and the two disappeared behind a vehicle. Ten minutes later, the captain's voice came over the loudspeaker: "The Soviet Army crossed the frontier to join us in the struggle against the Germans, the deadly enemies of the Slavs and of the entire human race. We cannot wait for orders from the Polish High Command. We must unite with the Soviet forces. Commander Plaskov demands that we join his detachment immediately, after surrendering our arms. These will be returned to us later."

Throughout eastern Poland, this scene was being repeated in one form or another. Some Poles learned of the Soviet incursion as crudely printed leaflets fluttered down on their towns, urging them in misspelled and inept Polish to welcome the "brotherly help" of the Red Army, whose soldiers came "not as enemies, but as your brothers in class solidarity, as your liberators from the oppression of landlords and capitalists." In other areas the invaders dispensed with verbal communication, getting their message across with gunfire. In one town they dragged a Polish general from his car and killed him before the eyes of his wife; in another they disarmed 30 policemen and then executed them; in still another they shot 130 schoolboys and cadets.

His former position with the foreign ministry notwithstanding, Jan had no way of knowing about a secret protocol attached to the German-Soviet Nonaggression Pact that had been signed on August 23, the day he had been called up to active duty. The protocol divided Poland into zones of Nazi and Soviet control. The young diplomat was caught up in the effect of this diplomatic agreement between two powers—one fascist and one communist—that professed to be mortal enemies of each other.

In the distance, a shot rang out. A rumor spread instantly through the ranks: A sergeant, it was said, had cried out in despair at the fate of Poland. Then he had raised a pistol to his temple and killed himself. Jan never learned whether the story was true.

"Officers to the right. Noncommissioned officers to the left," barked a Russian voice over the loudspeaker, jolting the assembled soldiers from "a dumb trance" of shock. The voice ordered the men to leave their weapons in a pile under a tree; too stunned to object, they obeyed.

Complying with Russian orders, the Polish throng formed ranks and began marching toward Tarnopol. In front of the column, to the rear, and along each flank rolled the tanks of Poland's new ally, with guns leveled at Polish soldiers.

∼

The crash of the boxcar's slamming doors was quickly followed by the clang of an iron bar as it fell into place, securely bolting them. Inside Jan sat, waiting in the darkness. The only sources of light in the car were a narrow ventilation slit that ran across the top of the walls and a round hole in the floor of the car that served as a toilet. As his eyes adjusted, he could make out the shapes of some of the fifty-nine other officers in his car, of the iron stove in the middle of the car, and of the small parcel of black bread and dried fish that had been apportioned to him.

Since Jan's car was one of the first of more than sixty to be loaded at the Tarnopol station that day, two hours passed before the train began moving. Finally, it pulled away from Tarnopol, passing into the Soviet Union within a few hours. Countless other boxcars would pass this way in the coming weeks, carrying over 250,000 Polish officers and soldiers into captivity. For tens of thousands, it would be a one-way trip.

The journey dragged on and on. Once a day, the train would come to a halt, and the cars would be opened. A ration of black bread and salted fish would be distributed, the boxcars' occupants would be allowed to step out under heavy guard for fifteen minutes of fresh air, and then the iron doors would shut them in for twenty-four more hours.

One officer in Jan's boxcar was Lt. Janina Lewandowska, a pilot in the Polish Air Force. The daughter of a well-known general, Lewandowska had been married for less than three months at the time of her capture. How and why she came to be included in the otherwise all-male prisoner transport is not known, but her rank, the fact that her husband was an officer, and her family's social status all may have marked her for special handling in the Soviets' eyes. Jan and the other men in the car knew little about the tall, blond woman who was enduring the journey with them. She sat quietly in the lingering twilight of the boxcar, keeping to herself. The gentlemen looked the other way when she needed to visit the hole at the corner of the car.

The temperature turned colder. The officers carefully husbanded the small pile of coal that had been allotted them. (Later Polish deportees to Russia, military and civilian, would rarely be afforded the luxury of fuel to keep them warm during their journeys.) Tending the stove was the only activity available to break up the monotony of confinement.

Five days after leaving Tarnopol, the train unloaded its occupants at a bare platform in a village called Kozel'shchina. Shivering in an icy wind and calculating the amount of time the train had traveled, Jan concluded that the village must be in an Arctic region of Russia. In fact, however, Kozel'shchina lies in central Ukraine, southeast of Kiev and just south of Poltava, where Peter the Great's Russian forces routed the invading Swedes in 1709. The train had covered a little over four hundred miles in five days. Actually, this was a good rate of speed; some other prisoner trains covered the same distance in nine days.

The Poles, many now weakened by colds picked up during the trip, were ordered to march from the station. After walking for some time along a road that passed through a forest, they reached a broad plain. They moved past a sawmill, several mud-and-thatch huts and a series of sheds. Straight ahead a warehouse faced them, a red star painted on its wall. Next to it was a taller building containing offices. The prisoners were led down a cobblestone road toward this settlement. In the distance they could see the onion dome of an Orthodox church, surrounded by a cluster of buildings. The compound was encircled by a barbed-wire fence with watchtowers at the corners. Passing a guardhouse adorned with the omnipresent red star and a portrait of Stalin, the defeated Poles shuffled single file through the gate. They had reached their prison.

~

Jan's group was the first to arrive at the Kozel'shchina camp, one of 140 such facilities that had been set up to hold Polish POWs.

Within the enclosure were the stables and barns of a collective farm, the buildings of a former boarding school, and a number of small houses that had served as the living quarters for a monastery before the revolution. At the center of the settlement stood the ancient church. "In this splendid and sublime baroque church," wrote a later arrival in his diary, "a podium rises in place of the altar. A club and Bolshevik cinema are housed in the shrine."

The Soviet authorities in charge of the camp, officers of the NKVD (the state security agency that preceded the KGB), made it immediately clear to the prisoners that they would be living under a new order. Officers of the Polish army, as well as anyone else with "bourgeois tendencies" or a history of "oppressing the Polish workers," would make up the lowest stratum of society in the camp. The long-oppressed "workers" (low-ranking enlisted men) would occupy the top rungs of the ladder under the new system, with noncommissioned officers somewhere in between.

In practical terms, these theoretical distinctions meant that Jan slept in a barn, while foot soldiers resided in the chapel and living quarters of the old monastery. His insignia identified him as a cadet officer rather than his true rank of second lieutenant because, despite having been promoted, he had not yet been formally commissioned when the war broke out. Thus he avoided classification as a full officer. He was also spared certain indignities that the Soviets meted out to captives who had held particularly "bourgeois" positions in civilian life. If Jan had been identified as a diplomat, he would have shared the fate of the doctors (quartered in a pig shed) or the policemen, lawyers, and judges (assigned to the yard of the monastery, where they were to build their own shanties). Realizing this danger, however, he had taken steps to head it off.

Jan had been carrying a diplomatic passport when he was taken prisoner. As soon as he grasped the peculiar modus vivendi of Kozel'shchina, he decided to get rid of this cherished status symbol. Discarding it presented a challenge in itself—he could not just throw away something that identified him so clearly. Over the course of a couple of evenings, Jan paid multiple visits to the various latrine sites around the camp. He shredded a small portion of the incriminating document each time, until all of the passport was safely disposed of.

Other officers took a little longer to comprehend the new system. On their first day in camp, Kozel'shchina's NKVD commander addressed them at roll call. Major Józef Konopka, a prisoner fluent in Russian, translated, though the Poles could understand much of what the commander said because of similarities between the two languages.

"You are exploiters and bloodsuckers," the commander announced in his welcoming speech. "You will learn how to work in our country. You will not be allowed the opportunity to exploit people any longer. You are prisoners of war. You will have to earn your keep. You will work just as the enlisted men work."

Konopka interrupted the commander. "We are officers," he protested. "The Geneva Convention states that officers are not to be used for physical work."

The commander didn't reject this argument out of hand. He nodded and said he would look into the issue. At the next day's roll call, he told Konopka and the others that he had checked with higher-ups, who informed him that the Soviet Union had not signed the Geneva Convention. "Consequently, you will be treated under the Soviet law," said the commander. "Under Soviet law, everyone must work."

The officers also skirmished with their NKVD warden over their dining arrangements. For their first few days in camp, Soviet troops prepared meals for them. But then the commander announced that the officers must begin cooking for themselves. Again Konopka raised an objection—this time with a half-smile on his face indicating that he knew what the response would be.

"Perhaps there are some cooks among the noncommissioned officers who can run the kitchen for us," ventured the translator.

The commander ruled out any such exploitation of the lower ranks.

"But *tovarisch* commander, there are no cooks among the officers," bantered Konopka.

"Well, then," responded the commander. "If you won't cook or can't cook, you can eat raw food."

They learned how to cook. But the next day, after preparing stew in iron kettles, they left the mess kettles unwashed, assuming that someone would come along to clean them.

"It is rather uncultured," commented the commander at roll call, "not to wash your dishes." Again he told the officers that they could not force the NCOs to do their dirty work. "If, however, you want to prepare food in dirty kettles," he said, "I will not interfere."

The call for kettle-patrol volunteers drew a sparse response. Most of the officers saw the chore as beneath their dignity—but not

Jan. He volunteered immediately. His first cleanup session confirmed his hopes: He could glean extra food from the sides of the kettles. Jan began enriching his diet in this manner after every meal. When the other officers, most of them many years his senior, reproached him for his "disgusting" behavior, Jan just smiled.

As harsh as conditions were at the camp, prisoners were not subject to physical brutality at the hands of their captors. Jan even developed a grudging respect for the depth of conviction displayed by some of the communists he encountered. From the moment he arrived at Kozel'shchina, however, he focused single-mindedly on getting out of the USSR. Like most other educated, upper-middle-class Poles, Jan viewed Russia as a barbarian land. And like other officers in the camp, he knew well the historical antecedents for his captivity—the imprisonment of thousands by tsarist Russia after the failed Polish uprisings of 1830 and 1863. The Russians had dispatched many of those Poles to permanent oblivion in Siberia. The Germans, on the other hand, represented western civilization to Jan. He could hate them for invading his country while still admiring their culture. He felt he had less to fear from the Germans.

The POWs of all ranks were put to work chopping wood in the nearby forest. The job fired Jan's imagination with thoughts of escape. But he knew he wouldn't get far in a hostile country.

As the month of October wore on, a tedious routine set in. At roll call each morning, the men stood for longer and longer periods in the biting autumn chill as the camp grew with the arrival of new captives. Meals and woodchopping were the only other official activities.

Unofficially, but with the permission of the NKVD, an enterprising doctor named Zbigniew Czarnek set up a makeshift clinic to treat medical problems in the camp, the greatest of which was a lice infestation. Clandestinely, the men gathered to analyze the news they were able to glean from Soviet publications and radio. More secretly, a chaplain, Major Jan Leon Ziółkowski, ministered to the camp's population and conducted at least one secret Mass, flouting Soviet directives that forbade religious expression.

Late in October, rumors began to spread of a possible way out of Soviet captivity. A swap of prisoners was in the works. The Soviets would hand over to the Nazis any Poles who were of German ancestry or who had lived in the parts of Poland now annexed to the Third Reich; the Germans would send to Russia the Poles they held who were of Ukrainian and Byelorussian origin. The rationale for this exchange is unclear, but it may have been related to Stalin's desire to claim eastern Poland as an extension of the Ukraine and Byelorussia.

Whatever the geopolitical implications, Jan saw a chance for freedom in the exchange program. As a native of Łódź, which had been incorporated into Germany, he had the necessary documents. And even though only privates were to be included in the swap, Jan's uniform was so badly soiled that it would not give him away as a lieutenant.

One big obstacle, however, lay in the way of Jan's participation in the exchange: his footwear. An officer was immediately identifiable by his boots. With patent leather uppers and soft calfskin extending almost to the knee, Polish officers' boots were at once handsome, durable, and comfortable. But Jan would have to get rid of his pair and get his hands on a soldier's boots.

Jan chose this moment to cultivate a friendship with a member of the enlisted corps. He got to know a private who had about the same shoe size and who, being of Ukrainian origin, was ineligible for the swap. A deal was quickly struck, and the two men arranged a rendezvous in the forest the next day. Dodging behind a large tree while on a log-splitting detail, Jan and the private quickly traded boots. Jan removed what was left of the insignia from his uniform and casually made his way to the church that had become the enlisted-men's barracks.

The NKVD was displaying less than its usual efficiency during this period and had not kept close track of prisoners' identities, merely issuing a number to which each man answered at roll call. After that evening's bed check passed without incident, Jan requested a meeting with the camp commander.

"I am simply a house painter from Łódź," Jan told the NKVD official in Russian a little more broken than what he had spoken as an officer. "My wife is expecting our first child. I want to return to be with her. It's not that I prefer the Germans. I just want to see my wife."

The warden gave the prisoner's documents a cursory glance and looked up with a slight grin. Jan was sure the commandant saw through his subterfuge. The officer rose from his desk and warily eyed the private who stood before him in a filthy uniform without insignia, wearing officer's breeches. Then he sat down, signed a sheet of paper on his desk, and began rifling through a drawer. Jan stood at attention, braced for the worst.

"Well, what are you waiting for?" the commandant barked, motioning toward the door. If he had suspicions, he apparently decided not to bother himself with them. The next morning, Jan and two thousand other Poles boarded a train and set out for Poland.

~

Of the Polish soldiers and noncommissioned officers Jan left behind at Kozel'shchina, a majority would soon be transferred to labor camps throughout the Soviet Union. Many of these prisoners would die during the coming years of harsh imprisonment. Some would live to join a Polish army reconstituted with Stalin's blessing after Germany invaded the Soviet Union on June 22, 1941. These soldiers would eventually leave Russia to fight under the Polish flag alongside the British and Americans in North Africa and Italy.

For most of the commissioned officers captured with Jan on the other hand, and for the other "bourgeois elements" in the camp—the doctors, priests, rabbis, lawyers, and others of prominence in civilian life—the Soviets had another plan. Within days of Jan's departure, the NKVD began transferring these prisoners from Kozel'shchina to three other camps in Russia and the Ukraine. On March 5, 1940, the Soviet Politburo issued secret orders regarding their final disposition. In April and May, 1940, the men were removed from the camps and taken to designated locations by train and specially designed prison trucks. Two NKVD functionaries dragged each individual to the edge of a pit, where a third held a 7.65mm Walther pistol to the nape of the neck and fired a single shot.

The executions took place at several sites, including prisons in the northern town of Kalinin (now Tver) and the Ukrainian city of Kharkov, as well as the location that gave its name to the massacre: the Katyn Forest near Smolensk. The NKVD "processed" some twenty-two thousand of Poland's leading citizens at these locations—members of the military and noncombatants, men and a few women, including Janina Lewandowska. By the end of May, most of the officers with whom Jan had been captured on the road to Tarnopol lay neatly stacked in mass graves, deep in the Soviet heartland.

~

The German officers stood in crisp uniforms at the end of the bridge, gazing serenely as Jan and the other ragged Poles shambled across. The town was Przemyśl; the river was the San, chosen as a line of demarcation when the Nazis and Soviets partitioned Poland. It was the end of October 1939, and the occupying powers were working smoothly together.

Once all of Jan's group had crossed to the German side and all of the former German prisoners had departed for the Soviet side, one of the German officers spoke to the Poles. The gist of his speech was that the men could count on work, food, and good treatment at the hands of the Nazis. The men were then provided with a ration of bread and ersatz honey before they were loaded onto boxcars. Shunted frequently onto sidings to make way for more urgent traffic, the train traveled for forty-eight hours before its doors were opened again at Kielce, a city on the rail line between Warsaw and Kraków. Passenger trains today cover the same distance in six hours or less.

Jan's illusions regarding the "civilized" Germans were quickly shattered as his group reached a new camp, located on the grounds of a Polish military base a few miles north of Kielce, on the way to the city of Radom. It was a model Nazi facility. In every aspect, it served to dehumanize its inhabitants utterly. Prisoners, addressed by the Germans as "Polish swine," received tiny amounts of inedible food that had almost no nutritional value. They slept on the bare ground. Although winter was approaching, their captors provided no blankets or overcoats. Men died regularly of exposure and disease; guards beat and shot others to death.

Jan endured his ten-day incarceration with the support of fellow inmates and a little help from an anonymous hand that tossed packages of food and medicine over the barbed wire fence. During his second week in the camp, he retrieved a package that included a note: "You are leaving the camp in a few days for forced labor." Forewarned, Jan began plotting an escape.

~

The cattle car offered a slight advantage over the boxcars Jan had come to know so well in recent weeks: Its ventilation portals, about a foot high, opened at roughly eye level, rather than in the upper perimeter of the car. Like the other trains that had transported him, however, the convoy that left Radom one morning in November was guarded by machine gun emplacements in its front and rear cars, as well as searchlights positioned on its roof. Sitting in the car, trying to ignore the mingled smells of cattle residue and unwashed humanity, Jan considered his options.

The train was headed south, in the direction of Kraków. Since transporting Polish prisoners in comfort and style was not among Hitler's war aims, the train was likely to move at a leisurely pace, and the journey would probably continue past nightfall. One of the men in the car, familiar with the rails and terrain in this area, had mentioned that the train would pass through a heavily wooded area. The ventilation slits in the car were too high for Jan to jump through unassisted, and it would not be right to do that anyway. The other men, who might suffer reprisals after his escape, should be given a chance to join in.

Jan, waiting for nightfall and watching the landscape, began quietly recruiting collaborators. By the time the train approached the forest, three other POWs had agreed to take part in the operation. Jan stood in the middle of the car and made an announcement:

"Citizens of Poland! I have something to say to you. I am not a private, but an officer. These three men and I are going to jump from the train. Poland is not defeated. I have information about a powerful Polish army in the woods, in the mountains." He had no such information, but he wanted to inspire the men in the car, most of whom seemed to be simple peasant inductees. "I cannot jump by myself," he continued. "Listen, I need three men to raise me and throw me out—carefully—at a point where there are no lights along the track."

The response to this oratory was not overwhelming. Several of the men in the car objected that they would be shot for Jan's escape. Some argued that the Germans would treat everyone well if they just behaved themselves. But enough others sided with Jan to shout down the opposition. Twelve men, including Jan, prepared to jump from the train, while others volunteered to throw them out.

The darkness, the thick forest, and a rain shower all worked in favor of the men. Jan organized them into a line. He watched anxiously as three prisoners hauled the first escapee into a horizontal position, paused, and on Jan's count of three, shoved him through the opening. No sound came from beyond the train. The team in the car quickly pushed four more men through the narrow aperture. At this point, shots rang out and the searchlight pierced the darkness.

The Nazis had spotted the escapees. Jan ordered the team to keep ejecting men until the train came to a halt. The prone figures continued to fly out of the side of the car into the darkness. There was no way of knowing how many of the escapees had been hit, but the Germans had not bothered to stop the train.

Jan went last. There was no time for reflection. His hands wrapped in rags torn from his uniform, he grabbed the edge of the window. The three-man team hauled him into position and launched him from the car. He landed on his feet, then stumbled and fell forward into wet grass. The searchlight had not found him, but the shots continued to pierce the night. He dashed for the forest and crouched behind a tree, watching the train roll on.

Shivering in the icy rain, Jan peered into the darkness in search of the others who had jumped. He spotted one soldier, who turned out to be a very young and frightened private. After trying to calm him, Jan set out with him through the woods. Jan decided to seek assistance from any Poles he could find. Hungry, exhausted, ill-clothed, and in unfamiliar territory, the men knew their only hope lay in the kindness of strangers—a quality that might be in short supply. Not only would anyone who helped them be subject to Nazi retribution, but if they encountered a *Volksdeutsche*, they would probably be immediately betrayed.

As dawn broke, they crept toward a sleeping village. Jan knocked on the door of the first cottage they reached. A gray-bearded old man answered. "Are you or are you not a Pole?" Jan demanded of the peasant. The man responded, with some bemusement and a little irritation, that he was a Polish patriot. After some further efforts to browbeat the man, Jan issued a demand: "You must help us and give us civilian clothes. If you refuse and try to turn us over to the Germans, God will punish you."

It was not the most polite way to ask for help, but it worked. The old man invited them inside; his wife prepared a meal of hot milk and black bread for them. Jan and his comrade bedded down on a lumpy mattress that was, they soon learned, infested with fleas. Under the circumstances, Jan could hardly complain—the peasants' hovel was the lap of luxury compared to the places he had been sleeping in recent months. Still, he did casually mention the infestation to the old woman when he awoke.

"Oh, of course," she said brightly. "Those fleas are always there. They're just a little more active with a stranger around, because they don't know you."

Late that day, carrying loaves of bread and wearing threadbare clothes furnished by the peasants, Jan and the young soldier set out for Warsaw. They reached Kielce within a few hours, but by that time Jan realized that the boy, who had continually whimpered and wept along the way, was experiencing an emotional breakdown. The trauma of his nation's defeat and the horrors he had witnessed as a prisoner seemed to have sunk in only after he had escaped. In Kielce, Jan found a Polish Red Cross nurse and asked her to take charge of the boy, whom Jan considered at risk of committing suicide.

Then he started walking toward Warsaw.

2
Apprentice to the Underground

Chafing in the peasant's ill-fitting suit, shivering without an overcoat in the November chill, his pockets empty, Jan trudged northward. Before he could begin to decide what to do with himself after losing his job and his country, he had to get home to Warsaw.

Six weeks after Poland's capitulation, refugees still thronged its highways. Jan was grateful for their company as he hiked toward Warsaw, a little over one hundred miles away. By blending with the masses, he minimized the chances of being identified by a German patrol. He was, after all, now a fugitive.

The arduous journey was merely one more challenge to his resourcefulness. Before long, Jan put his equestrian knowledge to good use, mending harnesses and salving galls for peasants along the way and bartering his services for rides on their carts, as well as for food and lodging. While making small talk with his fellow travelers, he gleaned information about the outcome of the disastrous military campaign of September and the current situation in the newly occupied country.

Jan was particularly eager to learn what had become of one Warsaw institution—the police force—after the city surrendered to the Germans on September 28. After asking around for a while, he found someone who knew the answer. The Polish police were still at their posts, serving in cooperation with the Germans, Jan was told. And what of Warsaw's chief of security, the commander of the police force, a certain Marian Kozielewski? Still at his post, according to the traveler.

The news concerned Jan deeply. It was simply impossible that his brother had become a traitor. But why was Marian still holding his office, serving under German control? Until Jan could find an answer, he could not return to his brother's home, where he had lived before the mobilization order came. Not only would he be unable to turn to his brother for advice on what to do next, but he would also have no access to what was left of his worldly possessions.

Six wearisome days after he left Kielce, Jan stopped at a train station. He had heard that tickets had become meaningless in the current chaotic environment. The word was that the rides were free—for those who could get on board. The size of the crowd at the station made it clear that the rumor was widespread. When a Warsaw-bound train pulled up to the platform, a panicked rush ensued. Fists and angry curses flew as refugees shoved each other out of the way. Caught up in the heaving crowd, Jan managed to reach a door and pull himself into a car.

He left the train at a suburban Warsaw station, fearing scrutiny from the Germans in the main terminal. Once again wandering with a crowd of refugees, Jan made his way into the city and walked toward the Praga district. The massive destruction inflicted on Warsaw disoriented him; the bombardments of the Blitzkrieg had reduced familiar landmarks into piles of rubble. Still, he could never have imagined how much less would be left of Warsaw by 1945.

The apartment building where Jan's sister Laura and her husband had lived had been spared. Chuckling at the thought that they might take him for a beggar in his present unshaven and ragged condition, he rapped at the door. Laura appeared, showing no surprise at his arrival, her face drawn, her eyes downcast.

Silently she gestured for him to enter. "What's wrong?" Jan asked. "Where is Aleksander?"

Laura fixed her gaze on a portrait of her husband across the room. "He's dead," she said quietly. "He was arrested three weeks ago. They questioned him and tortured him. He was finally shot."

Jan's brother-in-law had joined one of the more than two hundred resistance groups that sprang up spontaneously after Poland fell to the Nazis. The movement Aleksander had joined, like most at the time, was an amateurish operation, undertaken with little understanding of the Gestapo's ruthlessness.

Jan was torn between horror at Aleksander's fate and concern over his own. After offering such words of comfort as he could to his sister, he told her how he had reached Warsaw. His story upset Laura. She worried that the Gestapo had her dwelling under surveillance. He could stay long enough to get some rest and shave his matted beard. She would give him money and let him take one of Aleksander's suits. But then he had to go.

"Can you contact Marian?" asked Jan. He told Laura of his misgivings at learning that his brother had remained at his post.

It was easy enough to reach Marian. Laura dialed his office on the telephone. At Jan's insistence she did not mention his name over the possibly tapped phone line, but she made it clear that Jan was in town and was not sure whether to approach his brother.

"Marian says not to worry," Laura murmured blankly, as she hung up the receiver. "He told me how he wants to meet with you."

~

At the foot of Krakowskie Przedmieście, Warsaw's Main Street, institutions of church and state stood side by side. At Number 1 Krakowskie Przedmieście was the city's police headquarters. Next door, across a small enclosed yard, was the Church of the Holy Cross, a seventeeth-century cathedral best known for one of its relics, an urn containing the heart of Frederic Chopin.

Jan entered the church from the street. He knelt at a familiar pew near the front. There he prayed, and waited. Within a few minutes he heard someone approach from the rear of the church. He stared at the altar as Marian knelt next to him. Then both men bowed their heads.

"What are you doing still in function?" mumbled Jan. He surprised himself with his accusatory tone of voice; Jan had always been deferential to his much older brother, whose gruff manner intimidated him.

"Do you think I don't know what I'm doing?" Marian fumed under his breath. "I was fighting for our motherland's freedom before you were born!" Jan had heard this line before. Same old Marian.

Whispering prayerfully, Marian explained his situation to Jan. During the September campaign he had done his part in defending the city. Just before the surrender he had been awarded the Cross of Bravery by Mayor Stefan Starzyński. But he and the mayor faced a tough decision after Warsaw fell. The German authorities, wanting to maintain civil order, asked Starzyński to remain in his position and to keep the fire, police, and other public service departments functioning as before. Doing so, however, could be perceived as treason. And Starzyński also had to weigh the danger of remaining visible to the Germans rather than going into hiding.

The mayor had chosen to remain in office. At a meeting of policemen, Starzyński explained that he felt a responsibility to maintain whatever vestiges of Polish self-government he could preserve. He exhorted the police to stay on the job, but with a clandestine agenda. As the only Polish forces allowed to carry arms under German rule, said the mayor, the police needed to stay in place so that they could turn on the Nazis in the event of an uprising or an Allied invasion of the country. At the same time, the security forces would be in a position to gather valuable intelligence and to aid in counterintelligence against the Germans.

Implicit in Mayor Starzyński's reasoning was the assumption that a cohesive underground movement would emerge to fight the Germans. His confidence was based on Poland's history of revolt against oppression. Marshal Piłsudski had forged the modern Polish state out of a revolution against Austrian, German, and Russian rule during World War I, and many Poles who remembered the anti-tsarist unrest of 1905 were still alive. The revolts of 1830 and 1863 were the stuff of romantic legends. Of course there would be resistance. The question was how to coordinate it. Starzyński and the police could play a part in that coordination if they took advantage of the opportunities presented to them by the Germans. Some police officers resigned, fearing they would be seen as collaborators, but others, led by their commander Marian Kozielewski, stayed on.

Starzyński paid a heavy price for his decision to stay in office. The Germans soon decided that his services were no longer needed. He had already been arrested by the time Jan returned to Warsaw. Starzyński died in Nazi custody.

"Are you safe?" Jan asked, when Marian told him of Starzyński's arrest.

"So far, I don't see any danger," Marian replied. "What about you? How did you get away?"

Jan gave his brother a brief narrative of his adventures. Marian betrayed no admiration or concern over the perils Jan had endured. He was all business.

"You've got a good story, in case you are arrested," the older brother said curtly. "There are street sweeps going on. They're looking for people like you. I can get you some false documents within a few days. In the meantime, if you get picked up, stick to your story about lying your way out of the Russian camp. But tell them this, too: You decided to escape the Soviet Union because you hate the Bolsheviks, you hate the Jews, and you expected a better life among the Germans. Give them your real name. Since I am dealing with their authorities, I will learn about it if you're captured. I may be able to get you out."

Marian left much unsaid. He did not mention the "POL Insurance Co.," the code name for a conspiracy of policemen that he had helped to organize. He said nothing about his ambition of creating a unified resistance command that would encompass police cells all over Poland. There was no need yet to discuss his baby brother's role in the movement. They could get to that later.

Marian stood up. "You can stay at our place, as long as you come and go through the church," he said. "Wait a while here, and then cut across the yard." A few minutes later, Jan stepped out a side door of the cathedral and walked to his former home, Marian's apartment on the grounds of police headquarters.

~

Equipped with impeccably falsified documents that attested to his gainful employment in a key war industry, Jan moved freely around Warsaw in the days following his return. He sought out prewar friends, gathering as much information as possible from them about the course of the war to date, its future prospects, and the ins and outs of life under occupation. Nearly every rendezvous ran the same course: first a joyous reunion, then a discussion of current affairs, and then an invitation from the friend to join a conspiratorial group.

Each would-be warrior among Jan's acquaintances was sure it was his own destiny to save Poland. Each leaned close and whispered about his movement's elaborate plans to drive the Germans out. And to each Jan responded the same way: "Leave me out of it. I want to live in peace." After learning of his brother-in-law's fate, Jan might well have been wary of wildcat underground activities. In truth, however, Jan was merely constructing a cover for himself. A *real* resistance movement had already come into being, and Jan was about to become a member of it.

Marian spent the evenings explaining his own conspiratorial initiatives to his younger brother and discussing the dynamics of underground life. He also told Jan what he knew about the political developments that had followed Poland's defeat. The government in power when the war began had lost all credibility. Its top officials had fled the country and were now interned in neutral Romania. They had officially ceded power to Polish officials in Paris, which had long been a center for exiled opponents of the Piłsudski regime and its successors.

The most prominent of those opponents, Gen. Władysław Sikorski, had been named prime minister and commander-in-chief. French officials had allowed Sikorski to set up a Polish government-in-exile in the provincial city of Angers. Word of the establishment of the government and the recognition of its sovereignty by Allied governments had spread throughout Poland as soon as it was announced on the BBC and other shortwave radio broadcasts.

After several days, Marian finally called Jan into his office. He stood behind his desk as Jan entered. "Raise your right hand," he ordered sternly. Jan complied. "Repeat after me: In the name of the motherland—"

"In the name of the motherland," Jan said softly, looking into Marian's eyes.

"I swear before God, his Son, and the Holy Spirit—"

"I swear before God, his Son, and the Holy Spirit—"

"—that I will not divulge any of the information which I am about to receive, or any confidences to which I am privy in the future, except as authorized."

Jan repeated the words.

"I hereby pledge to resist aggression against Poland by all means at my disposal. I swear to God, that even under the most extreme circumstances, even unto death, I shall remain faithful to the Polish nation."

Jan completed the oath.

"I haven't told you everything before," said Marian. "There is an underground substitute government in this country. It represents the government of General Sikorski. I am in touch with it; my police network is subordinate to it. By the oath you have just taken, you are now a member of the underground movement."

Marian had held back from informing his brother about this "official" resistance movement until he could consult with one of its leaders about Jan's role. Impressed by what he heard about this rather accomplished young man, that leader had asked for a meeting.

~

The apartment door opened a thin crack. After Jan spoke the password his brother had given him, an elegantly dressed older man invited him in. He introduced himself as Marian Borzęcki, a former minister of the interior who had been ousted from his position by Piłsudski. "I know all about you," said Borzęcki. Himself a religious man, he viewed Jan's youthful membership in Sodalicja Mariańska as an important credential. "This tells me very much," he said. "I have no doubt that you are faithful, that you are a patriot."

Jan suppressed a smile as Borzęcki opened a desk drawer, produced a religious medallion and, placing it in Jan's left hand, ordered him to raise his right hand. Another oath! Clearly, Jan thought, his reputation for piety was getting out of hand. He repeated after Borzęcki, solemnly mouthing the same pledge he had pronounced to his brother.

"I hear that you know languages," Borzęcki said. "You know your way around Europe. I have been told that you lived in England, in Switzerland, in Germany. I have been told that you're a smart fellow. We need someone like you to help our movement communicate with the government abroad. I think you should be sent to France."

Jan took the news in stride. He had been considering whether he should try to leave the country and join the exiled armed forces, which were being reconstituted in France out of escapees. But he was a diplomat, not a soldier. If the underground movement wanted him to act as its ambassador, he would do it.

Borzęcki told Jan he would be back in touch soon.

~

Marian Kozielewski approved of the idea of sending Jan abroad. But he also had his own plans for his little brother. Before Jan could depart for the free world, there was work to be done in Poland.

Throughout the country, policemen were wrestling with the question that Marian and Mayor Starzyński had faced—whether to stay at their posts, or evade the German demands and go into hiding. Marian Kozielewski needed to keep in contact with those comrades regardless of their decisions, and he wanted to urge them to remain in place. The conspiracy would be more cohesive and the officers would be safer, he argued, if they stayed put.

Somebody had to communicate these arguments to policemen in Poland's other cities—no easy feat, especially since the country was now divided into three distinct zones. Western Poland, including the city of Poznań and Jan's hometown of Łódź, had been annexed to Germany. Towns and cities were given German names,

Poles were deported en masse, and the invaders tried to wipe out all traces of Polish culture. Central Poland, including Warsaw, Kraków, and Lublin, became a sort of Polish reservation under German control, known as the General Gouvernement. Eastern Poland, including Jan's college town of Lwów and the city of Wilno (now Vilnius, Lithuania), was under Soviet control. Soon after the Red Army marched into this area, a "plebiscite" had been arranged, in which the residents voted overwhelmingly (or so they were told) to annex their lands to the Ukrainian and Byelorussian Soviet Socialist Republics.

Marian's position allowed him to deputize Jan and to invent missions that would require him to travel to various cities on official police business. In the two German-occupied zones, at least, this technique was foolproof. At a time when all travel was restricted, and when any healthy young Pole on the streets could be seized and sent to a labor camp, Marian's trumped-up police missions offered Jan considerable security.

In the last two weeks of November and the first days of December, 1939, Jan set out on a whirlwind tour of his conquered country. He later reported to the Polish government in France that he had traveled through Poznań and Łódź in the western zone, Lublin and Kraków in the General Gouvernement, and Wilno in the Soviet-held territories. (How he was allowed to reach Wilno remains a mystery, since Marian had no authority there.) While helping to solidify the police conspiracy, Jan also took the opportunity to collect information and impressions from throughout the country that he could share with the government-in-exile when he reached France.

In Łódź, recently renamed Litzmannstadt, Jan witnessed the transformation of a Polish city into a "typical and neat German town," as he wrote two months later. Jan's report described his visceral reaction to the sight of his hometown profaned by the Nazis:

> It's not only that all streets, shops, offices, etc. have only German names; not only that Łódź is flooded with German flags, slogans, posters; not only that stupendous, massive portraits of Nazi dignitaries stare down from the windows and walls of homes; nor that hundreds of German newspapers, brochures, books are lying around nearly everywhere. What's most disturbing is that absolutely everywhere, you hear only and exclusively the German language. He who does not speak German is silent. . . . If someone in line for bread, fuel, or potatoes dares to speak Polish aloud, he runs the risk of being thrown to the end of the line, or not being served at all.

From contacts with aunts and uncles in the western territories, Jan learned more precisely how the Germanization was being carried out.

> Members of my family were forced to move out of Łódź, Zduńska Wola, and Cieszyn. It is forbidden to take along more than 20 kilograms (sometimes less) of food and clothing. A time limit is set for moving out of the apartment or home—2 hours. So systematic are the Germans, that a Gestapo officer instructed my aunt in Zdunska Wola that "the two hours are measured not from the time I arrive, but from the time I receive my orders."

When the Gestapo came to seize his uncle's home, they advised the man that he should "leave a vase full of flowers, 'or something of the kind,' on the table, as a sign that he was leaving peacefully."

Elsewhere in the territory annexed to the Third Reich, such civilities were not necessarily observed. At the Mlyńska Street prison in Poznań, those guilty of "crimes" committed on what was now German soil were dealt with in a manner befitting the Führer's medieval imagination: A headsman decapitated them with an axe. A guillotine at the same prison later dispatched thousands of recalcitrant Poles.

During Jan's travels, a friend who worked as a translator for the Germans told him about a conversation with a twenty-five-year-old Wehrmacht officer, one of the overlords of the new order. The army officer had explained to the Pole that brutality against civilians was simply an aspect of the "virile methods" that the occupying Germans felt obliged to employ. "Not just because they are effective, but also because they regenerate us, they make men of us, they make us aware of our position as the Master Race," the young officer explained cordially. "The Czechs, Slovaks, and Poles offer us a chance to be reborn, to become the grand, old, barbaric, forceful Germany, free of the smallness and weakness of soft cultures and Jewish Christianity."

The morale of the nation had been utterly shattered. "As a result of these pressures, anxieties, and humiliations, Poles are unbelievably depressed, fearful, and in despair," Jan reported to the Polish government in France. "The common people believe that the Antichrist has descended on earth." But desperation only hardened the Poles' will to resist. "Everybody," Jan wrote, "believes that to give in to this fate would mean inevitable death."

~

The sufferings of the Poles were great. But Jan was already acutely
aware that the Nazis had even more diabolical intentions toward
Poland's Jews. He had not been back in Poland long before he witnessed the Nazi noose tightening around the conquered nation's
Jewish community.

Given the persecution of Jews in Germany during the first six
years of Adolf Hitler's rule, anybody in Poland should have been
able to anticipate that the invaders would mistreat Jews in the conquered country. At first, however, there were no overt hints that a
program of mass extermination would be carried out on Polish soil.
The German authorities promulgated anti-Jewish restrictions gradually during the first months of occupation: in October, a law for-
bidding Kosher food preparation; in late November, a decree re-
quiring all Jews to wear armbands emblazoned with the Star of
David; in January, forced registration of Jewish-owned property;
and so on.

Still, Jan could already sense that an even more dire fate lay
in store for the Jews of Poland. Reporting to the government-in-
exile about his trip through the German-annexed western territories, he noted that the Germans were "cleansing the lands seized by
them of Jews, at the expense of Judaizing the General Gouvernement." And he understood that Polish Jews, at least in the western
area, were "intended . . . for destruction or removal."

In Lublin, near the eastern border of the General Gouvernement, Jan personally witnessed the emerging Holocaust. There he
happened upon a "gymnastics and hygiene lesson" that was being
inflicted in public on a few dozen Jews. Forced to sing humiliating
songs while carrying out their exercises, the victims were also subjected to constant taunting and physical abuse from the Germans.
In freezing weather, the Jews were doused with cold water. Old
people fainted from shock or exhaustion. Young boys were stripped
naked, mocked, and threatened by the guards. "The 'Master Race'
is truly a nation of madmen, of brutal haters, and heartless creatures," Jan wrote of the event.

This instance of abuse was no aberration. In a Warsaw marketplace, Jan watched a German soldier walk up to a Jewish peddler's
stand. The soldier picked up socks, combs, and other items, stuffed
them in the pockets of his greatcoat, and casually wandered off. The
Jew followed him, furiously demanding payment. Oblivious, the

soldier walked on. Other Jews tried to hold the peddler back, fearing for his safety. "What can he do to me?" the merchant howled. "He can only kill me. Let him kill me. Let him kill me. Enough of all this. I can't go on anymore."

The soldier glared briefly at the man. "Goddamned Jews," he muttered, and kept walking.

Also in Warsaw, while visiting the Gestapo's office to obtain a pass, Jan saw a pregnant Jewish woman asking for permission to be on the street after curfew, in case she should go into labor at night. A German secretary berated the woman: "You don't need a pass! We're not going to make it easy for you to give birth to a Jew. Dogs are dying from hunger and misery, and you still want to give birth to Jews? Out! Out!"

Such scenes must have horrified all who observed them. But the persecution of Jews had a particularly poignant resonance for Jan Kozielewski. The reason lay in his past.

~

The ghetto walls of medieval Europe that Hitler was destined to reconstruct during the war had been only a psychological presence in Poland. It was, in fact, persecution elsewhere in Europe that prompted the first waves of Jewish immigration to Poland in the early Middle Ages. Often prospering under a system of limited self-government, many Polish Jews isolated themselves in shtetl villages and Jewish areas of cities, speaking primarily Yiddish and rarely interacting with Poles. Others assimilated into Polish society, but even before the Nazi occupation, assimilation had limits that were codified by anti-Semitic regulations like the *numerus clausus*, limiting the Jewish presence in Polish universities.

By the time Jan was growing up, many Poles were openly hostile to Jews. Outbursts of anti-Jewish violence took dozens of Jewish lives in the chaotic days of November 1918, when the end of World War I created a law-and-order vacuum in Poland, and similar violence recurred on several occasions during the next twenty years.

The Kozielewskis' apartment building had been home to several well-assimilated Jewish families. Every autumn, in honor of the harvest holiday Sukkot, the Jewish men would construct a sukkah, a small hut decorated with fruits and branches, in the yard of the building. One of Jan's earliest memories involved his mother's response to the hostility of what she called "bad boys"— anti-Semitic youths—who were amusing themselves by sneaking up to the sukkah and, as the Jews prayed in the hut, tossing dead rats into it. For the remainder of the holiday period, Walentyna Kozielewska ordered Jan to stand guard discreetly at the edge of the yard each evening and to fetch her if the boys returned. She would deal with them, she said. Though terrified that the older youths would beat him up, Jan stood watch for several nights without further incident.

Jan took a cue from his mother's broad-minded Catholicism when he enrolled at the Józef Piłsudski Gimnazjum in 1927. Despite the deeply rooted anti-Semitism of much of the society surrounding him, including elements of the church to which he so fervently adhered, he quickly fell into a clique of Jewish boys who became his closest friends for the next four years. Jewish students ordinarily tended to keep to themselves, but Jan thought of a mutually beneficial arrangement with several of the Jews in his class. He would help the Jews, who were weak in Polish history and literature, and in return those Jewish students who were more talented in math and science would help Jan in his studies.

Jan took his idea to the oldest of the boys, Izio Fuchs. Fuchs, a poor student but a dominant personality among his peers, commanded respect from Jews and non-Jews alike by his piety; he was never seen without his prayer books. He assigned a talented student of the hard sciences, Kuba Przytycki, to tutor Kozielewski, on whom he hung the nickname "Kozioł" (Billy-goat). Przytycki would go through every returned test paper with Jan, scolding him when Jan performed below expectations. Others in Jan's crowd included Lejba Ejbuszyc, an aggressive, muscular, foul-mouthed native of the toughest neighborhood in Łódź; Sasha Goldberg, a chubby, rich kid who boasted that after graduation he would become a financier, since financiers were wealthier and more powerful than bankers; and Salus Fuchs, younger brother of Izio, an aspiring concert pianist whom Jan would remember as "the best-looking boy in Łódź."

Time and events had already eroded these friendships before the war came. In 1938, Jan returned to Łódź for a visit. Meeting Salus Fuchs in Sienkiewicz Park, near Jan's boyhood home, Jan heard about the rising anti-Semitism that in recent years had made life difficult for the Jews of Łódź. Salus told how his devout brother Izio, wearing his yarmulke while walking in public, had been set upon and thrashed by local thugs. Too proud to admit what had happened, or feeling that the authorities would do nothing about it, Izio had told police at the scene that he had merely fallen down. Ever since, said Salus, Izio had been in a precarious psychological

state, often secluding himself for hours of bitter prayer, during
which he would argue with God about the nature of justice and
injustice. Jan had wanted to see Izio during his visit, but Salus said
it would be a bad idea.

Whether any of Jan's Jewish friends from childhood survived
the war, or whether all were among the more than 160,000 Jews of
Łódź murdered by the Nazis, he never learned.

At Jan Kazimierz University, Jan again became close to several
Jewish students. The numerus clausus campaign, designed to reduce the prominence of Jews in professional positions by discouraging or preventing them from attending universities, reached a fe-
ver pitch during his last two years at the Lwów university. Cries of
"Jews to the back!" would often ring out as lectures and classes
began and Polish nationalist students intimidated the Jews into sitting or standing in the back rows.

Jan's favorite professor was Ludwik Ehrlich, a prominent
scholar in the field of international law. Ehrlich was a Jew by birth
who had converted to become an ardent Catholic. He was an intim-
idating presence in the classroom, both because he demanded so
much from students intellectually and because he required their
attendance at every lecture, taking roll to enforce this mandate. Like
other professors, Ehrlich refrained from confronting the right-wing
students openly. But more than once, Jan watched with quiet satisfaction as the professor looked toward the rear of the hall and
growled, "Why are you people standing in the back? There is plenty
of room up here. I cannot conduct my lecture with you hovering
back there. You disturb me. Have a seat in the front." No anti-Semite would dare to protest.

The activities of the right-wing students polarized and in-
flamed the campus. In response to anti-Jewish demonstrations,
some non-Jewish students mounted protest rallies in support of the
Jews. The nationalists frequently attacked individual Jews physically, and non-Jews sometimes came to the defense of the victims.
One of Jan's closest friends, a Catholic named Jerzy Lerski, involved
himself frequently on the side of the Jews, and finally suffered a
beating from the anti-Semites that left him hospitalized for several
weeks.

Jan himself, however, carefully avoided any public involvement with the Jewish cause, despite his disgust with the anti-
Semitism permeating the university. He knew that diplomats had
to steer clear of domestic political entanglements to maintain their

impartial standing within the government. And besides, as he later joked, "those thugs might disfigure my face, and I wouldn't be an attractive ambassador."

Jan's silence in the face of evil at the university would long haunt him. "I simply did not want to get involved," he would ruefully comment as an older man. When the chance arose, some years after college, to compensate for his inaction by coming to the aid of threatened Jews, Jan would seize the opportunity.

- -

By the time he returned to Warsaw in early December 1939, Jan had become an expert on conditions in Nazi-occupied Poland. From his discussions with policemen aligned with his brother, he had also learned much about the potential for effective resistance in his nation. He was soon to learn more.

Summoned to a second rendezvous with Marian Borzęcki, Jan found himself standing before not only Borzęcki but also four other leaders of the embryonic underground movement. Borzęcki, who assumed a more stiff and formal demeanor than he had displayed in their first encounter, chaired the meeting. "You have before you representatives of the most important political organizations in our country," he said to Jan. Turning to the four other men in the room, Borzęcki gave a glowing account of Jan's intelligence, linguistic talents, and resourcefulness—without revealing any information that would have identified him. "I have decided to send this young man to General Sikorski," Borzęcki continued. "In order to avoid any misunderstandings, I will tell you now what instructions he will carry. You will then tell me whether you agree or not."

The four men nodded gravely.

"The 1926 coup d'état that brought the dictator Piłsudski to power created the origins of our current plight," Borzęcki said. (That he and the Piłsudskite Marian Kozielewski were able to collaborate in the underground was indicative of the strange political bedfellows created by wartime conditions.) "The first concentration camp in Poland was established not by Hitler, but by Piłsudski," claimed Borzęcki, referring to the Bereza Kartuska camp where the Marshal's political opponents were detained in 1934. "Now, after our nation has been betrayed by the heirs of Piłsudski, we have seen numerous underground organizations emerging. None have any experience. They have no money. They have no support. As a result, these patriotic but misguided Poles have suffered tremendous losses.

"The problem, obviously, is that they all act independently. It is necessary, therefore, that all underground organizations be brought under the authority of General Sikorski as commander-in-chief and prime minister. If we fail to unify our movement, we will leave the way open for the prewar Piłsudskites to take control once more when the war ends. And they will do with General Sikorski what Piłsudski did with Paderewski," Borzęcki continued, referring to the exile of the much-venerated Polish statesman and pianist Ignacy Paderewski. In order to bring about unity in the underground, Borzęcki postulated, it was vitally important that Sikorski immediately appoint an official delegate in Poland who would act as the lawful representative within the underground of Sikorski's exiled regime. "There is no better man for this position than 'Pan Ryszard' [Mr. Richard]," concluded the resistance leader. "This young man will go to France with our recommendation in this regard, and he should return with the government's nomination of Pan Ryszard."

The four faction leaders each expressed support for Borzęcki's initiative in strong terms. Not knowing who the four men were, Jan had no way of knowing that a charade of sorts was being staged for his benefit. "Pan Ryszard," the unknown leader promoted by these men as the government's delegate in the country, was Ryszard Świętochowski, a confidant of Sikorski. And as Jan would learn only much later, Świętochowski himself was one of the four anonymous faction leaders in the room with Jan, vigorously promoting the candidacy of the mysterious "Pan Ryszard."

Yet again Jan took an oath from the conspirators, swearing that he would faithfully carry their messages and would return as soon as possible with instructions from Sikorski. With a paternal pat on the back, Borzęcki sent him on his way.

~

Jan's brother cut him off when he began excitedly describing the meeting. "I don't want to know what they want," he said. "Don't tell me. It is a burden to know too much these days." Marian had more than security concerns on his mind; he was also revealing his lingering antagonism toward the anti-Piłsudskite leaders who dominated the emerging underground. "They are the government," he told Jan. "You must obey them, and I obey them, too. But I too have a message for you to carry to France." Marian explained that the government-in-exile, while controlled by opponents of the prewar regime, did include one key figure who was a lifetime follower of Marshal Piłsudski. He was Gen. Kazimierz Sosnkowski, second-in-command of the exiled Polish army.

"When you go to France," Marian ordered Jan, "you will reach General Sosnkowski. You will identify yourself. And you will give him a message: 'The commander of police in Warsaw, Marian Kozielewski, considers General Sosnkowski as the successor of Commandant Piłsudski.' He will understand the meaning."

Marian spent several hours with Jan, discussing possible routes across the Polish border and working out the details of Jan's journey. As it happened, one of Marian's subordinates on the police force, a Jew, was planning to cross to the Soviet-occupied zone of Poland in order to escape the Nazis. Marian, who was already helping the policeman with his plans, decided to send Jan with him to Lwów. From there, Jan could try to reach Romania and then could make his way west. Though circuitous, it was the least risky route available. Jan would leave almost immediately.

"You boast and boast that you are a patriot, that you are such a good Pole," said Marian. "Now you will show what you can do for your motherland."

~

The train trip toward the edge of the German-held zone was lengthy, but no complications arose. Departing at a village and hitching a ride from the station on a peasant cart, Jan and the policeman reached the town of Bełżec before the sun went down. Walking to the outskirts of Bełżec, they located the guide whose name they had been given.

He was one of many local residents who specialized in escorting Jews into the Soviet zone. A rush for the border had followed the German invasion and the early abuses of Jews in Poland. Under Soviet rule, Jews had ostensible legal protection against anti-Semitism, and rumor had it that conditions were at least somewhat better for Jews in the Soviet zone than in German-held areas. Few Jews, especially those from the wealthier and better-educated classes, saw the Soviet Union as a truly inviting haven or harbored any illusions about the degree of freedom they would enjoy there. But flight to the East was the only alternative to Nazi rule.

The Germans had trouble keeping the line of demarcation effectively closed, but they did make efforts to keep Jews from escaping. The refugees had to sneak past the guards, with the help of a guide well versed in the local terrain, in order to reach the other side. Not everyone made it. Jan, stuck in Bełżec until the guide was ready to take another group across, saw what happened to those who were caught.

In his report to the government-in-exile early in 1940, Jan described the tableau of misery he witnessed:

> Near Bełżec, the Germans have created a camp of Jews. . . . An enormous proportion walked and slept under the open sky. Very many people were without proper clothing or other covering. While one group slept, the other waited its turn, so that outer garments could be lent to one another. Those who waited jumped and ran around so as not to freeze. . . . All are frozen, in despair, unable to think, hungry—a herd of harassed beasts, not people. This has been going on for weeks. A nightmare—not real. . . . Never in my life have I beheld anything more frightening.

Throughout the war years yet to come, grotesque ironies would often follow Jan's life. One of many such ironies was the fact that he would one day return to the general vicinity of Bełżec, there to behold events that would make him forget all about this visit.

～

After waiting three days in Bełżec, Jan and the policeman joined a large crowd of Jews one night at a predetermined meeting point in the snowy forest. A few mothers had brought their babies along, violating the guide's rules, but he let it pass. Clambering over icy rocks and through pitch-black woods, maintaining a desperate silence—even when the women slipped and fell, or ran into a branch, they found ways to keep the infants quiet—the fugitives traveled thirteen miles on foot. They reached the village of Rawa Russka (now Rava Russkaya, Ukraine), where many of the Jews celebrated their arrival joyously.

Jan and the Jewish policeman boarded a train for Lwów. The car was full of Poles, many of them drunk, who displayed no great fear of Stalin's secret police. They vented loud diatribes at each other, mostly dwelling on the Jews' responsibility for everything that had gone wrong in Poland. Jan worried about the policeman, who was asleep next to him, but he was not personally harassed.

The policeman took Jan to an apartment in Lwów and advised

him to wait there while he consulted with local members of the police conspiracy about the possibility of getting across the Romanian border. Jan waited for several days, rarely leaving the apartment. Lacking Soviet documents, he was much more at risk in the streets of Lwów than in Warsaw. When the policeman finally returned, he had bad news: The border had been heavily reinforced by Red Army troops. There was no chance of Jan's crossing safely.

Jan prepared to return to Warsaw. He would have to find another way to reach France. In a further disappointment, when Jan stopped at the home of Jerzy Lerski's family in Lwów, he learned that he had missed his friend by only days. Lerski had escaped and was on his way to France.

The trip to Lwów did yield one benefit for Jan—a new name. Before he left the city, he called on one of his old mentors from the university, Professor Eugeniusz Kucharski. One of the educator's sons had been among Jan's closest friends, and Jan hoped to learn that Witold Kucharski had survived the turmoil of the past few months. Jan rapped on the door of the Kucharski family's elegant home, which he had visited many times. When Professor Kucharski opened the door and recognized the visitor, Jan could see the blood visibly draining from his face.

"Get out of here," he pleaded, his voice a hoarse whisper. One son, he said, had already been arrested by the secret police. Witold had fled safely to France. But there was no time to talk. "Don't endanger me," the professor said. "You must never come here again. Go!" The door closed quietly.

As disheartening as the encounter was, it nevertheless provided Jan with valuable information. If Witold Kucharski was abroad for the duration of the war, then he certainly wouldn't mind loaning his name to Jan in case it was needed in a pinch. Knowing Witold's birthdate, his address, and the names of his family members, Jan could construct an airtight "legend" that he would have no difficulty remembering if he needed to recite it to the Gestapo.

Jan would take on many other names at different moments during the next few years. But within the underground, he would be known henceforth simply as "Witold." The name "Kucharski" would undergo certain mutations as circumstances demanded. Under one of these pseudonyms, he would depart in a few weeks on a second attempt to reach France. Removing a syllable, he would become Jan Karski.

3
Off to the Phony War

The waiting was over. Marian peeled off a few hundred zlotys from his bankroll and handed the bills to his brother. Jan stuffed the money into the pocket of his overcoat, already heavy from the weight of the gold coins that Jadwiga had sewn into its lining. After a hug from Jadwiga and a firm handshake from Marian, Jan left for the train station.

In the five weeks since Jan's return from Lwów, Marian had anxiously canvassed his police contacts for ideas on how to get his messenger to France. It was vitally important that Jan make the trip soon.

As months went by with no attack on Germany by France and England, the likelihood increased that the Nazi occupation would last a lot longer than most Poles expected. In such a case, Marian's position would become more and more delicate. Serving as police chief under German authority for a short time was defensible on tactical grounds, but long-term service might be regarded as treasonous collaboration when the time came for the Polish government to settle scores after the war—from which, few doubted, even now, that Poland would emerge triumphant. Of the many messages Jan would carry to France, none would be more important, for personal reasons, than a plea from the commander of police in Warsaw, seeking guidance from General Sikorski on how long he should stay at his post.

Now, on January 20, 1940, Jan was finally on his way. Marian could only hope that the itinerary he had so meticulously planned for his brother would work.

For Jan to reach Poland's southern border, the plan had to take into account all the restrictions imposed by the German occupiers as well as the inconveniences and difficulties that affected train travel in a war-torn country. The first leg of the trip was a ride from Warsaw due south to Kraków—a four-hour journey in peacetime. Forbidden by the Germans to travel on direct trains (which were reserved for the occupiers), Poles like Jan had to follow a hopscotch pattern of routes on dilapidated coaches that weaved across southern Poland: Warsaw to Częstochowa, Częstochowa to Kielce, and then, after many hours in the Kielce station, on to Kraków. Altogether, the trip lasted two full days.

As though the length alone were not enough to lend a nightmare quality to the journey, conditions along the way were wretched. Jan recalled the scene in a report he wrote soon after he reached France:

> The train is packed . . . It is mostly unheated, completely unlit, lacking many of its windowpanes. . . . The atmosphere is depressed, the passengers weary, impatient, severe, unforgiving. If conversations are carried on at all, their subjects are only food or war. All are complaining, cursing the former regime; all are embittered.

Many of those on board were smugglers, carrying foodstuffs to market in defiance of German efforts to confiscate Polish produce. Others were city dwellers, obliged by urban shortages to shop for food, clothes, and fuel in the provinces. Desperation was etched onto many of the faces Jan saw. These people, scrambling around Poland in search of better conditions, left Jan with the impression of a society running in circles. "The population is in constant flux," he reported. "Almost everybody is looking for somebody . . . trying to reach somewhere, to buy something, to sell something, to arrange something."

Another category of passengers was the large contingent of Jews in search of safer places to live. Under decrees already announced, Jews were forbidden to change their addresses without special permission from the Gestapo. Within a few days, they would be banned from the railways altogether. Though not yet subject to extermination, the Jews faced ever-increasing privation—and that fact suited some of the Poles in Jan's car quite well. In the absence of even the tenuous legal protections available under the prewar Polish regime, these Jews were at the mercy of Polish anti-Semitism. "The attitude toward the Jewish traveling companions is most often pitiless, severe," noted Jan. "Again and again they are abused with threats, ridiculed, pushed from the seats they have occupied. The Jews remain passive, submissive."

~

In Kraków, Jan spent a couple of days consulting with Marian's co-conspirators on the police force. Most Poles were avoiding public accommodations at this time, fearful of document checks by the Germans. But Jan, armed by Marian with secure documents and a good excuse for traveling, confidently took a room at the hotel Pod Róża (Under the Rose). He did discover upon returning one night, however, that someone had rifled through his backpack.

The train to Zakopane, the winter resort haven in southern Poland's Tatra mountains, was empty in late January. So were the streets, as Jan found when he reached the town. The scene contrasted starkly with the bustling crowds of vacationers he remembered from prewar days. A policeman waited at the station and, exchanging few words with Jan, took him to meet his guide, a Pole who had smuggled goods in peacetime and now made his services available to human beings. Jan took a room in a local hotel. It was unoccupied except for a few German officers on leave with their families.

Jan was an accomplished but out-of-practice skier. After a few days of brushing up his skills along Zakopane's famed slopes, he prepared to depart in the company of his guide and two other escapees. None of the skiers had any illusions about what would happen if they were caught crossing the border into Slovakia (the new nation created when Hitler seized Czechoslovakia and allowed its eastern territories to secede). Several Poles had already been executed at a cemetery in Zakopane for similar attempts.

At dawn on January 29, the entourage set out across the rugged Tatra peaks. Already, Jan had misgivings about the guide. The man claimed to be acting out of patriotic motives, but he had demanded five hundred zlotys—three times a typical worker's monthly salary—as a fee from each escapee. "Unbelievably greedy," commented Jan in his report to the government in France.

For two days, the skiers trekked in bright sunshine, the virgin snow crunching under their feet. Neither the Germans nor anyone else frequented these high slopes. The four men crossed the border on the first day, but they did not let down their guard. Even though

Hitler had not yet invaded Slovakia, its puppet fascist regime would seize and turn over to the Germans any Poles caught on Slovak territory. The skiers avoided mountain villages; each man had brought rations of bread, sausage, and brandy in his backpack. They slept in empty shepherds' huts.

Jan reveled in the freedom of this silent, frozen world, so distant from the terrors and misery of life in Poland. The solitude of the magnificent Tatras offered a few moments of peace and beauty in the midst of what had heretofore been an ugly journey. Unfortunately, Jan was in too much pain to enjoy the idyll fully. The guide had provided him with a new ski outfit in Zakopane, including brand-new boots. Not having broken in the stiff boots adequately, Jan soon found that they were rubbing agonizing blisters on both feet. Compounding the agony, he suffered frostbite on several of his toes.

By the time Jan reached the end of the skiing portion of the trip, he was barely able to walk. The mountain guide handed his clients off to a Slovak associate who, according to plan, would drive them to the Hungarian border. But the Slovak demanded payment in his country's currency, of which Jan had none. After a heated exchange, Jan hobbled off in disgust. He was on his own.

Jan quickly got his hands on a sum of Slovak crowns by selling most of the gold that he was carrying. The Slovak people, bound closely to Poland by tradition and linguistic similarities, were friendly despite their government's alignment with Germany. As Jan limped across this unfamiliar territory, making his way to the south on foot, by bus, and by train, he frequently stopped people to ask for information. The Slovaks he met were universally helpful.

One such encounter took place on a bus that sat at a depot, empty except for its driver. Once again out of Slovak money, Jan decided to take a chance. He climbed aboard.

"Are you a Catholic?" Jan asked, by way of introduction.

"Yes," said the man, squinting quizzically.

"Do you believe in God?"

"Yes."

"Are you an honest person?"

"Yes." The bus driver probably thought he had some sort of proselytizing religious fanatic on his hands.

"Well, I'm in luck," sighed Jan. "Sir, I am a Pole—in misfortune, with my nation gone, alone in a foreign land, penniless. I am sure that a Slovak will not harm a Pole. I'm fleeing from a destroyed homeland, a country stolen away and cast into despair and suffering. I'm going to Hungary. Please," he begged, "help me."

The bus driver proved to be more accommodating than Jan could have hoped. He not only briefed Jan on how to avoid the local authorities, but also introduced him to a taxi driver who was making runs across the Hungarian border and who would accept foreign currency. The taxi driver took him to Dobšina, a Slovak town that straddled the Hungarian border (Hungary had just annexed part of Slovakia). Bidding him bon voyage, Jan's chauffeur dropped him late in the evening at an opportune point in the town, free of Slovak guards. Jan walked across the border.

After presenting his diplomatic passport to Hungarian border guards (despite the fact that he was traveling under a different name), Jan was cordially received and given a free train ticket to Budapest.

~

At the Polish consulate in Budapest, a central processing point for all Polish refugees who reached Hungary, Jan at first encountered less courteous treatment from his own country's officials than he had received from the Hungarian authorities. He was still upset about it four years later, when the Polish government asked him to write a summary of his early activities.

Complaining about the officer who interviewed him upon arrival, Colonel Alfred Krajewski, Jan wrote:

> I cannot refrain from reporting that he behaved toward me in a disloyal manner, not befitting his office. He would not let me travel on to Angers unless I disclosed all my materials to him—moreover, despite my reservations that these materials were very confidential, he brought along to my interrogation the local II Division [Polish intelligence] chief.

Once Jan had convinced the Poles of the importance of his mission, he was still stuck in Budapest until arrangements could be made to move him on to France—a delicate matter, since the neutral Hungarians had promised Hitler they would not let refugee combatants leave their territory. Anyway, Jan was in no physical condition to travel farther just yet. After his initial interrogation, Polish officials checked him into a Budapest hospital for treatment of his swollen, mangled feet as well as a head cold that threatened to turn into pneumonia. He emerged three days later in much better shape, but some discomfort would linger for months. These infirmities, which would have amounted to no more than a painful nuisance in ordinary times, were destined to bring about consequences four months later that would change Jan's life forever, and very nearly end it.

Back on his feet and free to enjoy himself in Budapest until his new travel documents were ready, Jan took in the elegant charms of the Hungarian capital. He attended an opera performance, stopped by some of the more stylish cafés, and visited a spa. The Hungarians he encountered went out of their way to be friendly. Being familiar with neither the language nor the money of the country, Jan would hold out a handful of coins when boarding a tram, and the conductor would pick out the correct amount. Then others on board, recognizing Jan as one of the many refugee Poles in town, would embrace him or shake his hand, offering what Jan could discern as words of solidarity.

A week after Jan reached Budapest, officials at the Polish consulate presented him with his new documents. While en route to France, he would be "Jan Kanicki," a translator of French who worked in a Hungarian tourist office. The Hungarian government had authenticated these papers. Together with the false documents, the consulate dispensed first-class railroad tickets and a generous amount of pocket money to Jan. It also sent a secret cable ahead to Angers, advising the government-in-exile of his impending arrival.

Jan's train trip was almost as routine as any in peacetime. From Hungary the route led south through Yugoslavia, then west across northern Italy. Despite Mussolini's alliance with Hitler, the Italians had made no great effort to interdict passenger traffic into France. Although he had a ticket to Paris, Jan followed the instructions of the Budapest consulate and left the train at Modane, the first stop on the French side of the French-Italian border. On French soil, where his government was recognized as a sovereign ally, he could abandon the temporary identity he had assumed in Budapest. Walking up to a policeman in the station, he stated his business in French: "I am a Polish officer. Please direct me to the Polish military authorities in this city."

Once again, Jan faced an unpleasant reception from the Poles. A captain from the military intelligence division was assigned to deal with him. The man had received no word from Angers about

"Kanicki." He ignored Jan's requests to telephone the prime minister's office in order to clarify matters. The captain conducted a rote interrogation. With the weary sigh of a bureaucrat who has heard it all before, the man sent this refugee where he sent all the Polish refugees who streamed through his office—to a barracks in town, where they would be processed for induction into the army. The captain answered Jan's indignant protests with a blank stare.

A few hours after this encounter, the captain appeared at the barracks, anxiously looking for Jan "Kanicki." When he found Jan, he apologized profusely for the "misunderstanding." The captain had received a call from the prime minister's office—which apparently had inquired about Jan after realizing he was overdue—and now understood the situation. He was terribly sorry for the inconvenience, the officer said, leading the suddenly important visitor from the dank, overcrowded barracks. He had booked Jan a room at the best hotel in Modane.

A limousine arrived from Angers the next morning. By nightfall, Jan reached Poland's temporary seat of government, situated on the River Loire southwest of Paris.

~

At Angers, Jan still maintained a false identity in order to conceal his mission from the Nazi spies who infested France. Paweł Siudak, the official who retrieved Jan from Modane, had given him instructions during the limousine ride on how to remain under cover in France. Jan was to try to avoid the throngs of Poles in Angers and Paris. If he should happen to be recognized by one of the Poles, his story would be that he had come from Poland to look for a military assignment.

Jan's first contact at Angers was Professor Stanisław Kot, formerly of the Jagiellonian University in Kraków, now interior minister of the government-in-exile. Kot, a longtime adversary of Marshal Piłsudski's regime and the closest political adviser to General Sikorski, had a unique capacity for making enemies. Not only Piłsudskites but also many members of other political factions loathed him as an arrogant intriguer. Despite this antipathy, or perhaps in certain ways because of it, he wielded great influence in Sikorski's government.

Kot's lack of popularity stemmed in large part from the fact that he was smarter than most of his opponents. Jan, aware of the professor's reputation as a shrewd judge of people, was careful to be as open and candid as possible when he met Kot at a hotel restaurant in Angers. Jan knew he would be immediately suspect in Kot's eyes because of his family's connection to the Piłsudski regime. He also knew he had to win over the interior minister if he was to be allowed to return to Poland, as he had sworn he would.

Kot appraised the young Pole as they shook hands. "You look like a Parisian banker coming from a banquet," he said, eyeing Jan's new suit, not smiling. On someone who had just escaped from Poland, said Kot, one would have expected "wrinkled trousers and torn socks."

Jan explained that he had purchased the suit in Budapest, with funds provided by the government. But even in occupied Poland, he noted, most people still found a way to look presentable.

"Tell me everything about yourself," Kot ordered. "I want to know who you are, what you did before the war, and which underground group you are aligned with now."

Jan told Kot his true name, which he had been trying to keep secret even within government circles, both for security reasons and in order to avoid being branded a Piłsudskite because of his well-known brother's political affiliation. He gave the professor a complete history of his life and work, making a point of revealing his activity in the Piłsudski-oriented Youth Legion and the fact that his brother was Marian Kozielewski. There were limits to full disclosure, of course; Jan stopped short of telling about the message he was carrying from his brother to General Sosnkowski, the leading supporter of the old regime in the current government.

"It's a shame that people like you represent Poland's interests abroad," Kot remarked coldly. "You don't know your own country. You know nothing about Poland. It astonishes me how you were educated. You walk around with blinders on your eyes, seeing nothing but Piłsudski. But," he conceded, "you do seem to be honest."

Jan bit his tongue, restraining an urge to argue. He listened attentively as Kot briefed him on the often-chaotic political developments that had taken place among the Polish exiles since the Blitzkrieg. Then Jan reported on the similarly turbulent formation and disintegration of political alliances within the underground. This activity had a frantic character, said Jan, because everyone assumed that the war would end soon and all the leaders wanted personally to reshape the political landscape in postwar Poland. In response, Kot warned Jan that nobody should count on a short war, despite the current lull in military activities. Defeating Hitler could take a long time.

In the following days, the government minister summoned Jan to more discussion sessions, in which Kot lectured him about the recent history of Polish politics. The professor seemed intent on reeducating his pupil, whose mind was supposedly polluted with the anti-democratic notions of Piłsudski and his followers. Jan was to endure numerous tutorials from Kot during his sojourn in Angers and did, in fact, find them intellectually stimulating. Moreover, the very fact that Kot was spending so much time converting Jan Kozielewski from Piłsudski-worship suggested to Jan that he had made the right impression on this important cabinet member. In time, Jan developed a certain sympathy for Kot.

Kot took a great interest in the new arrival's news about conditions in Poland. Ordering Jan to dictate a report on life in the occupied country, Kot sent a stenographer to his Angers hotel room. Since this was to be a document for the eyes of cabinet members only, Kot asked him to be as frank as possible. The interior minister told Jan not to worry about polishing his prose but, above all, to work quickly. Such fresh news should be decanted as soon as possible, Kot stressed.

Speaking extemporaneously to the secretary in his room, Jan covered the four areas in which Kot had indicated a specific interest: the tactical details of his journey from Poland, general conditions of life in the country, trends in political thought among the populace, and the situation of Jews in Nazi-occupied Poland. Kot's wife was Jewish; he had indicated to Jan that he was very concerned about her family in Poland.

Jan's report on the increasingly desperate plight of the Jews provided rare and historically valuable documentation of the early stages of Hitler's anti-Semitic terror. When he handed it to Kot after a few days of work, however, Jan realized he knew a little too much for the government's comfort.

Jan's narrative on "the Jewish problem in the Homeland" was a devastating recital of the indignities and traumas to which Jews were being subjected in Poland. Included were Jan's own eyewitness accounts of episodes such as the verbal abuse of the pregnant Jewish woman at the Gestapo office, the "gymnastics and hygiene lesson" in Lublin, and the suffering of Jews at the holding camp near Bełżec. The report also included a survey of living conditions for Jews in each segment of the occupied nation. Jan reported that in the western areas annexed by Germany, "the situation of the Jews is clear, uncomplicated, easy to understand: They are outside of the law. . . . Jews are deprived there of practically all possibilities of living." In the General Gouvernement (central Poland), on the other hand, Jan sensed that "the Germans would like to create something along the lines of a Jewish reservation." And in the eastern areas seized by the Red Army, the Jews were often "better off both economically and politically than they were before the war," according to the report.

Addressing the issue of Jewish collusion with the Soviet occupiers, which had already produced howls of accusation and counteraccusation in Poland and abroad, Jan challenged the prevailing view among non-Jewish Poles. "It is generally believed that the Jews betrayed Poland and the Poles," he wrote, "that they are basically communists, that they crossed over to the Bolsheviks with flags unfurled." But Jan suggested that one could hardly blame some Jews for taking such a stance, given the depredations they had suffered at the hands of Poles before the war. "Their attitude seems to me quite understandable," he reported to the government.

"However," Jan continued, "there are worse cases, where [Jews] denounce Poles . . . [and where] they direct the work of the Bolshevik police force from behind their desks." (This observation foreshadowed similar accusations in the late 1940s from Polish exiles, who cited the prevalence of Jews in the first postwar Communist regime in Poland.) "Unfortunately," Jan reported, "it is necessary to state that such incidents are quite common."

Though all this information was appalling, it would not necessarily create major difficulties for the government-in-exile if it became public. For the moment, of course, all of Jan's reports were top secret. But Kot was so impressed with this recital of German abuses that he hatched the idea of releasing it in some form as part of the Polish propaganda effort. No Pole in exile, however, had the right to level public criticism at the Polish people during a war, Kot told Jan. The interior minister said his staff would recast some of Jan's original thoughts on Polish-Jewish relations so they would not cause a scandal, harm Polish morale, or injure Poland's image in the eyes of the Allies.

Jan understood Kot's motivations and did not object to this manipulation of the report. There was a war on, Jan explained later in life. No purpose would be served by airing the occupied nation's dirty laundry. Social problems could be addressed after the war; for now, unity was imperative. And the anti-Semitism described in the report, while certainly reprehensible, did not look quite as hideous in 1940, before any news of Hitler's mass extermination program had reached outside Germany, as it does today.

After Kot's assistants created new versions of four passages in the text, Jan appended these variants to the original document. On the cover of the copy sent to the information ministry for possible publication, a note in Jan's handwriting reads: "Attention—pp. 6, 9, 10, 11 have the double text." Karski may have been trying to assure that the sugarcoated version of the report would not be presented as fact to people within the government. His scribbled warning about the "double text" was not removed as the report circulated among Polish ministries, and Polish officials who read it did see the damning original pages.

There is no evidence that any portion of the report was ever released to the public. Nonetheless, the Polish government-in-exile's handling of it reveals what parts of Jan's testimony were considered too hot to handle. Two of the changes involved particularly flagrant distortions of what he had originally reported.

Speculating about the possibility of an alliance between Jewish and non-Jewish Poles against the common Nazi enemy, Jan originally wrote that "such an understanding does not exist among the broad masses of the Polish populace." In fact, said Jan, "a large percentage [of non-Jewish Poles] are benefiting from the rights that the new situation gives them." Jan was apparently referring to Polish expropriation of businesses and real estate abandoned by Jews. "They frequently exploit those rights and often even abuse them," he noted. "This brings them, to a certain extent, closer to the Germans."

The amended version of the same passage made exactly the opposite assertion: "The attitude of the Poles toward the Jews has changed in very many instances under the influence of what is happening. . . . In many cases, Poles display visible sympathy for the Jews."

Referring to efforts by Jews to bribe their way out of Nazi restrictions, Jan observed that "the Jews pay, pay, pay—and the Polish peasant, laborer, and stupid, demoralized, dim-witted wretch loudly proclaim, 'Well, they are finally teaching them a lesson!' 'We should learn from [the Germans].' 'The end has come for the Jews!'

'Come what may, we should thank God that the Germans came and took hold of the Jews,' etc."

The altered text of this passage reads: "The Jews pay, pay, pay—the Polish populace, however, more and more frequently, and in ever-wider circles, is thinking aloud: 'This is already too much. . . .' 'This must end with some horrible punishment for the Germans.' "

~

When Kot had extracted all the information he could get from Jan, he finally granted the young Pole's request to meet with the commander-in-chief. Toward the end of February, Jan traveled to Paris, where Sikorski presided over the Polish military buildup.

From the moment of their first handshake, General Władysław Sikorski instantly evoked in Jan a sense of awe tinged with fear. In his years of exile in France, Poland's prime minister and commander-in-chief had acquired a Gallic air of barely perceptible haughtiness; this was paired with the ramrod posture and gruff manner of a lifelong military man. Though Sikorski hardly projected warmth in any event, he was especially cool in receiving Jan. He made it clear at the outset that Kot had told him about Jan Kozielewski, and that he knew Jan came from a family aligned with his political enemy.

As Jan delivered the messages he was sworn to carry—one from his Piłsudskite brother, the other from the anti-Piłsudskite committee headed by Borzęcki—the general listened impassively. Jan could detect no reaction to Marian's plea for guidance on whether to stay in office, and he saw no change in Sikorski's facial expression when he presented the nomination of "Pan Ryszard" as government delegate. At the end of his oral report, Jan emphasized that he had solemnly promised to return to Poland as soon as possible with the government's responses. Only then did he get a reaction out of the commander-in-chief.

"Let me explain something to you, Lieutenant," growled Sikorski, leaning over his desk, his nostrils flaring. The last word had been hissed from between gritted teeth, the better to remind Jan that he was not a civilian diplomat but a mobilized officer in the Polish armed forces, even though he was not in uniform at the moment. "You are still subject to the authority of your superiors in the military chain of command," the general snarled. "You will do what they tell you to do, not what you want to do. I have assigned you to the Ministry of the Interior, to Professor Stanisław Kot. You will work under his direct supervision. Understand!"

This was not a question, but Jan answered it anyway. "Yes, sir."

Crestfallen, Jan boarded the train for Angers. He wondered how the government could be so insensate to the emerging underground's urgent needs as to ignore their requests altogether—and to turn their messenger into a petty bureaucrat. Was the fear and loathing of the old Polish regime truly so intense among Sikorski and his advisers that they would take Jan out of the war, just because of his distant ties to the Piłsudskites? Or had Jan made a *too*-favorable impression on Kot, so that the professor decided to keep him around for his own purposes? Either way, Sikorski's order appeared to leave both Jan's brother and Borzęcki's movement high and dry.

Soon after reporting to the interior ministry, Jan learned that Kot did not even have work for him to do. To the contrary, in the middle of a war, Kot wanted to send Jan on a vacation. "You've had a hard few months," the professor said. "Go to Paris, enjoy yourself, rest up. Go to the theater. Go to the concerts. We will send for you when we need you." Kot's only instructions were that Jan should maintain his cover and that he must avoid becoming ensnared in intrigues by the various Polish factions in Paris. Bewildered, Jan boarded the train once more, returning to the great city, where he had been ordered to have fun.

~

Back in Poland, Marian Kozielewski waited in vain for his brother to return. By April 1940, "Pan Ryszard" Świętochowski had given up on receiving any word from the government-in-exile about his candidacy to act as its chief representative in the underground. There was no sign of the courier that he and Marian Borzęcki had sent abroad three months earlier, despite the young man's sworn assurance that he would return. Frustrated, Świętochowski decided to go to France himself and deal with the matter personally. He made it as far as Slovakia before he was arrested. Ryszard Świętochowski died in Auschwitz in 1941. To Borzęcki, the courtly former government minister who had first suggested Jan's mission, the courier's delay made no difference. The Gestapo had seized him at the end of February. In the torture chamber, Borzęcki was beaten continually with iron rods for days on end, breaking nearly every bone in his body. When the Germans finally determined that he would not reveal any information to them, they shot him.

~

Jan took a room at a modest Parisian hotel and settled in to make the most of the *drôle de guerre*, the "phony war" between the complacent western Allies and Hitler's forces, which were biding their time.

As a first order of business, he resolved to contact General Sosnkowski, the Piłsudskite leader to whom Marian had sent his own conspiratorial message. Jan reasoned that Kot had not *forbidden* him to contact the general (though he probably would not be happy about the meeting), and that he could explain his action, if necessary, as a courtesy call or fact-finding mission. Under the name of Jan Kanicki, he asked for an appointment to meet the general. A meeting in a small, inconspicuous restaurant was scheduled.

Sosnkowski, who had served as Piłsudski's chief of staff during the struggle for Polish independence in the early years of the century, was even more old-school in his military demeanor than Sikorski. Immediately he reprimanded Jan for telling his adjutant freely on the telephone that he wanted to meet the general. "Don't you know that telephones can be tapped?" Sosnkowski chided him. "Now, tell me what it is that you want from me."

"Sir, I am carrying a message from a person in Poland," Jan said, getting to the point as quickly as possible. "The current commander of police forces in Warsaw, Marian Kozielewski, who remains in his prewar position at the moment, wishes me to convey that he considers General of the Army Kazimierz Sosnkowski as the successor to the Commandant, Marshal Piłsudski."

The old general raised one bushy eyebrow. "What binds you to Kozielewski?" he asked.

"Sir," replied Jan, "he is my brother."

Suddenly the warrior's hard edge disappeared. Sosnkowski rose from his chair, stepped around the table, and embraced Jan. "So you are ours," he said softly.

The general reminisced briefly about life in the Legionnaires and about his first contacts with a seventeen-year-old volunteer named Marian Kozielewski. He asked Jan about his background, nodding approvingly at the mention of his activity in the Youth Legion. Jan told how he had reached France, but said he was not sure whether he would be sent back to Poland. Sosnkowski frowned significantly when Jan revealed that he had been assigned to work for Professor Kot.

Jan explained his brother's decision to retain his position with the police and offered details about the police conspiracy. Sosnkowski gave his blessing to Marian's decision, saying that exiled leaders would have no business second-guessing it. Then he announced his response to the message Jan had brought.

"If you return to the Homeland," said Sosnkowski, "you will tell your brother the following: The soldiers of the Commandant should be everywhere."

The general paused, waiting for Jan to ask for an explanation. But Jan simply nodded. He had been exposed to the closed society of Piłsudski's followers long enough to become accustomed to oracular and conspiratorial statements.

"How long will you stay in Paris?" asked Sosnkowski.

"Sir, I don't know," said Jan. "Professor Kot told me that he will summon me back at some point. Every day I have to wait in my room until 9:00 in the morning, ready to go if he calls."

Sosnkowski told Jan he should not have to wander around Paris alone. "I will give you a good guide," he said, beckoning a previously unseen secretary to the table. "This young man is visiting Paris," the general said to her. "I know that most of the galleries are closed, but please take him to whatever is open, or wherever he wants to go."

Every afternoon for more than a week, the secretary picked Jan up and drove him around to see the sights of Paris. Jan grew weary of the tourism, but he had nothing else to do. One night, as Jan and the secretary dined at a restaurant she had suggested, an elegant woman strolled through the door. Jan recognized her immediately as Maria Garczyńska, known throughout Poland as "Marysia." Jan had dealt with her during his ill-starred tenure as leader of the Youth Legion in Lwów; she held a top position in that Piłsudskite organization and was considered highly influential in political circles.

Garczyńska rushed to the table and greeted Jan effusively. But he saw through her feigned surprise right away. This was no chance encounter. Sosnkowski's secretary had set him up for it. Though uninvited, Garczyńska took a seat at the table. In response to her persistent questions, Jan stuck to his cover story: He had come to Paris to join the army.

"There's something I want to talk to you about," Garczyńska said. "Tell me where you're staying, so we can get together." Unable to refuse politely, Jan gave her the name of the hotel.

In his room a couple of mornings later, Jan received a call from the front desk, telling him he had a guest. He invited Garczyńska to his room.

"I know you have been in Angers," Garczyńska said. "Do you know Kot?"

"Yes, slightly," Jan lied.

"Be careful around him. He is an intriguer," she said, forcing Jan to suppress a laugh. She should know about intriguers, he thought. "He is madly anti-Piłsudskite," said the woman. "He persecutes us all. He has spies everywhere. Sosnkowski is surrounded by spies. He is observed everywhere."

Garczyńska went on in this paranoid vein for some time. Finally, Jan interrupted. "Marysia," he asked, "why are you telling me these things? I am not interested. I'm looking for an assignment in the army."

"I'm telling you this so you will inform people in Poland," she snapped.

"Are you crazy?" cried Jan. "Where did you get the idea I'm going to Poland?"

"Janek," she said, calling him by a pet name he had shed after college, "I've been in conspiracies longer than you have. I simply added two plus two, and it came out to four."

Garczyńska dwelled at length on the shabby treatment that Sikorski and his followers had allegedly meted out to Juliusz Łukasiewicz, Poland's last ambassador in Paris before the war. At the time of the country's defeat in late September 1939, Łukasiewicz had played a key role in gaining French approval for the establishment of the government-in-exile. "This man is a patriot," she said, "and now they treat him like a leper."

Jan heard her out politely until she ran out of diatribes, then escorted her to the lobby.

Two days later, Jan was again summoned by the front desk. When he reached the lobby, a gaunt older man introduced himself: "My name is Juliusz Łukasiewicz. I am the former ambassador to France. I would like to have a few words with you. I hope you will not refuse."

Embarrassed at the humility of a man who was so senior to him in the diplomatic corps, Jan led him to the room.

"I know everything about you," said Łukasiewicz. "You have always been the first, always the best." He recited the highlights of Jan's record in the foreign service. "I know you are going back to Poland," he said. "I want to give you some names, some messages to take back with you. We are persecuted here. They don't even want to take us into the army. They deny us even the honor of fighting for our country. We are patriots. We were fighting from the very beginning under Marshal Piłsudski—" Flustered, Łukasiewicz paused to collect himself. "Will you carry this material for us?" he asked.

"Sir, there must be some misunderstanding," Jan answered. "I don't know anything about my going to Poland. I am here in Paris to look for a good assignment with the armed forces."

The diplomat looked into Jan's eyes. "I am sorry for this incident," he said.

The two men sat in silence for some time.

"Mr. Kozielewski," the visitor finally said, "I suppose that you write reports to your superiors about people you meet. May I ask that you not write a report about this conversation to your superiors? I am sure I was not observed."

"Mr. Ambassador, I will do as you ask," said Jan.

"Goodbye," said Łukasiewicz, leaving the room too quickly for Jan to escort him out.

～

At last the call came from Angers. Jan was happy to be out of Paris and away from its scheming Poles, even if he was only returning to a desk job at Angers.

Kot had a surprise for him: Jan was going back to Poland. The government, as it turned out, had intended all along to send him back. "I just didn't want to have you on hand," the professor explained. "You would have only gotten in the way." During Jan's extended vacation, the interior ministry had been busily preparing microfilmed documents for Jan to carry and gathering political information that he would commit to memory.

Back in Angers, Jan was surprised to encounter his college friend Jerzy Lerski, wearing a crisp, new Polish army uniform. The friends shared an awkward moment, as neither could say what he was doing in Angers. They arranged to meet later, and Jan eventually confided in Lerski about the nature of his mission. Jan encouraged his friend to apply for work as a courier himself. Kot was looking for other emissaries to send to Poland, and Jan could highly recommend Lerski's intellect and character.

Lerski declined Jan's offer to submit his name to Kot, claiming that he was not the right type for clandestine work. "I prefer to fight with an open mask," he said, flashing a smile.

"Don't be so sure," Jan replied. "Perhaps those who act secretly are as useful or more useful than those who fight in the front lines." The seed Jan planted in his friend's mind would bear fruit three years later, when Lerski did become an emissary to Poland.

Jan was dispatched to another meeting with Sikorski. The general did have responses to the messages Jan had relayed to him in their prior discussion—he had simply delayed passing them on so Jan would have no opportunity to create mischief in Paris by talking to Poles about Sikorski's positions on the issues involved.

As to the question of who should act as the government delegate, leading the unified underground movement, Sikorski said he would approve any candidate who had the support of all the major factions in the country. The candidate's own politics were of no concern to the government-in-exile; the key point was that the delegate should be chosen by a somewhat democratic process, through a consensus of the rival political movements.

Sikorski, like Sosnkowski, expressed support for Marian Kozielewski's decision to stay at his post. "He does not need to have any moral or patriotic scruples about remaining in function," said the commander-in-chief. "The government approves of his point of view." It was the affirmation Marian so desperately desired. Now Jan merely needed to deliver it to him.

Sikorski and Kot set out an elaborate array of principles to guide the underground forces in their activities. There were guidelines on how the military and civilian wings of the movement should relate to each other, how and when the government-in-exile could step in to resolve disputes among underground leaders, the duties and authority of the government delegate, how best to maintain a defiant attitude among the population, and how the resistance movement could communicate with the government. All this Jan committed to memory, together with the names of nineteen political leaders from various factions whom Kot told him to contact.

At the end of April 1940, Jan left Angers for his return journey. He covered the same route as before, but, with the advantage of careful planning by the government in France, he had a much smoother time of it. Still, there were difficulties. Again he was antagonized by his dealings with Polish authorities in Budapest, which he reached on April 28. Jan later complained to the government that "the director of our base there committed an abuse of my services" by forcing him to carry into Poland a package of money weighing over thirty pounds. This was a task ordinarily reserved for lower-ranking couriers. And again, Jan's feet were in great pain as he hiked over the mountains of Slovakia, now free of snow. The extra weight in his backpack cannot have helped matters. The aggravation of these injuries would soon have grave repercussions for Jan.

~

Hobbling into Kraków at the beginning of May, Jan made his way to the apartment of Tadeusz Pilc, a friend he had known since his high school days in Łódź. Eager though Jan was to reach Warsaw and report to his brother and others, he was physically unable to travel any farther at the moment. Besides, he did have business in Kraków—Kot had told him to contact several individuals there, including a socialist leader named Józef Cyrankiewicz.

Having persuaded Pilc to travel to Warsaw and tell Marian that Jan would arrive soon, Jan used the apartment as a meeting place while he convalesced. Pilc, whose own politics were even to the left of those of the socialists, was nevertheless a friend of Cyrankiewicz and arranged for a meeting. Jan received the socialist leader in bed. The charismatic Cyrankiewicz impressed Jan greatly with the no-nonsense approach to politics he displayed as he briefed Jan on the development of the underground in southern Poland. Although Jan had little sympathy for the socialist political program, he established a relationship with Cyrankiewicz that would prove remarkably durable. In 1974, Jan would have a friendly and emotional reunion with Cyrankiewicz, despite certain aspects of the past that divided the two men. Józef Cyrankiewicz, the Kraków socialist leader in wartime, was destined to become the prime minister of communist Poland.

Pilc returned with the message that Marian was anxiously awaiting Jan's return, and the sooner the better. Cyrankiewicz gave him contact information to help him reach various political leaders in Warsaw, and on May 7, 1940, Jan returned to the capital by train. As usual, he approached his brother's residence by entering the Church of the Holy Cross and then proceeding out its side door, across the courtyard of police headquarters. Still limping badly but grateful to be back home at last, he climbed the stairs to the apartment door and rang the bell.

Jadwiga appeared in the doorway, a pensive look on her face. "The Gestapo took Marian last night," she said, in a nearly whispered monotone. "Leave quietly. Don't attract any attention. They may be watching the building."

~

Having thoroughly infiltrated the police conspiracy, the Gestapo swooped down upon it with fury. In the wee hours of the morning of May 7, the Germans seized sixty-eight officers in addition to Marian, holding all of them for weeks of brutal interrogation at Warsaw's notorious Pawiak prison. Those who survived this experience, including Marian, were then shipped to the sleek new prison camp constructed on the site where the war began for Jan, at Auschwitz.

With the police conspiracy dissolved, "Pan Ryszard" arrested, and Borzęcki executed, Jan's original mission back to Poland was moot. But the underground evolved rapidly, despite the losses sustained among its leaders. The information Jan carried back from Angers was quite valuable to top figures in the resistance movement, even though some of its intended recipients were out of the picture.

In the process of contacting the factional leaders Kot had suggested he see, Jan quickly got his bearings within the emerging underground movement. The underground was becoming increasingly cohesive. Disparate political wings were agreeing to cooperate within the same umbrella organization, while a unified military movement was coalescing out of the scattered cells that had arisen spontaneously in 1939. This increasingly organized conspiratorial apparatus had come into being none too soon for Jan, who had to rely on it for food ration coupons, false identity documents, income, and safe places to live as soon as he returned to Warsaw.

Within a couple of weeks, Jan had met with numerous key personalities in the underground, sharing with them the government's thoughts about the governing principles of the insurgency. There was a general consensus on certain principles. Chief among these was the need to establish a complete, functioning, clandestine state that would symbolically maintain the authority of an independent Poland. Every other aspect of the struggle followed from that tenet. An absolutely uncompromising attitude toward the enemy, an army that respected civilian authority, a quasi-democratic ethos in the civilian underground, and a political climate that rejected the discredited regime of the Piłsudskites—all these steps were essential to maintaining the credibility of the underground movement's claims to legitimacy as a representative of the Polish people.

In late May, Jan was summoned to a meeting of the newly formed Political Coordinating Committee, a council composed of the leaders of each major political faction and the head of the underground military forces. The committee had been meeting weekly in various safe houses since March, constituting a rump parliament of sorts in the very midst of Nazi-occupied Warsaw. These parliamentarians sometimes overcame unusual obstacles to achieving a quorum, as when the Peasant Party's representative missed an early meeting because he had been plucked off the street at random and held with scores of other Poles as a hostage, to be shot if the resistance created any mischief during a certain period. Without missing a beat, the deputy chief of the party filled in until the leader was released.

The house of parliament du jour for the session Jan attended was the apartment of an old woman on Skorupki Street in Warsaw. The woman probably had no idea what her home was being used for, but simply volunteered it to the underground and got out of the way. Jan was ushered into the sitting room, walking into a scene reminiscent of his December meeting with Borzęcki and his allies. He was not given the names of the four men who awaited him in the room, but he learned who they were soon after the meeting. Each of the three political representatives had played a leading role in Polish politics before the war: Kazimierz Pużak of the Socialist Party, Aleksander Dębski of the National Party, and Stefan Korboński of the Peasant Party. All of these factions had been in opposition to the regimes of Marshal Piłsudski and his successors. The fourth man present was General Stefan Rowecki, commander of the Union for Armed Struggle, the military wing of the underground.

Gathered before Jan was the brain trust of the Polish underground movement. These leaders had put aside their partisan differences to engage in a common struggle, with the goal of not only liberating Poland, but also creating a new Polish state that could emerge from the war as a free and democratic nation. In recompense for their efforts, a cruel fate awaited all but one of the men. Rowecki would die at the hands of German captors. Dębski would be decapitated with an axe at the Poznań prison. Pużak, taken prisoner by the Russians after being invited to discuss cooperation with

them in 1945, would perish in his cell five years later. Only Korboński would survive, eventually settling in the United States.

Standing before the committee, Jan explained that he would
repeat the observations and suggestions he had heard from Sikorski
and Kot, speaking purely as a messenger, as though he were a recording. He would not inject his own thoughts into the discussion.
He proceeded to speak for two hours, often quoting entire sentences
from memory. In a memoir, Korboński recalled that Jan

> had an honest appeal and seemed truthful. What he said was not a
> great revelation to us. . . . What General Sikorski wanted to express
> through him and where he intended to go, we knew very well. Nev-
> ertheless, this excellent and detailed report deepened our orientation.
> We bade the emissary . . . farewell, more impressed with his person
> than his report.

In subsequent meetings, Jan became acquainted with each of
these leaders individually. How favorable an impression he made
is clear both from Korboński's reminiscences and from a memoir
left by socialist leader Kazimierz Pużak. Secretly recording his activities for posterity on scrap paper in his prison cell, Pużak praised
Karski as one of the most precise and objective sources of information then available to him. Jan's report to the underground council was "really a masterwork of precise recollection," Pużak recalled.

~

At the end of May, Jan was not surprised to learn that the Political
Coordinating Committee had decided to send him back to France.
He knew there would be a need for further consultations with Si-
korski on details of the underground administration.

In addition, the political leaders each needed to communicate
with their counterparts in exile. It would have been impractical, to
say the least, for each of the parties to send its own individual courier abroad for consultations. Thus it came to pass that the four political movements (the original three plus the Christian Labor Party,
a later addition), often miles apart in basic philosophy and in their
stands on wartime and postwar issues, all transmitted their most
intimate, strategic secrets through a lean, serious young man whom
they knew only as "Witold."

One by one, the leaders huddled with Jan to instruct him as a proxy to their brethren in the West. He listened intently as they explained their parties' positions and vented their petty jealousies and mutual suspicions. "The Socialist Party is well aware of what the nationalists are doing," Pużak told Jan in private. "They look fragmented now, but just wait." At the war's end, he said, the right-wing factions would unite to seize power in a fascist coup. From the National Party's representatives, Jan heard the inverse argument. The leftist parties, they said, were collaborating for nefarious purposes. "We know what they are after," nationalists in the underground confided to Jan. "When the war ends, they will try to create the same kind of popular front of peasants and workers as the socialist Leon Blum created in France before the war. They want to seize power. And behind them, we know, are Jews and international Freemasons. This is a conspiracy. We will not allow it."

Jan nodded along, somehow keeping a straight face.

Long after World War II, Jan Karski—the name he would keep—would speak modestly of many of his wartime activities. But he remained immensely proud of the trust placed in him by the contending political parties, who had faith that "Witold," as a man of honor, would never betray them.

LIFE ON THE EDGE
June 1940–September 1942

4
Sacrifice

Karski's month-long return visit to Poland had coincided with the eruption of hostilities in western Europe, after the long pause of the "phony war." By the time Jan prepared to travel back to Angers in early June 1940, German troops had swarmed through the Netherlands and Belgium in a second Blitzkrieg, penetrating deep into France.

In Poland, where many people were still waiting hopefully for an Anglo-French offensive that would swiftly defeat the Third Reich, an optimistic interpretation of events in the West prevailed. France had skillfully lured the Wehrmacht onto its territory, according to this rationalization. The German divisions, their supply lines overextended, would soon be encircled and destroyed by French and British troops.

Jan told anybody who would listen that he had seen no evidence of such a strategy during his time in France, that the French had boasted over and over about the Maginot Line of defense battlements that would protect them—a barrier the Germans had neatly sidestepped. Jan's friends and colleagues called him an alarmist.

Despite the queasy feeling that the Polish government-in-exile might not exist in France by the time he got there, Jan was determined to make the journey. Both the individual political parties and the collective underground council viewed his mission as urgent. Among other duties, he would seek the government's help in resolving an impasse that had kept the parties from deciding who would act as government delegate, the chief authority in the underground. All the factions agreed on Stefan Korboński for the position, except the nationalists, who considered Korboński too far to the left and threatened to pull out of the alliance if he were chosen.

As Jan stopped in Kraków on his way to the southern border of Poland, he had an encounter that increased his anxiety. He met with Tadeusz Surzycki, a lawyer and nationalist leader in Kraków. In the course of an otherwise routine meeting, one of several Jan had in the city, Surzycki brought out a roll of film and handed it to Jan. "It is important that General Sikorski should know the positions of the National Party in Kraków on certain home affairs," he said. "So we have prepared a selection of key documents for him."

Jan protested vigorously, explaining that he was under strict orders from the central underground authorities in Warsaw to carry all messages orally. He pleaded with the nationalist leader to understand that he was not supposed to have any incriminating materials with him. But Surzycki persisted in his demand. Weary of the argument and eager to maintain good relations with all the political factions, Jan gave in. He would carry the film.

~

During the first week of June, the underground's military wing sent Jan to a safe house in Nowy Sącz, a mid-sized town southeast of Kraków, fifteen miles north of the Slovakian border. At the apartment of a female soldier in the resistance, Zofia Rysiówna, he met the guide who would escort him on the first leg of his journey.

With much to fret about already, Jan took at least some comfort in learning that he would be in the most capable hands available as he crossed Slovakia on the way to Hungary. His escort introduced himself as "Myszka." The stocky, rugged-looking peasant's real name was Franciszek Musiał. Jan had heard from the military authorities in Kraków who organized his transit that Musiał was the champion courier guide on the Slovakian route. A veteran mountaineer who knew the Tatra terrain intimately, he had safely made thirty-one trips across Slovakia since the war began.

Musiał had heard that this client was on an extremely important mission. In the reticent, deferential manner that peasants typically adopted in speaking to city people, he laid out the details of the route to Jan. After crossing the border near his hometown of Piwniczna, they would hike through the mountains to the village of Stara Lubovna, eight miles into Slovakia. There they would catch a ride with what Musiał called a "taxi driver"—one of the smugglers who made a living by running refugees to the south. They would transit the narrowest portion of Slovakia, crossing the Hungarian border at Košice (another Slovak city annexed during the war by Hungary). From there, as before, Jan would be able to travel easily to Budapest and on to France.

Musiał explained the itinerary haltingly, with hesitations that suggested he was leaving something unsaid. "Is there something bothering you about this trip?" Jan asked.

"Sir, please," the guide stammered, "I know that my orders are to get you to Hungary as quickly as possible, but, please, let us wait a little bit."

"Wait? Why on earth should we wait?" Jan responded.

"There were some people who went through this route recently," Musiał revealed. "Two Polish Army officers and a guide. The guide was supposed to be back a few days ago, and he still has not returned. This is unusual. I'm worried, sir. I have a bad feeling about this. Perhaps if we wait a few days we can find out—"

Jan cut his guide short. "No, we have to go now. My mission is urgent." He had made a snap decision. People ran late all the time, Jan mused. People disappeared. People fled to France. People got arrested. Life in the underground was full of uncertainty and risk. If he delayed his work every time he was in danger, he would never get any work done. He was not going to be held up by a superstitious peasant.

Musiał accepted the decision without further comment. The next day, he and Jan left Nowy Sącz on a southbound train. They left the train that night at a tiny mountain village and proceeded toward the border on foot. The following evening, in a driving rain that dulled the vigilance of the German border patrols, Jan and his guide crossed the frontier into Slovakia. They hiked through the night, reaching Stara Lubovna in the early morning hours.

When Musiał made contact with his usual "taxi driver" in the village, he heard bad news. A crackdown by the Gestapo, who functioned openly in Slovakia despite the country's ostensible independence, had put all the "taxis" out of business for the moment. No amount of pleading would convince any driver to make the trip, at least until the Germans eased up. Jan and Musiał could not possibly stay in the town to wait indefinitely for a ride. And after their previous discussion of delaying the mission, Musiał knew there was no point in suggesting that they abort it and return to Poland. If it was impossible to arrange transport by car, they would simply have to travel all the way across Slovakia on foot.

The guide led Jan away from the village before daybreak. When the travelers had put a little more distance between themselves and the border, they halted at a cave, each taking turns on guard duty as the other fitfully slept.

Slogging on through the mud for two more days and nights, Jan became more and more aware that an old problem had returned. With his hobnailed boots completely soaked through, his feet and ankles were once again rubbed raw. They soon swelled to the point that he could not take off the boots. Every step was an exercise in agony. Jan said nothing at first. He trudged on, cursing his failure to foresee this predictable quandary.

By the fifth day of the journey, after covering more than fifty miles, he could walk no further. Desperate for rest, bandages, and a chance to dry out his boots, he finally told Musiał of his predicament. "Isn't there some place we can be put up for the night?" he pleaded.

Courier routes always included safe houses, but Musiał tried to avoid these as a general rule—any contact with the Slovakian population increased the danger a courier faced. He was especially eager to stay away from the established stopping points after the other guide failed to return from his last mission. Jan's request alarmed him deeply.

"I know how tired you are, sir," said Musiał. "But you must realize how dangerous it is to stop over, even briefly." Besides, he argued, they were not that far from the Hungarian border. On the horizon, they could already see the lights of Košice, some twenty miles away.

Jan shrugged helplessly. No matter how close they were to their goal, he could not go on in his present condition. Apologetically, he told Musiał that reaching Hungary that evening was out of the question.

The rugged, rustic mountaineer eyed his suffering client with thinly veiled disgust. "Have it your own way," he said. "There is a village where we can stop for the night."

"Don't be so pessimistic," Jan said with forced cheerfulness. "You will probably enjoy this rest as much as I will."

"I don't think so," Musiał replied gloomily. "I won't feel good until we're on our way again."

The hikers had to double back for a few miles in order to reach the safe house. Plodding to the north, they reached a road that led into a tiny village called Demjata. At about 11:00 in the evening they approached the sleeping hamlet. To avoid its main street, they left the road again and cut through the surrounding fields and forest. At the other end of the town, the men emerged from a copse of woods and crept toward a humble cottage. Musiał rapped gingerly on the door.

A peasant man greeted Musiał amiably. He invited the travelers into his home, asking excitedly about their adventures, offering bread and spirits. His hospitality seemed a little excessive to Jan; it set him on edge. But he was too tired to worry. To get off his feet was all that mattered.

The peasant, a Slovak of Polish descent, had hosted Musiał and other couriers before. Musiał immediately inquired about his colleague who had not returned to Poland. He asked anxiously whether "Antoni," his friend, had stopped at this house lately.

The peasant scratched his head, hemming and hawing, making a show of trying to remember "Antoni," whom he should have known well. "Oh, yes," he finally drawled. "He did come through here, on his way back from Hungary. Is anything wrong?"

Musiał said nothing.

The host moved on to other topics of discussion. At the first moment when he could interrupt the peasant's chatter, Jan excused himself and settled luxuriously into bed.

Jan Kozielewski had always considered himself a man of peace. As a child and a teenager, he had shunned rough play and fled from any threat of violence. He could have held his own physically in any schoolyard brawl or in confrontations like Lerski's battle with anti-Semitic thugs on the university campus. And he was not such a pacifist that he shrank from military service. But violence of any sort offended his sensibilities. Later in life he would turn off any television program that included violent scenes. He could not bear to be exposed to brutality.

Jan had managed to avoid it for the first twenty-six years of his life—until 3:00 that June morning in Slovakia.

~

The gendarme's rifle butt smacked Jan out of his deep slumber, crashing into the side of his head. A hellish cacophony of screams, whimpers, thuds, and throaty cries of "Hands up!" rang through his clouded mind. At this hallucinatory moment, unable to formulate any conscious thought, Jan nevertheless instinctively swiped the roll of film from under his pillow as he was being jerked out of bed.

Breaking free from the policeman's grip, he lunged across the room and plunged the roll into a bucket of water by the stove.

Suddenly the room fell silent. The two Slovakian gendarmes and their two Gestapo bosses froze, apparently fearing that Jan had tossed a grenade. When nothing happened, one of the Germans stepped over to the stove, thrust his hand into the bucket, and pulled out the film. He held it up for the others to see, pantomiming a wan smile.

The other Gestapo officer slugged Jan in the face. Caught by the other German as he staggered back, Jan stared woozily into the man's red face and bloodshot eyes. "Where is your knapsack?" Jan's captor yelled.

When Jan said nothing, the fist smashed into his face again.

"Did you come with anyone else?" Again a pause, and a blow.

"Are you hiding anything?" As Jan gaped mutely, blood trickling from his mouth, unable to answer even if he had wanted to, the Gestapo man struck him once more.

Amid the blur of events, Jan gradually became aware that his traveling companion was undergoing the same treatment across the room. He saw his guide look up at the host who had betrayed them. "Why did you do it?" cried Musiał.

The peasant shook his head, tears running down his fat cheeks. He said nothing.

The Poles were dragged from the house, loaded into separate cars, taken to the police station at the town of Kapušany, and then transported on to the larger town of Prešov. Jan was incarcerated at the military stockade in Prešov.

He lay on a straw pallet in a tiny cell, wiping the blood from his face and wondering what would come next. Tales of Gestapo torture had already taken on legendary proportions within the underground. There could be no doubt that the Germans would use any means available to extract information from him, nor would they place any value on his life once he was no longer of use to them.

Jan knew his only option was to stick to his "legend." He was Witold Kucharski, the son of a professor in Lwów. He was apolitical, not anti-Nazi. He was just sick of the war. He was leaving Poland in the hope of reaching his girlfriend in Switzerland. She lived at Rue de Lausanne 106, Geneva—the actual address of a girl Jan had known during his Swiss sojourn in 1936.

The problem with this scenario was the roll of film, the package

Jan had begged Surzycki not to give to him in Kraków. There was a glimmer of hope: If Jan was lucky, the roll had either cracked when he threw it into the bucket, allowing light to destroy the images on the film, or the water had seeped in to ruin it. Still stunned from the thrashing he had received at the cottage, Jan searched his clouded mind for an excuse for possessing the film. Eventually he hit upon a lie that might work. As a favor to a friend, he would say, he was carrying undeveloped photographs of the ruins of Warsaw. The friend hoped to get his pictures published in the West. He had offered to put Jan in touch with a guide if he would carry the film. The Germans would not like the idea of these pictures being published, but Jan could claim to be innocent of any truly subversive activity.

As Jan lay on the cot, two men entered the cell and wordlessly yanked him to his feet. One of them then spat on the bed. The guards prodded Jan out the cell door, down a hallway and into the bright sunshine. They shoved him into the back of a car and drove to the police station in Prešov.

At a small office in the station, several men milled about, smoking cigarettes and talking casually. They took no apparent notice when Jan was brought into the room. A thin, sandy-haired man in a Gestapo uniform sat behind a small table, staring at the papers in his hands. There was an empty chair across from him.

A guard thrust his fist into the small of Jan's back. "Sit down, Polish swine," he bellowed. Jan stumbled into the chair.

The man looked at Jan with a slightly bored expression on his face. He pushed the papers across the table. "Are these your documents?" he asked in German-accented Polish.

Jan gazed at the identity papers he had been carrying. Although he had rehearsed for this moment, he was paralyzed.

"You don't like talking to us?" taunted the man at the desk. "We aren't good enough for you?" The audience in the room laughed heartily.

The guard behind Jan grabbed his neck and squeezed it in a powerful grip. "Answer the inspector, swine!" he demanded.

"Yes," said Jan. "They are my papers."

"Thank you," the interrogator replied in a snide, nasal voice. "It is so good of you to acknowledge my question with a direct answer. As long as you are in that frame of mind, my friend, you won't mind telling me the entire truth about your connection with the underground?"

"I have no connection with the underground," Jan snapped back. "You can see by my papers, I am the son of a teacher in Lwów."

"I know, I know," said the inspector. "And how long have you been the son of a teacher in Lwów? Two months? Three months?"

Jan sat silently.

"Tell me, teacher's son," the Gestapo officer continued, "have you lived all your life in Lwów?"

"Yes."

"It's a beautiful city, Lwów, isn't it?"

"Yes."

"Someday you would like to see it again, wouldn't you?"

Jan said nothing.

"Tell me, why did you leave Lwów?"

Jan played up his desire to escape from the Soviets, hoping to establish his anti-Communist credentials with the Nazi. The interrogator skillfully twisted his words.

"You liked us and trusted us, but you wished to escape us? I am not a teacher's son," the Gestapo man said. "I do not understand."

Jan launched into the story of his romance with the imaginary girlfriend in Geneva, insisting that he merely wanted to see her and to escape the war.

"And did you not, by chance, want to go to France to join the Polish army?" inquired the inspector.

Jan's denials began to sound feeble even to him. He carried on with the rest of his story, volunteering a detailed account of how he had come to carry the film, even giving the true name and address of a friend in Warsaw (who had already escaped abroad) as the photographer who had sent the film.

The inspector gestured to a man with a writing pad in his lap. "Did you get all of that touching story down, Hans?" he asked. "I want to read it exactly as it is." He turned back to Jan. "Tomorrow," he said, "someone else will have the pleasure of hearing your tale. Your conversation with him will surely be a much more pleasant one."

The Gestapo man smiled thinly for a moment. Then he looked up at the guard and, in a voice suddenly fierce, grumbled: "Get the lying bastard back to his cell."

~

The next day found Jan back in the same chair, in the same smoky office, again surrounded by a chorus of guards who burst into sardonic laughter at every attempted witticism the interrogator made at Jan's expense. The inquisitor himself was a new Gestapo official, an obese man with excessively refined manners.

Jan had spent a sleepless night in anticipation of this session. He knew his story fooled no one. He had to stick to it, if only as a mantra that would focus his mind on keeping all the secrets he knew. His teeth chattered, and his knees nearly buckled as he entered the room. And then he saw the rubber truncheons that the guards held.

His heart pounding, Jan listened to the words of the fat interrogator. "We will not harm you if we are not forced to do so," the rather effete voice was saying. "You will sit opposite me. You must look directly into my eyes at all times. You must answer all my questions at once. . . ." Jan had the impression that the man had made this speech many times before. It was punctuated by dramatic silences.

"I don't beg you to confess," the inspector continued. "I don't give a damn whether you do or don't. If you are sensible and tell the truth, you will be spared. If you don't, you will be beaten to within an inch of your life."

Before asking the first question, the inquisitor briefed Jan on what he already knew. A courier and two Polish officers in his care had indeed been captured at the same peasant hovel where Jan was caught. From them the Germans had extracted considerable information about the courier routes. Now they wanted to know what all the traffic was about. He addressed Jan as "Mr. Courier."

His throat parched, Jan spoke hoarsely: "I don't understand you. I'm not a courier."

The German nodded to a man behind Jan's chair.

The sharpest pain Jan had ever known surged through his body. The baton had landed behind his left ear. He would later describe the feeling as "something like the sensation produced when a dentist's drill strikes a nerve, but infinitely multiplied and spread over the entire nervous system."

Jan tried to sit up straight and look directly into the eyes of his torturer, as ordered. The blow left him dizzy; a fear-driven surge of adrenaline made him nauseous. The Gestapo man started to ask another question, but bolted from his chair when he saw his victim gagging.

"Get him out of here," he told the guards, "before he throws up all over the place."

Carried swiftly to a washroom, Jan vomited in a urinal. Soon he was back in his chair, his arms pinned back by a guard.

The interrogation proceeded, with Jan meekly adhering to his cover story and the inspector coolly tearing it apart. None of Jan's lies worked. Every time he told one, he braced for another blow. The Gestapo officer exposed one aspect of his story as false, then another, then another, but nothing happened to Jan. Working up his courage, he denied with particular vehemence that he had carried a backpack on the trip—as a matter of course, he and Musiał had hidden their packs before stopping for the night, even though they had nothing incriminating in them.

This time, the officer nodded to a guard. A fist crashed into his face. Jan heard a crack. Through the blood filling his mouth, he felt a molar dangling by a root.

The questioning continued. Soon the truncheon again crashed against Jan's head. He pretended to faint, sliding from his seat, but his theatrical efforts brought only snickers from the men in the room. They hauled him back into the chair, assuring him they had seen that trick before.

Finally, frustrated, the interrogator rose from his seat and stepped toward the door. "Get to work on him," he told the guards. "Leave just enough to be questioned."

The henchmen pulled Jan from the chair. He was already too exhausted to resist. Two men propped his sagging body against the wall. A third slammed his fists into Jan's face and body, methodically pummeling him, pounding into him over and over. Then another man took his turn. Then another.

When they grew weary of playing with their human punching bag, the guards let it fall to the floor, unconscious.

After a couple of days, the Gestapo called for Jan again. This time, however, his captors first sent an aged Slovakian janitor and a barber to help Jan prepare for the encounter. His clothes were cleaned, he was allowed to wash up, and he was given a shave. The Slovakians explained the reason for all this attention to his appearance: One mustn't show up shabby and smelly, they said, for a meeting with an SS officer.

The news nurtured some slight hope in Jan. He could not imagine why a member of the elite Schutzstaffel (SS), the Third Reich's army-within-an-army, would want to see him, but at a time when things could hardly get worse, perhaps something good would come of this meeting.

The guards took Jan almost courteously to an office in the same military complex as the prison. Awaiting him was a tall, handsome, blond-haired man of roughly Jan's age, wearing the red swastika armband and gray uniform of a lieutenant in the SS. As an officer of either an intelligence department or the security hierarchy of the SS, he was the superior of the Gestapo men who had tortured Jan. He stepped forward and placed a hand on Jan's shoulder. "Don't be afraid of anything," he said. "I will see to it that no harm comes to you."

Jan could not conceal his amazement, but he remained wary. The officer invited him to his quarters and guided him down a hallway to an elegantly furnished suite. He gestured toward a pair of large maroon armchairs. Offering Jan a glass of brandy and a cigarette, the SS man took the seat opposite him.

"I have changed your status to that of a military prisoner," said the officer, "and have issued instructions that you be treated accordingly."

"Thank you," Jan replied. He considered briefly and then rejected the possibility that the lieutenant was telling the truth.

Quickly it became apparent that this meeting would be simply a less confrontational version of the interrogations Jan had undergone before. After making small talk for a few minutes and expressing his gratitude at finding a cultured man to converse with in this provincial backwater, the SS officer started probing for information. He politely inquired about Jan's underground activities; Jan politely denied them and claimed to be baffled by all this talk of underground activity. After a few minutes of this standoff, the lieutenant's demeanor hardened. "About that roll of film," he said sharply. "Tell me again what was on it."

"The ruins of Warsaw," Jan said wearily. At some level, he knew he was walking into a trap. The lieutenant had already said he had conclusive evidence of Jan's membership in the underground. Still, Jan clung desperately to his cover story.

The SS man got up and walked stiffly to the door. He summoned three Gestapo guards from the corridor. He stepped over to his desk, yanked open a drawer, and pulled out a roll of film. He stood in front of Jan's chair, stretching out the developed roll to its full length. Jan forced himself to look at it. The film was completely blank—except for the last three frames, which had not been destroyed. The officer handed enlarged prints of those frames to Jan. He took them with trembling hands. They were the last three pages of the report written by Surzycki's nationalist group. Jan dropped the prints in his lap.

"There must be some mistake," he murmured weakly. "I must have been misled."

"You'll never stop that idiotic drivel about your innocence, will you?" fumed the SS man, now livid with rage. He reached into the cabinet, from which he had produced the brandy a few minutes earlier, and took out a riding crop. "I thought that you were a gentleman!" he screamed in Jan's face. "I was prepared to treat you as a normal human being! You disappoint me. You are Polish swine!" He lashed the whip across Jan's face, then stepped aside to make room for the Gestapo men.

Hauling Jan out of the armchair and into the hallway, the men fell upon him enthusiastically, beating him with fists and truncheons. As his sensibilities waned, Jan heard a series of loud crunches and felt the teeth spilling out of his mouth. He had lost consciousness entirely by the time one of the guards capped the festivities, delivering a kick to the side that broke several of his ribs.

~

A klieg light fitted with a special reflector illuminated every corner of the cell. It blazed in Jan's swollen eyes as he came to. He lay on the damp stone floor, laboring for every breath, his physical agonies exacerbated by awful anticipation as he awaited the clap of the jackboots approaching down the hallway. There was absolutely nothing he could do to save himself. The Gestapo had truly made his existence a hell on earth.

Still worse was the fear of losing control. Jan knew far too much for the underground's good. He told himself that he would never break, would never disgrace himself and cause the deaths of colleagues by revealing information to the Gestapo. But how could he be certain that his resolution would hold through whatever intensified tortures the Germans were now planning for him? What if he lost his mind?

There was only one way he could deliver himself from this situation: suicide. Under the circumstances, he thought, it would hardly qualify as a brave act, given that the final blow from the enemy would surely be a bullet to the back of the head anyway. Suicide would be a violation of the faith to which he had so strongly adhered all his life; his religion taught that killing oneself was a mortal sin that left the soul in eternal peril. But none of that mattered. Jan was gripped by a pure desire for the deliverance of death.

The planners of his journey were supposed to have given him a vial of cyanide that he could take in just such a circumstance. But he had not been supplied with poison—a lapse later noted with consternation in the memoirs of the underground army's top general. He had, however, remotely considered the possibility of disaster as he planned his trip across Slovakia. Before leaving Warsaw, he had slipped a razor blade into the sole of one of his boots. He had thought that in a desperate situation this implement might come in handy for self-defense. Perhaps he had also sensed he might face a moment like the one he faced now.

Jan waited for the old Slovakian janitor to finish making his rounds. When the corridor fell silent, he tried to summon the strength to tear apart the boot. After a lengthy and painful effort, he extracted the blade.

What was one supposed to think about at a time like this? The thought of his imprisoned brother crossed Jan's mind, as it often had in recent days. Marian might be in the same predicament now, or might already be dead. The anonymity of Jan's impending death struck him. In all likelihood, nobody in Poland would ever know what had happened to him. And he thought bitterly of all the shattered dreams, all the unfulfilled promises he was leaving behind. But Jan had no doubts, no hesitation; he had made his decision. He did not pray.

He plunged the blade into his right wrist. No significant blood emerged. He stabbed again, leaning his weight on the weapon, sawing back and forth through his flesh. Pain was a relative matter at this point—his ribs hurt more than his wrists. Blood poured from the wound. Jan transferred the blade to the bleeding hand, finding it difficult to grip because of the damage he had done to the tendons of his wrist. He slammed his left wrist down onto the edge of the blade as hard as he could. The warm liquid now spurted from his left arm.

Jan fell back against the floor. As he felt himself weakening, he realized the blood had begun to coagulate. He thrashed about, re-opening the gashes. The flow went on. Jan found it harder and harder to breathe. With his last energy, he retched violently, then collapsed peacefully in the muck. The dim light through the cell door faded to black.

~

Suddenly awake, Jan struggled in vain to emit a scream of rage. He tried to thrash free of the bare wooden table to which he was strapped, but the transfusion continued. The world faded out again.

When it faded back in, Jan lay in a hospital ward, surrounded by ancient patients and antiseptic odors. Huge splints, which would have been comical in another time and place, were attached to his wrists. To his utter despair, he soon learned that the old Slovak in the prison had overheard his dying throes and alerted the authorities. The Gestapo had ordered local doctors to preserve their catch for further questioning. The cycle would continue—and now they would be on the lookout for his next suicide attempt.

That attempt would come nonetheless, Jan resolved. He had been deterred once, but it was absolutely imperative that he kill himself. Certainly there was no more to live for at this moment than there had been the night before.

A nun appeared at the bedside, holding a thermometer. "You understand Slovak?" she asked cheerfully.

Jan nodded.

"Listen carefully," she said softly. "It is better to be here than in prison. We will try to keep you here as long as possible. Do you understand?"

Here was a possibility. Perhaps the good sister had it in mind to provide him with a medical exemption from future torture. Interesting, but Jan still refused to allow himself to hope. His misery was multiplied a few days later, when the guard in his room tauntingly placed a newspaper in front of him. Its headline announced the surrender of France to the Nazis on June 22, 1940.

A week went by. Jan played along with the scheme that the nun, and later the doctor who had transfused him, had outlined in whispers over his bed. He made a point of appearing as weak and sickly as possible, to bolster the physician's claim that he had to stay longer at the hospital. But Jan knew he was only putting off the inevitable. On his seventh morning in the Prešov infirmary, two men from the Gestapo came for him. Over the doctor's strenuous protests, they hauled his limp form back to the prison.

Although deposited in his old cell, Jan remained there only a few hours. In an even more foul temper than usual, the Gestapo men returned to take him back to the hospital. The Slovak doctor had evidently convinced higher-ups among the Germans that their prized prisoner would perish without further treatment.

Now in excruciating boredom, still pretending to be near death, still expecting to face further torture as soon as the Germans thought he was ready for it, Jan lay in the hospital while days went by. Then, one day in early July, everything changed.

The Gestapo did come for him again. But after they shoved him into the back of the car, they drove in a different direction from the prison. Jan feared the worst: They could have been taking him to another prison, or even to an execution site. But he felt a glimmer of hope as he realized they were headed north, into Poland. His spirits soared when the car halted in Nowy Sącz—the very town Jan and his guide had left a month earlier, at the outset of their ill-fated journey.

The Germans deposited their cargo in a secured ward at the local hospital. His room, which he shared with several elderly patients, was guarded at times by Polish policemen and at other times by Gestapo men. Immediately Jan began considering the possibility of escape. If he could contact his colleagues in Nowy Sącz, then maybe, just maybe, they could free him.

On the other hand, any such attempt might play right into the hands of the Germans. They had sent him here for a reason, Jan thought. Surely they must have decided that if their prisoner would not tell them about the movement, he could be tricked into showing them some part of it. Jan decided that they were using him as bait. Nevertheless, he had to explore his new options. If the underground could not free him, perhaps it could at least help him commit suicide.

"What can I do to help you?" mumbled a young doctor, leaning over to change the soiled dressings on Jan's wrists. "Can I pass a message to anyone?"

Jan studied the physician's smooth, guileless face. The offer was tempting—but that was probably just how the Gestapo wanted it to seem. "No," pouted the patient, "I have nobody to send messages to. I don't know what you're talking about."

The doctor leaned closer. "Don't be afraid," he said. "I'm not a provocateur. We're all patriotic Poles here."

Jan turned his eyes away from the doctor. He was not about to fall for this trap.

From doctors and nurses alike, Jan heard the same advice he had heard in Prešov. "You are very sick," they kept telling him. "Stay that way." After a couple of days, he learned that the nurses were consistently logging his temperature two or three degrees higher than the thermometer read.

On his second day in the hospital, Jan hatched a plan. He began to moan feverishly, begging to see a priest. He was going to die, he wailed. He had to receive the last rites. The doctor and nurse on the scene reacted with ostentatious distaste in front of the guard, rebuking Jan for disturbing the other patients. But they helped him into a wheelchair and rolled him down to the chapel. The guard dutifully followed, but allowed the prisoner to enter the confessional alone.

"Forgive me, Father, for I have sinned. . . ." Jan had much to confess, given the sin he had tried to commit. But when he had finished asking the priest for absolution, he moved on to a more secular matter. He had qualms about raising it in this holy place, but he dismissed them by rationalizing that he was no longer at confession once he had received absolution.

Jan knelt silently after a final prayer with the priest. He tried to work up his nerve.

After a while, the voice came from the other side of the screen, "Son, go in peace."

Jan did not move.

"Son, go in peace," repeated the priest, a trifle irritated.

"Father, I want you to carry a message to someone for me," Jan finally whispered. "Her name is Zofia Rysiówna. She lives at number 2 Matejko Street."

"And what is it that you want me to tell her?" the paternal voice hesitantly asked.

"That 'Witold Kucharski' is at this hospital," said Jan, "and that he wants poison."

The priest almost wept as he scolded the parishioner on the other side of the booth. "My son, my son," he whispered, "you cannot use the confessional for such earthly matters. You cannot ask me to help you commit the very sin for which you have just received absolution. How can you think of such things?"

Jan kept his silence.

The priest paused. "Oh, my son, my son," he said. He seemed to be groping for words. Finally he spoke again, in a strained whisper: "What's her name? What's that address?"

~

A new nurse tended to Jan the next day, solicitously fluffing his pillow and taking his temperature. She was Zofia Rysiówna, the colleague at whose home Jan had prepared for his departure from Nowy Sącz. Jan's heart raced when he recognized her. The message had been delivered.

"Everybody's crying," Rysiówna mumbled as she hovered over the bed. "Everybody's worrying. What should we do?"

"Inform Józef," said Jan, not moving his lips. He told her that she could reach Józef Cyrankiewicz, the socialist leader, through Tadeusz Pilc, Jan's high-school friend in Kraków. He gave her Pilc's address. "If they can't save me," Jan mumbled, "let them send poison. I can't take any more torture."

Rysiówna went directly from the hospital to the hideout of her brother, Zbigniew Ryś, an official of the local division of the underground's military wing. After discussing the situation with him, she boarded the first available train to Kraków. There she found Pilc and delivered the message for Cyrankiewicz.

By contacting Cyrankiewicz, Jan increased the odds in his favor. Both the underground army and one of the political factions would now be aware of his predicament. Jan knew that Cyrankiewicz was on good terms with the leader of the unified military forces in southern Poland, Tadeusz Komorowski. Independently, however, the socialists also had their own small fighting units. One way or the other, Cyrankiewicz could see to it that something was done for Jan—if, in fact, anything could be done.

Two days after her first visit, Zofia Rysiówna returned to the hospital. Again fluffing Jan's pillow, she put one hand under it. "This is cyanide," she murmured. "It kills painlessly. But don't use it except in the most dire emergency. We will try to arrange your escape."

Komorowski, the military leader, authorized an escape operation, but the socialists agreed to finance it. The main cost would be a bribe offered to the two Polish policemen who would be on duty outside Jan's ward on the night of the operation. For this purpose, the socialists allocated the sizeable sum of twenty thousand zlotys. One of their party's underground officials accompanied Rysiówna on her return trip from Kraków. As soon as she arrived, bringing the cash from the socialists and the go-ahead from Komorowski's headquarters, her brother Zbigniew began organizing a team to carry out the mission.

~

In the shadow of the hospital, crouched on the wet grass, a three-man team waited for midnight. Zbigniew Ryś scanned the grounds in search of guards. The fact that his superiors had forbidden any direct engagement with the enemy had not sunk in on Józef Jenet and Karol Głód, his overanxious young subordinates. They had fairly oozed bravado from the outset—dangerously so. Sixteen-year-old Jenet had even produced a kitchen knife, with which he was ready to take on the Gestapo. Ryś had little faith that his whispered reprimand would have any effect.

The silhouettes of orderlies and nurses appeared occasionally in the corridors and stairwells. A bored-looking janitor was also visible, manning the lodge at the main entrance. The other windows were dark.

Inside the hospital, Dr. Jan Słowikowski emerged from the delivery room, the cries of a newborn fading in his ears as he paced the hallways. To his relief, he encountered none of the recuperating German soldiers who sometimes lingered in the hallways to enjoy a late smoke. Just before midnight, he climbed the stairs to the third floor. At the door to the secured ward, one of the Polish gendarmes was already asleep in his chair, an empty glass sitting on the table next to him. The other glanced briefly at Słowikowski, saying nothing. In the center of Nowy Sącz, church bells rang the hour. The doctor opened the door.

Jan lay still, watching the figure in the doorway, listening for any interruption in the steady breathing and snores coming from the other five beds in the room. Słowikowski, the baby-faced physician whose offer Jan had earlier rejected, had turned out to be a genuine underground member after all. He slowly pulled out a cigarette and lit it. Seeing this all-clear signal, Jan rose from his bed. He clutched the cyanide capsule tightly: Tonight he would be free or die.

Quickly, quietly, the patient took off his gown and padded naked toward the door. Dr. Słowikowski disappeared. The gendarme guided Jan to the stairway, then rushed back to his seat. The policeman gulped down the sedative-laced water in his glass and nestled into the chair next to his comrade.

Jan staggered all the way down to the ground floor and began fumbling with the lock on the stairwell window. He tried furiously to turn the lock, but couldn't muster the grip strength. Hearing the voices of nurses in the corridor, he stumbled up to the next landing. There through the open window he saw Zbigniew Ryś, who had climbed to the roof of an annex to the building.

Clambering over the windowsill, Jan fell into the arms of Ryś. The two men crawled across the roof. Ryś jumped to the ground ahead of Jan and then caught the naked fugitive on his shoulders as he climbed down. Jan glanced at the faces of his rescuers as Jenet and Głód slipped a jacket and trousers over him; he recognized none of them. Each throwing an arm around him, Jenet and Głód half-carried Jan toward the fence surrounding the hospital grounds.

Running, or even walking, was an ordeal for the weak, injured, barefoot escapee. Scaling the fence was out of the question. He held up his bandaged wrists in silent apology. The three underground fighters swept him up and shoved him over the fence in one swift motion. The escape team's lookout, Tadeusz Szafran, caught him on the other side. Ryś now led the group toward the River Dunajec, ignoring Jan's feeble plea for a brief rest. Every minute of delay due to Jan's frailty would leave the trail that much fresher for the blood-hounds. Signaling for the others to hoist their cargo onto his back, Ryś carried Jan the rest of the way to the river.

At the Dunajec, the three younger men under the command of Ryś fled into the darkness, their mission completed. Another underground member emerged from the rushes at the water's edge, pulling a rowboat to the bank. He and Ryś helped Jan into the boat and began rowing, against the current, toward the opposite shore of the broad river.

As the rescuers furiously paddled, the boat listed wildly from side to side. Jan, weak and dizzy, held on to the side of the boat as firmly as he could. But in the middle of the river, he tumbled over the side. Ryś, a powerfully built man, calmly set down his oar and hauled Jan back into the boat. Jan lay on the floor of the boat, shivering uncontrollably, until it reached the other shore. The crossing took more than an hour.

After hiding the boat in the rushes, Jan and his liberators fled through a forest and across a moonlit field. In agony all the way from his soggy bandages to his bare feet, but exhilarated by the promise of deliverance from the Gestapo, Jan alternately limped along with the two men and rode piggyback on them. They reached a country road and fell into a trot, racing the approaching dawn. As the first light approached, Ryś and the other conspirator led Jan through a foggy pasture and halted at a barn.

"We must leave you here," said Ryś. "Your host will pay his respects tomorrow. He will see to it that you are well hidden for a while. You will be contacted as soon as the Gestapo chase slackens off."

Jan, too excited and exhausted to speak coherently, tried to babble his thanks. Ryś cut him off.

"You better cut out all those thanksgivings," said Ryś. "I had two orders. The first was to get you out if I could. The second was to shoot you if I failed."

Jan concealed himself in a hay loft, awaiting further developments. The barn's owner, an ancient farmer who was a veteran of the anti-tsarist underground of 1905, brought food twice a day. After several days, two underground agents arrived to evacuate the fugitive from the Nowy Sącz area.

Buried under a small mountain of produce in a horse-drawn cart, Jan rode for hours on end. When he was allowed to emerge from the fragrant pile, he was on a remote rural pike southwest of Kraków, near the village of Kąty. A fresh-faced young woman awaited him there. Jan rode with her to a modest, isolated country estate, nestled in mountainous terrain. His escape was over; his quarantine—a standard precaution taken with any underground member who had been compromised—had begun.

~

At dawn on the morning after the escape, the two policemen in the hospital corridor awoke to find a formidable nurse hovering over them and inquiring none too politely about the whereabouts of patient "Kucharski." They looked at each other sheepishly, wondering aloud how they could both have fallen asleep at once.

As the nurse charged off to notify the authorities, the policemen scurried off to hang a rope from one of the windows of their floor. During interrogations, and later when they were on trial for negligence, the rope and the sedative residue in their water glasses would temporarily convince the Germans of their innocence.

The Gestapo investigation at the hospital hit a dead end. Doctors, nurses, and patients could offer no clues. A large bounty was posted for information leading to the capture of Kucharski and those who had helped him escape, but without effect. A dragnet around the Nowy Sącz area and house-to-house searches yielded nothing.

In the *Vigilance Gazette*, a newsletter distributed to police stations throughout Poland, Jan's photo appeared over the caption: "A dangerous bandit who is a threat to the people." The newsletter advised officials that the fugitive was easily recognizable by the scars on his wrists.

Obersturmführer Heinrich Hamann, commander of the Gestapo in Nowy Sącz, pursued the case relentlessly. His suspicions were heightened by a series of disappearances: First one of the acquitted policemen, then Dr. Słowikowski, then Zofia Rysiówna went into hiding. Then, in May 1941, the Gestapo somehow broke the case. How the Germans learned the names of those involved in the escape has never been determined with certainty, but local rumor had it that one of the excitable young conspirators under the command of Ryś—either Jenet, or Głód, or Szafran—bragged to friends about his exploits.

Rysiówna, captured in Warsaw, was imprisoned at the Ravensbrück concentration camp until it was liberated in 1945. Głód and Jenet were captured with another underground member who had helped to transport Jan out of the area. All three were sent to Auschwitz. None survived captivity. Szafran was held at the prison in Nowy Sącz. The second drugged policeman from the hospital, rearrested after his acquittal, was also detained at the prison. Unable to find Jan Słowikowski, the Gestapo jailed another local doctor, along with Słowikowski's brother Teodor. Unable to determine which of two local priests had carried Jan's message from the hospital confessional to the underground, the Gestapo imprisoned both. Dozens of other Nowy Sącz residents filled the jail as well, not charged with taking part in the escape, but simply held in retribution for it.

The Nowy Sącz prison echoed with the cries of the tortured throughout the summer of 1941 as the Germans tried to extract the whereabouts of the escapee from the Poles they held. By late summer, Hamann had apparently given up on finding the escapee. But he could still teach a lesson to the Poles in his custody.

The Polish underground made a specialty of jailbreaks, but there was to be no jailbreak in Nowy Sącz. The Poles also often managed to set up efficient lines of communication between prisoners and the outside world, generally by bribing guards to carry messages. After several months of captivity, one of the imprisoned priests smuggled such a message to the outside:

Tomorrow, on 21 August at 5:00 A.M., they will shoot us. We are calm and we wish you the same. It seems our beloved country needs this sacrifice. We shall pray for you at the Lord's throne. We forgive everyone and ask for your prayers for our souls. If we have wronged anyone, we are sorry. We apologize to all our parishioners.

As dawn broke the next morning, the crack of automatic rifles rang out from a brickyard in the nearby town of Biegonice. Thirty-two Poles fell dead, punished for their real or imagined parts in the escape of "Witold Kucharski."

5
A Routine Existence

Oblivious to events in Nowy Sącz, or anywhere else within the underground for the most part, Jan spent the next seven months in forced semiretirement from the movement. Since resistance leaders could not be certain that the Germans had not allowed him to escape as a means of exposing the underground, security considerations required that he break contact for a time with all the conspirators he knew.

Jan was literally put out to pasture. His new home was a spacious but simple mansion, situated on a few dozen acres of farmland just outside of Kąty. Its owners, a couple named Sławik, had earned the money to acquire it by emigrating to the United States for a few years. Their daughter Danuta had met Jan as he emerged from the produce-laden cart, amused and embarrassed to compare his own bedraggled and emaciated appearance with the lithe, healthy figure she cut.

Jan became Danuta's "cousin from Kraków," sent to the countryside to recuperate from a persistent illness. Perhaps it was assumed that his penchant for long-sleeved shirts, even on the hottest days of July, arose from embarrassment at his scrawny physique— rather than from a need to hide his mangled wrists from scrutiny. He posed as a gardener by trade, though he knew next to nothing of the land and its bounty. In this position he could easily make himself scarce when the Germans came around to collect the "contingent" of agricultural products that each farm was required to render up every few weeks.

To curious villagers and laborers on the estate, Danuta and her parents put the word out that the cousin from the city was a bit of a coward, a malingerer who had evaded military service. Jan got into the habit of encouraging that impression by slipping the occasional pro-German remark into his conversations with the locals.

When he first arrived, Jan reveled in the joy of freedom, the crisp freshness of the country air, the luxury of a healthy diet, and the opportunity of convalescence from his injuries. But the tedium of the bucolic life wore on him quickly. He could have no social life beyond the estate, aside from a few visits with the Sławiks to a neighboring mansion (this one more authentically aristocratic, owned by a count). After a while he thought Danuta might have a crush on him, but now was no time to get into a romantic entanglement, however much he enjoyed her cheerful company and admired her spunky attitude. There were few books in the house. There was a gramophone, but with a limited selection of disks, and Danuta played one popular recording, a love song called "Fernando," frequently enough to drive Jan to distraction.

Most grating of all was the enforced isolation from the movement for which he had been ready a few weeks earlier to give his life. Jan understood the necessity of the security quarantine, but chafed under it nonetheless. When the chance arose to initiate some limited work for the underground once more, he leapt at it.

Weeks after his arrival, Jan learned that the Sławik family's involvement in resistance work went beyond sheltering him. Danuta had a brother, Lucjan, an underground member who lived in hiding. Lucjan regularly visited his sister at night, rapping gently on her window. Danuta eventually let Jan in on the secret, and he began attending their midnight meetings in the garden. Lucjan did not discuss his activities during the visits, but Jan knew he held a high-ranking position in the area command of the underground. After hearing Jan complain repeatedly about his inactivity, Lucjan finally decided to assign him some "safe" work.

Jan's new part-time job involved the generation of "black propaganda" for Action N, a resistance cell devoted to undermining the morale of the occupier. His contribution was his imagination. Taking on the personae of German soldiers and civilians discontented with aspects of the war effort, he would write letters and leaflets to be distributed among the Germans. The writings would be more believable, Lucjan told him, if he would avoid overtly dissident arguments. Instead, Jan should pose as a loyal supporter of Hitler, unhappy with the way the Führer's underlings were carrying out his will.

Jan wrote in Polish, since he did not have enough confidence in his command of German to be sure of avoiding a slipup; a skilled linguist within the movement translated his work. The letters were then copied onto German brands of paper and mailed from a point within the German-annexed western area of Poland territories, which had been incorporated into the Reich's postal system. Recipients were chosen at random, through telephone books and similar sources. The leaflets were strewn in cafes, coffeehouses, brothels, and other places favored by German troops in Poland.

Lucjan gave Jan free rein to write about any morale-weakening conflict he could imagine. Often Jan posed as a grousing footsoldier, writing home anonymously—the letters generally included a passage to the effect of "You know me, but I can't identify myself in this letter"— to complain of the hardships he was facing. For instance: "The Polish people are not as friendly as Göbbels' propaganda makes them out to be. . . ." In other epistles, Jan became the concerned German civilian: "As a good Catholic, I am ashamed of what our authorities are doing to the Jews, God's chosen people. . . ." "Hitler is a man of destiny, but he doesn't realize how many of his subordinates are little people, greedy people, like Göring—a drug addict who steals artistic treasures from galleries. A true German nobleman would never do such things."

Jan never had much faith in the effectiveness of these psychological-warfare efforts. But they gave him something to do, providing some minuscule contribution he could make to the war effort. He threw his full energies into the job. Still, he chafed at his indefinite quarantine and took every opportunity to plead with Lucjan for parole. Since Lucjan did not tell him what had happened in Nowy Sącz after his escape, Jan could not know just what a sought-after fugitive he was and thus how necessary an extended quarantine was.

In February 1941, Lucjan finally brought Jan the news he had awaited from the underground command: He was free to go. Expressing his gratitude to his new friends Danuta and Lucjan and to their parents for the months of hospitality, Jan left the Sławik estate. After spending a long period in a seemingly secure environment, he found it hard to readjust to a life of constant danger as he returned to Kraków to resume his full-fledged involvement in underground activities.

Only later did he learn how lucky he was that his leave of absence ended when it did. Some months after Jan's departure, the

Germans arrested the entire Sławik family. Lucjan endured brutal interrogation and imprisonment, but he and his mother and father survived the war. After months of imprisonment and torture, Danuta Sławik was executed by the Gestapo in 1942.

~

It was only natural that Jan should seek out his contacts from the Socialist Party when he returned to Kraków. After all, they and the underground military wing had saved his life.

Despite his aversion to partisan politics in general and to the tenets of socialism in particular, he gravitated toward the charismatic Józef Cyrankiewicz and others in the socialist camp, as well as his even more leftist friend Tadeusz Pilc. (It should be noted that Cyrankiewicz and his followers espoused a parliamentary brand of socialism that had little in common with the so-called socialism of postwar communist slogans.) "They were against the Germans," Karski later explained. "It didn't make any difference to me. I had much more faith in Cyrankiewicz at the time than in any of that stupid black propaganda."

To his dismay, Jan learned upon arrival in Kraków that he would have to remain in the black-propaganda business for a while. Colonel Komorowski, the Kraków military chief who had helped to rescue him, had appointed him deputy director of Action N for the Kraków area. Jan knew he could not go back to acting as a courier— with the scars marking his wrists, and with the Gestapo still freshly smarting from his escape, any encounter with the Germans could lead to devastating consequences not only for Jan but for the entire underground. Still, he felt that he was wasting his time on propaganda that would accomplish little or nothing.

At the first opportunity, he arranged for a transfer to a division that monitored foreign radio broadcasts. Here he could at least put his linguistic talents to use. He was still risking his life, of course: A German edict in December 1939 had made possession of a short-wave radio a capital offense. But Jan found an ideal place to live and to carry on his work, right next door to the occupier.

He settled into a room in the ample and luxuriously furnished apartment suite of Bronisława Langrodowa, the wife of a diplomat whom Jan had known during his stint in Geneva in 1936. Because her husband had been trapped abroad by the Blitzkrieg, she had been left alone to raise a young son under wartime conditions, under a regime that would have treated her as a Jew if her mixed ancestry had been revealed. Langrodowa had gradually sold off personal possessions since the war started, and now she had been reduced to renting out rooms to make ends meet. In the spring of 1941, she had two tenants: a member of the Polish underground and a German army officer.

Since Langrodowa served as a top assistant and confidant to Józef Cyrankiewicz, she often hosted conspiratorial meetings as well as Jan's radio work. She insisted that the Wehrmacht officer's presence in nearby rooms provided a perfect cover—she could tell that he didn't suspect anything (it helped that he spoke no Polish) and other Germans would have no suspicion because he was there. Jan and his landlady carried on their activities discreetly, keeping a polite distance from the other lodger. Jan's living situation was rife with both dangerous and comic possibilities, but fortunately or unfortunately it did not last long.

One day in late March 1941, Cyrankiewicz came to the apartment for an appointment with Komorowski's chief-of-staff, the deputy commander of the Union for Armed Struggle. The military man did not show up on time. Cyrankiewicz reacted with fury. Punctuality was absolutely crucial to conspiratorial work, but, as he fumed to Jan and Langrodowa, people from the army couldn't even get to a meeting on time. Wasn't it just typical of the inefficient, politically backward military functionaries who had run Poland before the war? Well, someone needed to teach Komorowski's deputy a lesson. Cyrankiewicz told Langrodowa that he was going to the tardy conspirator's apartment.

"Józef, don't go!" Langrodowa pleaded, suddenly alarmed. "You don't know what may have happened to him."

Cyrankiewicz brushed off her concerns. "I'll be back in two hours," he promised.

Jan and his landlady passed two dread-laden hours together. Cyrankiewicz did not return. Langrodowa did not hesitate; she began packing immediately. "I am sure that even under torture, Józef will not reveal my name," she told Jan. "But I'm leaving Kraków anyway." She soon departed for Warsaw.

After arresting Komorowski's adjutant, the Germans had used him to "set up a kettle," as underground members referred to a time-honored anti-conspiratorial tactic. Instead of taking the prisoner directly to jail, the secret police kept him in his apartment and waited to see who would come to meet him. Cyrankiewicz came.

With a single blow, the Gestapo had instantly threatened a

huge portion of the underground movement in Kraków, in both its military and its political dimensions. Cyrankiewicz was imprisoned at a jail in Kraków, from which some of his colleagues resolved to spring him in a guerrilla raid. Jan knew of this plot and tried to join in it, as a way of returning a favor, so to speak. But the conspirators refused to include him, and their plans were foiled when Cyrankiewicz was transferred to Auschwitz.

Cyrankiewicz was actually lucky to be sent there. He possessed false documents so thorough and convincing that the Gestapo had no inkling of his true identity. Considering him an unimportant nuisance, they consigned him to the oblivion of Auschwitz without taking the time for a torture session. Cyrankiewicz not only survived captivity but helped to organize an underground movement at Auschwitz.

The arrests introduced Jan to the underground habit of changing addresses like clothes. Forced by Cyrankicwicz's seizure to seek new accommodations on a few hours' notice, he moved into an apartment at a housing cooperative run by his childhood friend from Łódź, Tadeusz Pilc. Jan felt reasonably secure in these quarters, since Pilc was not a socialist and did not consider himself in danger.

Jan stayed with Pilc for six months, continuing his radio monitoring work. But as the Gestapo crackdown continued, he felt less and less safe. Finally, after learning that Komorowski had moved to Warsaw, Jan decided that his future prospects in Kraków were too dim to justify remaining there. Pilc agreed that Jan should leave town, though he still felt secure himself. Through contacts with a Peasant Party representative in Kraków, Jan obtained the name of an official in Warsaw who could find a position for him in the underground movement there. Jan left for Warsaw in October 1941.

Arrested days later, Tadeusz Pilc perished in 1942 at the Buchenwald concentration camp.

~

In the seventeen months that had passed since Jan left Warsaw on his doomed mission through Slovakia, Poland's capital had been transformed. Nightly sorties by Soviet bombers had destroyed or damaged much of what was left after the German barrages of September 1939. Whole neighborhoods had been leveled by the air force of a nation that had invaded Poland under the pretext of friendship in 1939, had collaborated with Hitler, and now presented itself once again as Poland's ally. After Germany's invasion of the Soviet Union on June 22, 1941, the Polish government-in-exile (now based in London) had concluded an uneasy alliance with Stalin.

As mind-boggling as Jan found the destruction in Warsaw, he was equally amazed to see the extent to which resistance to the enemy had become a fact of life in the city. The first evidence he noticed was the omnipresent graffiti scrawled on the fractured walls of Warsaw's ruined buildings. Praise of General Sikorski, abuse of Hitler, and commemorations of Allied battle successes confronted Jan on nearly every street. In a popular taunt at the occupiers, Polish youths would alter one letter of a propaganda poster the Germans had posted throughout the city: Instead of "Deutschland siegt an allen Fronten" (Germany stands tall on all Fronts), the slogan would read "Deutschland liegt an allen Fronten" (Germany lies fallen on all Fronts). On walls all over the city, a simple, hurriedly drawn "V" affirmed the Poles' faith in Allied victory.

These outward signs reflected growing self-confidence and boldness among the Poles struggling against the Nazi forces. Hitler and his minions had miscalculated in their attempt to convert Poland into a nation of serfs, cowed into submission by mass terror. The pervasive and random nature of German repression and abuses served not so much to terrify the Poles of Warsaw as to convince them they had nothing to lose by fighting back.

In many ways, those affiliated with the movement were the safest residents in Warsaw. At a time when any able-bodied Pole could be snatched off the streets and shipped to Germany for forced labor, the underground's first order of business was to protect its activists from random danger. In order to give the Germans an incentive to leave one of its members alone, the resistance movement needed to create an identity that marked the individual as a worker essential to the Reich's war effort—in a business supplying the Wehrmacht, for example, or in one of the German offices set up to administer the conquered territory.

The conspirators often stole blank forms and official seals as raw material for their document-manufacturing operations. When the real thing was unavailable, underground forgers went to work. They became so proficient that even experts could not always tell the difference between real and faked documents. To back up the papers carried by underground members, well-placed conspirators would enter parallel forgeries into the German-held files that recorded the issuance of these documents. With typically Germanic

thoroughness, the occupiers had established bureaucracies that required all Poles to carry a large volume of personal documentation.
There were identity cards, employment cards, ration cards, travel
permits, residence permits, curfew passes, and so on.

Taking on a new identity, therefore, meant more than simply
growing a beard and obtaining a fake driver's license. In addition
to falsified versions of several different official documents, a good
set of false papers typically included other evidence corroborating
the individual's identity—for instance, a few letters to the newly
created person, with falsified postmarks proving that he or she had
gone by the name before the war. And forged papers were only the
beginning. The underground member had to memorize an extensive biography, including both the data given in his documents and
other information that might convince the Gestapo of his or her
identity.

The movement had these defensive measures down to a science by the time Jan arrived in Warsaw, but their tactics were far
from foolproof. In spite of these concealment efforts, and despite
rules designed to limit the amount any one member knew about the
organization as a whole, Gestapo actions took a constant and fearsome toll on individuals and entire sections of the conspiracy. Resistance fighters, whether caught in the act of sabotaging German
property or merely rounded up after the Germans extracted their
names from tortured colleagues, were marked for special treatment
by the Gestapo. The lucky ones would face life, or death, in a concentration camp. Of those less fortunate, some would face a firing
squad; others would be left dangling from a public gallows for days
after their execution, to serve as examples to their fellow "Polish
bandits."

~

They also serve who carry out tedious chores. In Warsaw as before
in Kraków, the burgeoning underground bureaucracy assigned Jan
to labors that were a far cry from his glamorous service as a courier.
Upon returning to the city, he joined the Bureau of Information and
Propaganda, a civilian-oriented outpost within the military arm of
the resistance movement. His new boss was Jerzy Makowiecki, an
engineer before the war, one of many highly educated operatives in
the bureau.

Makowiecki initially asked Jan to act as a liaison between the
leaders of various underground factions, reporting to him about

their political thinking. Jan agreed to take on this function, but after some consideration his instincts told him it would compromise his reputation for nonpartisanship. He went back to Makowiecki and begged off, citing as a pretext the concern that his scarred wrists might make it especially dangerous for the leaders to be in his company.

As a second choice, Makowiecki put his new employee in charge of analyzing the underground press. In view of the perils, hardships, and material shortages confronting them, Poland's myriad underground factions produced an astonishing number of publications. The majority expressed at least some degree of loyalty to the government-in-exile in London and to the resistance movement aligned with it, made up of the four main political parties, the government delegate, and the Home Army (as the Union for Armed Struggle was renamed early in 1942). But communists, extreme nationalists, and other splinter groups from the far left and far right pursued their aims independently, and even under the umbrella of the London-aligned movement there were dozens of factions. Each had its own newspaper or journal.

Jan's analytical work, like many other underground functions, depended on the assistance of a cadre of "liaison girls"— young women who functioned as messengers and guides, facilitating communication between higher-ranking conspirators who could not risk meeting each other in person regularly. The contact personnel also eliminated the need for operatives like Jan to carry any compromising material on their persons or to know the addresses of locations where underground activities took place.

Jan had to follow a rigorous procedure for every working session. At a predetermined time, a liaison woman would stroll past the apartment building where he lived. Jan was required to be ready to step out the front door at precisely that moment. The woman would walk on without acknowledging him in any way. He would follow. She would lead him to one of the many sites the movement had established for activities like his, usually an apartment, and he would follow her inside. In every location, the same device had been installed somewhere in the flooring: a spring-loaded floorboard that, with the press of a hidden button, would pop open to reveal a compartment full of underground periodicals. The guide would show Jan where the device had been installed. Then she would leave.

For a set length of time—generally three or four hours—Jan

would stay in the room, reading through the batch of publications and writing reports for the Home Army's high command on the political tendencies revealed in the writings. He found the level of political thought depressingly low in many cases. There were broadsheets calling for the establishment of a monarchy in postwar Poland; there were syndicalist tracts full of dense theoretical arguments; there were articles setting out chauvinistic, expansionist views of a "Greater Poland" stretching from the Baltic to the Black Sea; there were incessant anti-Semitic diatribes. The futility of it all depressed Jan. It seemed ridiculous to him that he risked his life, and the liaison women risked their lives, and the publishers themselves often lost their lives, just to disseminate and analyze such worthless polemics.

At the end of the working period, the same woman who had led Jan to the room would reappear. After placing the periodicals back in their compartment, he would give the assistant his handwritten notes. She would take them to be typed and would route them to the appropriate recipients. After guiding him back to his home, she would be the first to enter his apartment while he waited to see if the coast was clear. Then he would follow her in, and she would move on to her next assignment.

Not surprisingly, the liaison cadres suffered heavy losses throughout the occupation years.

After a few weeks, Jan became so fed up with working on the periodicals that he requested a new assignment from Makowiecki. He took up a new position monitoring Allied and neutral radio broadcasts, much as he had done in Kraków. In an unheated villa a few miles outside of Warsaw, Jan, still wearing his hat and coat for warmth, would work shifts of several days' duration, listening to the BBC and other foreign-language services and sending reports back to his superiors through a contact person.

~

Makowiecki, Jan's boss, once paid him a compliment after watching him operate for a while within the movement. "You do a great job of withering into the background," he said. Such was the goal of every underground member whenever he or she stepped onto the street: to walk, dress, and look in every way like an average person. Standing out from the crowd only invited trouble. Jan had mastered the art of blending in.

It was not just a matter of cultivating a personal image of plainness. Jan was also extremely careful to avoid being seen at places that had become underground hangouts. If he heard that his compatriots were frequenting a certain bar or café, he stayed away from it at all costs. Aside from the dangers all the conspirators faced, Jan had to consider the added peril created by his wrists. Even the most casual contact with a German or a Polish informer—say, a glance across a crowded room, at a moment when his sleeves had ridden up on his arms—could lead to disaster. For the same reason, he said nothing to any of his friends in the movement about what had happened during his trip through Slovakia.

Keeping a low profile was not always enough to prevent danger from closing in. One day in the spring of 1942, Makowiecki told Jan that his liaison woman had been arrested. There was no way of knowing how much she might reveal under torture, and she knew Jan's current name and address. "Did you leave anything important at your apartment?" Makowiecki asked.

"Nothing incriminating," Jan told him. "Some personal stuff."

"Leave it," ordered his boss. "If nothing happens, you can recover it in a few weeks." After staying one night with the family of Bogdan Samborski, a foreign ministry official who was abroad, Jan headed for the country.

Remote estates were among the underground's favorite hiding places for members who had become "hot." Makowiecki placed Jan at a grand home near Puławy, east of Warsaw. The owner, a certain Madame Siemiątkowska, seems to have operated an underground hotel of sorts; Jan later placed his brother there and encountered a number of movement members there who shared his plight, having fled after the arrest of comrades put them in danger.

One of these refugee conspirators was a young woman named Renee with whom Jan, having little else to do, spent a considerable amount of time. Long afterward, he would insist that their relationship had been quite innocent. The burdens, attachments, loyalties, and trust of romantic affairs were incompatible with wartime conditions, and the underground frowned severely on such goings-on among members. But the relationship between Jan and Renee reached a point of some seriousness during the weeks they spent on the estate, and it continued after both returned to Warsaw. By his account he made no commitment to her, but she considered herself his fiancée. Many months later, when he reached England, Jan still felt a close enough bond that he sent his greetings to Renee in a coded telegram transmitted back to Poland. And after he received a large payment of dollars in England, he arranged for five hundred dollars to be transferred to her through underground channels. The relationship did not survive the war, but Renee did.

Jan's impromptu vacation was not to be his last visit to Madame Siemiątkowska's "hotel." Soon Makowiecki would send him back, on a mission of mercy.

~

Amid the tides of humanity washing through the Warsaw train station, Mrs. Weinberg clung tightly to her husband. Her terror was etched on her face. She was truly a novelty in this crowd—an obviously Jewish woman, out in the open long after the city's Jews had been herded into their own urban prison camp, the Warsaw Ghetto.

Dr. Weinberg was more composed. Perhaps his stoicism arose from a sense of resignation. Forced to leave their hiding place in Warsaw, he and his wife had placed all their hopes for survival in a tall, hollow-cheeked Pole who called himself "Witold." Either he would guide them to safety, or they would perish. Either way, worrying would accomplish nothing.

Jan had been laying the groundwork for this expedition for a couple of weeks. When Makowiecki first told him that the Weinbergs needed to be evacuated to a hiding place outside the city, Jan had agreed to scout for a suitable location. He paid a courtesy call on Madame Siemiątkowska, explaining who the two Jews were and why the underground attached particular urgency to saving them. Not only was Dr. Weinberg the father of two Home Army soldiers, but he was also a veteran of Marshal Piłsudski's legions who had retired as a colonel. It was impossible to save more than a few of the country's oppressed Jews, but a man who had rendered such service to Poland should surely be one of the few.

The estate owner had agreed, but with conditions. Heeding Jan's warning that the woman looked very Jewish, Siemiątkowska refused to put the couple up in the manor house. "It's too great a chance to take," she said. "I have other people there who would be endangered. But I can find a place for them in one of the sheds on the property."

Delighted, Makowiecki had given the go-ahead for the operation. The riskiest moment would come at the train station in Warsaw, but Jan thought the general chaos of the place would work in their favor.

All went well for the first few moments. Having purchased the tickets, the party found its platform and settled as casually and inconspicuously as possible against a wall. They waited . . . and waited . . . and waited. The train was more than half an hour late. A short distance away, Staszek and Romek Weinberg stood, arms folded, intently watching Jan and their parents, who did not acknowledge them.

Passengers passed back and forth in a continuous stream in front of the departing trio. Suddenly one man halted.

"So, Dr. Weinberg!" the Pole said through his teeth. "I know who you are. You're a Jew. You may not remember it, because you did it to a lot of people, but I sold you my blood, and you paid me peanuts. Now you will pay me!"

Mrs. Weinberg turned and plunged her face into her husband's sleeve, whimpering in staccato bursts. Dr. Weinberg stared straight into the blackmailer's eyes, silent. Jan, appalled but not entirely surprised, took the man aside. He was prepared for this contingency.

"Listen," Jan told the extortionist, "we both deal in Jews. You want to make money, I want to make money. I think you understand that if the Germans learn you wanted to make money off these Jews, you would be in deep trouble. They might execute you and me both, and of course they'll kill these Jews. There's a simpler way to deal with this situation. They paid me well. How much do you want?"

The man named a figure.

Jan pulled a large stack of zlotys out of his wallet. "There," he said. "Get lost."

The blackmailer walked off without a word. But Jan saw that he was still in the station. Staszek and Romek looked on with anguished expressions. Then the train finally pulled in.

Jan stepped aboard with the Weinbergs, quickly taking a window seat so he could keep an eye on the blackmailer. If the man boarded the train, they would be subject to further blackmail or immediate denunciation. Mrs. Weinberg continued to cower and whimper. Jan himself was trembling. But as the train left the station, the man stood still, apparently satisfied with what he had already collected from the travelers. Perhaps Staszek and Romek would have a word with him.

The Weinbergs settled into a shed on Madame Siemiątkowska's grounds, as planned. What Jan could not plan for was the scarcity of vodka in eastern Poland. In the area of Puławy, where the estate was located, the Gestapo had established an incentive program for parched residents of the countryside. For each hidden Jew turned in to the authorities, a peasant would receive a liter of vodka. Two Jews, two liters—not a bad deal. Dr. and Mrs. Weinberg had been there only a few weeks before a worker on the estate spotted them in the shed and denounced them to the Germans, who killed them on the spot.

~

It was Jan's business to know what was happening in Warsaw. He thought he knew what went on behind the walls of the Warsaw Ghetto—though, as he was to learn, knowledge and comprehension are two different states of awareness. He knew that about 450,000 Jews were imprisoned in the Ghetto. He knew that their sufferings had long surpassed even the most vicious torments inflicted on the non-Jewish population. And, being well informed, he knew that something even more horrible had begun on July 22, 1942, when the Nazis started liquidating the Ghetto.

Jan had heard some of the earlier rumors about massive atrocities against the Jews. He could not know with any certainty about the activities of the German Einsatzgruppen (special-duty squads), which had systematically cleared all traces of Jewish life from eastern Poland during the past year, leaving over one million bullet-riddled corpses piled in trenches that the victims themselves had dug. Nor did he have any first-hand knowledge of the more technologically advanced procedures in use at Chełmno, near his hometown of Łódź, where hundreds of Jews per day were being forced into vans whose exhaust pipes had been routed into hermetically sealed passenger compartments. Nor did he have any definite information about the even more efficient operations at Treblinka, Sobibor, and Bełżec, the three "Operation Reinhard" death camps (touchingly code-named after one of their most enthusiastic boosters, SS Obergruppenführer Reinhard Heydrich, whose May 1942 assassination had been avenged by the obliteration of the Czech town of Lidice). Still, Jan had heard enough to be fairly sure that an unprecedented effort was under way to annihilate the Jews.

The most ambitious Nazi designs had been fulfilled in more remote areas; Warsaw itself had not seen the full effect of Hitler's extermination plans. Everything changed on July 22. When the Nazis began herding the Ghetto's residents onto boxcars that day, they maintained the pretense of carrying out a "resettlement" to the East. Within a few weeks, the Nazis abandoned that charade and resorted to brute force to drive the residents toward the train siding. Each train traveled a short distance out of Warsaw to Treblinka, disgorged its passengers, and returned to the city. The passengers—again through deception at first and later through force—were induced to disrobe and to enter chambers in which they were put to death by carbon monoxide gas. (Zyklon-B, the poison gas that represented the pinnacle of Nazi achievement in the field of mass-murder technology, would come later.) In the first month of the Ghetto's liquidation, over two hundred thousand victims would be processed at Treblinka.

Reports of the true fate of those who had been "resettled" made it back to Warsaw soon after the deportations began. Polish railroad workers in the underground and escaping Jews both brought news to the capital. The Poles outside the Ghetto reacted in a variety of ways to this information. Some ignored it, too busy with their own difficult lives to concern themselves over a matter about which they could do nothing. Some—perhaps not many, but some—took a degree of satisfaction in the elimination of the Jews in their midst: Now they would have Warsaw to themselves after the war. And some—again not many—were personally transformed by the abomination that was taking place, seeing in it an issue of transcendent moral significance, sensing that some countervailing action, however futile it might be, was imperative.

Zofia Kossak was such a person. A novelist renowned in Poland and beyond, whose works were imbued with a passionate Roman Catholic vision, Kossak had founded the Front Odrodzenia Polski (FOP), or Front for the Rebirth of Poland, early in 1942. The stated purpose of the clandestine movement was to promote "Christian moral rebirth" as a means of restoring Poland to wholeness. "Only deep, conscious and continuous religious faith," announced its manifesto, "can assure the magnificence of Poland and the fulfillment of the role given to the nation by God." Kossak and her followers campaigned against the German administration's systematic attempts to corrupt the population—the brothels, pornography, and other base amusements that the occupiers had introduced as a means of diverting the attention of the Poles and fomenting internal conflict among them. But she believed that the unprecedented crime against the Jews tainted the Polish national character more profoundly than anything else the Nazis had done. The mere fact that it occurred on Polish soil—aside from any questions of Polish complicity—imposed on all Poles a responsibility before God to fight the perpetrators of such evil.

Neither Kossak nor many of her acolytes were naturally inclined to lend support to the Jews of Poland. The FOP was heavily
weighted with activists whose political sympathies were to the right
of center; some were members of underground parties that called
for the forced emigration of any Jews remaining in Poland after the
war. Some of these parties, in fact, were so conservative that they
refused to take part in the underground's coalition government
alongside the socialists.

In the increasingly anti-Semitic environment that had prevailed in the years between the 1935 death of Marshal Piłsudski and
the beginning of the war, these individuals had not been among the
minority of non-Jewish Poles who came to the defense of the Jews.
Kossak herself held strong rightist views both before and during the
war, at times when Poland's Jews were widely suspected of harbor-
ing communist sympathies. Some of her prewar political writings,
and even some of the pronouncements of the FOP, were tainted with
anti-Semitism. And of course, twenty more years would pass before
the Catholic Church began to make its peace with Judaism at the
Second Vatican Council; anti-Semitism held particularly deep roots
within Polish Catholicism.

Yet, in the name of Catholicism, the Front's members put their
lives on the line to support the Jews. They encountered the hostility
not only of the Germans, but also of elements within the Church
establishment. A Vatican official who was in contact with Poland
during the war wrote of the "intense battle" waged by traditionalist
priests against the FOP. The group's members, wrote the official,
"lacked any serious dogmatic foundation." Their publications "were
crammed with false ideological propositions whose frank heresies
made them really dangerous." These people had no history of philo-
Semitism, yet they took up the cause of Jewry in the face of major
obstacles; something must have changed in their hearts.

Although Jan had generally tried to avoid associations with
underground factions that might cast his nonpartisanship and objectivity into doubt, he took an interest in the FOP soon after it was
formed. The war had not diminished the ardent faith of his youth.
He liked Kossak's novels, and when he heard of her efforts, he
sought her out through his underground contacts. Still using the
name Witold, Jan told her about his upbringing, about his beliefs,
and about his admiration for her work. Kossak, a large, jolly
woman, fifty-two years old, seized Witold in a bear hug and planted
sloppy kisses on both cheeks. He was in the movement.

"From that moment the closest friendship developed," Karski later recalled. "But she considered me as a schoolboy, a nothing. I considered her, and called her to our friends, our 'Popess.' Others called her 'Ciotka'—'Auntie.' " Soon he was writing articles for the Front's underground publication, *Prawda* (Truth). He still attempted to remain aloof from any political involvements arising from his association with the right-wing political figures in the Front, but he could not hide his devotion to its charismatic leader. His feelings came through when he suggested in a 1943 report to the government-in-exile that Kossak's escape from Poland should be arranged "because her especially rare moral values could be greatly beneficial to propaganda." Later in the war, Karski would describe her as "the inspiration and the finest flame of Polish underground life." And in an interview fifty years after his first meeting with her, he stated: "I loved her. Very simply. I was not in love with her, but I loved her. I admired her."

During the time Jan was affiliated with it, the FOP could do nothing but raise its voice—one voice of many dozens in the cacophony of the underground press—to vent Kossak's articulate outrage at the atrocities occurring in Warsaw. Condemnations flowed from her pen: of the Polish police in Nazi service who pursued Jewish beggar children in the streets outside of the Ghetto, of the propaganda posters warning Poles that Jews carried typhoid and lice, of blackmailers, and of other underground organizations that were not doing their part to help the Jews.

Later, the words became deeds. On September 27, 1942, Kossak and other FOP members as well as representatives of underground political parties and the Home Army founded the "Konrad Żegota Committee" for aid to the Jews. Among the cofounders was a twenty-one-year-old FOP member, Władysław Bartoszewski, who was destined to become one of the most active members of the pro-Jewish cell. Decades later, after the state of Israel voted to recognize Bartoszewski's wartime exertions by making him an honorary citizen of the Jewish state, Karski would take pride in having introduced the young activist to Kossak in the summer of 1942.

Kossak employed her talents as a fiction writer to invent Mr. Żegota, whose name was used in conversations to take the place of the dangerous word Żydów (Jews). Żegota, and a successor organization set up in December 1942, helped thousands of Jews in hiding throughout Poland for the remainder of the war, despite a chronic shortage of funds. After continuing her efforts for a year, Kossak was arrested in September 1943 and sent to the women's camp at Auschwitz-Birkenau. Like Józef Cyrankiewicz, however, she possessed sufficiently convincing forged papers to conceal her true identity from the Germans. She was released in July 1944 and later wrote a book, *From the Abyss,* about her experiences at the camp.

~

As the maelstrom of the Jewish tragedy raged in the Ghetto, underground leaders elsewhere in Warsaw were preoccupied with their own problems. The endemic squabbling among factions continued, the Gestapo was getting more and more adept at rooting out resistance, and now the movement faced a new kind of adversary: Communist agents provocateurs. In the eastern territories and increasingly in Warsaw as well, cells of Communist fighters began to appear after Germany's June 1941 invasion of the Soviet Union. There could be little doubt that they were under the control of Moscow—most were well armed, and some were Russians rather than Poles. Of the Poles, many were known to have fled to the East at the outset of the war. They had returned to Poland by parachuting from Soviet aircraft.

The Communist partisans set up their own underground military force, the *Gwardia Ludowa* (People's Guard), as a rival to the Home Army. Implacable enemies of the Home Army, GL detachments did all they could to undermine its prestige. Unable to carry out large-scale operations, they launched many small sabotage and assassination actions against the occupier, provoking the Germans into massive retaliation against the communities where they operated. The GL would then either blame the Home Army for recklessness or, taking credit for the actions itself, accuse the non-Communist forces of cowardly passivity. Communist sympathizers, meanwhile, tried to infiltrate the underground political parties, especially the Socialist Party. Without openly declaring themselves Communists, the operatives agitated within the underground for closer ties to the Soviet Union. They avoided being drawn into discussions about the question of Poland's borders with the USSR, which Stalin wanted to shift westward. And they denounced the government-in-exile (which had set up shop in London after the fall of France) as a reactionary clique that did not represent the people of Poland.

The Communists' activities became a source of deep concern to the London-aligned underground movement. There was no reason to worry that their arguments would persuade any significant number of Poles to shift allegiances, but there was plenty of cause to suspect that their goals had nothing to do with democratically winning over the populace. Despite the fact that most of its members were stoutly anti-Soviet, the Home Army and the underground movement had sought to establish a working relationship with the Communists, acting on the principle that the common struggle against Germany outweighed all political considerations. In exploratory meetings between representatives of the two sides, however, the Communists showed no willingness to cooperate, while at the same time asking many sensitive questions about the structure and leadership of the Home Army and political parties. And after each meeting, non-Communist underground leaders discovered Communist agents trailing them home. The implication was clear: If the Soviet-directed elements could learn the secrets of the underground, they could eliminate their rivals either by denouncing them to the Gestapo or by denouncing them to the Soviet secret police after the Red Army reoccupied Poland.

Relations between the underground and the government in London were also far from ideal. Political disputes created tensions among and between the factions in London and Warsaw, but communication difficulties also caused great problems. The legitimacy of both the underground movement and the government-in-exile depended on maintaining the appearance of coordination between the policies of each body. With Poland and most of the rest of Europe under the Nazi yoke, the barriers that stood in the way of such coordination were obviously enormous. The underground was in contact with London by means of several hidden radio transmitters through which it sent and received coded telegrams on a daily basis. These had to be kept brief, however. The Germans had developed listening devices that could track the transmitters while they were in operation.

The only other available method of communication—and the only possible way of conveying complex information and lengthy documents—was the courier system. The Home Army and the political representation each sent emissaries to London regularly, traveling along three general routes: via Hungary, on the path Jan had taken in 1940; as stowaways on cargo ships between Poland's Baltic ports and neutral Sweden, and on to England on British diplomatic flights; and through Germany, France, and Spain to Gibraltar or Lisbon. The envoys returned to Poland by parachute, jumping from flights coordinated by Britain's Special Operations Executive, which also dropped arms, ammunition, and equipment into the country. The two great drawbacks to communicating via courier were danger and delay. Many couriers, naturally, were captured as they attempted to cross occupied territories on false papers. And those who escaped the notice of the Germans could take several months to arrive, as they were stalled at various points on their routes by changing military and security conditions.

By late summer of 1942, these shortcomings had become a particularly acute problem for the underground leadership. Confident of the Allies' ultimate victory despite the current strength of Germany's stranglehold on Europe, the leaders had to consider the future. The possibility that the Red Army would push Hitler's troops back across Poland raised political issues that were all the more pressing now that Stalin's agents were creating havoc within the country. There was a real need for closer communication with the London government.

6
Witness

The deepening twin crises of deteriorating Polish-Soviet relations and the Nazi extermination of Jews in Poland loomed over the underground as the summer of 1942 wore on. Yet when Jan received orders for what would become his most important mission, neither of these factors was the direct motivation. Indeed, the mission developed from the most petty origin imaginable—careerism, on the part of both Jan and a top underground official.

Jan's relations with his brother Marian had grown distant since both returned to Warsaw. Marian had assumed an important security post in the underground movement after his release from Auschwitz (releases of non-Jewish Poles were not uncommon, although Marian's may have been caused by a bureaucratic error), but he had never fully reconciled himself to cooperation with the multiparty coalition that controlled the movement. Marian remained a Piłsudskite, with little taste for any alliance that included the prewar opposition parties. When Marian Kozielewski realized that his brother had strayed from the path of Marshal Piłsudski, developing contacts with all kinds of different factions and maintaining particularly friendly relations with the socialists, he was shocked and angry. After a few confrontations, the brothers avoided each other as they went about their work in Warsaw.

Not every Piłsudskite held views as rigid as Marian's. Jan remained on good terms with several political figures he had met through his brother. One of these men, an underground official named Tadeusz Miklaszewski, suggested in mid-1942 that Jan make contact with Roman Knoll. Knoll had been one of Poland's best-known diplomats before the war, having served at times as acting foreign minister and envoy to Germany. He now headed a section in the civilian underground dealing with foreign affairs. "It is not a bad idea to get acquainted with a man like Knoll," advised Miklaszewski. "Who knows? He may be the foreign minister after the war."

Despite his absorption in the war effort, Karski had not forsaken his long-standing professional ambitions. Someday the war would end; after the victory over Hitler's Germany, Jan would resume his diplomatic career in the new Poland. He readily agreed with Miklaszewski, who arranged an introduction to Knoll. Soon Jan was meeting regularly with the senior diplomat.

Jan was initially taken aback to learn that Knoll was living under his real name in his prewar apartment, protected from harm by close contacts with Italian diplomats in Warsaw. Jan's visits quickly took on more than a social character, as Knoll learned that Jan was privy to information that was not reaching him. As an employee of the Home Army's Bureau of Information and Propaganda, Jan was listening to the BBC every night and sending news summaries up the Home Army chain of command. The military authorities, however, were not sharing this information with Knoll— much to his consternation. Jan felt that Knoll had a right to know what he was hearing on the British broadcasts, so he gave Knoll frequent briefings. A mutually beneficial relationship developed between the career-oriented young diplomat and the underground's foreign-affairs officer.

One day, greeting Jan at the apartment door, Knoll addressed his guest in French. Playing along, Jan conversed with him in this language for a while. Then Knoll, apparently satisfied with Jan's linguistic skills, made a proposition. "How would you feel about going abroad again, to London?" he asked. Knoll had only one purpose in mind: He wanted Jan to help him secure from the government-in-exile an official nomination as the director of a full-fledged "department" of foreign affairs. Once given the "cabinet" rank it currently lacked, Knoll's division would have more authority within the underground. Maybe the Home Army would even start sharing the BBC reports with him. And the prestige of this enhanced position would make Knoll a stronger candidate for the foreign minister's job in a postwar government.

If Jan was amazed at the pettiness of the cause for which Knoll was asking him to risk his life, he didn't let it show. After all, his exertions might indeed serve valuable purposes, apart from Knoll's desires. There was a legitimate need to improve communications between London and Warsaw. And after over a year and a half of wide-ranging underground work, Jan was well prepared to serve as a representative in the West. The trust he had earned from the political parties during his mission to Angers had deepened. Knoll had already raised the idea of sending Jan on a mission with top civilian officials of the underground and had received a positive response. The personal attributes that made Karski well suited for courier duty in 1940 were still there: the photographic memory, the quick-thinking resourcefulness, the physical stamina—though the latter was considerably worn down by the poor nutrition that plagued all of Poland. The scars on his wrists remained a danger, but Jan lived with that peril every day. He was ready.

"The delegate wants to see you," Knoll told Jan. "He will tell you more about the mission."

Cyryl Ratajski, delegate of the government, didn't look like the leader of an underground movement. Fat, in poor health, he hardly projected the image of competence and daring that Jan might have expected of the top civilian official in Poland's clandestine state. There was, in fact, widespread dissatisfaction with his leadership among the underground's factions, although he personally was held in high esteem. Within days of Jan's departure from the country, the political parties would ease Ratajski out of his position. A month later, he would be granted the ultimate luxury in Nazi-held Poland: a natural death.

Jan's meeting with the government delegate was brief. "All of the party leaders have agreed," Ratajski said. "They want to send you as their man. They trust you. And from what I have learned about you, I trust you as well. You will also carry my messages. Will you go?"

"Naturally," Jan replied.

~

By now, "Witold" knew what to expect from his meetings with representatives of the underground political parties. As in 1940, he heard diametrically opposed theories, evaluations, and statements of fact from various faction leaders. And once again, he committed each group's arguments to memory, swore he would keep its information secret, and promised to report fully and faithfully to its counterparts in exile.

The depression he had felt months before, on reading the mis-

guided underground publications, reasserted itself as he listened to
these leaders. Each clique was sure it had the support of large segments of the population. Each was ready to wield the balance of
power in postwar Poland. Each claimed to be the dominant power
in the underground movement. Jan nodded along, soberly committing to memory every diatribe, every grievance, every quixotic assessment, all the wildly divergent ideas about Poland's future social
system, from the right, the left, and the center of the political spectrum.

There was unanimity on one key point, however. Among all
the individuals Jan met in the weeks leading up to his departure—
from party leaders of all stripes, to the delegate and his officials, to
the Home Army commander and his underlings—virtually everyone
implored him to spread the news of the Communists' malicious underground activities in Poland. There was no meaningful division
among the factions on this topic; all knew that Stalin's machinations posed a threat to Poland's very existence. The underground
leaders begged Jan to make Allied authorities understand the difficulty of their position, and to emphasize the movement's desire to
cooperate with the Communists against the common enemy. Although skirmishes between the Communists and Home Army fighters had already broken out, the leaders insisted they were only fighting in self-defense. They didn't want to give Stalin any excuse to
claim that the Poles were disloyal to the Allied cause. The Allies
needed to understand that.

But so did the Polish government-in-exile itself, some underground operatives insisted. The leaders said Jan needed to impress
the gravity of the situation on them, too, suggesting that London
had drifted out of touch with affairs in the Homeland. This suggestion concerned more than the issue of Communist infiltration and
agitation. Those who were sending Jan, and Jan himself, probably
had something approaching a clandestine agenda for the mission:
not merely improving communications with the Poles in London,
but objectively gauging their true attitudes and the true position of
Poland vis-à-vis its allies. In the early weeks of his visit in London,
Jan would discreetly search for answers to these questions on behalf
of underground leaders in Poland.

Although Jan was to be a political courier, the military wing
of the underground would handle most of the logistics of his transit
across occupied Europe. Because of this involvement, and because
Jan was nominally an employee of the Home Army's Bureau of In-

formation and Propaganda, he was in close contact with military officials as he prepared for his departure. When his secret plans became known to the BIP, they set in motion a chain of events that would change Jan's life forever.

The Bureau of Information and Propaganda was a primary point of contact between the Polish underground movement and the suffering Jews of Poland. Many of its functionaries were intellectuals, including some of the nation's most prominent educators, historians, and scientists. Anti-Semitism was less widespread in this class than in other segments of Polish society, and several bureau officers took a sympathetic interest in the plight of the Jews. Moreover, some Jews served in the BIP. The unit's Jewish connections would eventually kindle the ire of right-wing Poles. Fascists in an underground splinter group, intent on "rooting out the Jews from BIP," were later blamed for the murder (or betrayal to the Gestapo) of several BIP employees. Only after the killing of Jerzy Makowiecki and his wife in 1944 would Jan learn that his immediate supervisor's mother had been Jewish.

The Jewish resistance movement was in an embryonic state as the liquidation of the Warsaw Ghetto began in July 1942, although efforts to organize it had been under way for some time. The brutal German sweeps settled a debate that had preoccupied the Ghetto's Jewish leaders in previous months. Some wanted to take up active resistance against Hitler's henchmen, in whatever desperate form might be possible. Others counseled against resistance, arguing that any such action would not only be doomed to failure but would also provoke the Germans to abuse the Ghetto's residents even more savagely. The dispute had split the Jews roughly along prewar political lines. Left-wing Zionist youth groups and the socialist Bund movement, among others, gravitated toward confrontation, while many prewar members of the Right Labor Zionist and General Zionist parties held positions in the German-directed Ghetto administration and took an accommodationist stand.

Only one group of Ghetto dwellers had any meaningful weaponry. The Jewish Military Union had been formed soon after the German occupation of Warsaw, drawing much of its membership from the far-right Revisionist movement. The Revisionists had enjoyed the support of the prewar Polish government in their campaign for a Jewish homeland in Palestine. (This support surely grew out of a desire to reduce Poland's Jewish population through emigration, rather than any deep commitment to the establishment of a Jewish state.) The right-wing Jews had even been allowed to set up bases in Poland before the war to train a paramilitary force that might someday fight for Israel. A Revisionist leader and corporal in the exiled Polish Army eventually led such a force in a revolt against the British authorities in Palestine; his name was Menachem Begin. Many of the Jewish Military Union's fifty members had similar backgrounds, and some were able to parlay their prewar ties with Polish military leaders into a small amount of smuggled pistols and ammunition. But the group had not yet used its weapons in battle, and its politics isolated it somewhat from other residents who were inclined toward resistance.

On July 28, 1942, as the first wave of mass deportations was under way, left-wing militant youths and other factions in the Ghetto proclaimed the establishment of a resistance cell that was to become the Jewish Fighting Organization. Despite political differences, this movement and the Jewish Military Union cooperated to some extent. Completely lacking in weapons, however, this movement could accomplish little during the peak deportation period of late July, August, and early September 1942.

The nascent Jewish underground had several representatives beyond the ghetto walls in Warsaw. These were generally individuals whose physical features did not identify them as Jews; they entered and exited the Ghetto through secret passageways. There was Arie Wilner, a militant leader from the leftist Hashomer Hatzair youth group. There was Adolf Berman, a prominent Zionist figure before the war. There was Menachem Kirschenbaum, one of the very few General Zionists to take part in underground activity. And there was Leon Feiner, probably the most important Jewish leader outside the Ghetto. A lawyer and labor leader whose activities had landed him in a Polish prison before the war, Feiner had returned to Warsaw from Russia in 1941 to head the socialist Bund movement in occupied Poland. "With his distinguished gray hair and whiskers, ruddy complexion, erect carriage, and general air of good health and refinement," Jan would later write, Feiner "passed easily as a Polish 'nobleman.' "

Through sewers and other secret passages, Feiner and others entered and exited the Ghetto regularly. The Bureau of Information and Propaganda, in turn, maintained contact with these Jewish leaders, gathering information on conditions in the Ghetto and the relentless progress of the extermination campaign. Beginning in September 1942, the BIP also relayed urgent requests for weaponry from the Jews to the Home Army's high command. The questions of how responsive the military movement was to these pleas, what it could have possibly done to help the Jews of Warsaw, and why it didn't do more have been subjects of often-bitter debate between Poles and Jews since the end of the war. The Home Army did provide some guns and ammunition before and during the ghetto uprising of April and May 1943.

Jan had no contact with the Jewish underground in the ordinary course of his work for the BIP. But he clearly shared the sympathy for the Jews that prevailed in the bureau; his attachment to the ideas of Zofia Kossak cannot have been a secret from his BIP superiors. Jan did not ask to add Jewish concerns to his mission. Those who knew him and knew of his impending travels, however, knew he could be counted on to act as an advocate for the Jews in the West. It was almost certainly someone within the Bureau of Information and Propaganda who let the Jewish leaders in Warsaw know that a courier would soon depart for London.

~

At twilight on a late-August evening, huddled over a single candle in a bombed-out house, two Jews and a Polish Catholic conversed in excited whispers about the ruin of European Jewry. The Catholic was Jan. He had learned through underground channels that Jewish leaders wanted to see him, and after receiving clearance from Delegate Ratajski he had agreed to a meeting. As usual, he did not know the true identities of the men he was encountering. He knew only that one represented the Bund and the other was a Zionist, and that the leaders were emphasizing the solidarity of disparate Jewish factions by meeting jointly with him. Future scholars would speculate about who the men were. One was clearly Leon Feiner of the Bund. Various writers have identified the other, a younger man, as Adolf Berman, Arie Wilner, or Menachem Kirschenbaum. Most evidence suggests he was Kirschenbaum, the General Zionist leader.

Karski wrote two years later:

> It was an evening of nightmare, but with a painful, oppressive kind of reality that no nightmare ever had. . . . I sat in an old, rickety armchair as if I had been pinned there, barely able to utter a word. . . . [Feiner and the Zionist] paced the floor violently, their shadows dancing weirdly in the dim light. . . . It was as though they were unable even to think of their dying people and remain seated.

Feiner led the conversation and did most of the talking. Karski was to relay large portions of his lengthy lecture verbatim to authorities in London. The Zionist leader chimed in occasionally to express his agreement with the Bundist. Feiner was all business, exuding stoicism, displaying the steely-eyed determination for which a postwar writer would label him "the man whose nerves and arteries became wires." In contrast, the Zionist struggled to control his emotions. Before the discussion of Nazi atrocities had gone far, the Zionist burst into tears.

"What's the good of talking?" he sobbed, head in hands. "What reason do I have to go on living? I ought to go to the Germans and tell them who I am." Nobody could ever understand the horrors that had befallen the Jews, moaned the Zionist.

Jan sat perfectly still.

Feiner laid a calming hand on his colleague's shoulder. As the Zionist apologized for his outburst and tried to regain his composure, Feiner recited a catalogue of Nazi-inspired horrors to Jan. "You Poles are also suffering," said Feiner. "But after the war, Poland will be restored. Your wounds will slowly heal. By then, however, Polish Jewry will no longer exist. Hitler will lose this war, but he will win the war he has declared against the Polish Jews."

There was no power in Poland that could help the masses of Jews now facing imminent destruction, Feiner continued. Neither the Polish nor the Jewish underground movements could offer more than marginal assistance. Therefore, the responsibility for at least making some effort to help lay with the governments of the nations allied against Germany. "Let not a single leader of the United Nations be able to say that they did not know that we were being murdered in Poland and could not be helped except from the outside," declared the Bund leader. History, he added, would hold them responsible if they failed to act.

Feiner and the Zionist then laid out a series of demands to be carried to various parties in the West. Jan was to seek out certain Jewish leaders in London and relay the following demands, which were then to be presented to Allied leaders:

First: There was to be a public declaration by the Allies that prevention of the physical extermination of the Jews would henceforth be among the official war aims of the coalition fighting Hitler. The two Jews insisted that this goal should be incorporated into the overall strategy for the conduct of the war.

Second: Allied propaganda was to inform the German nation of Hitler's crimes through radio, air-dropped leaflets, and any other available means. The names of German officials taking part in the genocide and the methods of murder being employed should be widely circulated, so that the German populace could not claim ignorance about what was being perpetrated in its name.

Third: The Allies should appeal publicly to the German people to bring pressure to bear on Hitler's regime so that the slaughter would stop.

Fourth: The Allies were to declare that if the genocide continued and the German masses did not rise up to stop it, they would be considered collectively responsible for it.

Fifth: In the event that none of the other steps effected a halt in the extermination program, the Allies were to carry out reprisals in two forms: through the bombing of selected sites of cultural importance in Germany, and through the execution of Germans in Allied hands who still professed loyalty to Hitler after learning of his crimes.

When Feiner and the Zionist reached the point about retaliation against Nazi sympathizers, Jan spoke up. "Gentlemen, it is impossible," he said. "It is against international law. I know the British. They will not do it. It is hopeless. It weakens your case."

"No!" spat the Zionist in a hoarse whisper. "Say it! We don't know what is realistic or not realistic. We are dying here! Say it!"

Jan nodded, promising to carry the message faithfully. Later, as he predicted, this demand fell on deaf ears in London.

In addition to the demands Jan was to present to Jewish and Allied leaders, the two spokesmen in the ruined house also set out appeals to other persons. They asked Jan to tell the figurehead president of Poland, Władysław Raczkiewicz, about the fate of the country's Jews. They suggested that Raczkiewicz approach Pope Pius XII and ask the prelate to use all means at his disposal, including excommunication, in an effort to dissuade Nazi officials from carrying out the liquidations. The Jews also sent word to Prime Minister Sikorski, requesting that he issue an order to the population of his occupied nation urging Poles to render assistance to Jews in hiding. Polish blackmailers should be sentenced to death by the underground's justice system, argued the Jews. Polish authorities later agreed, and a decree published in March 1943 vowed punishment for any Pole who attempted extortion against imperiled Jews. The underground eventually executed several Poles who had black-mailed Jews.

Feiner and the other Jewish leader went on to appeal for what-ever material assistance could be provided. Jan was instructed to tell Allied leaders that they could help some Jews to escape by pro-viding hard currency for bribes and blank passports, which might allow Jews to be included in exchanges of Allied and Axis nationals. The free world would have to grant asylum to Jews who somehow escaped the cauldron of Hitler's empire—an indulgence that the western governments had been slow to grant in the past. And living provisions for Jews in hiding were direly needed. Jan was to urge Allied governments and Jewish organizations to provide such aid, explaining that it could be dropped into Poland by the RAF flights that were already delivering supplies to the Polish underground. The movement could then convey money and materials to their in-tended recipients through its efficient clandestine channels.

All hopes for succor of any kind hinged on making nations beyond Hitler's reach comprehend what was happening to Europe's Jews. Understanding this fact, and knowing that the Jews had no official advocate for their cause in Allied councils, Feiner desper-ately exhorted the Polish Catholic huddled with him to convince Jewish leaders in London of the situation's gravity. "Let the Jewish people do something that will force the other world to believe us," hissed Feiner. "We are all dying here; let them die too." The Bund leader said the Jews of Britain and America should go on a hunger strike, blockading the offices of Allied leaders, dying a slow death, if that was what it took to "shake the conscience of the world."

Finally, the Zionist, Feiner, and Karski came to the end of their long discussion. All three were physically drained. Feiner raised one last point. "Witold," he said, "I know the English. When you describe to them what is happening to the Jews, they will probably not be-lieve you." If Karski went to London and simply repeated what he had heard from two overwrought Jewish leaders, the result would be no different than the results of Feiner's earlier efforts to spread the news—for he had sent telegrams and detailed written reports to London before. No, Witold would need to present more tangible evidence. He would need to see the Nazi extermination machine in operation. He would need to be a witness.

It could be arranged, if Jan would agree to go along. Jan agreed.

~

Between August 20 and 25, 1942, the wave of terror in the Warsaw Ghetto briefly abated; the German murder network was busy clearing the Jews from several outlying towns. In an area already shrunken to a fraction of its former population, the Ghetto's remaining inhabitants were momentarily free to go about the business of living and dying—mostly dying, of starvation, disease, and suicide—relatively unmolested. The tenuous social order that had been enforced by the Nazi-directed Jewish administration of the Ghetto had dissolved by this time. It was a convenient by-product of the chaos that nobody was likely to notice a stranger on the Ghetto's streets.

In the guise of ordinary Poles, Karski and Feiner entered an apartment building at number 6 Muranowska Street, on the "Aryan side" of the ghetto wall. A janitor who went by the name "Staszek" greeted them and guided them to the cellar. Awaiting them there was a twenty-two-year-old member of the Jewish Military Union, "Dudek" Landau. He knew little about this Pole's mission to the Ghetto; his commander had told him only that a very important man was coming to visit and that it would be his responsibility to guard the secret tunnel by which the guest would enter. A squad of Jewish children under the command of the Jewish Military Union had excavated the tunnel, digging from the cellar of a building on one side of Muranowska (which was divided lengthwise by the wall) to the basement on the other side of the street. Landau led Karski and Feiner through the earthen passageway, which extended nearly forty yards at a height of no more than four feet. The men crawled through the cramped darkness in silence, aside from the curse Karski muttered when his head hit a pipe.

When they reached the opposite side, a member of the Jewish Fighting Organization took over from Landau as escort. Feiner and Karski donned ragged clothes adorned with the Star of David. Thus disguised, the men crept out of the building into the daylight.

The first thing that amazed Jan as he and Feiner emerged in the Ghetto was the utter transformation the Bund leader had undergone. Moments before, he had played the part of the jaunty, self-assured Polish magnate. Now he was a bent, sickly, pitiful old Jew, just another victim awaiting his fate. Jan tried to project the same appearance, stooping in his threadbare suit, cap pulled down over his eyes. During a second meeting, Feiner and the Zionist leader had assured him that a trip to the Ghetto involved a minimum of risk. Jan hoped they were right.

Karski and Feiner shuffled down the street with the Jewish underground member at their side. This had never been a posh area; that was why the Germans made it a ghetto. The buildings were older and smaller, the streets narrower than in most of the rest of Warsaw. The Germans had ordered the street signs to be printed in elaborate Hebrew characters. As in the rest of the city, there were demolished homes on every block—but none of the makeshift rebuilding efforts visible in the rest of Warsaw were in evidence here. The streets were packed with humanity and its remnants. "There was hardly a square yard of empty space," Karski recalled. "As we picked our way across the mud and rubble, the shadows of what had once been men or women flitted by us in pursuit of someone or something, their eyes blazing with some insane hunger or greed." The cries of the mad and the hungry echoed through the streets, mingled with the voices of residents offering to barter scraps of clothing for morsels of food.

Jan identified the stench just as he discerned the unclothed corpses. Strewn in the gutters were the bodies of the old and young, all as naked in death as they had been in birth.

"What does it mean?" Jan asked under his breath.

"When a Jew dies," Feiner calmly replied, "the family removes his clothing and throws his body in the street. Otherwise they would have to pay a burial tax to the Germans. Besides, this saves clothing."

The visitors reached the Plac Muranowski, a square at the northeast corner of the Ghetto that had once been a park. Mothers crowded the benches, nursing emaciated infants. Stunted children filled the area, some sitting listlessly, others cavorting in the dirt.

"They are playing, you see." Jan thought he heard Feiner's voice break with emotion. "Life goes on. They play before they die."

"These children are not playing," responded Jan. "They only make believe it is play."

On the streets, Feiner relentlessly pointed out every macabre example of the zone's bestial conditions. Over and over the men would come upon human forms crumpled against the sides of buildings, their catatonic stares fixed on nothing, only a slight rustling beneath their rags betraying the fact that they were still breathing. At each instance, Feiner would stop for a moment. "Remember this," he said, over and over. "Remember this."

As the tour continued, a commotion ensued on a side street.

People were fleeing. Suddenly, Feiner and the other Jew grabbed Jan by the arms and hustled him into an apartment building. "Hurry!" Feiner growled at the confused Pole. "You must see this."

The men clambered up several flights of stairs. Outside, Jan heard gunfire. Feiner pounded his fist on an apartment door. A haggard and frightened face appeared in the doorway. Feiner charged past the occupant and looked out the apartment window. It faced the rear of the building. The Bund leader dashed across the landing to the opposite apartment, again pounding on the door and demanding entry. The door opened.

"Don't worry—we are Jews!" Feiner yelled at a woman and her whimpering son as he led his comrade and Jan toward the window. Pulling down the blinds, he shoved Jan down into position at the side of the window. Through the gap between the blinds and the window frame, Jan could see two adolescent boys dressed in the crisp uniforms of the Hitlerjugend—the Hitler Youth, the cadet corps of the Third Reich.

"Look at it! Look at it!" Feiner hissed in Karski's ear. "They are here for the hunt."

The boys stood in a deserted street, broad smiles on their faces, their blond hair glistening in the sunlight. One had drawn a pistol. His eyes canvassed the surrounding buildings. The other said something that made him laugh. Then the first boy raised his gun and fired. Jan heard the tinkling of broken glass and a moan of pain from an adjoining building.

The boy who fired the shot let out a victorious whoop. His fellow "warrior" congratulated him. It was another successful *Judenjag*—another "Jew hunt." The Hitler Youth turned and strolled serenely away.

Jan remained crouched by the window, still frozen in horror, long after the boys left. Then, noticing a hand on his shoulder, he turned to find the woman who lived in the apartment standing behind him. "You came to see us? It won't do any good," she said. "Go back, run away. Don't torture yourself anymore. Go, go."

Jan insisted on leaving immediately. With Feiner and the underground's escort, he returned to the building on Muranowska Street. "Dudek" Landau was waiting in the cellar. Within minutes, the visitors had passed once again into the world of the living, beyond the Ghetto.

"You didn't see everything," Feiner said, in parting. Karski nodded, offering to return for another visit if necessary.

Two days later, Jan and a different guide repeated the Ghetto tour. This time they spent three hours within the walls. As Karski met with Jewish underground leaders in an apartment, listening to their pleas for help from the outside world, he was offered a glass of water and a slice of bread—a parody of hospitality amid the savagery of a prison city. Jan's reaction was the talk of the Jewish underground for days: He gently pushed the bread away from his place at the table. Everyone understood. Jan did not need to say that he could not, in good conscience, accept even a morsel that might otherwise feed the starving.

~

Feiner was not finished with Witold. The courier would have to see even more if he was to bear witness effectively to the world. What he had seen so far was brutality on a mass scale. The agonized hordes of the Warsaw Ghetto—and of scores of other urban prison camps throughout Poland and other Nazi-occupied countries—posed a problem for their German masters. But the Germans, a resourceful people, had devised a "final solution" for that problem. The Jewish resistance could arrange for Jan to see that solution in practice. Doing so would involve a much more dangerous fact-finding mission than the Ghetto tours. But Karski agreed without hesitation to carry out the unprecedented mission: to walk into a Nazi death camp of his own free will.

A few days after his second trip to the Ghetto, Jan arrived at a rendezvous point outside Warsaw's central train station. The Jewish underground was to furnish a guide who would get him to the site of the camp. Jan immediately picked his guide out of a crowd, and his heart quickened with anxiety as the young man approached. With olive skin, jet-black hair, and an elongated nose, the underground member appeared so obviously Jewish that Jan was afraid even to be seen with him, not to mention collaborating on a perilous mission with him. In a whispered conversation, Jan conveyed his fears as politely as was possible under the circumstances. After some consideration, he decided to go ahead with the mission. But Jan insisted that his escort ride in a separate train car; if he was going to be caught, Jan did not want to be in the vicinity.

The Pole and the Jew boarded a train bound for Lublin. The train moved southeast at a snail's pace, arriving in the city after nearly six hours. There, the guide had arranged for another form of transport. Jan and his escort rode out the main highway to the east of Lublin—a birch-lined allée in some places, a country road through rolling fields in others. They passed ox-drawn wagons piled high with potatoes. Among the rows that sliced through the black soil to the horizon, they saw peasants toiling to meet the production quotas imposed on them by the Germans.

In mid-afternoon, the conspirators reached a small town, situated where the highway met a rail line. The Jewish guide took Jan to a hardware store and handed him over to its proprietor, a member of the Polish underground. As planned, Jan found the uniform of a Nazi-affiliated Ukrainian militiaman (bribed to take the day off) awaiting him at the store. Not long after Jan finished donning the uniform, another Ukrainian guard appeared at the store, having also accepted a bribe to take this curious Pole through the camp.

The guard spoke perfect Polish, but he and Jan did not say more to each other than was necessary. Jan was to follow him, to avoid attracting attention, and to make sure he did not come into contact with other Ukrainians who might spot him as an impostor. The two "militiamen" set out on foot along a road that passed through a forest, leading away from the village.

Before long, Jan could hear an otherworldly keening from the direction in which he was headed. As Jan drew nearer, he thought he detected the stench of burning flesh. Emerging into a clearing, he approached the camp from a slight rise. He could see a barbed-wire fence about twelve feet in height, camouflaged with branches stripped from the surrounding trees. The fence enclosed a sizeable area. A walled wooden ramp extended from the camp to the nearby railroad track. Within the enclosure were a few small sheds or barracks. Several gates were cut into the fence. At one of them, Jan's Ukrainian escort lazily saluted two of his German masters. They casually gestured for the men to enter.

Spread out before Jan was a broad, open space. To Jan, it seemed to be completely covered by "a dense, pulsating, throbbing, noisy human mass" of "starved, stinking, gesticulating, insane" Jews. Of all ages and both genders, some in various states of undress, the captives sat and lay on the ground. Like the stupefied figures slumped along the Ghetto's streets, many of these victims appeared to be in shock. Here and there in the vast crowd—there must have been thousands—a guard was beating or kicking a Jew.

From his sparse conversation with the guard and from stories circulated in Warsaw, Jan had some idea of how the Jews had gotten to this point. They had probably been deported from the Warsaw Ghetto. They had exchanged existence in that hell for several days'

confinement in sealed boxcars without food, water, or sanitary facilities, followed by further torments and neglect upon their arrival
at this place. (He was mistaken about where they had come from,
but correct about the rest.) The guard had explained that the Jews
were encouraged to bring up to fifteen kilograms of personal belongings with them when they left for "resettlement." When they
reached this camp, their last belongings were snatched from them
and they were left under the elements until the system was ready to
deal with them further.

Behind the mass of humanity stood a long line of boxcars
rolled onto the rail siding. Jan could see some of his Ukrainian "colleagues" lining the cars with a thick layer of white powder, as the
guard had told him they would. It was quicklime, calcium oxide.
Jan made his way along the fence, taking up the position indicated
by the guard.

At a signal from a German officer, several of the Ukrainians
formed a cordon around the Jews on the ground and began herding
them toward the boxcars. Jan stood by the fence and observed the
procedure, carefully keeping his distance from the "other" Ukrainians. The guards moved steadily forward against the chaotic mass
of flesh, striking out with clubs and rifle butts to force the victims
toward the ramp leading to the boxcar doors, shooting and bayo-
neting any too weak or traumatized to move.

The low moan of misery that emanated from the crowd on the
ground gave way first to shrieks of pure panic as the Jews stumbled
up the ramp, then to echoing wails of agony as they were packed
into the boxcars and felt the quicklime burning their skin and lungs.
The guards fired at random into the crowd on the ramp, hurling the
dead and wounded into the car to land on the heads of those already
packed in. When no more bodies could be crammed into a car, a
Ukrainian slammed its iron doors shut, crushing any protruding
limbs.

Jan watched the Nazis fill several boxcars in this manner. He
estimated that thousands of human beings were being packed into
the cars. He visualized the fate awaiting them, these creatures who
had endured not only ghetto life but also the hideous trip to this
way station, followed by days of brutal confinement here—only to
meet such an end.

Jan could not be sure how the victims would finally be dispatched; he had heard various reports. There were reports that
when trains like this one pulled away, they would take the Jews

directly to a nearby camp. There, so it was said, the Nazis would unload it to the accompaniment of an inmate orchestra, with guards forcing the Jews toward the gas chambers as the strains of Mahler or Wagner echoed in the ears of the damned.

On the other hand, perhaps the train would merely grind to a halt on some remote siding. There the train might sit for days, a mobile oubliette, the last vestiges of life ebbing from its cargo. As bodily fluids came into contact with the quicklime on the floor, chlorine gas would be formed. The quicklime itself would eat away the flesh of the dead and living alike, finally combining with wounds, illness, starvation, and dehydration to bring a "merciful" end to the suffering of the humans within.

Jan's survival instinct, which had served him so well throughout the war, evaporated. Weeping and gesticulating, Jan lost control of his emotions. When the Ukrainian escort's angry shouts of "Follow me! Follow me!" roused him from his stupor, Jan did not know how long he had been in a fugue. Hustling the Pole from the camp, the guard vented his fury through clenched teeth: "You acted like you were crazy in there! Your crazy gestures! You endanger people! You've got no business being here! Come on!"

The Ukrainian led his shellshocked "comrade-in-arms" back to the hardware store in town, then disappeared. Immediately Jan locked himself in the bathroom. The merchant found an unholy mess when the door opened: Jan and the room were soaked.

"What the devil have you been doing?" the proprietor yelled.

"I washed myself, that's all," Jan mumbled. "I was very dirty."

Moments later, Jan rushed outside and vomited. He collapsed under a tree and fell asleep. Soon he awoke, shivering in a cold sweat, dimly remembering a nightmare about the tableau of human agony he had beheld. He vomited again, and then again, until he could heave up only blood. The store's mortified proprietor appeared in the yard, demanding to know if his disease was contagious. Assuring him that he had no disease, Jan begged the man to bring him a bottle of vodka.

Jan gulped the liquor gratefully, desperately hoping to obliterate his consciousness. He fell once more into fitful, nightmare-ridden sleep. The next day, Jan managed to return to Warsaw in the company of the Jewish underground guide who had left with him.

Later in life, Karski would be asked frequently to bear witness to the scenes he encountered at the Ghetto and the camp. Sometimes he would attempt to do so. More often, he would refuse to go into detail, instead conveying his experience in a simple sentence: "I saw terrible things."

~

At some point, either in the course of the day's travels or earlier, a misunderstanding had arisen. Although it would have no effect on Jan's mission, it was destined to mystify historians for a half-century after the war. Feiner had told Jan, and his guide had confirmed, that he would be taken to see the Bełżec death camp, the killing center east of Lublin that was the subject of fearsome rumors in underground Poland. It was said that deportees from Warsaw were murdered en masse at Bełżec, that the exterminations were carried out by electrocution in a specially wired chamber, that the bodies of the dead were processed into soap and fertilizer. These rumors were all false. Nevertheless, over a half million Jewish lives did end at the tiny town of Bełżec—the lives of Jews from outside Warsaw, extinguished by gas, not electricity.

The village Jan reached was not Bełżec, nor did Jan think it was while he was there. When he first spoke of this mission after reaching London three months later, he described the site as a "'sorting point' located about fifty kilometers from the city of Bełżec"—although in the same statement he referred to the camp's location as "the outskirts of Bełżec." (The actual Bełżec death camp was in the town of Bełżec, within a few hundred feet of the train station.) In an August 1943 report, Karski at first placed the camp twelve miles, then twelve kilometers outside of Bełżec. By the time he began retelling his story publicly in 1944, the town he reached had become Bełżec itself.

Scholars of the Holocaust have long realized that the camp Karski described could not have been the Bełżec death camp. Clearly, Karski confused certain details as time went by. The fact that he had witnessed early persecutions against Jews in Bełżec in 1939 must have contributed to the confusion. Just as clearly, however, Karski believed he had reached a site that was part of the murderous system centered on the Bełżec extermination camp. In this supposition he was correct.

Jan was in the town of Izbica Lubelska, precisely the midway point between Lublin to the northwest and Bełżec to the southeast—forty miles from each locality. Izbica was indeed a "sorting point"; Karski had this fact right and the distance from Bełżec nearly right in his earliest report. His description of the downhill slope between the town and the camp also matches the terrain of Izbica. The camp played an essential, if little-known, role in the extermination of hundreds of thousands of Jews. A sanitation worker who was employed in the town during the time of Karski's visit testified in 1946 about the town's function:

> The Germans brought Jews from all of Europe to Izbica. Most of the Jews came from Czechoslovakia. In Izbica the various groups would be held for a couple of days (sometimes up to ten days), specifically for the purpose of robbing them of all their valuables. From conversations with the Jews, I have learned that the Germans had told them, as they were being moved out, that they were being taken to work. That is why the Jews took everything they had with them, especially their valuables. After the Jews were robbed and after some of them were murdered in Izbica, the rest were taken to the extermination camp at Bełżec.

Aside from serving as a looting station for the Nazis, Izbica also functioned as a holding camp, allowing the Germans to regulate the flow of traffic to Bełżec. The fact that the Polish worker had been able to talk with Jewish victims suggests that security was lax at Izbica—lax enough to allow someone like Jan to wander the camp, and even to suffer a nervous breakdown there, without being detected. Such slackness on the part of Hitler's henchmen was not unusual: At Bełżec and other eastern death camps, guards were typically drunk on the job and even some S.S. officers kept Jewish women as concubines. The Nazi death factories operated with something less than Prussian efficiency and discipline.

An anecdote related by the same Polish sanitation worker in testimony for a war-crimes investigation suggests that what Karski witnessed was not an unusual sight in Izbica:

> Once, in November 1942, I rode my bicycle to Izbica. It was a rainy day, thoroughly cold. The marketplace there was incredibly muddy. . . . Suddenly there stood before me the Gestapoman [Kurt] Engels [sic; the defendant's name was Engel], revolver drawn, and he yelled "Halt!" He didn't shoot. Why? I don't know. . . . I stood there, and just behind him I noticed a black mass in the marketplace. Engels approached it and yelled; the mass raised itself from the morass. It was Jews, women and men, 100 in number, maybe 200, maybe even 300. . . . On the command of Engels the entire mass moved, formed itself into rows and tried to push itself toward the tracks some 100 m

away. During this time Engels shot three Jews in the head. In the marketplace, on the pavement, remained more than ten, maybe twenty, thirty, forty half-naked small children. They didn't cry anymore, although some still slightly waved their bare little hands and feet. Between the children lay ten to twenty old Jews and Jewesses. I don't know whether they were ill or just weak. Either way, they did not lift themselves upon the command of Engels. Engels suddenly halted the columns and asked the Jewish women to take the children. The women didn't know what to do. Then the Ukrainians started to beat the women with the butts of their weapons, and this brought success: The Jewish women leaped forth and took the children, every one. Engels then walked back to the marketplace, stepped toward the row of those remaining, and shot each one in the head. . . . In this manner, the transports to Bełzec were organized.

~

Back in the Polish capital, Jan tried to focus on the journey ahead. By the beginning of September 1942, preparations for the political substance of his trip were nearing completion. Tactical arrangements were taking longer. The delegate telegraphed the first notice of the planned trip to the government-in-exile in London on September 3. Another month would elapse, however, before Jan could depart for London—a month of frustration for Jan, whose mission had taken on a previously unimaginable significance. With each passing day, he realized, thousands more would die. But organizing a courier's passage across occupied Europe took time.

Jan spent his days and nights in a final round of meetings with political leaders. On the evening of September 1, as Soviet bombers pounded German positions in Warsaw, Jan huddled in the basement of the Warsaw Polytechnic with Peasant Party leader Stefan Korboński. "The drywall was cracking and chunks were falling on our heads," Korboński recalled in a memoir. "We looked like two priests who were receiving confession from one another by candlelight." The two men and Korboński's wife Zofia, who was crouched in the shelter with them, could not have imagined that they would spend the four decades following the war as neighbors in an American suburb.

The Home Army's Bureau of Information and Propaganda, with its contingent of Jews and intellectuals sympathetic to the Jewish cause, had meanwhile begun assembling written information on the Jewish crisis for Jan to carry. The bureau was charged with producing a roll of microfilm that would contain all the documentary material to be carried by the envoy. Jan handed over to its technicians various reports and letters that he had been given in the course of his meetings, including a ten-page letter from Leon Feiner with crucial information about the Holocaust under way in Warsaw. There were also several documents written by political leaders and destined for their counterparts in exile, as well as a few samples of Jan's own analysis of underground publications, written some months earlier.

To this cache, three BIP officials added a report that carefully detailed the atrocities of recent weeks throughout Poland. It included a copy of orders issued by the German-run Jewish Council, mandating deportation procedures at the outset of the Warsaw Ghetto liquidation on July 22. It included a section on the process of liquidation that then ensued in Warsaw and towns surrounding the capital. It included the account of a policeman who had worked in the Warsaw Ghetto. It included a report on Bełżec, written in July. And it incorporated several other accounts of the systematic destruction of Jews in Poland.

Also included in the material to be microfilmed was a late arrival, an eloquent protest from Zofia Kossak's Front for the Rebirth of Poland (FOP). This broadside had hit the streets of Warsaw in early September, days after Jan returned from his trip to eastern Poland. Its text made clear that Jan had told Kossak everything he had seen:

> In the Warsaw Ghetto, behind the wall that cuts it off from the world, several hundred thousand of the condemned are awaiting death. The hope of rescue does not exist for them; no help is coming from anywhere. Assassins speed through the streets, shooting anyone who dares to leave his house. They also shoot anyone who stands at the window. Unburied bodies are strewn about the streets.

The protest went on to summarize the progress of deportations in the Ghetto. Then it described what happened to the deportees:

> At the ramps, boxcars are waiting. The hangmen push up to 150 of the condemned into each one. A thick layer of lime and chlorine is spread on the floors, with water poured over it. The boxcar's doors are sealed. Sometimes the train leaves as soon as it is loaded; sometimes it sits on the track—perhaps for a couple of days—but it doesn't matter to anyone anymore. Of the people packed so tightly that the

dead cannot fall and continue to stand shoulder-to-shoulder with the living, of the people slowly dying in the fumes of lime and chlorine, deprived of air or even a drop of water, none will live. Wherever, whenever the death trains arrive, they will contain nothing but corpses. . . .

We do not want to be like Pilate. We have no means of actively opposing the German murders; we cannot overcome them or save anybody. But we *protest*, from the bottom of our hearts, which are filled with compassion, loathing, and horror. That protest is demanded of us by God—God, who has forbidden us to kill. It is demanded by the Christian conscience. Every creature calling itself a man has the right to the love of his neighbor. The blood of the helpless calls to the heavens for vengeance. Whoever among us does not support this protest is not a Catholic.

Kossak's statement concluded on a jarring note, blaming the "stubborn silence of international Jewry," among other factors, for the lack of action by the Allied nations to help the Jews. But in the coming months, as the protest was reprinted throughout the world, its abridged version would omit that sentence. The famous writer's declaration, which incorporated (and may have been motivated by) the horrific tales Jan told after his visits to the Ghetto and camp, was to achieve lasting recognition. It was one of at least four documents from the Front for the Rebirth of Poland to be included on the microfilm prepared by the BIP, out of a total of thirty to forty items.

All this material was to be shrunken to fit on a tiny roll of film. That film would then be stuffed into a hollow house key, which would then be welded shut. All Jan had to do was carry it across Hitler's empire.

The key would be the source of some irony. The courier who carried it was an eyewitness of the Nazi extermination program that had so often been rumored and so often been disbelieved in the West. Mere written reports of Nazi atrocities had been sent before, without effect. Yet it was the material in the key, reaching London by clandestine means before Jan himself did, that was destined to shock the world.

TERRIBLE SECRETS
October 1942–September 1943

7
Carrying the Message

Warsaw was still dark when the curfew ended at 5:00 A.M. on
October 1. Bundled to ward off the chill of an early frost,
blending in with the early-rising greengrocers and newsstand atten-
dants, about a dozen men and women made their way toward Krakowskie Przedmieście. One by one, they entered the rectory behind
the Church of the Holy Cross. Jan was the last to arrive.

Father Edmund Krauze greeted him with a silent smile at the
door, and those gathered in the parlor stood as the guest of honor
entered. With handshakes, hugs, and murmured benedictions, each
of Jan's comrades wished him a safe and successful journey. It was
a varied crowd: Zofia Kossak, Jan's matronly muse, standing next
to Renee, his sometime girlfriend; Witold Bieńkowski, who had
helped to found the pro-Jewish Front for the Rebirth of Poland,
across the room from Jerzy Iłłakowicz, leader of the anti-Semitic
National Party. Many Poles would later blame Iłłakowicz's right-
wing troops for the 1944 murder of Jerzy Makowiecki. This morning Jan's boss stood alongside Iłłakowicz at the farewell Mass.

Before a makeshift altar in his parlor, Father Krauze quietly
spoke the words of the liturgy, answered in hushed tones by the
assembled conspirators. After administering communion, he led
Jan's friends in reciting the blessing for travelers from a prayer
book. Jan bowed his head, eyes welling with tears.

The priest summoned Jan to the altar, told him to kneel, and
asked him to open his shirt. In his outstretched hands, Father
Krauze held a golden, pillbox-sized locket, known in church ter-
minology as a pyx. It contained a single communion wafer. "You
will wear Christ's Body throughout your journey," said the clergy-

man, draping the talisman over Jan's neck. "If danger approaches, you will be able to swallow it. It will protect you from all evil and harm." The priest knelt next to Jan and silently prayed with him.

After the service, Jan's thoughts narrowed to a single focus—not the journey he would begin later that day, but the vial of cyanide taped between his legs. Ever since he had resumed underground work after the escape from Nowy Sącz, he had dutifully carried the poison he would need if the Gestapo ever caught him. Since the scars on his wrists made him so readily identifiable, there could be no excuse for any repetition of his failure to carry an efficient means of suicide during his 1940 mission. As a practical matter, carrying the capsule entailed an unpleasant ritual for Jan: In order to guard against the danger of a leak, he had to pull the tape from behind his scrotum every few days—ripping hairs from his skin along with it—to change the dressing.

As Jan strolled with the consecrated Host around his neck, the thought of simultaneously keeping open the option of suicide—a mortal sin—suddenly struck him as blasphemy. God would not be fooled. In a frenzy of religious fervor, Jan rushed back to his apartment. He removed the cyanide from its hiding place, broke open the capsule, and washed its contents down the sink. He would travel across Europe with a clear conscience. And he would dispense with the painful annoyance of repackaging the poison at regular intervals.

Jan now hurried to a dental appointment. The dentist was not in the underground, but he could be trusted. Jan had approached him a few days earlier with an odd request: "Look, don't ask why, but I need a dental problem. What can you do to make my jaw swell for a few days, with a minimum of discomfort?" The dentist had promised to find a way, and today he gave Jan an injection that produced the desired tumidity. The swelling, together with the all-too-real gaps left in Jan's mouth after the Gestapo beating, would provide a perfect excuse not to carry on conversations with passengers on the train.

Avoiding such encounters had taken on particular importance when Jan learned what papers he would carry on the first leg of his journey. Taking advantage of the thousands of French laborers who had volunteered to work in German-run industries in Poland, the underground had prevailed upon one of those laborers to spend his vacation on a Polish estate (where he would be lavishly pampered), and to hand over the German-issued documents that would have allowed him to return to France on holiday. Jan became that Frenchman. His command of the French language was excellent, but he worried about his thick accent. Since he would share compartments all the way from Warsaw to Paris with real French workers, keeping his mouth shut became a key security issue.

Jan's dental ploy worked just as planned. As he boarded the westbound train later that day, he held a handkerchief to his swollen mouth and feigned chronic pain, nodding and mumbling disinterestedly at the greetings and perfunctory sympathy of others in the car. No one tried to strike up a conversation with him as the train crawled toward Berlin. Late that night, Jan crossed the Polish border. Thirty-two years would pass before he touched his native soil again.

In the capital of the Reich, an overcrowded train station offered Jan safety in numbers: The Gestapo had better things to do than check papers in the midst of such chaos. Changing trains in Berlin, he set out on another agonizingly slow journey as a low-priority passenger on the wartime rails. By the time he reached Brussels, after a thirty-six-hour ride, Jan's dental ruse was working so well that a Belgian passenger felt a humanitarian duty to help the suffering traveler in his compartment. The Belgian went for help, and an officious German nurse soon appeared on the platform, clutching a medical bag and demanding to know where it hurt. Unable to escape from these well-meaning tormentors, Jan reluctantly opened his mouth. The nurse swabbed the empty sockets of his gums with anesthetic, reprimanding him for taking such poor care of his teeth. She sternly handed him an orange and ordered him to eat nothing but soft fruit until he saw a dentist.

~

"Jestem Witold od Waci" (I'm Witold from Wacława), said the tall young man who appeared at the counter of a Polish-owned fashion boutique in Paris. The woman behind the counter smiled, excused herself, and disappeared to the back of the shop. A middle-aged Polish man emerged and introduced himself. Jan gave the password again. The man beckoned him behind the counter.

Jan's contact was Aleksander Kawałkowski, chief of the Polish underground in France. A former consul at Lille, Kawałkowski had stayed behind when France fell in order to lead a resistance movement made up of Poles who lived in France—mostly coal miners and other laborers, but also a number of intellectuals. By 1942, the

Polish government in London was claiming that about five thousand Polish agents were operating in France. They worked independently from, but in harmony with, the French resistance.

Kawałkowski's cadres were responsible for arranging Karski's transit from Paris to the border of neutral Spain. Covering this relatively short distance was a considerably trickier affair than getting from Warsaw to Paris, and Jan had arrived at a particularly difficult moment. As the Germans prepared to consolidate their control of France by imposing direct rule over the southern zone governed by the puppet Vichy regime, they had moved to crack down on resistance in Vichy France. In August, the Gestapo had arrested hundreds of Poles from Kawałkowski's group. And before Jan could leave France, on October 17 and again on October 23, Gestapo teams equipped with special sensors homed in on Polish radio transmissions to London and raided the clandestine stations, arresting key personnel, seizing documents, and heightening fears in London for Jan's safety.

In such a perilous environment, Kawałkowski moved slowly and deliberately to arrange the emissary's passage. He may also have been caught somewhat off guard by Jan's arrival. He appears to have relayed a complaint to Warsaw via Interior Minister Stanisław Mikołajczyk in London, who sent an irritated dispatch to the government delegate in Warsaw: "Why didn't you provide him any personal authentication [false papers], mail, or money? It makes further expedition difficult." Jan may have lacked the necessary forged documents to move freely in Paris, but he certainly was carrying plenty of cash—the delegate had appropriated the extravagant sum of thirty-seven thousand złotys (roughly $550) for Jan's journey, mostly in the form of gold coins. The complaint that he was not carrying "mail" (smuggled documents destined for the London government) must have arisen from confusion. Jan had handed his key to Kawałkowski during their meeting at the boutique. Kawałkowski would make use of his consular connections to send the key out of France in the diplomatic pouch of a neutral country. The key, bearing microfilmed "mail" that would shock the world, was to arrive in London about ten days before Jan.

In order to ensure Jan's security in Paris, Kawałkowski procured false papers that allowed him to pose as a Polish worker. The agent billeted Jan with a Polish priest, telling the visitor to relax and enjoy himself while awaiting an opportunity to move south. The priest asked no questions of his visitor, although after a few days he began to express anxiety about Jan's lengthy visit. Jan had no such worries. He knew French, he knew Paris, and he was long overdue for a vacation. By day he wandered the city as a tourist; after dark he haunted the cafés and nightclubs of Montmartre. The war seemed far away—except when a Wehrmacht battalion goose-stepped past him on a boulevard, or when he saw French women clamoring to dance with German officers in the clubs. The rail-thin Pole, whose nation's foodstuffs had been plundered so systematically as to bring about mass-scale malnutrition, gorged himself at the amply supplied restaurants of Paris until the rich food made him sick. At the nightclubs he could arrange to satisfy other long-repressed desires as well.

Jan's Parisian interlude lasted almost two weeks. When Kawałkowski finally presented him with a new identity and train tickets to Lyon, he journeyed uneventfully to that city. At the railway station, he was surprised to find that his Lyon contact was none other than Bogdan Samborski, the former foreign ministry official in whose Warsaw home Jan had hidden a few months before. At the news that his wife and child were alive and well, Samborski wept.

At Lyon, Jan was again delayed while the underground worked out arrangements to move him farther south. At least two weeks passed before he traveled on to Perpignan, where the frustrating pattern repeated itself. With Gestapo activity in the Vichy territory on the upswing, Jan remained cloistered for a week at the home of a Polish agent in Perpignan. One day the agent came home and tossed him a French copy of Lenin's *The State and Revolution*. "Read it," he said. "You are about to become a Communist."

The agent had at last found a guide to escort Jan across the Pyrenees and into Spain. Such smugglers were plentiful, charging ten to twenty-five thousand francs per cross-border transit. As rumors spread that Germany would seize Vichy France, however, escorts had become scarce at any price. But José, Jan's partner in the mountain trek, was motivated by more than financial gain. As a communist, he was an exile from Generalissimo Francisco Franco's Spain, where he had been on the losing end of the civil war. José's specialty was helping fellow party members infiltrate his country.

"He is fanatically, stupidly Communist," the Polish agent in Perpignan told his houseguest. "Witold, I told him that you are a Polish Communist on a mission. So be careful: As long as you deal with José, you are a Communist. The guy is crazy. If he discovers you are a fake, he will cut your throat, or will leave you in the mountains alone to die of exposure."

Jan digested the slim volume of Lenin's thoughts with the enthusiasm of a Comintern member. For three days, as the former prisoner of the Soviets and the Spanish true believer trudged together over the Pyrenees, Jan debated the nuances of Marxist dogma with his guide as vigorously as José's broken French would allow. José's single-minded devotion to his cause greatly impressed Jan, notwithstanding his own antipathy to Communism. Accepting Jan as a comrade, José went to great lengths to take care of him during the arduous journey through snow-covered terrain, sharing rations with him, offering him vodka to keep warm, building fires, covering Jan with his own fur jacket, and huddling together with him as they slept in hillside shepherds' huts. Long after the war, Jan would still remember José as "a noble, noble man."

Crossing the Spanish border without incident, Jan and his unlikely companion hiked to a village, where José purchased train tickets. They rode together to Barcelona. There José deposited his client at a safe house operated by Spaniards. The next morning, a limousine with diplomatic license plates appeared at the house, and an English-speaking man invited Jan for a ride. Within a few hours, Jan was in Madrid.

Aside from its delays, the journey had come off without a hitch. Jan had no idea, however, how close he had come to disaster. The arrest of the radio operators in October, as well as the simultaneous discovery that German agents posing as couriers from Poland had infiltrated the Polish network in France, raised the possibility that his mission had been exposed. ("There is no conspiracy [in France] anymore; everybody knows everything about everybody," an alarmed Home Army chief Stefan Rowecki radioed to London on October 22.) Jan was not informed of this danger. Moreover, the German seizure of Vichy France on November 11, 1942, would effectively close off the escape route Jan had taken. Within a month of Jan's trip across the Pyrenees, the Germans had completely sealed the Franco-Spanish border. If Jan had encountered further delays, he might well have had no other option than crossing to Bern, Switzerland, where Polish diplomatic and military officials had already been advised of his possible arrival. In all likelihood, he would then have been unable to leave Switzerland for the duration of the war.

Even though he was in the hands of diplomats, Jan did not yet

Jan Kozielewski as a Polish Army cadet, 1935.

On maneuvers with the Fifth Horse Artillery, 1938.

A scene from the Soviet prison camp at Kozel'shchina, sketched by one of the Poles detained there. In the autumn of 1939, Karski was held at the camp for eight weeks. He won his release by deceiving the Soviets into thinking he was not an officer. Many of his fellow officers were executed a few months later, on the orders of Stalin. (Courtesy of Stanisław Westwalewicz, Tarnów, Poland)

General Władysław Sikorski, commander-in-chief of Polish armed
forces and prime minister of Poland's exiled government, 1939–43.

Stanisław Mikołajczyk, prime minister of the Polish government-in-exile
after Sikorski's death in 1943.

The boundaries of
Poland have changed
many times in its his-
tory. The map shows
the boundaries and
Polish territory during
the period the events
in this book took place
up to the present.

At work on *Story of a Secret State*, late spring 1944. Karski composed the book in a New York hotel room, with the assistance of stenographer and translator Krystyna Sokolowska.

Karski opens an exhibition on the underground struggle sponsored by the Polish government-in-exile, 1944.

Ex Libris... *By William Sharp*

WHEN THE NAZIS OVERRAN POLAND, LT. JAN KARSKI JOINED THE UNDERGROUND.*

AS COURIER, HE WAS THE CONTACT WITH THE *GOVERNMENT IN-EXILE.*

NUNS IN NAZI PRISON HOSPITAL HELPED HIM ESCAPE FROM GESTAPO!

HE VISITED NOTORIOUS JEWISH DEATH CAMP, DISGUISED AS ESTONIAN GUARD,

STORY OF A SECRET STATE
by JAN KARSKI
BOOK-OF-THE-MONTH CLUB SELECTION

Promotional cartoon for *Story of a Secret State* produced by the Book-of-the-Month Club, 1945. The lower two frames are not quite accurate. Karski's book did mention that he had been aided in his escape from the hospital by an underground member dressed as a nun, but Zofia Rysiówna, the woman who helped him, later denied that she had been disguised in this manner. For security and political reasons, Karski wrote that he had worn an Estonian uniform while in the death camp; in reality, he was dressed as a Ukrainian guard.

Karski, 1944.

Polish-British artist Felix
Topolski, who helped arrange
Karski's London contacts in
1943, executed this charcoal
sketch in 1986.

Karski toured Asia as a State Department lecturer in 1955. Top: He enumerates the evils of Communism to a Pakistani audience (Lahore, August 28, 1955). Bottom: Karski poses with the reception committee at the Mandalay, Burma, airport, October 31, 1955.

In 1985, the government of Israel presented a nineteenth-century Torah, which had survived the war in Europe, to Georgetown University in the name of Professor Jan Karski. Left to right: Georgetown president Timothy S. Healy, S.J., Israeli ambassador Meir Rosenne, visiting Israeli professor Haggai Erlich, and Karski. (Photo by Mitchell Layton, courtesy of Georgetown University)

Karski speaks in the U.S. Capitol rotunda after receiving the Eisenhower Liberation Medal from the United States Holocaust Memorial Council, April 11, 1991.

Karski at home. (Photo by Gay Block, from *Rescuers: Portraits of Moral Courage in the Holocaust* by Gay Block and Malka Drucker [New York: Holmes & Meier, 1992]. Reprinted by permission.)

let down his guard. As soon as he entered the limousine, he asked the agent: "May I have some instructions as to what will happen if I am arrested?" The agent reassured him. Franco was no longer dallying as enthusiastically with Hitler as he had in the past. If Jan had been caught early in the war, the agent told him, the Spanish would have shipped him back to Germany. A little later, they would have put him in a detention camp and informed the Germans. Of late they had become a little less confident of German victory and thus a little more eager to please the Allies. If they caught him now, said the agent, Jan should say nothing. His release would be swiftly arranged.

In Madrid, a pair of English-speaking agents took charge of Jan. They seemed to have orders to cater to his every need, shuttling him around the city to purchase clothing, toiletries, and anything else he wanted, all at their expense. They warned him that consumer goods were in short supply in England and recommended that he buy whatever he would need while in Spain. Jan reveled in the opportunity to dress in the style to which he had been accustomed before the war. First he was fitted for a custom-cut suit, then he and the agents roamed the city in search of the Italian shoes he had preferred as a civilian. When Jan demanded custom-fitted silk shirts, though, his handlers were rather taken aback. As a tailor took his measurements, Jan listened carefully to the sotto voce chatter of the agents. "Gee whiz, never in my life have I worn a silk shirt," muttered one agent, loud enough that he probably meant to tease the young Pole. "Sissy, just sissy."

"Gee whiz" was the clue Jan had been looking for—proof positive that he was in the hands of American rather than British intelligence. Until this point, he had been unable to identify the men's nationality by their accents. His curiosity was now satisfied. In Washington ten months later, he would meet William J. ("Wild Bill") Donovan, head of the Office of Strategic Services (OSS). Donovan would cut Jan's formal presentation short, asking him about his trip through Spain. Did some people take care of him there? Did they identify themselves? Did they treat him well? Were all his needs met? Jan said he didn't know who the agents were, but he gave a glowing report on their work. Beaming, Donovan turned to the Polish ambassador, who was sitting in on the meeting. "My boys!" he exclaimed, thumbs jabbing his chest. "My boys!"

There is evidence, however, that British secret services played a role in Jan's transit as well. A senior officer of Britain's Special

Operations Executive (SOE) later wrote to a Foreign Office official that "Mr. K. was brought out under our auspices but Mikołajczyk probably doesn't know this." And it was an SOE operative who sent word to the Poles on November 25 that Jan was in Gibraltar.

He had reached the Rock through a procedure that seemed quite routine to all involved, except Jan. The American agents had driven him to Algeciras, the Spanish town just opposite Gibraltar, where they booked him into a hotel. In the wee hours of the morning, they awoke him. After insisting that he accept a large sum of British pounds, the agents escorted him to a small motor launch. The boat trolled out into the Straits of Gibraltar for a rendezvous with a Royal Navy patrol boat, which took Jan on board and steamed toward Gibraltar. The next day, after dining with Mason MacFarlane, the colony's governor, Jan boarded a flight to England.

On the night of November 25, 1942, Jan Karski arrived at a Royal Air Force base outside London. The flight on a military transport had lasted more than four hours. Together with Jan in the frigid, unpressurized cargo bay were five other men in civilian clothes, none of whom ever spoke during the trip. After his transit through Spain was handled so efficiently, Jan gave no thought to any formalities that might be necessary upon arrival. He expected that he would be able to begin carrying his various messages to their intended recipients immediately.

Jan was in for a surprise. Not only were no Polish officials waiting for him as he stepped off the airplane, but the British authorities who led him from the aircraft refused his request to telephone the Poles in London. As a matter of standard procedure, they told him, he would remain in quarantine until his case had been resolved. Jan was being treated as an ordinary refugee.

The next day he was transferred to the Royal Victoria Patriotic Schools (RVPS), located in the southwestern London suburb of Wandsworth. The Patriotic Schools served as a holding facility for certain categories of newly arrived aliens, including refugees from enemy-held territory. MI5, Britain's primary security agency, handled interrogations at the facility. Obviously it was important to screen all arriving foreigners: At least ten Nazi spies were discovered during the war among purported escapees from the continent.

Major Malcolm Scott, the intelligence officer who greeted Jan at the RVPS, set out the ground rules in a friendly but firm manner, speaking fluent Polish. Jan would not be personally searched, but his suitcase would be examined. He would not be allowed any contact with the outside world while in custody. He would be questioned in detail about his activities during the war and the route of his escape. As soon as His Majesty's Government could be satisfied about the accuracy of his representations, he would be released.

Jan smiled at the irony of his situation. He had been a prisoner of the Soviets, then of the Germans, and now he was in British captivity. Despite his frustration, he understood that Major Scott was simply doing his duty. And Jan would do his duty. "I will tell you absolutely nothing," he said, as pleasantly as possible. "I consider myself a diplomatic courier. Please contact the office of the Polish prime minister. My mission is to the prime minister and commander-in-chief, General Sikorski. If you are interested in the content of my mission, I'm sure he, as a loyal ally, will be happy to tell you what you need to know."

The amiable expression never left Scott's face. "Mr. Karski," he said, "we will keep you here until you provide us with the information we need, even if you stay until the end of the war." He directed Jan to his dormitory-style room.

~

At the Polish government's headquarters near Buckingham Palace, an irate General Sikorski ordered his foreign ministry to lodge a formal protest with the British government over its treatment of the newly arrived envoy from Poland. A British diplomat noted that "the Poles are more concerned with the person of their 'emissary' rather than with any documents that he may have been carrying." But concern over the detention of the messenger was overshadowed by alarm over the message he carried. The microfilm in the key had reached London by November 17, and Polish officials had condensed its information on the Jews' persecution into a two-page report in English.

"News is reaching the Polish Government in London about the liquidation of the Jewish ghetto in Warsaw," the text began. It told of Himmler's order to exterminate half the Jewish population in Poland by the end of 1942. It told of the first phase of the "resettlement" that commenced on July 22 and of the suicide the next day of Adam Czerniakow, the Nazi-appointed Jewish leader of the Ghetto. It told how the Germans had printed fewer and fewer ration cards as the months went by—proof that the number of ghetto residents was diminishing. It told of a "digging machine" operating "ceaselessly" to bury the dead at Treblinka. And, borrowing details from the protest issued by the Front for the Rebirth of Poland (and thus, in turn, from Jan's experiences), the document described the cramming of Jews into overloaded boxcars lined with quicklime. It told how the trains would either transport the victims to extermination camps or simply sit in oblivion as those trapped within died in agony. Over a million Jews, the report concluded, had perished at the hands of Hitler's forces in Poland.

It was not the first report of Nazi monstrosities against the Jews to reach the West, or even to reach the Polish government-in-exile. Rumors and scattered reports of atrocities had begun to emerge early in the war. In the months before Karski arrived, an increasing amount of compelling testimony about crimes against humanity had leaked out of occupied Europe by various means. The SS was unable to keep its operations completely secret for long. In May 1942, what turned out to be a very accurate report by the Bund on the early stages of the Holocaust—the Einsatzgruppen mass murders in the East and the extermination camp at Chełmno—reached London, transmitted with the help of Swedish businessmen in Warsaw. The Poles made the bulk of this information public. But the Polish government had several motives for treating the Bund report with caution.

The news presented the regime with myriad political concerns. If true, the Bund report threatened to overshadow the great sufferings of non-Jewish Poles in the eyes of the world. The West might demand more vigorous action by the Polish underground to save the imperiled Jews, upsetting the movement's strategy of undertaking only carefully targeted actions until the time was right to mount a massive uprising. Moreover, by appearing as an advocate for Jews, the government would antagonize anti-Semitic Polish factions both in London and in Poland. (Just how prominent and influential these factions were has been the subject of rancorous debate since the war, but their existence is indisputable.)

The Polish government incorporated all these factors into its political calculus, but its overriding concerns involved the degree to which the report could be believed. The Bund account described a shocking level of bestiality. Only a quarter century earlier, lurid tales of this kind had become standard fare in Britain's war propaganda against Germany, and after the war the stories were revealed as fabrications. Polish Foreign Minister Edward Raczyński's reaction to the May 1942 report was probably typical: "It seemed to

me so devilish, it seemed to me so horrible," he recalled, "that at
first I thought it was exaggerated."

Polish officials also had to take into account the reaction of
other parties in the free world. The British, American, and Soviet
governments had shown no eagerness to involve themselves in the
issue of atrocities against Jews. To the extent they pondered the fate
of these noncombatants, Allied leaders probably thought that while
Hitler was surely mistreating them terribly, he would want to preserve them for slave labor.

And then there were the Jewish leaders in London, New York,
and the British colony of Palestine. Details had reached them
through their own channels as well as Polish and other Allied
sources—the World Jewish Congress office in Geneva had gathered
intelligence on events in occupied areas; individual Jews in Poland
could sometimes send letters to neutral countries, written in veiled
language to dodge the censor; some Jewish refugees were still coming to Palestine from Europe, telling tales of horror. Yet throughout
most of 1942, many Jewish political, religious, and journalistic observers received the news from Europe with reserve, if not outright
skepticism. Jerusalem newspapers denounced each other for sen-
sationalism in articles on alleged massacres. A Polish Jewish leader
accused the non-Jewish world of "exaggerating [the Nazi persecu-
tions] twofold and more." Jews harbored the same suspicions as
others in the West about atrocity propaganda, coupled with a deep-
seated inclination to deny that anything so hideous could really happen in the twentieth century.

By the beginning of September, Jewish leaders in London and
New York had read an account of the grand design behind all the
atrocities: the Final Solution of the Jewish question in Europe. Gerhart Riegner, an official of the World Jewish Congress in Geneva,
cabled a summary of his discussions with an "informant stated to
have close connections with highest German authorities" whose reports were "generally reliable." The informant, a German industri-
alist, told of a plan hatched "in Führer's headquarters . . . according
to which all Jews in countries occupied or controlled [by] Germany
numbering 3½ to 4 million should after deportation and concentration in East be exterminated at one blow."

Leaders of American and British Jewry had reacted with
alarm, but also with caution. Riegner himself had warned that he
could not confirm the "exactitude" of his informant's information.

The leaders heeded the counsel of the British Foreign Office and the U.S. State Department: They refrained from publicizing the Riegner telegram.

As Riegner's information was being discussed in Allied capitals and Karski's microfilm was being digested into a report by the Polish government, the Jewish Agency in Jerusalem was preparing a third account of the Holocaust. On November 14, a trainload of Jews had arrived in Palestine from Europe. Most of them were Palestinian citizens who had been caught in Poland at the time of the Blitzkrieg; the Nazis had agreed to exchange them for German detainees in the West. They came from all over Poland as well as Germany, Belgium, and the Netherlands. Not only had they witnessed atrocities across this wide geographical range, but during their journey they had also been in contact with some of the four hundred Jews remaining in Vienna—out of a prewar population of two hundred thousand Jews. The Jewish Agency, a semi-autonomous organization in British-ruled Palestine, interviewed the exchangees as they arrived. Prior, more fragmentary reports had left open the possibility that rogue German units were engaging in widespread but uncoordinated acts of terror. These interviews, however, painted a vivid portrait of a coherent Nazi policy of extermination.

The Jewish Agency made its findings public on November 23. On November 24, after learning that the U.S. State Department had independently confirmed the essence of Riegner's report, Rabbi Stephen Wise of the World Jewish Congress in New York called a press conference to release the Riegner telegram. Wise said that of the five million Jews in Nazi-held territory, half "had already been destroyed." The revelations from New York and Jerusalem had an immediate impact on public opinion, particularly in Jewish circles.

These reports came from Jews themselves; some might still dismiss the accounts as the exaggerations of a people under stress. But a non-Jewish source came forward the same day with a third account of the unprecedented wave of terror against Jews. On November 24, the Polish government released to the press its two-page digest of the reports carried by Karski. Many newspapers around the world carried the news; most treated the report's release as a minor story.

On the morning of November 26, two prominent British Jews called on Richard Law, parliamentary undersecretary for foreign affairs. A.L. Easterman, a top British official of the World Jewish Congress, and Labour M.P. Sydney Silverman insisted to Law that immediate action was needed in light of the Polish revelations. If Britain's position was that nothing could be done to help the Jews now, Silverman emphasized, then nothing could ever be done. He suggested various measures that might be taken—a promise of retribution; radio broadcasts to encourage the remaining Jews—but he left Law with the impression that he realized such measures would be futile. Law, reporting on the meeting to his colleagues, referred condescendingly to "Silverman and his friends" and warned that "unless we can make them some kind of gesture they will cause a lot of trouble." The only realistic explanation for such a callous response to news of genocide is that Law did not believe Karski's report. Still, careful to cover his bases, the diplomat added another warning: "I think that we would be in an appalling position if these stories should prove to have been true and we have done nothing whatever about them."

~

On the morning of November 27, as Sikorski's government released more of the new information emerging from Poland, Jan Karski took his seat in an interrogation chamber at the Royal Victoria Patriotic Schools. After his British captors had agreed to the presence of two Polish intelligence officers as observers, Jan consented to undergo questioning. "He told a very lengthy story of his underground work in Europe," noted a senior officer of MI5, in a letter responding to Foreign Office inquiries about Jan's detention. "Karski appears to have done astonishing work for the Poles over a very long period of time," he added. "They had every reason to consider him a hero."

The interrogation lasted about three and a half hours. Meanwhile, the diplomatic wrangling continued, with the Poles insisting on Karski's release and the British counterintelligence bureaucracy insisting on its right to investigate him. MI5 beat a tactical retreat the next day, finally releasing Jan at 3:00 on the afternoon of November 28 while continuing to fight a genteel war of words with the Foreign Office over the principles involved.

Paweł Siudak, the Polish interior ministry official who had met Jan when he arrived in France on his 1940 trip, showed up to retrieve him from the Patriotic Schools. At last Jan was free; at last he could begin carrying out his duties. But he was torn by conflicting emotions: the exhilaration of freedom, the annoyance of his detention by the British, the horror of what he had witnessed in Poland, and above all an awful sense of responsibility. The mental toughness that allowed Jan to press on with his tasks after enduring the horrors of the Ghetto and Izbica began to elude him. As Siudak drove to his apartment, where Karski would live for the next two months, he noticed that the new arrival seemed agitated. Jan wasn't saying much.

When they reached the flat, Siudak offered Jan half a glass of Scotch. "Drink," he said. "It will strengthen you."

Jan—no veteran tippler—emptied the glass in one gulp. Suddenly he collapsed, gasping for breath. Siudak took hold of him and led him to the toilet, where he vomited.

Later that evening, Stanisław Mikołajczyk, who had taken Professor Kot's place as interior minister, arrived to debrief Karski. Mikołajczyk greeted him warmly, but Jan brusquely interrupted his government's third-ranking official. He rattled off the names of Polish cabinet members from various parties to whom he was carrying messages, as well as other Poles like Tadeusz Bielecki, the extreme Nationalist leader in London who had been excluded from the coalition government and was a bitter enemy of Sikorski. But those official missions were only part of the story, Jan insisted. There were other issues at stake, matters of life and death. "The Jewish leaders in Warsaw have begged me to approach the British government. Without their help the Jews will perish. I have to see Churchill!" he shouted. "Immediately! I have important information!" He paced back and forth across the apartment floor, gesticulating wildly as he described the atrocities he had witnessed.

Mikołajczyk and Siudak looked at each other apprehensively, then left the room together. When they returned a moment later, Mikołajczyk approached Jan and placed a hand on his shoulder. "You are tired," he said softly. "You have to rest. We will give you all the newspapers, in Polish and English. First, you should read everything you can get, so you will know what the situation is in London. Eat well. Get some sleep."

Jan's voice trembled with frustration. "But I swore I would deliver—"

Mikołajczyk cut him off curtly. "You will not establish contact with anybody until I authorize you to do so. You must stay here for several days."

"Several days" would turn into two months of loosely enforced quarantine for Karski. He would meet the Poles he was supposed to meet, and under the tightest secrecy he would meet a few British officials with special interests in Polish covert operations. Otherwise, he would stay on ice at Siudak's apartment. One reason for the isolation was that Sikorski had departed for the United States and Mexico just as Karski was arriving. The commander-in-chief's unforeseen absence (plans for the trip had been kept secret for security reasons) in itself thwarted Jan's plans for a quick return to Poland. But the state of mind in which he arrived gave the government cause for grave concern: Jan appeared to be a potential loose cannon. Two months after his arrival, responding to a resentful complaint from Jan, Sikorski would explain his quarantine bluntly: "You were crazy when you got here. We couldn't let outsiders see you in that shape."

Siudak did accede to one urgent request from Karski the morning after his release from the Patriotic Schools: He needed to see a priest. Siudak drove him to the Polish church on Devonia Road where many of London's exiled Poles worshipped. Monsignor Władysław Staniszewski didn't bat an eye at the borderline sacrilege of allowing a layman to carry the Holy Host as protection against evil; perhaps he had seen others employ this technique during the past three years. After hearing Jan's confession, Father Staniszewski took the pyx from him, removed the Host from the locket, and administered communion to Jan. When Jan asked if he could keep the locket as a souvenir, the priest replied that he had a better idea. "I will hang it on the church's portrait of our Madonna of Częstochowa, as a votive in commemoration of your safe journey." It hangs there to this day.

Jan went to work the next day, Monday, November 30, dictating a detailed report on his missions to various political factions among the Poles—the first of scores of reports he would file in the next eighteen months, keeping the government apprised of his activities. He emphasized the nonpartisan nature of his political missions in this first report, warning the government that he was not entitled "to explain officially, to clarify, or to analyze the work and personnel" of any faction for whom he carried information. "My character is wholly that of a courier," he explained.

Still in an agitated state psychologically, he hurried through this report and began dictating another, on the extermination of the Jews. The stenographer, horrified by his bloodcurdling stories and flustered by his excited, rapid-fire delivery, asked him to speak more slowly and distinctly. Karski yelled harshly at the woman and ordered her out of the apartment. As the door slammed, Jan paced the floor, trembling in shame over his rudeness, furiously smoking a cigarette.

~

On December 2, Jan reported to the two Jewish members of the Polish National Council, Szmul Zygielbojm and Ignacy Schwarzbart. Zygielbojm, representing the Jewish socialist Bund movement, had assumed the worst about the fate of the Jews in Europe for some time. His had been a lone voice, without much influence in Polish or Jewish circles. Schwarzbart, a member of the prewar parliament in Poland, had close ties to the World Jewish Congress and had shared the pragmatic and cautious outlook that prevailed in that organization as the early stories of Nazi atrocities filtered out of Europe. The day before the meeting, December 1, when he perused the full text of the documents Karski had carried, Schwarzbart saw that attitude shattered. Reeling from shock, Schwarzbart immediately sent a telegram to the World Jewish Congress in New York:

> HAVE READ TODAY ALL REPORTS FROM POLAND COMPULSORY ORDER JEWISH COUNCIL WARSAW FOR DEPORTATION STOP THEY EXCEED BY HORROR SUFFERINGS OF OUR NATION EVERYTHING FANTASY CAN PICTURE STOP JEWS IN POLAND ALMOST COMPLETELY ANNIHILATED STOP READ REPORTS DEPORTATION TEN THOUSAND JEWS FOR DEATH STOP IN BELZEC FORCED TO DIG THEIR OWN GRAVE MASS SUICIDE HUNDREDS CHILDREN THROWN ALIVE INTO GUTTERS DEATH CAMPS IN BELZEC TREBLINKA DISTRICT MALKINIA THOUSANDS DEAD NOT BURIED IN SOBIBOR DISTRICT WLODAWSKI MASS GRAVES MURDER PREGNANT WOMEN STOP JEWS NAKED DRAGGED INTO DEATH CHAMBERS GESTAPOMEN ASKED PAYMENT FOR QUICKER KILLING HUNTING FUGITIVES STOP THOUSANDS DAILY VICTIMS THROUGHOUT POLAND STOP BELIEVE THE UNBELIEVABLE STOP. . . .

Although the suffering of the Jews was not the primary factor motivating Karski's mission, the meeting with Zygielbojm and Schwarzbart was the first formal briefing given by the courier. The two National Council members received Jan in a small conference room at Stratton House, the building near Piccadilly that was the seat of the Polish interior ministry. If they needed any further evidence in order to "believe the unbelievable," Karski certainly provided it. He told of the naked corpses in the Warsaw Ghetto, of the Jew hunt by the Hitler Youth, of the hollow-eyed children wearing their yellow stars. He reported the liquidation of the Jews of Otwock, where thirty-two hundred victims perished in a single all-night orgy of gunfire. He related the tale of a contingent of Latvian policemen arrested for refusing to carry out brutalities. He spoke of a Gestapo officer who murdered Ghetto dwellers for sport, marking his daily tally of victims in chalk on the doors of the victims' homes. And he described, in painstaking detail, the machinery of extermination that he had seen in operation near Bełżec.

Jan fielded questions from the two Jewish leaders for some time. When the questions ended, he told the leaders that one portion of his report was to be delivered confidentially from the Bund in Poland to Zygielbojm. Schwarzbart excused himself, rising unsteadily from his seat, as though staggered by the burden of what he now knew. The emissary sat alone with Zygielbojm at the conference table. The Bundist leaned forward expectantly, his dark eyes glaring at Karski. His cheek twitched with a nervous tic. Jan explained that he would repeat as exactly as possible what the Bund leader in Warsaw had told him. He relayed Feiner's rejection of half measures and empty protests. He repeated the Warsaw Bund leader's call for retaliatory bombing, leafleting, and the execution of Germans in Allied hands. Then, without notes, Karski began reciting verbatim the final plea he had heard from Feiner in the ruined house:

"We are only too well aware that in the free and civilized world outside, it is not possible to believe all that is happening to us. Let the Jewish people, then, do something that will force the other world to believe us. We are all dying here; let them die too. Let them crowd the offices of Churchill, of all the important English and American leaders and agencies. Let them proclaim a fast before the doors of the mightiest, not retreating until they will believe us, until they will undertake some action to rescue those of our people who are still alive. Let them die a slow death while the world is looking on. This may shake the conscience of the world."

Zygielbojm jumped from his seat. He paced violently back and forth across the small room. "It is impossible," he said, "utterly impossible. You know what would happen. They would simply bring in two policemen and have me dragged away to an institution." Zygielbojm peppered Karski with more questions, seemingly at random, about the gory details of what he had seen. He became more and more frantic, less and less coherent. By the end of the interview, he was begging Karski to believe that he had truly done his best to help the Jews of Poland. It was as though Zygielbojm had assimilated not only the information Jan had carried, but also the emissary's precarious mental state.

Zygielbojm read a speech on the BBC two weeks later. "It will actually be a shame to go on living, to belong to the human race," he declared, "if steps are not taken to halt the greatest crime in human history." The Bund leader continued his desperate efforts for five more months, as news emerged of the doomed uprising in Warsaw and the final liquidation of the Ghetto. Finally, Zygielbojm apparently decided to heed Feiner's call for self-sacrificing protest. Leaving a note with one last exhortation to the world to take action on behalf of the Jews, Szmul Zygielbojm committed suicide on May 12, 1943.

~

The news was getting out. On November 30, 1942, work stoppages and mass protests erupted among Jews in Palestine. Jewish newspapers throughout the world began appearing with black-bordered pages. The Chief Rabbinate of Palestine declared December 2 a worldwide day of mourning, prayer, and fasting. "The homicidal mania of the Nazis has reached its peak," proclaimed the lead editorial in that day's *New York Times*, declaring that five million Jews faced extermination. Over a half million Jews and non-Jews in New York City stopped work for ten minutes of protest and mourning.

At the British Foreign Office, skepticism and caution were being overtaken by events. One official suggested on December 1 that the Poles were merely taking up a Jewish issue in order to prove they were not anti-Semitic, but by December 5 the same official was citing the Polish reports as "the most complete and authoritative account of what has happened." On December 7, Foreign Secretary Anthony Eden advised the British ambassador in Washington that he now had "little doubt that a policy of gradual extermination of all Jews, except highly skilled workers, is being carried out by the German authorities. Polish government have recently received reports tending to confirm this view," added Eden. "They regard these reports as reliable and they read convincingly."

The Polish government-in-exile pressed the case for action on behalf of the Jews. Secretly, it interceded with the major Allies to advocate retaliatory bombing of German cities, as well as other steps such as the dropping of leaflets to inform the German public of Hitler's crimes. During his visit to Washington on December 4, Polish Prime Minister Sikorski handed a copy of his government's report on the atrocities to a senior State Department official. Publicly, the Poles issued a ten-page diplomatic note on December 9 which reiterated the revelations brought to light by Karski and politely challenged "the civilised world" to find a way of restraining the Nazis from committing future atrocities. By December 14, Prime Minister Winston Churchill had reviewed this note and asked the Foreign Office for more information on the subject. With Churchill actively engaging the issue, his underlings in the British government could now ill afford to ignore it.

On the morning of December 17, Anthony Eden rose in the House of Commons in response to a question from Sidney Silverman. Eden read the text of a joint Allied communiqué, approved by the governments of eleven nations at war with Germany. After reviewing a catalogue of barbarities committed by the Germans against the Jews, the statement denounced "this bestial policy of cold-blooded extermination." It promised that "those responsible for these crimes shall not escape retribution."

The communiqué was as noteworthy for what it did not say as for what it did say. It carefully avoided promising that Jews who somehow escaped the terror would be given refuge in Allied nations or in Palestine. It did not address the question of dropping leaflets. It did not threaten reprisal bombing in Germany or executions of Nazis in Allied hands. Leon Feiner, in the letter to Zygielbojm that Karski had carried out of Poland, had warned that "decisions taken to punish the Nazi murderers after the War" would be "without effect and unimportant"—but the free world was offering nothing more. The official line from the Allied governments would henceforth be that only victory could help the Jews, and that their sufferings, however horrible, could not be allowed to influence the military effort.

The statement did, on the other hand, acknowledge unambiguously that the Jews of Europe were being subjected to a "policy" of extermination, and not simply to random atrocities. And it represented a milestone in international law, promising a type of postwar punishment never before officially meted out by victorious nations. It was the Allies' first decisive step toward the Nuremburg trials.

Privately, Jan denounced the Allied policy as inadequate. Many Jewish observers agreed—but not all. Five months later, a senior official of the World Jewish Congress would write that "[m]any of us believe here that the threat of retribution has not been without result; there is evidence that it has been effective, at least on a small scale, in the Balkans and France." On the day of Eden's speech, the same official had instructed Easterman in London that "we must forget about reprisals" because "we cannot hope to beat the Nazis at their own game."

When Eden concluded his speech, parliament member James de Rothschild took the floor. Another member described the scene: "[H]is voice vibrating with emotion, he spoke for five minutes in moving tones on the plight of these peoples. There were tears in his eyes, and I feared he might break down; the House caught his spirit and was deeply moved. Somebody suggested that we stand in silence to pay our respects to those suffering peoples, and the House as a whole rose and stood for a few frozen seconds. It was a fine moment, and my back tingled."

Karski's mission had helped to produce this and other "fine moments" of symbolic resistance to the Final Solution. But Nazi propaganda chief Josef Göbbels knew how much such moments would accomplish. On December 18, he wrote in his diary: "At the Wailing Wall they invoked the Old Testament Jewish curse against the Führer, Göring, Himmler, and me. So far, I haven't noticed any effect on me."

~

Jan, meanwhile, was carrying out the political portions of his mission in a series of meetings with representatives of the competing Polish factions, as well as a full meeting of the exiled government's council of ministers. The Poles of London were bitterly divided and full of intrigues, and yet Karski generally won their trust. He gained credibility from the risks he had already taken and those that lay ahead when he returned (as the plans still had it) to Warsaw. "His tales of heroism amid cruel persecutions and torture remind one of the early Christians in the catacombs," wrote Foreign Minister Raczyński after meeting the envoy. "The courage of those now fighting in Poland is of the very highest order, as is their idealism and love of country," Raczyński continued in his diary. "Side by side with this, as is usual in Poland, there are fierce, relentless, and intolerable party struggles."

To keep Jan from becoming embroiled in the London versions of those internecine struggles, government officials still kept his contacts with exiled Poles tightly circumscribed. Complicating this security effort was the fact that there were Poles in London who had known Jan Kozielewski before the war. One night Karski went to a restaurant with a secretary from Sikorski's office. Just as they were being seated, Jan spotted a familiar face across the room—Karol Kraczkiewicz, a diplomat who had served as a mentor to him when he first went to work at the foreign ministry. Although he remembered Kraczkiewicz warmly, Karski knew he could not speak to him. Jan asked for a table on the other side of the restaurant and sat with his back to Kraczkiewicz, who soon finished his meal and left. Jan's dining companion assured him that he had not been spotted. Later, when Jan asked for the check, the waiter told him that his meal had been paid for. The waiter handed Karski a note written on a napkin, reading: "Bon appétit, et bonne chance!—K.K." The diplomat had known better than to ask why Jan had suddenly appeared in wartime London.

As a side task, on behalf of the underground movement as a whole, Karski was at work on a project intended to make it easier for couriers like himself to reach England. As he explained to the government, clandestine communication from Poland to the West was in a very poor state. Little record has survived of his efforts to improve it, aside from two mysterious telegrams Karski sent on December 4 through the government's secret radio channels:

Delegate.
I am in the midst of reporting my mission. All materials arrived safely. Break contact with the Frenchman indicated by me. He is dishonest. I have arranged the itinerary. Some knowledge of German language required. It will be possible to send up to six persons after my return. I am returning at the end of January. God bless you.
—Karski

For my brother:
Let Lusia find out necessarily from Madame the name and address in Paris of the French laborer Lucas, whom she knows, who worked this year on Fort Wola. Regards to Renee.
—Karski

Jan had a young niece named Lusia; "Madame" was one of Kossak's nicknames; Fort Wola is near Warsaw. Perhaps "Lucas" was a Frenchman involved in the illicit transit of Poles like Jan;

perhaps Jan felt that the Frenchman somehow double-crossed him during his journey. And there may be some connection between the scheme described in this veiled language and Jan's suggestion, a few months later, of six key underground personalities who would be good candidates for escape to the West. (Kossak was one of them.) The full significance of these dispatches is surely lost to history, though, just as it was intended to be lost on the Germans.

On December 9, Karski was received by the figurehead president of his exiled nation, Władysław Raczkiewicz. The emissary transmitted a secret plea from the Bund and Zionist leaders in Warsaw to the head of state. The Jews asked Raczkiewicz to intercede with Pope Pius XII on their behalf. "Poland is a Catholic nation, and some of those being killed are Catholics of Jewish descent," Jan told the president, again repeating the Jews' arguments verbatim. "Many of the Germans are Catholic; even Hitler is a baptized Catholic," he continued. Surely the Pope's moral suasion, or even threats of excommunication, could sway some Nazis in some way.

Raczkiewicz listened to Jan, his face betraying no reaction to the Jews' plea. He soon changed the subject to political matters within Poland, asking Jan for detailed information about the relations between underground parties. In his diary, the president made lengthy notes about this political discussion. He did not mention the plight of the Jews.

Years later, however, Jan would learn that Raczkiewicz reacted to his pleas on behalf of the Jewish leaders, secretly sending a letter to Pius XII. The missive implored the Pope in the strongest terms to speak out against those who had left "[t]he laws of God trampled under foot, human dignity debased, [and] hundreds of thousands of men murdered without justice." Referring to Kossak's Front for the Rebirth of Poland, the president cited the example of Catholics in Warsaw who protested the murder of Jews, implicitly asking for a similar pronouncement from the Holy See. "This is the prayer of my suffering nation," wrote the Polish president, "which I place at the feet of Your Holiness."

Six weeks later, the Pope replied with a peevish and defensive letter to Raczkiewicz. He said he had already done all he could do for those suffering in Poland.

8
In Official Circles

The sights, sounds, and smells of a more carefree time and place greeted Jan as he entered the basement of Monsignor Staniszewski's North London rectory on Christmas Eve, 1942. Government ministers and their wives carried on boisterous conversations across banquet tables from smartly dressed officers of the Polish army, navy, and air force. Jan's friend Jerzy Lerski, soon to become a courier himself, hailed him from across the room. Jan took the seat Lerski had saved for him, opposite Foreign Minister Raczyński and his wife. Jan drank in the warmth, the good cheer, the Polish hospitality. A bishop offered his blessing to the gathering; a soprano performed; one of the cabinet members made a brief and patriotic speech that brought tears to the eyes of many in the room. For the moment, this basement was Poland.

That night, and often in subsequent months, Jan pondered the surreal twists of fate that had led him to London. He felt detached from the events that seemed to swirl around him, considering himself an "automaton" or a "human tape recorder," operating on one plane physically and another emotionally. After three years of almost constant peril and privation, Jan now awoke every morning in a comfortable bed. He opened the door of his new apartment on Dolphin Square, just down the river from Whitehall, to find toast and tea left by his kindly old landlady. But he shrugged off security and comfort as he had shrugged off fear and hunger in Poland, throwing himself into his work and trying not to think too much about himself.

Reminders that he was still in a war zone did come every few nights, as the wail of air-raid sirens sent Jan scurrying for shelter along with the rest of London's population. Usually, he heard only the muffled rumble of distant explosions from the basement of his apartment house. One night, however, a nearby blast rattled his shelter. Jan ventured out the next morning to see where the bomb had fallen in his neighborhood. Reduced to rubble, an office building had taken a direct hit. The smell of cordite lingered in the air.

In front of the smoldering ruins stood a short, grimy man in overalls, hands behind his back, staring grimly ahead as pedestrians bustled past. Jan vaguely recalled buying boutonnieres from the man at the floral shop in the building. The florist had salvaged a plank from the wreckage and laid it across a pair of broken chairs. On this makeshift counter were three broken bottles, each brimming with singed, half-dead carnations. Behind the man was propped another plank, unevenly lettered, with the words "Business as Usual."

Jan approached the stoic-faced merchant. "Sir, I would like to buy a flower," he said. After paying the man for the boutonniere, Jan leaned over to hand it back to him. "Sir," he said, "I don't need this carnation. Keep it so you will sell to somebody else."

The florist glared fiercely at Jan. "You bought it, you keep it!" he shouted, clearly in no mood to suffer the pity of a foreigner in civilian clothes. Jan smiled and inserted the limp flower into his lapel. Walking away, he felt tears of pride welling in his eyes. That Englishman's spirit, he thought, is what will win this war. Before going on to work, Jan stopped at a church. He prayed for Britain.

~

Although he had informed the underground authorities in his December 4 telegram that he would return to Poland at the end of January, it was quickly becoming evident that Jan would be abroad for quite a while longer. Consequently, he recommended that Lerski be sent to the Homeland, carrying responses to some of the queries Jan had brought from the conspirators. In the coming weeks, Jan would work closely with Lerski in preparation for the mission. Lerski parachuted into Poland in February, arriving safely and making contact with key personalities in the underground.

As Jan awaited Sikorski's return from the United States and Mexico, he stayed busy with as much activity as his semi-quarantine would allow. In late December, Mikołajczyk decided that the secret visitor from Poland could be exposed to one of the Polish government's most secret operations, the radio station "Świt." Świt ("dawn," in Polish) broadcast news, propaganda, and underground directives throughout Poland, ostensibly from a clandestine base somewhere in the country. The station gave the Germans fits; they spent fruitless man-hours trying to trace its signal, without success—for Świt was headquartered at Woburn Abbey in the English countryside. A select team of Poles, under the dual command of Mikołajczyk and officials of the political intelligence division of the British Foreign Office, had been beaming the broadcasts into the occupied country since the spring of 1942. Very few other Poles or Britons knew the truth about the station. Świt received the latest news by radio from Stefan Korboński, one of a handful of underground members in on the secret. A street roundup or execution that took place in Warsaw at 10:00 A.M. could be reported to England within hours and denounced during Świt's evening transmission. The broadcasters would sometimes even hurriedly sign off, claiming that the Germans were closing in on their hideout. Karski's visit to the station was the beginning of a sporadic relationship that would continue for almost a year. The British officials would repeatedly ask Mikołajczyk to send him—sometimes to make broadcasts, other times merely to boost morale among the Poles at the station. "He has infused new life and spirit into the work here and has also been an inspiration to the others," wrote one of the officials after Jan's first visit.

Mikołajczyk was beginning to loosen restrictions on the emissary, but the interior minister continued to direct Jan's movements and monitor him carefully. Aside from his fragile emotional state, the London Poles may also have had another consideration in mind when they first ordered Karski to lie low. Experience with previous couriers had probably convinced them of the need to acclimate arriving underground fighters to what could be called the London point of view. The government-in-exile operated with a constant awareness of, if not anxiety about, the tenuous nature of its political authority. Events in the Homeland always had the potential to make London irrelevant, and underground politicians knew that. Although theoretically the various underground ministries and the Home Army worked in lockstep with their counterparts abroad, in practice the underground frequently asserted its independence. A man like Karski would bring certain preconceived notions about the underground struggle to London. It was important to make sure he toed the government's line when he spoke to Allied leaders.

Evidence that the government had good reason to worry about

Jan's point of view emerged in the course of his first meeting with
a British diplomat. At the end of December he was introduced—in
even greater secrecy than usual, and under still another assumed
name, "Kwaśniewski"—to Frank Savery, an official of the British
embassy to the Polish government-in-exile. Savery, an old hand at
Polish affairs, had developed many contacts in Polish political circles before the war. The two met several times over the course of
about three weeks. Jan's encounters with Savery were particularly
dramatic, and each party wrote a detailed account for the perusal
of his government. Savery's minutes of his meetings with "Kwaśniewski" record the impression Jan made in his first contacts outside Polish circles:

> He is an active member of the underground patriotic movement, al-
> though he speaks very modestly of his own position in it. He intends,
> if possible, to return to Poland. I am inclined to think that before the
> war he was working in the Polish Ministry of Foreign Affairs but I
> have no certain information. In any case he is clearly a man of edu-
> cation, breeding and intelligence who musters his facts well. . . .
>
> He came to me with the direct blessing of Monsieur Mikołajczyk
> who had told me beforehand that he wished me to see him. Our first
> conversation took place in the presence of a member of the Polish
> Ministry of the Interior [probably Siudak] and on that occasion he
> confined himself to giving me information about conditions in Po-
> land. On the second occasion however, when only another English-
> man was present, he began to ask me questions in his turn. He has
> certainly been told by his superiors in Poland to establish direct con-
> tact with Britishers here—he speaks English fairly well. . . .

The dialogue touched on military matters. Because the underground always had to balance the desire for immediate action
against the Nazis with the certainty of German retaliation against
innocent civilians, and because its guiding strategy called for the
hoarding of military resources until the time was right for a mass
uprising, the movement lay exposed to charges of shrinking from
the fight. Indeed, Soviet propaganda had already begun airing this
criticism. Jan left Savery with the impression that the underground
fighters were "almost morbidly afraid of being suspected abroad of
passivity and resignation." In his report, Savery took pains to assure
his Foreign Office colleagues that the underground's cells were carrying on the struggle: "If even in the most confidential reports few
details are given of the acts of sabotage and arson carried out by

these organizations, it is not because there is little to chronicle but only for prudential reasons," the diplomat wrote. "Not infrequently the secret Polish press attributes acts of sabotage to German officials frightened of seeing their pilferings exposed. . . .

"As regards the persecution of the Jews," Savery noted, "Kwaśniewski's views were all that they ought to be." The British official added that "before leaving Warsaw he had seen the Bund representatives there and promised to report on their behalf to their friends in this country."

These matters were of interest, but Savery devoted the bulk of his minutes to Jan's comments on Polish politics. On one issue, Jan took a stand that amounted to a threat of outright mutiny by the underground against the London government. As Polish-Soviet relations had begun to degenerate (amid differences over both the present status of Poles in the USSR and the future border between the countries), the British were keen to learn how much room for maneuver the underground would allow the Sikorski regime in negotiating with Stalin. Savery probed the Polish courier with several questions on the subject, finally asking what the underground movement's response would be if Sikorski came to a compromise with Stalin that involved some limited amount of territorial concessions to the East. Jan's response was unequivocal: The resistance movement in Poland would denounce the London government and set up a rival national government within the occupied country, along the lines of the revolutionary government formed during the 1863 uprising, claiming that it alone represented Poland's sovereign interests.

The tenor of Jan's remarks shows that after a month in London he still saw himself as a representative of the underground movement, not the London government. He spoke very frankly to Savery of the underground's misgivings about Sikorski and his regime, asking about the government's prestige in Allied eyes and even seeking reassurance that the London Poles were not "trying to re-insure themselves against the possibility of a German victory." Regarding Sikorski himself, Jan expressed "very little, if any, of that warm devotion and blind confidence which was felt towards Marshal Piłsudski by many thousands of Poles." Seemingly reflecting the mistrust felt by the underground leadership, Jan also inquired about the possibility of setting up an independent link through which Warsaw could communicate directly with British authorities, bypassing the government-in-exile.

Many years later, Karski would offer an alternative explanation
of his political agenda in the conferences with Savery: "It is very
possible that I asked him such questions in order to convey to Sikorski his answer," he said. By acting as a double agent, he could
thus gather valuable intelligence about the true attitudes of top British officials toward the Polish leadership. Since Sikorski himself
was in North America at the time of this meeting, however, it is
unlikely that he personally assigned Karski a mission of such sensitivity. And although the emissary did later inform the prime minister that he had discussed the "attitude of society toward the Government in London" with Savery and others, his report on the
meetings with Savery covers almost none of the issues mentioned
in Savery's report.

From Jan's perspective, getting acquainted with Frank Savery
brought about an ugly epiphany. Even though Jan had been one of
the best-informed members of the underground by virtue of his job
as a translator of foreign radio broadcasts, Jan had shared the general view of Poland's fighters toward the western Allies: True, the
West had failed to defend Poland in 1939, but Great Britain must
surely be in complete solidarity with Poland now that it, too, was
in a battle for its freedom. The underground Poles harbored no illusions about Stalin's intentions toward their nation, but surely
Britain would stand behind Poland in rejecting any Soviet mischief
related to the border issue (which was moot anyway at the moment,
since the German line was still deep in Soviet territory). Surely Sikorski had been assured of at least that much British support when
he concluded the 1941 treaty of alliance with the invaders who had
pillaged eastern Poland less than two years earlier. Jan had voiced
grave misgivings about that agreement within Polish circles after
he arrived in London, but he was prepared to tell Allied officials
that the underground did support the treaty, if grudgingly, since the
common struggle against Germany had to supersede all other issues.

Jan had no idea, however, of the lengths to which Churchill's
government was prepared to go in order to maintain a solid relationship with the Soviets. Only during his last encounter with Savery did Jan confront the devastating truth about his country's real
standing among the Allies. It came in the form of two sheets of
onionskin paper.

As the meeting began, Savery swore Jan to secrecy. What Jan
was about to read was not an official statement by His Majesty's

Government, said the diplomat. Jan could not keep a copy of it; its contents must not be circulated in London. He might find it encouraging or might find it discouraging, Savery said, but either way he could now go back to Poland and convey to his underground comrades some sense of the attitudes of British authorities toward Polish territorial issues. Savery handed the typewritten, single-spaced document to the Pole.

Jan read Savery's note at first with amazement, then with depression. "Slavic minorities"— the Ukrainians and Byelorussians claimed by Stalin—had only weakened prewar Poland, wrote Savery. "There is a conviction among the English that this part of the country is more detrimental to Poland," he added. So England was prepared to do Poland the favor of ridding it of its "detrimental" eastern territories! The note elaborated on the value of the Soviet war effort and the possible shape of postwar relations between Britain and the USSR. "England does not want a powerful Russia; it wants a strong Poland," it continued. "But that does not necessarily mean that the English do not appreciate the necessity for compromise in the issue of Poland's eastern borders."

Jan stared at the paper, trying to make sense of it. Great Britain was prepared to see Poland, an Allied nation, dismembered as though it were a defeated aggressor—and was making plans for this partition while Poland was still under Nazi control. What was the use of the underground struggle, if these were really the major Allies' plans? Jan scanned the pages again, committing the words to memory. His promise to Savery be damned: He would tell his government about this. Jan handed the sheets back to Savery, struggling to keep his composure. "This is an unfortunate note," Jan said coolly. "The Polish nation has an entirely different point of view on eastern issues."

Dragging a wastebasket from behind his desk, Savery set fire to the note.

~

Sikorski droned on. Karski stood before the general's desk as Sikorski leaned back in his chair, a rare smile on his face, recounting his recent adventures in Washington. He had returned to London in mid-January. The future was bright, Sikorski assured Karski. Maybe Britain was leaning too far toward the Soviets, but the Americans would protect Poland's interests. Sikorski bragged of the personal friendship he had established with Roosevelt, of the intimate level of communication between the two leaders. "The Polish position is gaining in strength in the Allied camp," he assured Jan.

The general had not called him in to talk politics, though. He stood and edged closer to Jan, gazing into his eyes. "Young man, you have worked hard in this war," said Sikorski. "Because I like you personally, and have known you through a long and difficult time, because you have honest eyes, because they gaze upon me with friendship, I would like for you to accept this gift from me."

Sikorski produced a silver cigarette case, etched with his signature, from his desk drawer. He handed it to Jan. It was not the first reward Jan had received for his work as a courier: Sikorski had also arranged for him to receive twenty-five hundred dollars in American currency soon after he had arrived in England. Having little use for this substantial sum, since the government was already taking care of all of his needs, Karski had sent most of it to Poland through the government's fairly efficient channels for the transfer of funds. The delegate's office was to distribute the bulk of the cash to Marian Kozielewski and smaller amounts to Zofia Kossak, to Jan's girlfriend Renee, and to his niece. Jan later learned that all of the money reached its intended recipients.

Sikorski also bestowed one other gift of sorts on the envoy. At one point during their conversation he paused and stared intently at Jan. "What happened to your mouth?" he inquired in his usual sinister tone. Jan explained that he had lost most of his teeth during his Gestapo torture session. "What?" Sikorski huffed. "A diplomat! A horse-artillery officer! Without teeth? You will go to a dentist." He gave Jan the name of a well-regarded dentist and told him he would authorize the Ministry of Finance to cover the cost of reconstructive oral surgery.

The cigarette case, Sikorski told Jan, was a token of personal esteem. As prime minister and commander-in-chief, on behalf of the nation, he would present another award to Karski in a few days: the order Virtuti Militari, Poland's highest military decoration. At a private ceremony on February 3, 1943, in the presence of several generals and cabinet ministers, Sikorski pinned the medal to Jan's lapel.

The event marked a coming out of sorts for Karski: His first official meetings with top Allied leaders were now scheduled. For the past couple of weeks, Jan had been taking part in intensive briefing sessions with members of the government. He was instructed in precisely which issues to raise and briefed on the likely reactions that various officials might have to his report. He spent long hours in an empty room at Stratton House, rehearsing his basic presentation with a stopwatch. Mikołajczyk had told him to prepare a twenty-minute talk for delivery at the beginning of each meeting. The talk would cover the issues the underground and Jewish leaders had asked Karski to raise with the British and Americans, while simultaneously raising the points the government-in-exile was most eager to get across: the valiant and well-organized struggle of the underground, the horrors of life under occupation (including the plight of the Jews), and an issue not raised by the Poles in the past—the damaging effects of Soviet-inspired underground activities in Poland.

Although underground leaders had begged Jan to alert the western Allies to the Russians' treachery, he had avoided this topic in his prior contacts with most exiled Poles and with Savery. It was such a sensitive area, cutting as it did to the very essence of Poland's war effort and reflecting on an alliance with Stalin that had never been popular among London's Poles, that Mikołajczyk probably ordered Karski to keep the matter secret until Sikorski could return to deal with it personally. Spreading news of the Soviet misdeeds in Allied top echelons carried the risk that Poland would be seen as a troublemaker, undermining the valiant efforts of an ally that had just borne the brunt of Hitler's fury at Stalingrad. But the Poles were nearing the end of their rope with Stalin. On January 16, the "Great Leader" proclaimed that all Poles on Soviet territory—and hundreds of thousands of those deported into Russia in 1939 and 1940 were still there, either imprisoned or merely prevented from leaving the country—would henceforth be considered Soviet citizens. As furious as Sikorski was at this affront, he and his closest advisors had been privately fretting for over two years about a smaller number of Poles—some fifteen to twenty thousand officers and civilians captured by the Red Army during the 1939 campaign. Until the spring of 1940, all of them were known to be in three Russian and Ukrainian holding camps. And then every trace of them had disappeared.

At this anxious moment, the Polish government placed high hopes in Jan's discussions. By convincing Allied officials of the legitimacy of the underground government, the tenacity of the Home Army's struggle, and the perfidy of the Soviet agents, Karski could perhaps make the Western powers less sympathetic to Stalin's expansionist designs. Sikorski knew the young emissary needed a "handler" who could help him exploit the excitement of his story, and he knew where to turn for such help. Sikorski called in Józef Retinger.

Retinger was unquestionably the most fascinating personality involved with the Polish government-in-exile. To this day, though, it is still impossible to discern clearly between the truth about Retinger and the mythology that grew around him. He may or may not have been born near Kraków in 1888; one or both of his parents may or may not have been Jews. He was said to be a practicing Roman Catholic at certain times. (Later, he may or may not have been affiliated with the Jewish organization B'nai B'rith, but he definitely managed to draw the ire of Jewish leaders by making what were interpreted as anti-Semitic comments while traveling with Sikorski in December 1942.) There is evidence that he was a confidant of Joseph Conrad in the Polish-born writer's later years; Conrad called him an "unofficial intermediary between the British and French Governments" in 1916. Retinger was known to be fluent in English, French, German, and Spanish as well as Polish, and it is clear that he traveled widely. At various times he held British, French, Austrian, and Polish passports. Although he was seen in the company of British Prime Minister H. H. Asquith during World War I, an exclusion order was issued against him in the United Kingdom after he was discovered in 1917 acting as an illicit courier for the Japanese embassy in London. He was reportedly expelled from France in 1918. It was widely believed in Polish circles that Retinger had taken part in revolutionary activities of some variety in Mexico in the 1920s. A Polish historian claimed he was "closely connected with the fighting in North Africa during the Abd-el-Krim rising in the early 1920s." A dossier purportedly culled from Scotland Yard, MI5, Foreign Office, and U.S. State Department documents portrays Retinger as having been under suspicion of communist activity throughout the years between the world wars. This compilation and another source assert that he was arrested in St. Louis in 1921 for carrying an outdated passport and that he was suspected of sabotage in the United States. Those who tried to track him between 1931 and 1937 could not determine his whereabouts.

"In American [perhaps FBI] records, Retinger . . . is recorded as a person to whom one should not entrust work of a confidential nature," notes a wartime report on Retinger prepared by Poles who may have been hostile to him. "He is described as a man who is untrustworthy." This was the man assigned by Poland's prime minister to accompany Karski as he carried out important talks with Allied leaders.

It would not be the last sensitive mission for Retinger. Over a year later, on April 4, 1944, the aging and nearsighted *eminence grise* would jump from a British bomber over Poland, carrying out orders from both the British and Polish governments. Almost four months later, he would board another bomber in a muddy potato field somewhere in the occupied country and would return to London. And after the war, Retinger would play a role in the development of what became the European Community.

What people said about Józef Retinger made no impression on General Sikorski. All that mattered to the Polish prime minister were his unswerving loyalties—to the Allied war effort, to Poland, and to Sikorski personally—and his connections. Despite the reservations of British intelligence and law-enforcement authorities, Retinger had the trust of a wide range of government officials in the UK, including Churchill.

The adventure-loving Retinger clearly felt an immediate fondness for Jan when Sikorski introduced them to each other. Since Jan's reputation for daring had preceded him, Retinger had already coined a nickname for the envoy; over Jan's protests Retinger hung it on him during their first meeting: "Piorun." It translates as "Lightning Bolt."

Retinger took part in the last few days of Jan's preparations for the upcoming round of meetings. "Don't try to be Rejtan," he advised, alluding to Tadeusz Rejtan, an eighteenth-century political figure revered as an ardent Polish patriot. "Don't try to give lessons. Don't give them advice. Don't ask embarrassing questions. Try to create goodwill. You are going to meet the most powerful people in England, and we need their help."

Jan had heard of Retinger's connections and hoped to make the most of them. "Will I be able to see Churchill?" he asked.

Retinger smiled. "With Churchill we must use a special procedure," he said. "Every prima donna from every little country in Europe wants to meet with him. He is overwhelmed with such requests. What we have to do is to make *him* want to meet *you*. Piorun, you will make the rounds of British leaders. He will learn of you. Churchill is very anxious to know everybody. He is very curious about details. Trust me—he will call for you."

~

"Damn!" said Anthony Eden. "There's no time for tennis now." He stared out the window contemplatively, as though it had just dawned on him that the war had deprived him of his favorite sport.

Britain's foreign secretary (and future prime minister) had greeted Jan warmly. The young Pole had mentioned seeing Eden on a tennis court in Geneva seven years before, when Jan had been an apprentice diplomat there.

Eden had come to the meeting with a hidden agenda. He had reviewed Savery's report and considered its implications important enough to warrant further debriefing of the Pole in question. Since Retinger was accompanying Jan, however, Eden could not hope to elicit the underground's perspective on any sensitive issues. He listened politely to Jan's presentation, but asked few questions. "He didn't show any reaction," Jan wrote in his report on the meeting. "Without encouragement from him, I managed to present all the Polish questions according to the outline." Eden seemed particularly uninterested in hearing about the underground's difficulties with Soviet agents. He perked up when Jan began discussing the plight of the Jews, but at the mention of leaflets and retaliatory bombing as possible methods of counteracting Nazi terror, the foreign secretary raised his hand and gently interrupted. "The Polish report on the atrocities has already reached us," he said. "The matter will take its proper course."

Karski was unaware that his government, which had begun to fear that the Germans intended to process the non-Jewish population of the occupied country through their murder machinery, had been pressing the British and Americans in recent weeks to take more decisive action. The major Allies remained adamantly opposed to both the dropping of leaflets in Germany detailing Nazi crimes and the bombing of specially targeted sites in retaliation for the atrocities.

Eden's questions did not cover the report he had just heard, but the details of Karski's adventures as a conspirator and courier. Although he had seemed to give Jan's presentation only perfunctory attention, Eden appeared deeply moved by the underground agent's personal exploits. "Step over to the window," he told his visitor. "I want to look at you more carefully. I want to see what an authentic hero of this war looks like." He lavished praise on Jan, marveling at how much the contributions of selfless men like him had aided the Allied effort. Jan stammered his thanks, surprised and overwhelmed that Britain's second most important leader would address him so sympathetically. And then the thought ran through his head. Before he could stop to recall Retinger's admonitions, the words came out of his mouth:

"Sir, will I have the honor of reporting to the prime minister?"

A businesslike expression came over Eden's face. "No," he said, "I am not going to allow it."

Jan stared at the floor, crestfallen. He immediately knew he had disobeyed Retinger's instructions and blown his chance at a meeting with Churchill.

"People do not realize our prime minister is no longer a young man," explained Eden. "There are tremendous burdens on his shoulders. He creates an impression that he's strong, but he's not so strong. He receives hundreds and hundreds of people. I can assure you that your report to me will be reported to the War Cabinet, and the Prime Minister is the chairman of the War Cabinet. He will be informed," promised Eden. (He kept this promise, sending a report to the War Cabinet on February 17.) "But I will not allow you to take his time."

"I understand," said Jan. He apologized to Eden for making the request.

When the thirty-minute meeting was over, Retinger barely made it out of the building before he exploded at Jan. "What were you thinking?" he demanded, throwing his hands in the air as he stood in front of the Foreign Office building. "You closed your way to Churchill forever! Now, even if Churchill wants to see you, you have forced Eden to tell Churchill that it is not worthwhile, to save his face." The tirade went on for several minutes.

"He abused me in the most vulgar terms," Karski would recall.

"I don't want to have anything to do with you!" Retinger finally shouted. "I'm going to tell the general I wash my hands of you."

Jan took him by the hand. "Please, Dr. Retinger, don't give up on me," he begged. "You're right. I made a stupid mistake. I will be more careful now." Retinger stormed off. Karski skulked back to his apartment.

An hour later, Retinger called to invite him to dinner. Jan was forgiven—this time.

Eden wasn't finished with the Polish envoy. He sent word several days later that he would like to meet Jan again. Since Eden didn't invite Retinger to come along this time, Karski had to go alone. Jan arrived at the Foreign Office at 6:00 in the evening, his jaw throbbing in pain; he had undergone the last in a series of dental operations that morning. Eden made friendly and flattering small talk for a few minutes, then got to the point.

"You've made a good impression on us," said the foreign secretary. "We consider you not only a Polish soldier, but an Allied soldier. We trust you. I want to ask you a question, and I expect that you will answer regardless of your own feelings. Will you do it?"

"Yes," Jan answered, already sensing that he had stumbled into a no-win situation.

"Polish-Soviet relations are not as good as we desire," said Eden. "They ought to be improved. The main problem seems to be territory, Polish boundaries. But perhaps there is a way around this problem. Perhaps Stalin's demands can be satisfied without such severe losses to Poland," he speculated. Jan immediately realized that Eden was leading the conversation in the same direction Savery had taken it. "Suppose General Sikorski makes an agreement with the Soviet government, publicly agreeing that certain eastern territories will be ceded after the war to the Soviet Union," Eden continued. "My question is: If this agreement will not involve substantial losses, and if His Majesty's Government will approve such an agreement, and will guarantee the new Polish boundary, what will be the reaction of the underground movement?"

Jan tried to think fast. The chief architect of Great Britain's foreign policy had gone to a lot of trouble to isolate him and set him up for this question. What would the consequences be if he refused to answer? Should he give the same answer he gave Savery? And on whose behalf was he answering? The London government that he now served, or the underground movement that had sent him to England in the first place?

"Sir, they would denounce General Sikorski," Jan answered. "They would probably form a secret national government in Poland. There was such a precedent in history, during one of the Polish uprisings. It would be completely impossible. For the prime minister to allow a change in territory *during* the war—no one would understand it."

Eden interrupted, leaning over to clap Jan on the shoulder. "The Polish arguments are known to me," he said with a grim smile.

There was a knock at the office door; a distinguished-looking man entered. "This is Lord Selborne," said Eden. "On behalf of His Majesty's Government, His Lordship is interested in underground resistance movements." Eden would say no more about Selborne, nor did he need to. Karski knew which British organization had a mandate to assist underground movements, although the existence of the organization was a secret guarded almost as tightly as the identity of its director. Roundell Cecil Palmer, the third Earl of

Selborne, was in charge of the Special Operations Executive (SOE).

Selborne had taken on the covert-operations job a year earlier, after being summoned to Chequers, the prime minister's country residence, for a Sunday lunch with Churchill. "When I arrived at Chequers, I was ushered into Winston's bed-room and found him in bed," Selborne recalled after the war. "The first thing he said to me was 'Have you any conscientious objection to murdering Hitler?' I said: 'None at all.' The[n] he proceeded to say he would like me to come and help him as Minister responsible for SOE."

Eden soon excused himself from the meeting. Selborne fired a barrage of questions at Karski about underground life and subversion, many of which the Pole was unable to answer. Specifics of the Home Army's activities, tactics, and supply needs were beyond his knowledge or authority; the military wing sent its own couriers to the West quite frequently to discuss such matters. Jan did tell the peer about the problems the Soviet partisans were causing, and for once he found a receptive audience. Selborne intimated to Karski that as far as he was concerned, "Polish underground authorities [could] go as far as necessary in self-defense against the Soviet agents." When Selborne asked about German repression in Poland, Karski seized on the question as an opportunity to emphasize the magnitude of the Jewish tragedy. Here, however, the SOE chief was less forthcoming.

Funneling hard currency and gold to the Jews, so that some could bribe themselves out of captivity, ought to be a high priority, Jan insisted. Selborne's reaction was instant and negative.

"No prime minister, no political leader will comply with this kind of demand," Selborne said, an unpleasant edge on his voice. "If we sent gold and hard currency, we would probably be able to keep it secret during the war. But eventually it would become public. No leader can take responsibility for subsidizing the Nazi regime with resources that would allow it to buy raw materials and weapons to harm our own men. This is impossible."

Karski abandoned the notion of convincing Selborne to use SOE channels to steer aid to the Jews, but he thought he might make some impression with his own stories of Nazi atrocities. Selborne seemed to listen intently to the horrific anecdotes. When Jan finished, he spoke. "During the First World War," he said, "there were rumors all across Europe that the German soldiers liked to seize infants by their feet and crush their skulls, just for fun. Of course, we knew that those rumors were untrue, but did not do anything about them. They were good for the morale of the population." He told Jan he was doing an excellent job. "Inform as many people as possible about what you saw," said Selborne. "We stand behind you."

~

Moments after Karski returned from the day's meetings, his telephone rang. It was Retinger. "What happened?" he asked, eager to learn the details of a meeting from which he had been excluded. In veiled language—since no telephone could be trusted—Jan conveyed the essence of his talk with Eden.

There was an extended pause. Jan could sense Retinger's fury through the line. "Piorun," he said, "don't interfere with matters that are none of your business. People don't like it!"

The next morning Karski was sitting at his desk in the grand hallway of the government-in-exile's headquarters when Sikorski strode into the building. Jan looked up from his newspaper. The general marched briskly past him, eyes fixed straight ahead, without the usual perfunctory words of greeting. Less than a minute passed before Jan's telephone rang. He was summoned to Sikorski's office.

"I understand you had a meeting with Eden yesterday," said the commander-in-chief.

"Yes, sir," said Jan, standing at attention.

"What was the subject of this meeting? Lieutenant, you will tell me everything, word by word!"

Jan tried to explain the situation. He told Sikorski what Eden had asked about the underground's possible reaction to territorial compromise—though he left out the fact that he had freely discussed the same issue with Savery. And he told of his response.

"Who authorized you, Lieutenant, to make such a declaration to the foreign secretary of Great Britain?" demanded Sikorski.

"Well, he asked me, and—"

"You have been here a short time. And already you start promoting your own policies, just like every other Polish politician!" the general fumed, leaning out of his chair. "It is not your job to be mixed up in such affairs. You forget what you are. As though you have soda water in your head!" Sikorski said, employing a common Polish term of abuse. "To whom did you speak about this conversation?" he asked.

"Only to Dr. Retinger," said Jan.

"I forbid you ever to mention this conversation with Eden to anyone else. If I learn that you have spoken about it, there will be consequences." Sikorski began to shuffle the papers on his desk. Without looking up, he waved his hand to dismiss Karski.

It was a good thing Karski had built up so much personal capital among the Polish leaders by his services earlier in the war. His mission to the Allied governments was off to a most inauspicious start. But Jan persevered, and the Polish government maintained its faith in him. As other meetings followed in quick succession throughout February and March, Jan never blundered again as badly as he had with Eden. That's not to say he considered these meetings any more successful or satisfying.

The outlines of a coming abandonment of Poland became more and more clear with each discussion Karski held with the men who shaped Britain's foreign policy. Not only did they show little or no sympathy for the underground as it passively endured the treachery of Soviet agents, but they were also firmly convinced that Poland should cede part of its territory to the USSR. At a dinner meeting with Richard Law, Jan heard the term "Curzon Line" thrown around for the first time during the war. A legacy of one of Britain's earlier efforts to set other countries' boundaries, the line proposed by Lord Curzon in 1919 as the eastern frontier of the reborn Polish state ran more or less concurrently with the border set by Soviet Foreign Minister V. M. Molotov and German Foreign Minister Joachim von Ribbentrop in their secret 1939 partition of Poland. The fact that Stalin had explicitly renounced the 1939 border agreement when he signed the 1941 Polish-Soviet pact apparently mattered little now; Britain was prepared to grant Stalin what Hitler had granted him before. It was bad enough that Savery and Eden had spoken of some fairly minor alterations in the border which, nevertheless, violated the principle of Polish sovereignty. But now the full extent of the future losses was becoming clear: Almost half of prewar Poland would be annexed to the Soviet Union. Jan dutifully reported what he had heard to his superiors, who continued to put a brave face on the situation. His discussions with Law, Jan wrote, had left him with "the most dispiriting impression of all my conversations."

Meetings with Frank Roberts of the Foreign Office, Colonel Peter Wilkinson of SOE, British ambassador to the Polish government-in-exile Owen O'Malley, and other key Britons did nothing to lift Jan's spirits. His first contact with the United States government seemed more promising on the surface, but Jan knew by now not to put much faith in such impressions.

Anthony (Tony) J. Drexel Biddle, Jr., was the American ambassador to the Polish government-in-exile. As the double-barrelled name suggests, Biddle was one of the many East Coast aristocrats among Roosevelt's appointees. From the same illustrious Philadelphia family, another descendant, FDR's Groton classmate Francis Biddle, now served as attorney general; Karski would meet him later. Tony Biddle had served as prewar ambassador to Warsaw, escaping the capital during the Blitzkrieg in a harrowing trek to Poland's southern border under constant bombardment. Jan had seen the ambassador once, at a 1939 diplomatic reception, but had merely caught a glimpse of him across a crowded room.

"Ah, of course, I remember you very well," intoned Biddle, after Jan mentioned that he had been in Poland's foreign service before the war. (Intent on concealing his true identity, Jan did not often mention this fact in his meetings; in this case he thought it might break the ice.) Perhaps thinking that Jan remained sympathetic to the prewar Polish regime he had served, the ambassador went on to wax nostalgic about Józef Beck, whose foreign policy was now thoroughly discredited. Jan tried to conceal his embarrassment.

As Karski launched into his prepared presentation, Biddle began taking voluminous notes. Afterward, Biddle was full of perceptive questions and encouraging remarks. The meeting stretched on for more than three hours as he probed Karski for information on the activities of the Soviet agents in Poland. "Most clearly of all the people I have talked with," Karski reported afterward, Biddle expressed "disapproval of the Soviet methods." The ambassador told Jan to convey to the underground his assurances "that the American government and especially Roosevelt support and always will support Poland." Biddle promised to send a report on the Soviet-agents issue back to Washington and assured Jan that Roosevelt would read it.

The American's reaction to Karski lent credence to the idea that the United States might serve as a bulwark against Soviet designs on Poland and British acquiescence to those designs. Sikorski had certainly returned from Washington in January with this notion firmly planted in his mind. But Jan already had his doubts. Were the Americans really going to confront both of their major allies on behalf of Poland?

Biddle did report on his meeting with Karski in a "strictly confidential" memorandum to Secretary of State Cordell Hull on March 3, 1943. (Whether FDR ever saw the memo is impossible to determine.) The lengthy report fully and accurately reproduced Karski's points. Citing his meeting with an unnamed "leading officer of the Polish Government-directed Underground Organisation, who has recently arrived in London," Biddle wrote that the underground was expressing "growing concern over Russia's potential aims in Poland. The movement's fear was that the 'Communist-guided underground movement in Poland' was engaged in "subtle attempts to 'liquidate' the 'Government-directed Underground' and to ferment [sic] revolution." Biddle's report went on to cite examples of treachery on the part of Communist elements in Poland, including their attempts to discredit the legitimate underground in the eyes of the Polish people and, when possible, to penetrate it and denounce its members to the Gestapo. Biddle continued:

> As a result of the foregoing examples of Russian disloyalty . . . a "horrible situation" had developed in Poland. Moreover, the "Government-directed Underground" had become deeply concerned lest it be considered here as disloyal to Polish-British relations, if it were to take measures against the aforementioned Russian activities. . . .
> My informant concluded by emphasising that he and his associates "at home" were deeply worried lest any measures they might take . . . be construed . . . as contrary to the spirit of the United Nations' Front. He was, therefore, most anxious that we understand the predicament in which the "Government-directed Underground" was being placed by what it conscientiously considered deliberate subversive activities directed from Moscow.

By late March, Karski had made all the contacts he could make in the upper echelons of Allied governments. In addition to the foreign policy specialists, he had reported to Labour leader Arthur Greenwood, Tory leader Lord Cranborne, Board of Trade chairman Hugh Dalton, and other officials. The government was in no hurry, however, to return him to Poland. Not only had Lerski already fulfilled part of Jan's return mission, but Sikorski and his aides had to be concerned about the political consequences of sending Karski back home. If the underground learned of Britain's attitude on the border question, there would surely be trouble. Even before Karski met Anthony Eden, his return was already in doubt: Eden reported to the War Cabinet that "it is no longer certain that he [Jan] will return to Poland."

There was still plenty for Jan to do. In his spare time during the past few months, he had been dictating a massive report on the attitudes of underground political parties and other segments of the population. He was not necessarily telling the government what it wanted to hear, given the chaotic spectrum of political opinion in the country as well as the persistence of anti-Semitism and other ethnic conflicts amid certain segments of the populace. But just as Jan had reported in complete objectivity to each Polish faction when he first reached England, he now felt he had a duty to convey the unvarnished facts of life under occupation to the Polish authorities in London.

Jan's attempt to maintain a nonpartisan stance was tested one day when he received a call from Tadeusz Bielecki, the far-right nationalist leader who was not a member of the coalition government in London. In exile as in Poland, Karski had managed to maintain the confidence of factional leaders representing the entire gamut of political views—even Bielecki, who now made a career of lambasting Sikorski's regime in speeches and articles in the London-based Polish press. Jan wondered what else he and Bielecki would possibly need to discuss, but he consented to come to a meeting.

Soon after Jan arrived, another man walked into the room. It took Jan a moment to recognize him in civilian clothes: It was General Sosnkowski, to whom he had carried the message of solidarity from his brother in 1940. Sosnkowski had resigned from the government when Sikorski signed the treaty with the Soviet Union in 1941. Within a few months of this meeting Sosnkowski would unexpectedly take command once more of the Polish armed-forces-in-exile, but for now he was on the outside looking in. Jan greeted him with unease.

"I understand that you have been in London for some time," Sosnkowski said. "You reported to everybody. I understand you even reported to the British spies. You didn't come to me."

"Sir, General, I had no message for you," said Jan.

"And this was enough for you? In Paris, you brought information to me about a man dear to both of us. What has happened to him?" Despite his hostility, Sosnkowski was careful not to reveal Jan's identity by mentioning his brother's name. Jan told of Marian's arrest, captivity in Auschwitz, and release.

"And he also did not tell you to come to me?" demanded Sosnkowski.

"No." Marian had known nothing of Jan's mission until he sent the telegram from London announcing that he had arrived safely.

"This is unbelievable!" Sosnkowski yelled. "You have become a soulless bureaucrat. You told me in Paris you are a Piłsudskite. Such a Piłsudskite!"

Bielecki came to Jan's defense. "He is in the hands of Sikorski and Mikołajczyk," the rightist leader told the embittered general. "He does what they tell him."

"They treat our Motherland like their real estate!" Sosnkowski shouted.

Karski prepared to leave. "God willing, we shall meet in better times," said Sosnkowski. They never met again.

～

As Jan embarked on a second tier of contacts in March and April 1943, he was granted considerably more latitude and independence. He scheduled many of his own meetings, and Retinger rarely came along. Left somewhat to his own devices, Karski devoted more of his energies to spreading the word about the fate of the Jews in Europe.

Although Jan had learned painful lessons about the necessity of following the Polish government's rhetorical line, he felt that both Poland and the other Allies had fallen far short in their responsibility to do something about the Holocaust. He made his feelings clear to Ignacy Schwarzbart when they met for the second time on March 15. "As a Pole and as a human being generally," he told the Polish Jewish leader, "I have to agree that there is a substantial difference between the sufferings of the Poles and the sufferings of the Jews. One can fittingly speak about a biological liquidation of the Polish intelligentsia, whereas you have to speak in relation to the Jews about the liquidation of a whole people." Jan told Schwarzbart he was "flabbergasted by the lack of understanding of this difference on the part of the Polish government." Raczyński's note of December 9 was "pale and weak," he said—and noted that he had said as much to the Britons he had met at the Foreign Office. If the Poles could not convince the other Allies of the need for "exceptional steps," including reprisals and the dropping of leaflets, insisted Karski, then the Jews were "doomed to perish."

Schwarzbart concluded in his diary that Karski had adopted a "really democratic and human approach to the problem." He noted, however, that "Mr. Karski was this time a little bit more restrained than during our first conversation. Of course," Schwarzbart added, with a hint of sarcasm, "he learned something already in London."

Elsewhere in his diary, Schwarzbart wrote that Karski was "a rare phenomenon among the Poles. If he thinks as he talks, and if a majority of Poles would act as he says, things would be better." Ultimately, however, Jan's philo-Semitism failed to overcome Schwarzbart's bitterness over the fate of the Jews. Late in the war, Schwarzbart commented that he had lost confidence in what he heard from the Polish underground couriers he had met over the years, "for in none of them, even in Karski, did I feel a heart for the Jews."

As the Poles sought to influence public opinion through Jan, he made secret, off-the-record contacts with a number of leading journalists and literary figures during this time. Powerful forces somewhere evidently took an interest in arranging these discussions: A writer named Derek Tangye, whom Jan knew as a friendly newspaper journalist, was in fact an MI5 agent under orders to help Karski get his story out. Jan brought up the entire range of Polish concerns in these meetings, but it was the urgency of his pleas on behalf of the Jews that most impressed Tangye. The writer later recalled the drama of his first encounter with the young Pole, "thin like a taut wire," who sipped coffee by a log fire in an upstairs room of his home, curtains drawn for the blackout, and told of the barbarities he had witnessed. "He spoke calmly without heroics," wrote Tangye, "and yet I had a strange sense that he knew the hardest part of his assignment was in the present. He had to convince people that he was *speaking the truth*."

Tangye set up meetings for Jan with a number of London journalists. He described the effect Karski's tales had on one writer, Associated Press bureau chief Frederick Kuh: "I arranged lunch in one of the cubicles at Simpson's-in-the-Strand and Freddie Kuh arrived, cynical, slick, disbelieving," Tangye recalled, "but by the end of lunch the emotion of the story had sunk through his thick mind, and I guessed he would be thinking of it in the dark of night with horror."

Polish émigré artist Feliks Topolski, famous for his portrayals of the British war effort, also assisted Karski in making contacts. In his memoirs, Topolski, who would later become a close friend of Karski and his wife, recalled the image the courier projected: "He was then a modern warrior—pentathlon-modelled, not a hefty legendary knight, but ever on the leap." The artist threw a party in Jan's honor at which he was introduced to such leading intellectuals as Penguin publisher Allen Lane and his competitor Victor Gollancz, the editors of two London newspapers, parliament member Eleanor Rathbone, and writer Arthur Koestler. Gollancz and Koestler, who, like Topolski, were Jewish, questioned Jan intently about the mass murders in Poland.

Koestler, some of whose relatives had already perished in the extermination camps, soon scripted a BBC broadcast about the atrocities, written in Jan's voice. The script was later included, together with contributions by writers Alexei Tolstoy and Thomas Mann, in a widely circulated pamphlet entitled *Terror in Europe: The Fate of the Jews*. Koestler also wrote a novel in 1943, *Arrival and Departure*, which treated the subject of genocide by a Hitlerian regime. Its protagonist is based closely on Karski.

Gollancz, already engaged in a campaign to raise public awareness of the Jews' sufferings, was reduced to what his biographer would term "a state of near-hysteria" by Jan's eyewitness accounts. Within weeks of meeting Karski, Gollancz suffered a debilitating nervous breakdown.

Meanwhile, Biddle's report on Soviet treachery in Poland was creating a stir in Washington, just as "Karski's Report" on the Holocaust had set London abuzz. On April 9, Elbridge Durbrow of the State Department's Eastern European desk sent an analysis of the report to others in his department. Moscow's Polish machinations, he concluded, "point to the possibility that the Soviet Government may desire to cause a break with the Polish Government-in-Exile and set up a Moscow-controlled 'Free Poland.' "

Durbrow could not have been more prescient. Four days later, German radio announced the discovery of a mass grave in Russia's Katyn Forest, containing the bodies of thousands of Polish officers. The Germans claimed that the Soviets had shot the men. The West generally accepted Stalin's denial and believed the Germans were cynically trying to score propaganda points with murders they had carried out themselves. Sikorski had kept his silence about the missing officers up to this point, but the Poles knew that the men had disappeared long before the German-Soviet war had started. In the face of overwhelming evidence that the Soviets had exterminated thousands of Poles, the government-in-exile could not possibly continue to keep quiet in the name of Allied unity.

Stalin had engaged Poland in a game of chess, every move of which was laden with tragic inevitability. Sikorski announced that his government would accept the German suggestion that an independent delegation from the International Red Cross visit the execution site to examine the evidence. The media and governments of the United States and Great Britain howled in outrage: How could the Poles be so stupid and disloyal as to fall for German provocation? On April 21, Stalin accused the Poles of "collusion" with the Nazis. On April 25, the Soviet Union severed diplomatic relations with the Polish government-in-exile.

9
Defeat in Victory

The Katyn disaster plunged the Polish government-in-exile into a deep crisis, threatening to rip apart the shreds of sovereignty that the London Poles had managed to maintain since they fled their homeland in 1939. At the beginning of May 1943, Sikorski's regime seemed to be passing through its darkest hour as it reeled from Stalin's perfidy. The Poles could not know how many more blows would fall upon them in coming months—in June on a Warsaw street, in July at Gibraltar, in December at Teheran.

With the government's survival depending on the goodwill of its remaining allies, any thought of returning as valuable a propaganda asset as Lieutenant Karski to Poland had again been put on hold by early May. Instead, Sikorski decided to send him in the opposite direction. Within days of Moscow's cutoff of diplomatic relations, the commander-in-chief called Jan into his office and ordered him to prepare for a trip to the United States.

On May 5, Poland's foreign ministry sent a secret telegram to the ambassador in Washington, asking that he obtain a visa for Karski. Officially, the mission would involve reporting to the Americans about "the situation at home with regard to the occupant," cabled the foreign minister. But in an eyes-only postscript for the ambassador, the dispatch suggested Jan's real agenda: "He's carrying news about Soviet partisans."

Karski would later credit Anthony Drexel Biddle with suggesting his mission to the United States, as well as arranging his eventual meeting with President Roosevelt. A report from the Office of Strategic Services (the OSS; a forerunner of the Central Intelligence Agency) also stated that Biddle arranged the presidential audience, but no record of such an intervention exists in Biddle's voluminous and intimate correspondence with FDR. The American ambassador may have played a role; there is cause to doubt, however, that his interest in the Polish cause was as benign as Karski believed.

Biddle did approach the president about a Polish issue just as Karski was preparing to leave for Washington—he denounced Professor Stanisław Kot, who had recently become Karski's immediate superior once more as information minister. In early June, the ambassador sent a lengthy memorandum advising FDR on how the Polish cabinet might be restructured to satisfy Stalin, who refused to consider resuming ties with Poland until there were new faces in the government. Biddle insisted that Kot and other "troublemakers" had to go. "Kot is a pronounced egoist, ambitious in the extreme," wrote the American envoy. The Polish official had "no particular liking for the United States or for Britain," and had an abiding hatred of Russia, according to the report. Kot had even worked to undermine Sikorski as a way of furthering his own postwar political goals. Not only should Kot be forced out of the Polish government, concluded Biddle, but for the duration of the war he should be sent to "some distant land with a healthy climate where there are no other Poles with whom to intrigue."

Whether Biddle was involved in the inception of Karski's American mission or not, his embassy did know of it from the earliest planning stages. By May 12, a State Department telegram from London about Karski's prospective mission was already circulating in the upper echelons of the OSS.

The formalities of arranging the secret trip during wartime took more than six weeks. On June 2, Karski was granted a U.S. diplomatic visa. A week later, two government ministers sent him on his way with letters of introduction citing "his splendid memory and great precision" as well as "extraordinary intelligence." Mikołajczyk, having assured Jan that he would be able to return to Poland as soon as he came back from the United States, gave the government delegate in Warsaw less assurance in a mid-June dispatch: "Karski departed for three months in America. When he comes back I will decide about his eventual return to you."

On June 10, Jan sailed from Scotland. The journey across the Atlantic was not without peril, but after heavy losses from Allied attacks in May, the German high command had recalled most of its U-boats from the North Atlantic. Jan's ship docked in New York on June 16.

~

"This will be your room. It was my son's room." For Ambassador Jan Ciechanowski, assigning his young visitor these second-floor quarters in the Polish embassy was a gesture of deep affection. Ciechanowski's son Władysław, a fighter pilot who had enlisted in the RAF, had been killed in action seven months earlier.

Poland's ambassador to the United States would serve as Karski's guide and mentor during his American visit. Ciechanowski was an urbane man of wealthy and, perhaps significantly, somewhat Jewish origins. Fellow diplomats considered him one of the best-connected envoys in Washington. Although Ciechanowski was on good terms with many American policymakers, he had made enemies among both Polish-Americans (many of whom considered him aloof) and some American officials. An OSS report written just before Karski's arrival complained that the ambassador had unleashed "most undiplomatic blasts" in an interview, including irate accusations that certain United States propaganda officials were not only anti-Polish but were even German or Soviet agents.

So stoic an aristocrat that he omitted any mention of his son's death from his published memoirs of the war years, Ciechanowski nevertheless betrayed the psychological effects of his personal anguish in his reaction to Jan. With a paternal sense of admiration and pride, he later described his first meeting with the "tall, dark young man, of striking appearance," who came to bear witness to his nation's struggle. The emissary "looked as if he had gone through great suffering and hunger, and his burning eyes reflected keen intelligence coupled with childish candor," Ciechanowski would recall.

After summoning a photographer to take Jan's portrait, the ambassador insisted on keeping a print for himself that had not been retouched to hide the scars left on Jan's face by the Gestapo and acne. Ciechanowski sent his guest to a dermatological specialist in New York for ten days of treatment before introducing him to anyone in Washington. Upon Jan's return, the diplomat established a routine of walking his poodle along Sixteenth Street with Jan by his side, the young Pole listening patiently to the tales of diplomatic frustration that beset the embassy on a daily basis.

Despite his warm feelings toward the envoy from the Homeland, the ambassador laid down strict rules for him. The mission was to be strictly secret, and Washington was swarming with spies, said Ciechanowski. Therefore, Jan would remain confined at the embassy for the duration of his mission. All meetings were to take place there.

Ciechanowski would relax the rules eventually. Some meetings could not be held at the embassy, and Jan chafed at his detention in the baroque-style mansion. The boredom of waiting for the next meeting began to weigh on him quickly, as did Washington's trademark dog-day weather. (OSS officer James G. Rogers, recording day after day of ninety- to one-hundred-degree temperatures in his diary that summer, wrote in exasperation: "The whole town sleeps naked.")

The ambassador frowned when his young charge begged for permission to go to a movie, but allowed a few such excursions under one condition: "Avoid the Poles like a pest!" The Washington area's substantial Polish-American population would try to latch onto Karski and involve him in petty intrigues, warned Ciechanowski. He gave Jan a list of right-wing Poles who were known to be critical of Sikorski for having made peace with Russia in 1941. "They will probably learn you are here," the diplomat told Karski. "Certainly all of them will want to meet you. You will not meet anyone. If they force you to make an appointment, make it. But don't keep it. You will offend. Too bad."

Faced with the paradoxical duty of calling attention to Jan in Washington's corridors of power while maintaining his secrecy, Ciechanowski devised a skillful public-relations scheme. He planned a month-long series of meetings that would not only expose key decision makers to Jan, but would also manipulate the elite into supporting the ultimate goal of an audience with President Roosevelt. The similarity to Retinger's earlier strategy for securing a meeting with Churchill was obvious to Jan; this time he would be more careful not to frustrate the plan.

Reporting back to London, Ciechanowski explained that it would have been easy enough for him to arrange a ceremonial meeting at the White House, where he himself had good access. But in order to obtain more than just a handshake from FDR, he needed to pique the president's curiosity. The ambassador must have appreciated the almost childlike fascination with the minutiae of covert military operations that led Roosevelt to spend hours engrossed in bull sessions with OSS head Bill Donovan, hatching such projects as the famous fruit-bat drop over Japan—an initiative intended somehow to undermine morale, but which was cancelled after the bats in early experiments consistently froze to death at high altitudes. If a man like Roosevelt learned that a cloak-and-dagger specialist like Karski was in town, surely the president would invite him over to play.

In a report prepared midway through his stay in the United States, Karski made a record of the diplomatic instructions he had received from Ciechanowski prior to his first meetings. These included two guiding principles: "1. Don't exaggerate; the truth about the Homeland is the best propaganda." and "2. Don't get involved in polemical political-ideological discussions. Don't color the information. . . . Cause the person to gain trust in you as a reporter." Aside from these general guidelines, "every discussion was prepared in advance, with the Ambassador indicating what should be emphasized and what should not be mentioned," Jan reported. "I always told the truth," he added, "if not the whole truth."

The truth is a malleable thing in wartime. Karski may well have considered himself truthful at this point, but the exigencies of his work had already compelled him to deceive his listeners. Before he had left London, Sikorski told him to present himself as an emissary not of the London government, but of the underground movement—one of those less-than-"whole" truths, given that he now took his orders from London. In order to make his reports seem more fresh, the London authorities spread word that Karski had come from Poland in February or March 1943 rather than November 1942, even giving Ciechanowski this date in one of Jan's letters of introduction. The accounts of individuals who met Karski show that he consistently repeated false arrival dates during his American visit.

Even the bond that developed between Ciechanowski and Karski did not preclude a certain amount of intrigue on the part of the younger man. On orders from Retinger, he maintained a secret channel of contact with London, sending reports to Mikołajczyk and Kot through Tomasz Kuśniarz, a special agent based in New York who was securing supplies clandestinely for the Home Army. Some of the reports Karski sent back criticized the ambassador for his combative relations with Polish-Americans and U.S. officials.

~

By the beginning of July, the ambassador felt ready to unveil his secret emissary to Washington's elite. On July 3, he sent out notes inviting several top policymakers to "small informal men's dinner[s]" in the coming days, where those attending would "have the opportunity of talking with one of the outstanding people of the Polish underground movement."

The next day, thousands of miles away, Sikorski dispatched a telegram to President Roosevelt:

> I WISH TODAY, THE FOURTH OF JULY, TO PAY MY SINCERE HOMAGE TO THE GREAT AMERICAN NATION, ESPECIALLY AS I AM SPENDING IT AS A GUEST OF THE GOVERNOR OF GIBRALTAR, WHERE I HAVE MET SOME OF YOUR OFFICERS. I AM CONVINCED THAT UNDER YOU, MR. PRESIDENT, THE INSPIRED LEADER OF THE AMERICAN NATION, AND IN CLOSE COLLABO-RATION WITH GREAT BRITAIN, THE VICTORY WILL SOON COME TO THE UNITED NATIONS. THIS VICTORY WILL NOT ONLY CRUSH THE ENEMY BUT ALSO BRING INTO BEING YOUR PRINCIPLES OF FREEDOM AND JUSTICE.

On July 5, another telegram was rushed to FDR: "General Sikorski, his daughter, and his chief of staff met their death by plane accident at Gibraltar yesterday."

The Polish regime's already bleak prospects suddenly looked even bleaker. Sikorski's death was only half of a double blow, the other element of which the Poles kept secret: Only days before, on June 30, General Stefan Rowecki had been arrested on the street next to one of his clandestine offices in Warsaw, the victim of a Gestapo informer. Efforts to arrange an exchange of Rowecki for a captured German general showed some initial promise, but were later dropped for fear of offending the Soviets. After being held at the Oranienburg concentration camp in Germany for over a year, Rowecki was executed in August 1944, as the Polish underground's general uprising began in Warsaw.

Ciechanowski and Karski forged ahead with their mission, even as political turmoil over Sikorski's successor raged and depression reigned among their superiors in London. Karski's first meeting with American officials took place as scheduled on July 5.

It cannot have been a coincidence that Ciechanowski brought together three of the administration's most prominent Jews to hear Karski's report in this initial meeting. Presidential adviser Ben Cohen, Assistant Solicitor General Oscar Cox, and Supreme Court Justice Felix Frankfurter had helped to shape Roosevelt's New Deal policies. Each man was close to the president and well connected in Washington. Ciechanowski wanted to get Roosevelt's attention; Karski carried dramatic news that would presumably interest

American Jews. Therefore, the ambassador would set his strategy in motion by inviting FDR's top Jewish advisers to meet Karski.

This plan was unquestionably sound with regard to Oscar Cox. More active in Jewish matters than most of the numerous other Jews in the administration, Cox had approached Ciechanowski in September 1942 to discuss the possibility of a United Nations commission on war crimes. Jan's tales of Jewish suffering would induce Cox to do exactly what Ciechanowski wanted: The day after the meeting, he wrote to two of the most powerful people in Washington—journalist Walter Lippmann and Roosevelt's right-hand man Harry Hopkins—to recommend that they meet with Karski and listen to his "bloodcurdling" stories.

Cox's activism, however, represented an anomaly. Far more typical of the attitude toward Jewish issues of Jews in Roosevelt's inner circle was Felix Frankfurter's reaction to news of the emerging Holocaust. The son of Austrian Jews who had emigrated when he was a child, Frankfurter did express concern about anti-Semitism and did sometimes intervene behind the scenes to deal with instances of possible bias. In June 1943, for instance, he took aside former ambassador William C. Bullitt (whom Karski would also meet) to lecture him about the appearance of anti-Semitism in his public statements.

But the news from Europe in recent months had not energized Frankfurter. The difference between Frankfurter's attitude and Cox's was evident in each man's reaction to the Riegner telegrams, with their accounts of mass murder on a scale never before witnessed on earth and their plea for action from the West. When Cox came into possession of the still-secret telegrams, he sent copies to Ciechanowski and urged him to investigate the allegations. When World Jewish Congress leader Nahum Goldmann showed the dispatches to Justice Frankfurter in October 1942, he found himself "very badly impressed by Frankfurter, who is an egoist and who, having read the terrible cables, started immediately to talk of his speeches."

The dinner meeting with Cohen, Cox, and Frankfurter lasted until nearly 1:00 in the morning. Jan held forth on the organization of the underground, the troubles caused by Soviet partisans, and other subjects, while also giving an objective description of the persecution of Jews in Poland. Over dinner, he referred only in passing to what he himself had witnessed—but the stories were still enough to "make your hair stand on end," as Cox wrote to Harry Hopkins.

Frankfurter, who had delayed a vacation in order to meet the mysterious young Pole described by his friend the ambassador, lingered after the other guests left the embassy. Adjourning the gathering from the table to a quiet ballroom, Ciechanowski took a seat to Karski's left. The Supreme Court justice sat opposite Karski, looking into his eyes. "Mr. Karski," asked Frankfurter, "do you know that I am a Jew?" Karski nodded. "There are so many conflicting reports about what is happening to the Jews in your country," Frankfurter said. "Please tell me exactly what you have seen."

Jan spent half an hour patiently explaining how his missions to the Ghetto and the camp had come about and precisely, in gruesome detail, what he had witnessed. The jurist asked a series of technical questions, such as how Jan got into the Ghetto and the death camp. When Karski had answered the last of these queries, he waited for the visitor to make the next move.

Frankfurter silently got up from his chair. For a few moments, he paced back and forth in front of Karski and the ambassador, who looked on in puzzlement. Then, just as quietly, the justice took his seat again.

"Mr. Karski," Frankfurter said after a further pause, "a man like me talking to a man like you must be totally frank. So I must say: I am unable to believe you."

Ciechanowski flew from his seat. "Felix, you don't mean it!" he cried. "How can you call him a liar to his face! The authority of my government is behind him. You know who he is!"

Frankfurter replied, in a soft voice filled with resignation, "Mr. Ambassador, I did not say this young man is lying. I said I am unable to believe him. There is a difference."

After a forced exchange of pleasantries, Frankfurter left the room in the company of Ciechanowski. Jan sat alone in the vast room as their footsteps echoed away.

Frankfurter was not the first person in Allied circles to react to Karski's atrocity stories with disbelief, but he was the most prominent. The effect this rejection may have had on Jan, coming in his first U.S. meeting, is difficult to determine. Both the available documentary evidence and his own recollections, however, suggest that Karski may never again have brought up his own horrifying experiences of the Final Solution in meetings with U.S. government officials during his 1943 visit. He would mention them to Jewish leaders later, and in the conversation with Roosevelt he would discuss the *issue* of Nazi atrocities, but Jan would refrain from mentioning

what he had witnessed. It is possible that he decided, or that Ciechanowski asked him, not to bring up his experiences for fear of
encountering reactions like Frankfurter's.

Without knowing whether Karski would have told what he had
witnessed in the death camp and Ghetto, it is impossible to assess
what difference could have been made if he had met Treasury Secretary Henry Morgenthau. Jan was scheduled to meet Morgenthau
in late July, but for unknown reasons the rendezvous did not occur.
When Morgenthau became convinced in December 1943 that the
Nazis were in fact carrying out a crime of unparalleled magnitude
and that many Allied officials were turning a blind eye to it, he
succeeded in pressuring Roosevelt to take more decisive action on
behalf of endangered Jews and to threaten the Nazis more vigorously with postwar punishment. Perhaps Karski could have spurred
Morgenthau into action sooner, saving thousands of lives, or perhaps not.

~

Undaunted by the Frankfurter debacle, Ciechanowski and Karski
met with other officials in quick succession. On July 7, Assistant
Secretary of State Adolf Berle came to dinner, along with State Department Eastern Europe specialists Loy Henderson, Elbridge Durbrow, and Charles Bohlen. The dinner-table talk, which again lasted
past midnight, centered on the political implications of Sikorski's
demise. With the death of Sikorski, Poland had lost not only a leader
with international credibility, but also the only political figure capable of holding together the fractious elements that constituted the
government-in-exile. Berle noted the magnitude of this loss in his
diary:

> We are endeavoring to work out with the British some method of
> reducing the tension between the Russians and the Poles and perhaps
> getting them to re-establish relations. But General Sikorski's death
> does not help. At the Requiem Mass for him today I was thinking that
> Sikorski, as a man, had been able to bridge the huge gaps between
> the positions which Poland must somehow bridge to continue as a
> nation; and there is no replacement for him. Possible replacements
> are dying by the hundreds in the German concentration camps. Un-
> fortunately, we have pretty clear evidence of this; the eye witness
> account of Karski, an escaped member of the Polish underground,
> given by the Polish Ambassador to Loy Henderson, Durbrow, Bolan

[sic] and myself last Wednesday night, makes this all too abundantly clear.

Some in Washington thought the war might end in 1943, and Berle wanted to know whether the underground movement was prepared to surface and maintain public order in the aftermath of Poland's liberation. Karski assured him that a complete state existed in hiding, ready to take up all governmental functions. Berle and the State Department experts also wondered how the resistance fighters were funded and whether their funding was adequate. "The government sends us money," Karski told them. "They are serious about it." There was enough for guns, ammunition, and organizational needs, he said, but not for personal expenses—hardly the truth in his own case, as he had been generously funded by the underground. "People get sick from hunger and exhaustion," Karski told the men. "Any amount sent, every gun delivered, will be put to good use."

The following day, Ciechanowski made Karski available to several officers from U.S. military intelligence. A Polish military attaché sitting in on the meeting recorded his impressions of the underground emissary in his diary: "Karski is polished and straightforward with everybody he meets," wrote the officer. "It looks as though he is accustomed to dealing with such situations. But probably as a result of his conspiracy work, or perhaps as a result of the Gestapo interrogations he underwent, he has learned not to answer questions immediately. He recapitulates the last point of the previous question in order to have time to compose his answer to the question at hand. It's not a bad method, but a little irritating."

The same diarist offers the only indication that Jan may have mentioned his own death-camp and Ghetto experiences to U.S. government officials after the Frankfurter meeting, noting that "Karski told us terrible, horrible things, things that cry out for God's punishment, about what the Germans were doing to the Polish Jews, about pogroms and massacres."

Other meetings included a daylong background briefing for a hand-picked group of journalists. Among the writers in attendance was the foremost columnist of the era, Walter Lippmann, who apparently had already been invited when Cox wrote to him about Karski. The contacts Karski made here resulted in several positive articles about the underground in leading periodicals, including a major story in *Collier's* magazine and an article focused on Jan's own adventures in *The American Mercury*. Lippmann listened to the envoy's presentation, including his information about the extermination of the Jews, but wrote nothing about Karski. Like Frankfurter, Lippmann was a Jew who gave Jewish issues a wide berth in his public life.

Ciechanowski's admiration for Jan was growing as he watched the young Pole handle himself with aplomb in every meeting. "I have never met a man," he later wrote, "who could with such simplicity, such telegraphic brevity, and such absolute frankness, de scribe events and complicated situations."

On July 9, Karski and the ambassador met with several top officials of the Office of Strategic Services. In attendance at the embassy on this muggy Friday afternoon were most of the leaders of the OSS, with the exception of Bill Donovan, who had gone abroad for the Allied invasion of Sicily. (Karski would meet Donovan in August.) James G. Rogers, chairman of the OSS planning group with responsibility for covert operations, noted in his diary some impressions from "an amazing day" spent with Karski:

> The Poles have a whole government underground, an executive, an army, parliament, guerrillas, courts, all managed by wireless from London. Every Pole can be ordered out, as a duty, but only a few hundred thousand belong. Six man cells, false names and papers for every participant; so each has a double or triple personality. . . . They use American dollars to buy guns and information. Trouble with the Russian partisans whom Sikorski (now dead) would not allow them to attack but who raided towns, provoked reprisals. Two undergrounds not at war but undermining each other! They have an escape route across Germany, France to Lisbon. Wireless—seven circuits in Warsaw alone for operation orders. They wait for "insurrection day." They try to pledge us, in return for aid, to a Poland to be but we cannot promise. No one can promise anything for the U.S.A. We have no leader at all, whose policy will get countenance.

This last sour remark reflects the Republicanism of Rogers, who had served in Herbert Hoover's State Department. The fact that Republicans were heavily represented in the OSS upper ranks helps to explain why Karski's mention of "trouble with the Russian partisans" hit a hot button with the men gathered at the embassy. Karski's own account of this session dwells at length on the OSS men's concerns regarding Soviet intentions.

~

After a few days of meetings, Ciechanowski had succeeded in showing Jan off to some of the most important American officials involved in Polish affairs, as well as some of the most influential individuals in the nation's capital. Yet, however masterful the
ambassador's strategy for Karski may have been in form, its substance doomed any hope of diplomatic success. Contemporary reports make clear that the London government's overriding goal in
sending Karski to the United States was to illustrate the depths of
Soviet perfidy through the medium of an authentic underground
hero from Poland. His mission was designed as a continuation (and,
in light of the deterioration in Polish-Soviet relations, an intensifi-
cation) of the attempts he had made to enlighten British authorities
about Stalin's Polish agenda.

Nowhere in the voluminous reports on the American tour sent
to London by Karski, Ciechanowski, and other diplomats is there
any indication that the government instructed its envoy to stress
any other themes in a significant way. The fact that Jan would later
be able to help his underground comrades obtain twelve million
dollars in American credit was purely a matter of coincidence. The
fact that he raised the issue of the Jews would be testimony to his
own concern about their plight, not his government's.

An OSS report would later remark, in a neutral tone, that "Karski's specialty seems to be propaganda against the Soviet." The per-
ception that the envoy had been sent to sow disunity among the
Allies can only have been damaging to the government-in-exile's
ultimate interest—marshaling Allied support for the preservation of
Poland's independence and territorial integrity. But the London
Poles' tactics were a measure of their desperation. Jan knew his
nation's hopes for achieving an honorable peace were slim by the
time he arrived in Washington. Ciechanowski, an astute political
observer of long expertise, cannot have entertained many illusions.
Back in London, Mikołajczyk—the new Polish prime minister—and
others were clearly moving toward the conclusion that their job was
to salvage the best deal possible for Poland in the coming postwar
order.

Yet no one aligned with the government-in-exile could publicly
advocate any meaningful compromise with the Soviets. How would
a soldier from the eastern city of Lwów, fighting with the free Polish
forces in Italy, react to the news that his exiled government had

ceded his hometown to Stalin? And how much credibility would the London politicians maintain among their underground counterparts in such a case? Trapped in this dilemma, the Polish government-in-exile chose to stick to its principles, however unrealistic they might have become.

There was ample evidence available, if the Poles had chosen to take notice of it, that the Allied authorities would give a chilly official reception to anti-Soviet agitation. The Poles could not know, however, that the Allies were already discussing the postwar partition of the Polish nation. In March 1943, just weeks after his meetings with Karski, Anthony Eden secretly arrived in Washington to hammer out a joint Anglo-American policy on Eastern Europe. Meeting with Roosevelt, he spoke of Stalin's moderation and goodwill toward the region. Russia wanted "very little" from Poland, said Eden—nothing more than all the territory east of the Curzon Line, and a Polish government with "the right kind of people" (by Stalin's standards) in charge. Eden was repeating almost verbatim the arguments he had heard from Soviet ambassador Ivan Majsky in a briefing before he left England.

Roosevelt concurred with Eden's assessment. Left unspoken, but always on FDR's mind, was the hope that Stalin might eventually help the United States attack Japan, as well as the countervailing fear that Russia would turn on the West and conclude a separate peace with Germany as the Bolsheviks had done in World War I. In such circumstances, the last thing an American commander-in-chief needed was a quarrel with Stalin over an issue as insignificant as the frontiers of Poland. The three main Allies would decide Poland's borders "at the appropriate time," said the president, adding that he "did not intend to go to the Peace Conference and bargain with Poland or the other small states."

Roosevelt's attitude rendered Karski's mission utterly futile before he ever reached American shores. The betrayal that would take place at Teheran in December 1943 and would become evident at Yalta in February 1945 was already foreordained. Poland had already suffered what Ciechanowski would later call its "defeat in victory."

The Poles did find kindred spirits in Washington's right-wing circles, where the popular wartime image of Stalin as America's brave and benign comrade-in-arms was fading fast by 1943. In fact, among Republicans and others opposed to Roosevelt's coddling of Stalin, Karski's efforts to raise a red flag concerning Soviet misdeeds

may have been a little *too* successful. At a time when the Polish
government in London was desperately seeking protection from the
Americans and British against Stalin's designs, Karski would soon
be able to excite the interest of several influential Washington policymakers in Poland's plight. In the process, however, he would unwittingly become aligned with one faction in an intramural battle
within the U.S. foreign policy community.

"He was a guy we were counting on to help out quite a lot
against the Soviets," Elbridge Durbrow recalled in a 1992 interview.
Durbrow was part of a right-wing bloc at the State Department
which, together with leaders of the OSS, former ambassador to
Moscow William C. Bullitt, and others, began to advocate a tougher
line toward Stalin in 1943. Tony Biddle's March report on Karski's
revelations, and later Jan's visit to the United States, would provide
Durbrow's group with ammunition.

Opposing the right-wing faction were some of the president's
closest advisers and Roosevelt himself—as well as the First Lady.
Karski, and the Polish government that directed him, chose the
wrong horse.

~

Viewed from today's perspective, William C. Bullitt was a remark-
able prophet. Well ahead of most of his contemporaries, he predicted the rise of a despot in a remilitarized Germany after World
War I. Immediately after World War II, he foresaw a nuclear arms
race. And at a crucially early stage in that conflict, he discerned
Stalin's true intentions in postwar Europe. On January 29, 1943, he
wrote to President Roosevelt: "We have to demonstrate to Stalin—
and mean it—that while we genuinely want to cooperate with the
Soviet Union, we will not permit our war to prevent Nazi domination of Europe to be turned into a war to establish Soviet domination of Europe." Bullitt repeated his warnings almost verbatim in
letters to Roosevelt on May 12 and, shortly after both men met Karski, on August 10, 1943.

Bullitt, who had become the first United States ambassador to
the Soviet Union in 1933 and then occupied the same post in France
until the surrender of Paris in 1940, held the official title of special
assistant to the secretary of the navy. He functioned, though, as a
more or less freelance gadfly, with ready access to the president. At
the time of his meeting with Karski, Bullitt was embroiled in both
public and private struggles. On July 17, 1943, he declared his can-

didacy in the Philadelphia mayoral election, pursuing a path suggested by FDR. And for years, he had been maneuvering strenuously
behind the scenes to force the resignation of Undersecretary of State
Sumner Welles.

One night in 1940, Welles had gotten drunk and propositioned
a sleeping-car porter aboard a train in Alabama. Bullitt, who viewed
Welles as one of his main rivals for power in the foreign policy
community, was determined not to let Welles live down his indiscretion. Bullitt's connections were legendary; not too surprisingly,
then, he happened to know some top executives of the Southern
Railway who obligingly provided him with an affidavit from the
porter. In 1941, Bullitt had presented the damning evidence to Roosevelt. The president, already aware of Welles' indiscretion, refused
to oust Welles despite Bullitt's assertion that the diplomat "was subject to blackmail by foreign powers" as a homosexual. In the spring
of 1943, stories of the event on the train began to surface in the
Washington rumor mill. FDR and press secretary Steve Early called
Bullitt on the carpet on May 5, accusing him of leaking the lurid
tale. Bullitt, calling this allegation "a complete lie," told the president: "Our intimate friendship has ended."

Welles resigned in August. Roosevelt later gave his opinion of
Bullitt's machinations to Vice President Henry Wallace. For what
he did to Welles, said the president, "Bill ought to go to hell."

There could not have been a less auspicious time for Bullitt to
adopt Karski's cause as his own. Bullitt's differences with Welles
had involved another dimension besides gay-bashing; Welles was a
leading exponent of an accommodationist policy toward the USSR,
while what William L. Shirer would later call "Bullitt's hysteria
about Communism" was well entrenched. Now Welles was out of
the way, but Bullitt was in no position to sway Roosevelt in a new
direction.

Into this turmoil stepped Karski, coming to Bullitt's home
(where the latter was recuperating from a broken leg) with his tales
of Soviet-inspired treachery. The Communist agents, he told Bullitt,
"are not numerous; their propaganda is not effective; we fear not
their force, but their method. We could easily eliminate them. But
we cannot do that without the government's order, and the government does not want to cause the collapse of the great coalition and
supply arguments for enemy propaganda." Karski told Bullitt that
what Poland needed was visible support from the United States and
Great Britain. "We believe that the Russian government is not doc-

trinally imperialistic," he said. If the other allies would only call his
bluff, Stalin would back down.

Bullitt's response filled Karski with hope. "Young man," he
said, "I think you probably don't understand just how important
your mission is and how much good it may bring." Not only Poland,
but other nations as well might benefit from it. If word of the Soviets' bad faith got out, the former ambassador suggested, the western Allies might be induced to use the opening of a second front as
a cudgel against Moscow. If Stalin didn't shape up, England and
the United States would hold off on invading Europe, thus increasing the military pressure on the Red Army.

"The ambassador takes Bullitt's announcement very seriously,"
Karski noted in his summary of the conversation. "My nonpartisan,
honest report . . . (according to the Ambassador's opinion, as well
as that of Americans such as Bullitt) . . . may have an entirely surprising influence on the political line of the American government
toward the Russians and on the swaying of American public opinion."

~

Bullitt's encouragement raised hopes at the embassy for a diplomatic breakthrough. In a report written on July 24, Karski noted
that Bullitt had "told the President about my information and encouraged him to gain firsthand knowledge of it. We are awaiting his
reaction." When Roosevelt did decide to send for the young Pole
that several aides had mentioned to him, Karski attributed this
much-hoped-for stroke of fortune to Bullitt:

> The invitation came suddenly after Mr. Bullitt, a former U.S. ambas-
> sador to France, had met with the President. Mr. Bullitt pointed out
> to the President the particular significance of my information con-
> cerning the activities of communist agents on Polish territory. The
> following day, at 8 A.M., the Ambassador received a telephone call
> informing him that the President expected us at 10:30 A.M.
>
> Before the meeting, the Ambassador gave me instructions on
> how to make my presentation and what to emphasize. He said he
> would try to refrain from interrupting my presentation so that it
> would not appear as though he was directing me, with the exception
> of helping me out with my linguistic shortcomings and a possible
> political discussion, if such took place between him and the President
> as a result of my presentation.

Karski and Ciechanowski were escorted to the second floor of the White House by way of an ancient elevator that Theodore Roosevelt had installed. They were taken to the Oval Room—not to be confused with the Oval Office, which is located in another wing of the structure. Because of his disability, FDR preferred to conduct business in this more accessible presidential study on the same floor as the living quarters. The American president sat behind a desk cluttered with memorabilia; on the wall behind him were nearly a dozen paintings and photographs of sailing ships. He bellowed a hearty greeting, beckoning the visitors with his trademark cigarette holder. Jan was aware of his paralysis, but to him Roosevelt looked completely healthy. "He really projected majesty, power, greatness," Karski would recall. He had the aura of "a master of humanity."

Karski and Ciechanowski took their seats across the desk from the president and Jan began expressing his gratitude for the invitation. "For those of us who are fighting in the Homeland, the fact that the president is interested and wants to be informed about us has enormous significance," he said. "Perhaps you yourself are unaware that your reputation in Poland exceeds all others. The people of Poland look to you as the one man who can bring us liberation and organize a peace based on justice and human principles."

Jan had not gotten far into his well-rehearsed presentation when the president interrupted. "Is the situation in Poland as bad as they say?" he inquired.

Jan knew plenty about this subject. He precisely described the tiny amounts of black bread, marmalade, and coal parceled out to the Poles under the Nazi rationing system. And he told the president how the Germans used material deprivation not only to starve the Poles but to demoralize them as well. During a sugar shortage in September 1942, he said, the Nazi governor of Poland had made a speech that was broadcast through the ubiquitous loudspeakers that the Germans installed at street corners. In mocking tones, he had thanked the population for making sugar available to the "heroic German army, which fights self-sacrificingly to protect Poles from Communism, British and American imperialism, and international Jewry."

"That's amazing," commented Roosevelt. "Their perfidy is just beyond understanding."

Karski continued with a detailed recitation of his nation's suffering under occupation. He compared the pervasive deprivation in Poland with the relative bounty available in occupied France, and he told how he had become ill in Paris on his trip across the continent. "After two and a half years in Poland, Mr. President, my system could not handle all the fats, meat, and sugar that a Frenchman can consume, even under rationing," said Jan.

"Ah, yes. How is the mood in France?" Roosevelt asked.

"I didn't have contact with many Frenchmen," Karski replied, choosing his words carefully. "But my general impression is that the broad classes of French society simply want life and peace." What he didn't say would speak volumes, thought Jan: The French were a lot of sniveling collaborators, as far as he was concerned. "I suppose that the mood is different in underground circles," he said, adding that Poles in France cooperated with the Resistance.

The president shot one question after another at Karski. He wanted to know about German expropriation of Polish agriculture, about the underground movement's bribery of Germans to obtain weapons and materiel, about the state of morale within the German army, about rumors that prisoners and mental patients in Poland were being sterilized. Karski, well informed about all of these topics, briefed Roosevelt fully.

"Tell me about the German methods of terror," Roosevelt said at one point.

"They're different than the Bolsheviks' methods," responded Karski, eager to shift the subject to Soviet abuses. The Russians had deported hundreds of thousands of Poles to the Soviet Union during their occupation of eastern Poland, he noted, and even now they were sending "agents and provocateurs" to penetrate and unmask the underground movement. "The Germans have other techniques," he said—techniques of mass terror. "They find a doctor in some small town who's involved in the underground movement, and they arrest most of the doctors," Jan reported. "They find a printing press, and they arrest everybody living for several blocks around." In street roundups in July 1942, they had arrested thirty-five thousand people in the space of a couple of days, sending them to labor and concentration camps.

Jan named Auschwitz as "the most horrible concentration camp," a place where eighty to one hundred thousand members of the Polish intelligentsia had already perished. Only sketchy reports of the extermination camp for Jews at Auschwitz-Birkenau had leaked out by the time Jan left Poland, since it began operations later than most of the other death camps. He ticked off the names of other camps "for Poles"—Majdanek, Treblinka, Bełżec, Stanisławów, Dachau, Oranienburg, Mauthausen, Ravensbrück—most of which actually held primarily Jews.

But Karski soon steered the conversation from the suffering of the general population to the treatment of the Jews. "I am sure that many people are unaware of just how horrible the situation of the Jewish population is," he said. "More than 1,800,000 Jews have been murdered in my country." Echoing his remarks to Schwarzbart some months earlier, and drawing a distinction that some within the Polish government had hesitated to draw, Karski emphasized to Roosevelt that Jewish suffering was of another magnitude entirely: "There is a difference between the German-orchestrated systems of terror against the Poles and the Jews. The Germans want to ruin the Polish state as a state; they want to rule over a Polish people deprived of its elites. . . . With regard to the Jews, they want to devastate the biological substance of the Jewish nation. I have brought with me the official declaration of my government, the government delegate, and the commander of the Home Army. Their message: If the Germans don't change their method of dealing with the Jewish population, if there is no effort at Allied intervention, whether through reprisals or other action, barring some unforeseen circumstance, within a year and a half of the time I left the Homeland, the Jewish people of Poland (beyond those actively working in the Jewish underground in cooperation with us) will cease to exist."

America's most prominent Jewish leader, Rabbi Stephen Wise, had been in the same office less than a week earlier, saying the same things to Roosevelt. Karski was not telling the president much that was new. But his mention of the Jewish underground movement piqued Roosevelt's interest. He asked about the level of cooperation between these Jews and Karski's organization, and he listened as Karski described some activities that the Polish underground had undertaken to help Jews. (A special division for aid to Jews had been established after he left Poland; Karski overstated somewhat the financial resources allocated to it.) He emphasized that the penalty for aiding Jews was death, often for the entire family involved, and that ultimately the Poles could do little to help the Jews. Only Allied retaliation could have any meaningful effect, he said.

The facts that Karski witnessed atrocities and told Roosevelt about the Final Solution have often been juxtaposed in writings about the Holocaust to suggest that the Polish courier actually gave the president an eyewitness account of the slaughter he had witnessed. Ciechanowski even writes in his memoirs that Karski did so. But in his contemporary report, Karski did not claim to have told Roosevelt about his death camp and Ghetto visits. Karski later denied having mentioned the experiences to the president.

The conversation moved on to other subjects. Roosevelt wanted to know more about the structure and workings of the underground. Predictably, he pried about the nuts and bolts of clandestine work: How did the fighters in Poland communicate with the government in London? Had the neutral Swedes helped to carry messages back and forth? Could airplanes from England land secretly in Poland, perhaps in the snow after being fitted for skis?

Then Roosevelt raised the issue of Poland's borders. The formerly German land of East Prussia, he assured the Poles, would definitely belong to their country after the war. There would be "no more corridor," said the president, referring to the disputed Danzig Corridor and Poland's prewar struggles with Germany over access to the Baltic Sea. As reassuring as this guarantee sounded on its face, Jan had heard enough talk of this sort from British officials to smell trouble in what was unsaid. Roosevelt had failed to mention the real border issue—the status of the eastern boundaries of Poland. Karski deferred to the ambassador, and Ciechanowski changed the subject as soon as possible.

The ambassador seized a chance to press the case that (as he and Karski supposed) Bullitt had begun making for them with the president. After Ciechanowski interjected that Karski had important information on Communist activities in Poland, Karski gave a report on this topic that lasted at least twenty minutes. The president said very little in response beyond "That's a very tough situation" and "Old Joe [Stalin] is playing a wily game." Karski's own record of the conversation leaves the distinct impression that FDR had no interest in discussing the issue of Communist agitation in Poland.

After one further brief exchange about the underground's plans for administration of Poland in the immediate aftermath of liberation, the president looked at his watch and announced that he was a half hour late for another appointment. The conversation had lasted an hour and fifteen minutes.

"Your story is very important," Roosevelt said as he shook Jan's hand. "I'm glad I heard it. I wish you success and a happy return to your country. I hope you will come back to America." Karski, emphasizing the importance of his visit to "all fighting Poles," asked for permission to repeat FDR's words to his comrades in Poland. "Naturally," replied Roosevelt, who then turned to thank Ciechanowski for bringing Karski to him. "I was really thrilled," said the president, thanking Jan for allowing him to learn more about "the wonderful resistance and spirit of Poland."

Karski left the office in awe of FDR—so much so that he walked backwards toward the door of the study as he took leave of Roosevelt. (Ciechanowski ribbed him about this later.) Yet he also left with a sense of disappointment. At one level, his mission required that he simply impress upon Roosevelt the stalwart conviction and bravery with which Poland resisted the Nazis, and he undoubtedly accomplished this stated goal. But he had hoped to spur FDR to take action on Poland's behalf—to tame Stalin and to save Jews. Nothing Jan had heard in the meeting suggested that these actions would be taken.

Karski long believed that his attempt to move Roosevelt to action on behalf of Europe's Jews had been a failure, and it may have been. But John Pehle, whom the president appointed as the first head of the War Refugee Board on January 22, 1944, later insisted that Karski had made a difference. Roosevelt's willingness to set up the Refugee Board in an attempt to help those Jews who were still alive—a mission in which it succeeded to some extent—resulted from his deeply moving encounter with Karski, according to Pehle. "Overnight," said Pehle, the Karski mission "changed U.S. government policy from . . . indifference at best to affirmative action." Other factors, however, also motivated FDR to set up Pehle's agency—chiefly, pressure from Treasury Secretary Morgenthau.

Ciechanowski reported to London that the meeting had been a rousing success. "Having so many times had the opportunity to get acquainted with the mood of President Roosevelt through conversations," wrote the ambassador, "I find that never before have I seen him so deeply interested, and even completely absorbed, as upon this occasion. . . . It was obvious from his attitude that his view of Poland was ripening in a direction beneficial to us. I emphasize the fact that the president, who so enjoys dominating conversations himself, listened to Mr. Karski without interrupting him and held his questions until Mr. Karski had finished with each topic. Also, special attention needs to be given to the fact that he made a categorical announcement relating to the annexation of East Prussia to Poland. It was obvious how greatly the president was impressed by the disloyalty of the Soviets toward Poland," Ciechanowski concluded—clearly putting the bravest possible face on the situation.

The boost to morale among Poles in London as a result of the underground courier's visit with the great American leader was evident to an OSS observer in London months later. "The Poles are obviously highly pleased by what they consider to be a great success at the White House," reported the agent. Details of the meeting reached Poland in April 1944, when a courier parachuted into the country with a report that Karski had written, in which he too gave a relentlessly upbeat assessment of Roosevelt's attitudes on all Polish issues.

Secretary of State Cordell Hull provided a glimpse of FDR's attitude toward Karski when he saw Ciechanowski a few days later. "The President seems so thrilled by his talk with your young man," said Hull, "that he can talk of nothing else."

HEARTS AND MINDS
September 1943–July 1945

10
Unmasked

A few hours after the meeting with Roosevelt, as Jan was dictating a transcript of the conversation, a messenger from the White House arrived at the embassy. The president had sent a list of dignitaries whom he thought Karski ought to see. This helpful gesture was a little late, since Jan had already met with many of the individuals listed and had meetings scheduled with others.

In fact, the agenda for his final six weeks in the United States had grown quite full. Dozens of engagements in four different cities lay ahead. For many who would have a chance to meet Poland's undercover emissary, the encounters would hold a unique fascination. For Jan, they would constitute a wearisome grind, all the more so because any meeting would be anticlimactic as he basked in the glow of his session with FDR.

By now, after all, Jan had repeated his report scores of times. He had seen more of the high and mighty than he ever imagined he would see, but many of these encounters had been rote affairs before bored audiences. Many of the appointments the ambassador had made were defensive in nature, scheduled out of fear of leaving out someone important. In the weeks leading up to his summons to the White House, Karski had met Attorney General Francis Biddle, Secretary of War Henry Stimson and his chief assistant John McCloy, Roosevelt economic adviser Herbert Feis, Catholic leaders including Father Edmund Walsh (the Georgetown University official who would later hire Karski for his faculty), Polish-American members of the Federal Reserve Board and Congress, and assorted other personalities, as well as all the political, press, and intelligence figures he had seen earlier in July. Shortly after the Roosevelt meet-

ing, Secretary of State Cordell Hull would receive him, speaking in
a mumbled Tennessee drawl Jan could not decipher. (In addition,
there were appointments scheduled with Treasury Secretary Henry
Morgenthau and FDR's top aide Harry Hopkins that did not take
place.)

None of these encounters made any meaningful impression on
Jan, and none produced results of any kind except the discussions
with McCloy and Feis. Those meetings were devoted to Poland's
request for an additional $12 million in Lend-Lease funds to pur-
chase equipment for the underground movement. The ambassador
trotted out Jan as an example of the Poles' valiant struggle. Ciechanowski felt that the good impression Karski made was partially
responsible for the approval of the loan, which came through just
after the audience with Roosevelt.

Originally, Karski's schedule had been even more crowded. In
a report to London, the envoy referred to "the second part of my stay
in America—conducting wide propagandistic action with lectures in
front of many people, developing contacts with organizers of the Polish or American society." It is difficult to imagine how Karski could
have taken on such a high public profile and still kept his identity
secret so that he could return to Poland as planned. Ciechanowski
foresaw another problem: If Jan went into the open after meeting so
many important U.S. officials in strict secrecy, he would lose credibility among the Americans he had met.

Shortly after meeting Roosevelt, therefore, Karski and the ambassador decided to scrap the idea of public appearances. The fact
that they cabled London for permission to make this change suggests that the ill-conceived notion may have been forced on them
by the government in the first place. London agreed with their argument. Karski would schedule no new meetings "after fulfilling
orders from the Socialist group," he wrote. These were the orders
of Leon Feiner's Jewish socialist Bund movement, whose representatives Jan would soon meet in New York City. Almost a year after
Feiner gave him a mandate to alert Jewish leaders in the West to
the full dimensions of the tragedy in Poland, Karski still considered
himself duty-bound to carry out that obligation.

On August 6, Jan traveled to New York, where consular officials had arranged a series of meetings for him with union officials
and Jewish organizations. Separate dinner meetings were held for
leaders representing Jewish workers and for those from main-
stream organizations. This division had the necessary virtue of in-

suring that only unions from the American Federation of Labor (AFL) would be represented on one evening (since the Jewish unions were tied to the AFL) and only unions from the rival Congress of Industrial Organizations (CIO) on the other.

The purpose behind the meetings with labor leaders is unclear (no record of their content has survived), but evidently the Poles felt that it might be useful to give the politically powerful labor movement (and the important Jewish leaders within it) a glimpse of their underground struggle. The dinners brought Jan into contact with some of the most important figures in American labor. At the gathering of CIO affiliates Karski met Sidney Hillman, the president of the Amalgamated Clothing Workers Union (ACWU), who was also a senior CIO official and an adviser to President Roosevelt on labor matters. Presiding over the dinner for AFL leaders was International Ladies' Garment Workers Union (ILGWU) chief David Dubinsky, one of organized labor's most formidable personalities— and a native of Jan's hometown of Łódź.

~

Karski's main task on this trip was to report to several Jewish organizations that had offices in New York, the city with the world's largest Jewish population. Espousing divergent views politically, socially, and to some extent in religious matters, a number of groups representing Jews had come into being in the years before and after World War I, when the idea of establishing a Jewish state was beginning to gain momentum. Some were focused primarily on harnessing Jewish political power to better the lives of American Jews, others on creating a Jewish state, and still others on improving the lot of Jews elsewhere in the world. Karski was set to meet with personnel from seven Jewish groups during his visit: the World Jewish Congress, its affiliate the American Jewish Congress, the American Jewish Committee, the American Jewish Joint Distribution Committee, the Bund, the Representation of Polish Jewry, and the American Federation of Polish Jews.

The differences in outlook that prevailed among these organizations did not prevent them from working together on initiatives to respond to the crisis of European Jewry. The frustration of viewing the Holocaust from a distance, however, drove them apart almost as much as it drew them together. Antagonisms surfaced between leaders of various groups: Thus Rabbi Stephen Wise, founder of the World Jewish Congress, referred in an internal memorandum to the "swinishness" of his counterparts at the American Jewish Joint Distribution Committee. But while relations among Jewish groups were somewhat shaky, the Polish government's relations with these bodies ranged from poor to miserable.

The motive of Polish officials for making Karski available to leaders of the Jewish groups is not hard to gauge. Clearly, the government intended the visit as a peacemaking gesture. Although there were Jews on the Polish National Council, one of whom (Ignacy Schwarzbart) was affiliated with the World Jewish Congress, Sikorski's and Mikołajczyk's regimes had remained embroiled in many of the disputes with Jewry that had dogged their prewar predecessors. Now war, along with the greatest irritant imaginable, the extermination of Polish Jewry, caused further discord.

There were frequent complaints of anti-Semitism in the exiled Polish army. There were complaints that the government had failed to make a clear commitment to equal rights in postwar Poland for those Jews who managed to survive. There were complaints that it had not shared its information about the Final Solution in a timely manner. And there were still complaints, despite the government's efforts, that it had not done enough to mobilize the Allies on behalf of Europe's endangered Jews.

The ill will extended to Poland's embassy in Washington—where Ciechanowski seems, in fact, to have acquired a reputation as an equal-opportunity curmudgeon, antagonizing Poles, Americans, and Jews alike. Schwarzbart had warned his colleagues in the World Jewish Congress that Poland's ambassador had a negative attitude toward Stephen Wise and Nahum Goldmann. Just as the widely held belief that Józef Retinger was born a Jew had not insulated him from opprobrium when he was accused of making anti-Semitic comments, Ciechanowski's Jewish origins did nothing to endear him to American Jewish leaders.

If anything, Ciechanowski's ancestry stoked the fires of disgust with the Polish government in American Jewish Committee chairman Morris Waldman. With obvious gusto, Waldman recounted in his memoirs an occasion when, responding to an appeal from Ciechanowski for Jewish support of the Poles in their diplomatic struggle with Stalin, he had rebuked Ciechanowski sharply and asserted a strongly pro-Soviet position. "The ambassador's face became white, either with fear or anger, probably both," wrote the American Jewish Committee leader. "I was certain that I had not made a friendly hit with the gentleman. I am told that he is a converted Jew," Waldman added, inaccurately.

Despite this background, Karski to some degree viewed the upcoming meetings as more of the same—recite the standard report, answer questions, avoid controversy, make friends. Here, though, the encounters would be more intense. Probably for the first time since his demoralizing encounter with Felix Frankfurter, Jan would speak of what he himself had witnessed. He had recounted the tales of atrocities with some regularity in England, but it had never been easy to speak of such horrors, and Frankfurter's disbelief had made it even harder. Karski altered the "boilerplate" language of his standard presentation in several ways when he spoke to these Jewish audiences: He included full eyewitness accounts of his exploits in the Warsaw Ghetto and Izbica, as well as his rescue of the Weinbergs (without mentioning their names). And he spoke of the failure of British and American officials to take meaningful action on behalf of the Jews after he brought his harrowing reports to England—a subject he obviously could not have brought up in his Washington discussions without creating controversy.

Aside from these changes, Jan's set speech when he met Waldman of the American Jewish Committee on August 10 was identical in every way to his earlier presentations. Non-Jewish elements had gotten considerably less attention, however, when he spoke the previous day to the Representation of Polish Jewry. A verbatim transcript of this meeting shows that Karski gave a much more extended report on the terror in Poland. Perhaps he felt that a Polish organization would want more details than the American groups.

"Because of the real impression that the loss of Jewish life in Poland has made on me," he reported to the government later, "I would like to help the Jews to the best of my abilities." As committed as he felt to the cause of the Jews in Poland, however, Karski still kept in mind what his government (represented in each meeting by a consular official) wanted out of the meetings. His mission was to engender goodwill toward Poland. Certainly, there were things Jan could not say. He could not voice the opinion he had offered to Schwarzbart some months before, that his government's response to news of the Final Solution was inadequate. He could not tell the Jews of his own confrontation with a blackmailer of Jews, or of his frustration at reading anti-Semitic underground periodicals, or of his revulsion at witnessing the Poles' "pitiless" harrassment of Jews on the train as he left for France in January 1940.

Still, he spoke frankly of the relations between Jews and Poles. He admitted to the Representation of Polish Jewry that there was an anti-Semitic element in the underground press, and he conceded

that his examples of Polish support for the Jews did not mean that
"all Poles have changed their attitude against the Jews." In the same
conversation, he rejected the accusation, then current in certain
Polish army and government circles, that "the Jews are pro-Soviet."

The reactions of some of the Jewish leaders were fairly positive. Although "almost everybody kept diligently asking if there was
still anti-Semitism in Poland," Karski felt he won the skeptics over.
"In the current atmosphere back home," he told his audiences, "it
is simply impossible for any Pole, regardless of political convictions,
to proclaim himself freely as an anti-Semite or to express solidarity
with the German methods." Wise, the most important of the leaders,
had responded to Karski's presentation by professing his admiration for the underground's struggle. "Poland will rise again!" Wise
declared, pledging his support for the postwar rebuilding of "a great
and independent Poland, in which the Jewish nation can live freely
and with equal rights."

Aside from such platitudes, Jan also heard concrete proposals
from the leaders. Members of the American Jewish Joint Distribution Committee, which tried to send aid to the Jews of occupied
Europe, indicated that they wanted to funnel $500,000 to the Jews
of Poland and asked him how best to go about transmitting the
funds. Top officials of the American Jewish Congress told Jan they
wanted an immediate communications link with the Jewish underground movements, independent of Polish government control.
Rather than expressing any resentment at the obvious mistrust of
the Polish regime implicit in this demand, Jan went along with it.
Sure, he said, the Jews could set up their own link. Here's what they
would need to do: Come up with four or five "young, strong, athletic
Jews," knowledgeable in languages, and send them "legally or semi-
legally" into Hungary—not too difficult a feat to arrange. With the
help of the Jews in Hungary, and perhaps the Hungarians and Poles
there as well, let them make their way into Poland as Jan had done
in April 1940. Then they could locate the Jewish leaders, using contact information provided by the Poles in London.

Of course, Karski told the officials, "in all likelihood, three or
four out of those four or five will fall into the hands of the Gestapo."
It was very important, he stressed, to make sure they were "resourceful and hardened," since those who were captured "must be
prepared for the fact that their ribs will be broken and their teeth
will be knocked out." After this little brainstorming session, wrote
Jan, "my interlocutors no longer insisted so much on their demand

for the organization of 'communications with the country independent of and not controlled by the Polish government.'"

The Representation of Polish Jewry raised the question of whether the underground could help selected Jewish leaders escape to neutral countries. Jan encouraged this initiative, explaining that the underground had already taken steps to help some Jews escape (referring perhaps to the efforts then under way to smuggle Jan's Kraków colleague Bronisława Langrod and her son to Switzerland). Shortly thereafter, the Representation of Polish Jewry presented the Polish government in exile with a list of potential escapees. Included were Menachem Kirschenbaum and Adolf Berman, one of whom may have been the Zionist leader Karski met in August 1942, as well as Emanuel Ringelblum, the famous chronicler of the Warsaw Ghetto. The rescue efforts, however, did not materialize. As for the money to be transferred, the Joint Distribution Committee and other groups did send large amounts to the Polish government, but it is unclear how much reached the remaining Jews of the occupied country.

Karski informed London about his meetings in an upbeat report, stressing what he perceived as the increasingly friendly disposition of American Jews toward Poland. But he presented a rather selective portrayal of events. He did not mention, for instance, that he had discussed the rescue of Jews by the underground; the government learned of this initiative only when the Representation submitted its list. He similarly neglected to inform the government of a commitment he made after Representation leaders complained about anti-Semitism in certain underground newspapers. He had promised the Representation that he would make the government aware of "the damage that the anti-Semitic press in Poland is doing to the Polish cause"—and he did call attention to the problem by mentioning the complaint in his report. His version of the conversation, however, was that he told the Jews he could not do anything about the matter because his role "consisted solely and exclusively of *informing* them." These omissions from his reports may suggest that Karski wanted to conceal the full extent of his commitment to the Jewish cause, so as not to get on the wrong side of certain parties in London who did not share that commitment.

Jan also avoided telling London about one encounter that, if mentioned, would have considerably darkened his bright assessment of Polish relations with the Jewish groups: his meeting with Morris Waldman of the American Jewish Committee. Although

Karski's reports say nothing about this conference, Waldman's minutes speak volumes.

After Karski finished his presentation, Waldman delivered a short speech of his own. He spoke briefly of his hopes for Poland's future, and then he set out an indictment of its present leaders, the purpose of which, he said, was to allow Jan to "judge whose fault it is that our relations with your officials here have been meaningless." He blasted various government representatives, including Sikorski, whom he faulted for creating "a great deal of publicity about the Jewish tragedy in Europe, without even asking us if we considered it wise." At the same time, Waldman alleged that the Poles were "count[ing] on the continuance of the war and the massacre of the Jews in Poland to settle the problem of the Jews in Poland." He said he had "scrutinized" the members of the government-in-exile with an eye toward determining their "integrity as human beings," and implied that he had found them lacking. At the end of this preamble, he made "one practical suggestion"—proposing that his organization and the Polish government set up a joint committee to discuss Polish-Jewish relations. For some reason, Jan did not see fit to transmit this proposition to the government.

In his unpublished postwar memoirs, Waldman was as scathing toward Karski as he was toward other Poles. "Later he wrote a book which received favorable press notices by reviewers who obviously were not familiar with East Europe," Waldman noted, referring to *Story of a Secret State,* the account of Karski's adventures published in 1944. "I checked up carefully on Mr. Karski," added Waldman, "and got reliable information that some of his statements were untrue and on the whole the information he was circulating was not reliable." A close reading of Waldman's minutes of the conversation does reveal two inaccuracies: As elsewhere, Karski did give February 1943 as his arrival date, and for security reasons he intentionally misstated the nationality of the (Ukrainian) uniform he wore at the death camp (he told Waldman it was Latvian, but in a meeting the day before he had said it was Estonian). Aside from these instances, though, everything in the minutes can be confirmed as historically accurate.

Waldman may not have been the only Jewish leader who did not believe what he heard from Karski. Despite his warm words to Jan, Stephen Wise may also have had certain reservations. Two months after their meeting, commenting on a Polish report about the liquidation of the Kraków Ghetto, Wise wrote: "I still believe that the reports of the Polish Government are frequently based on imagination or phantasy [*sic*]." The Kraków Ghetto had in fact been liquidated the prior February.

~

Karski returned to Washington for a lunch date with the leadership of the Office of Strategic Services (OSS) on August 12, this time with OSS chief William Donovan in attendance. As James G. Rogers recorded in his diary, Jan "told again the drama of the Polish underground, its legalism—'a complete state in hiding, army, courts, legislature, parliament.' Torture and escapes." The escape from occupied Europe was of primary interest to Donovan, who took the opportunity to brag about the services his "boys" had rendered to Jan.

Within a few days, Karski was in transit once more. He traveled to Chicago, home of a large and politically active Polish-American population. His agenda there included background briefings for local journalists, including the formidable publisher of the *Chicago Tribune*, Colonel Robert McCormick, as well as meetings with other influential figures in the city. There was also to be a gathering of prominent Polish-Americans in his honor on August 17—just a discreet little soirée, with a few big names, at the apartment of the Polish consul general in Chicago.

Karski recoiled in horror as he entered the apartment. No fewer than fifty-seven eager-faced Polish-Americans awaited him: fifty-seven enthusiastic babblers, fifty-seven sets of loose lips to blow his cover. Furious at the consul general, he struggled to maintain his composure throughout the five-hour affair. He gave his usual report; the Chicagoans replied with a bombastic resolution praising the courage of Jan and his underground colleagues for enduring "the hecatombs of sacrifice" in their struggle with "the barbarian invader."

The next day, Jan met with Samuel A. Stritch, archbishop of the Chicago diocese (and a future cardinal). When he expressed his hope that the city's Catholic charities would keep the unfortunate Poles in mind when they made their distributions, Stritch stared icily at him. He rather doubted, he said, "that the socialists and Jews who play such a prominent part in the [Polish] government will distribute our money to the sincere and God-fearing Catholics of Poland." Jan reacted deftly to this provocative statement. He assured the prelate that people of all persuasions were fighting in the underground for Poland's independence, and he made a point of mentioning that he himself was a devout Catholic. After a while, not only had Stritch's hostility disappeared, but he was even promising to look into the possibility of sending money for distribution in Poland.

The emissary made a final gesture of piety, perhaps for purely spiritual reasons or perhaps in order to cement his relationship with the cleric. "At the end of the talk," Jan wrote in his report on the encounter with Stritch, "I asked him for a benediction upon the Poles, upon the secret Catholic organizations working in Poland, upon the secret council of priests working in Warsaw, and upon myself. The Reverend Archbishop solemnly dispensed those blessings, and he commended us all fervently to the care of the Lord."

After a brief stopover in Detroit to meet with other members of the American Catholic hierarchy, Karski moved on to New York. A second visit to the city had been necessitated by a leak concerning his first trip there. An organization of Polish-American journalists, incensed at being left out of the secret visitor's itinerary, had written an angry letter to Ambassador Ciechanowski. They told what they had learned of Jan's U.S. activities—demonstrating that they had quite accurate information—and they expressed particular outrage that Karski had been allowed to meet (in the company of Morris Waldman) with a Jewish journalist known for his pro-Soviet and anti-Polish views.

The threat that the Polish-American scribes would create mischief was implicit, and Ciechanowski decided to make Karski available to them. He gave orders, however, that no mention was to be made of the Soviet partisan issue, and any questions about it were to be evaded. "The ambassador was afraid that some particularly indiscreet journalists . . . would use this information in a manner counterproductive to our current political line," explained Jan. The last thing the London government needed at the moment was pressure from right-wing journalists to take a harder line against Stalin. Stepping out of his nonconfrontational persona, Karski used the meeting to scold the journalists over the damaging effects of continual speculation in the Polish press about the weakness of the government-in-exile.

When Karski returned to Washington in the last days of August, a confusing surprise awaited him. Among a handful of congratulatory telegrams from London was one from Professor Kot. He too offered congratulations on the envoy's completion of such a successful visit to the United States, but Kot was also writing to offer Karski a job in London: "Upon your return I would like for you to take over one of the leading positions in [the Ministry of] Information, where your qualifications and experience could bring great benefit in such a decisive moment for Poland." Karski wondered what on earth the minister could be thinking about. He was not about to take a job in London; he would stop there only long enough to make arrangements for a parachute jump. His duty was to return to Poland.

~

Karski's ship arrived at Liverpool on September 19, 1943. As soon as he made it back to London, he rushed to Mikołajczyk's office. "Mr. Prime Minister," he said, "my mission is complete. When do I go to Poland?"

"Never," said Mikołajczyk, reaching into his desk. He produced a document and handed it silently to Jan. It was the transcript of a Nazi propaganda broadcast:

> A certain Jan Karski has been busying himself in the United States lately—or at least that's the name he goes by. He has hidden his past, and in reality he's a Bolshevik agent, in the service of American Jewry.

Jan handed the paper back to Mikołajczyk. "I've been deciphered," he said quietly.

There could be no question of his returning to Poland, Mikołajczyk told him. "There's no way of telling what else they know about you," he said, "but you would be a marked man in Poland. I will not send you back there to a certain death." Karski feebly tried to argue with the prime minister's logic, but it was incontrovertible.

Jan sank into a seat, head in hands. He tried to imagine how his identity had been compromised. It had to be the Americans' fault, since the broadcast made no mention of his British activities. There was the mention of the Jews; maybe one of them had talked too much and a German agent had gotten wind of the story. Or perhaps someone from among the horde of Polish-Americans at the Chicago consul's apartment had bragged of the hero he had met. Or maybe it was someone in Washington. Whoever was responsible had made it impossible for Jan to proceed with his plans.

Within a few days, Mikołajczyk convened a conference with Karski and several government officials who had worked with him

during the past ten months. The purpose was to decide what to do
with the unmasked envoy. Jan said he wanted to join the army. The
exiled Polish Second Corps, based in Scotland, had already made a
name for itself in the North African and Italian campaigns. But Mikołajczyk vetoed this idea immediately. There was also some discussion of sending Karski to an embassy as a diplomatic officer.
But the consensus view was that Jan would be more useful to the
government if he stayed in London and made himself available as
an exemplar of the Polish struggle—just what he had been doing
for the past eight months, only now on an open and public basis.

In retrospect, it is clear that the government had a very strong
motive for keeping Karski out of the army—and, for that matter,
out of Poland. He knew far too much. There was the danger, of
course, that he might be captured and might reveal important political intelligence to the Germans under torture. But even more
pressing was the danger that he would tell Poles in the army or the
underground what he had learned about Allied attitudes toward the
Polish cause. The possibility cannot be excluded that the government-in-exile manufactured the supposed propaganda broadcast
because it had decided that Karski knew too much to be sent back
to the Homeland. No evidence of such a deception has been found,
but neither has any evidence emerged that the broadcast actually
took place.

Soon, the government determined that even having Karski in
London was too great a risk. At a time of the utmost political sensitivity, with the integrity if not the existence of the Polish state at
stake, he could easily become a pawn in the intrigues of London's
Polish factions—no matter how carefully he tried to steer clear of
such dangers. By November, the Poles would be planning to send
Jan back to the relative isolation of the United States. When the
original purpose for this trip (a projected summit between Mikołajczyk and Roosevelt) fell through, the government would send
him anyway the following February, offering him free rein to carry
out such propaganda work as he saw fit while collecting a handsome
salary. His days in London were numbered.

For the time being, Mikołajczyk and Kot made use of Jan as
best they could. Although Jan had been out of Poland for a year
now, they turned to him with various questions about underground
life and sought his advice on propaganda issues. In early October,
the British managers of Świt asked that Karski be made available
once more to the secret radio station. They were not so much in-

terested in putting him on the air as having him "lend his assistance in keeping up the morale" of personnel at the station—morale stretched thin by the staff's battles with the Britons over the degree to which they would be allowed to attack the Soviets.

Karski's personal attitude toward the Russians, as expressed in memoranda to government members, had remained very moderate in comparison to the bitterness of many other Poles. Without actually admitting the extent to which he knew the Poles had already lost their struggle with Stalin, he advocated a conciliatory approach. In the short term he thought every effort should be made to cooperate against the Germans, and in the longer term he felt that Poland had to take into account the Soviet Union's legitimate desires for a friendly and stable western neighbor. He told Poles such as the Świt broadcasters that his views prevailed among his underground colleagues (though they probably did not). The British overlords of the radio station naturally welcomed this attitude. They reported to Mikołajczyk that they considered Karski to be "very much respected" by the Polish staff, and that they "always regarded his influence as most helpful in the work" of Świt.

When he was not busy with these diplomatic and propagandistic errands, Karski took the first steps toward emerging as a public personality. Before the end of September, he had granted his first "open" interviews to British journalists, and in the next few months he was the subject of numerous articles in English and Scottish newspapers. He seems to have fed a different tidbit of underground lore to each journalist—one story focused on the underground press, another on clandestine education and Nazi attempts to corrupt Polish youth, another on daring exploits of the underground. Karski spoke before various Polish and British societies, at a Labour Party conference on Poland (after which London's pro-Soviet paper, the *Daily Worker*, accused him of "attacking Russia"), at a gathering of parliament members interested in Poland, and at a meeting of the PEN Club of London, a group of writers interested in human-rights issues.

Polish émigré poet Antoni Słonimski arranged for Jan to address the PEN Club, and afterward introduced him to its most illustrious member, the aging science-fiction writer H.G. Wells. "He was a little man, rather pompous," Karski would later recall. Wells reacted to Jan's mention of the extermination of the Jews with a cryptic comment: "Mr. Karski, there is room for very serious research on the subject: What are the reasons that in every country the Jews reside, sooner or later, anti-Semitism emerges? Have you thought about it?"

From Washington, Ciechanowski arranged for Jan to meet with journalist Martha Gellhorn Hemingway, who was traveling to London to cover the war for *Collier's*. The ambassador advised the foreign ministry that Hemingway might well provide the Polish regime with good press; although she was "of a radical persuasion," Ciechanowski wrote, she was "not uncritically pro-Soviet." After several meetings with Karski in early November, the writer was impressed enough to feature his adventures in an article. ("He was tall and dark," she wrote, "good looking, too thin.") At the time, Mrs. Hemingway was sending regular cables to Cuba, trying to convince her husband Ernest to come to London and meet some of the fascinating people she was encountering. His refusal removed the possibility of what would surely have been a noteworthy meeting with Karski, given the novelist's taste for adventure.

That was not the only tantalizing exploit in which Jan would barely miss becoming entangled during the coming months.

~

In the capital of Iran, the leaders of the three major Allies met at the beginning of December 1943 to deliberate the future of Poland. During the same month, Karski published an article on the development and organization of the Polish underground movement in an official government newsletter. The Foreign Office's reaction to Jan's article reflected the attitudes that Churchill and Roosevelt had carried with them to Teheran, providing an indication of just how hopeless the cause of a free Poland had become.

In the article, Jan repeated an assertion he always made in discussions about the underground—that it had the unswerving support of virtually the entire Polish population. Allied officials had accepted this statement as true earlier in the war; after all, the movement was built upon a broad coalition of parties that had garnered support democratically in prewar Poland. But Stalin's propaganda, both before and after the break in relations with Poland, had chipped away at this assertion and tried to sow doubts about the benevolent intentions expressed by Polish leaders. A Foreign Office expert betrayed the extent to which western diplomats had been swayed by Soviet arguments in his comments on Jan's article:

One thing it tends to skate over (but which the Russians would affect to regard as crucial) is the extent to which [the movement's] discipline is willingly and unanimously accepted by all sections of the population, rather than being imposed by the militant but highly organised four-party political representation. There are features of the present underground state which savour of totalitarian dictatorship (although a broadly based one)—conscription into the underground movement, ostracism or execution by People's Tribunals of those who disobey.

There was a danger, added the official, that the present rift with the communists would increase, resulting in much greater discord "or even dismemberment of the country" after the Germans withdrew. The implications of all these observations were clear: On the one hand, the underground movement affiliated with London now seemed to exhibit the kinds of antidemocratic traits that might make it unfit for continued British support; on the other hand, the surest way to avoid chaos would be to support the Soviet Union's position. Strengthening this argument was the evolving military situation. The Red Army was routing the Germans in the East and had begun the relentless march that would finally take it to Berlin. Within a month, the first regular Soviet troops would cross Poland's prewar boundaries.

In Teheran, meanwhile, Allied potentates were huddled over maps of Eastern Europe. Churchill and Eden were swapping ideas with Stalin and Molotov. Roosevelt, less than eager to have his fingerprints on any business that might not sit well with the Polish-American voting bloc, sat in a corner of the room and feigned sleep. Stalin complained that the London-directed underground was collaborating with the Germans in order to kill off the partisans he supported. Churchill did not reject this charge; he changed the subject. How the British prime minister might have responded if Karski had been able to speak to him about the underground's struggle against Hitler and Soviet misdeeds in Poland is anyone's guess. But at the moment he declined to challenge Stalin on this claim, it became evident that every effort Karski and the Poles had made to impress the British with their fidelity to the Allied crusade had been a failure.

By the end of the Teheran conference, the major Allies had secretly agreed to shift Poland to the west, taking away its territory

east of the Curzon Line and bestowing on it the former German
lands east of the Oder River. The Polish government had played no
part in making these decisions. More and more forcefully after Teheran, however, British leaders began pressing the London Poles
behind closed doors to concede the territorial issue to Stalin as a
prerequisite for the restoration of diplomatic relations with the
USSR.

As a consequence of his increasingly close relationship with
Mikołajczyk, Karski was aware of the losing battle the Polish prime
minister was fighting. After gauging the attitudes of both British
and American authorities at close range during the past year, Jan
came to the conclusion that Poland had, once and for all, lost the
war. He shared this conclusion with fellow courier Jan Nowak, recently arrived from Warsaw, speaking (as Nowak later recalled)
"coldly, almost cynically" of the implications of Teheran. "If our
politicians had the courage to confront reality," Jan told Nowak,
"instead of relying on wishful thinking, they would sit down together and conceive a plan for *how* to go about losing the war." The
government, he said, should quit fighting against impossible political odds in the Allied capitals and begin thinking about "how to
prepare our country for what will inevitably come."

Nowak, who emigrated to the United States after the war and
headed the Polish section of Radio Free Europe for many years,
eventually came to respect Jan's clear-minded analysis. "In com-
paring Karski's comments with what actually happened later," Nowak wrote in his memoirs, "I see that he understood our situation
better than anyone else I met in London at the time."

Mikołajczyk refused to give in to British pressure on the border
issue. Aside from the principles involved, he felt that such a con-
cession would be so bitterly opposed within Poland that his government would lose its authority. Annoyed, Churchill would finally rise
in the House of Commons on February 22, 1944, to announce publicly the Teheran agreement on Polish borders. The government-in-
exile's protestations would then become empty words. The border
issue would be settled.

Even before this announcement, Churchill, Eden, and others
began considering the thorny matter of reaction to the new borders
within the underground and other elements of the Polish population. If the Polish government would be of no help, Britain would
have to take measures on its own in an effort to avoid open conflict
between the Poles and the advancing Red Army. It was time to es-

tablish direct contact with the Polish underground, without the government-in-exile as mediator—along the lines, in fact, of the feeler Karski had put out in his meetings with Frank Savery back in December 1942.

Jan was at sea when Churchill made his devastating speech about Poland in Commons; he had sailed from Scotland on February 21. He carried with him a letter from Mikołajczyk to Ciechanowski, spelling out his mission in the United States. One passage from this secret document puzzled him when he later saw it, and continued to do so for a number of years after the war. "Currently," wrote the prime minister about Jan, "he needs to be presented as someone staying outside of Poland until the end of the war. However, for your information," the letter added, there was still a possibility that he would be "quickly sent back to Poland. . . . Perhaps he will be called to come to London much earlier. In that case, he would have to interrupt all of his projects." As things turned out, Karski did not return to London for the remainder of the war.

∼

One afternoon in the 1950s, the telephone rang in the Georgetown University office of associate professor of political science Jan Karski. He picked it up. Without preliminaries, in a matter-of-fact voice, as though he had last seen Karski the day before rather than in 1943, Józef Retinger asked if Jan was free for lunch the next day.

On arriving at the restaurant of Washington's Mayflower Hotel for the meeting, Karski found a shrunken, feeble man, now blind, walking with the help of a young assistant. Retinger did not reveal the purpose for his trip to the United States, and given his history of secret dealings, Karski knew better than to ask. The old man and his former protégé swapped memories for a while, and eventually Jan raised the subject of Retinger's April 1944 parachute jump into Poland, which had become legendary in Polish exile circles.

"Piorun, I will tell you about it," said Retinger, "because I saved your skin." At the beginning of 1944, he explained, he had been summoned by certain friends he had in the British government. "They told me they would like to send an emissary to Poland who would be totally independent," he recalled. "His role would be limited. He would get access to all British secret documents referring to the position of the Polish government on the international scene. His mission would be to convey this information to the highest authorities of the underground in Poland, so that they would realize what kind of position the Polish government is now faced with, particularly in view of the territorial demands of Russia. The English asked me, what do I think? Would Karski be good for such a mission?

"I told the British: 'Karski is good,'" Retinger continued. "'He is faithful in his reports and he has wide experience in underground activities. However, Karski has no political standing. When he comes to Poland and meets with the political leaders, telling them such things and discussing the inevitability of a compromise solution, they will not take him seriously.'" Retinger had gone on to recommend himself for the mission, which he was allowed to carry out after overcoming the resistance of British officials concerned about his age and physical condition. Churchill himself gave the final go-ahead.

After finishing his tale, Retinger asked what time it was. When Karski told him, Retinger was alarmed. "Hail me a taxi!" he ordered Jan, struggling to his feet. "I'm late for a meeting with Dulles!" Whether he meant CIA chief Allen Dulles or Secretary of State John Foster Dulles, Karski never learned.

11
Fame in Vain

Karski's war was not over yet. Though he could not go back to his embattled country, and though the prospects for a free and democratic postwar Poland were declining just as Allied armies were advancing on the Third Reich, he still hoped to contribute to the struggle.

After arriving in New York on February 27, 1944, Karski set about the task of promoting the Polish cause in the United States. The vehicle he had in mind for that promotion was a project he had first suggested to the government during his prior visit to the United States: a film about the underground movement. While making his rounds in London, Jan had developed a habit of spending the time between meetings in theaters, where he would nap through whatever matinee was playing. He could sleep peacefully through any fare, even horror films and murder mysteries. "It is warm," he explained to a reporter, "and I know these things are not happening to me."

The government in London had indulged his idea of a movie dramatizing Poland's unyielding resistance to the Nazis, especially in the wake of an unabashedly pro-Soviet film, *Mission to Moscow*, that had come out in 1943. But the regime was not prepared to fund such a production. Jan would have to arrange financing for the picture on his own. To pitch the concept, he brought with him a script approved by the government-in-exile as well as translations of several secret documents, authenticated by the government, with which he could buttress the credibility of his tales.

Aside from this project, the authorities in London wanted Jan to do whatever else he could do to call attention to the under-

ground's struggle through public appearances and media contacts.
As before in his secret conferences with key Allied figures, he would
use his own experiences (though they were now more than a year
out of date) to acquaint audiences with the resistance movement in
general. Apart from these broad directions, Jan would be a free
agent for the duration of the war. Drawing an ample salary from
the embassy in Washington, he would act as he saw fit to spread
the word of Poland's undying fight against Hitler and its unfair
treatment by Stalin. Though he had no orders from London to pub-
licize the Jewish tragedy, he would take it upon himself to raise that
subject with the American public as well.

Jan's first month in the United States was a whirlwind of activity. By March 17, he reported back to London that he had "established communication with the most important firms in Hollywood." He found the film to be a tough sell. Movie moguls were
wary of Poland as a subject, fearing they would be drawn into the
Polish-Soviet controversy. They also worried that any such movie
might be overtaken by events, given the fast pace of both military
and political activity in early 1944. And, with the defeat of Germany
seen as inevitable, producers sensed that the public would soon
have little taste for flag-waving war movies.

Karski still expressed hope for the cinematic project in the
March report, but in the meantime he busied himself with his other
propaganda efforts. He had already given lectures in Washington
and New York, had been interviewed on a national radio program,
had persuaded the *Washington Post* to write a story on the Polish
underground based on his information, and had met with editors
from *Collier's, Time*, and *Life* magazines (laying the groundwork for
the *Life* cover story he would write a few months later). Through
contacts provided by the Polish embassy, Jan had also begun contacting public-relations firms and literary agents about a possible
fallback project, in case the film did not work out—a book about
the Polish underground.

~

Before the end of March, Karski had found the man who would
make that book a reality. Emery Reeves called himself both a literary agent and a publisher. In an era when agents wielded far less
power and influence than they do today, he did indeed serve as the
American literary representative for such prominent figures as Winston Churchill and Anthony Eden. But he was not listed in direc-

tories of literary agents, nor did his Cooperation Publishing Company actually publish any books. In essence, Reeves was an entrepreneur, trading in fame. Karski's job was to thrust himself into the limelight; Reeves could help him accomplish that goal.

In their first meeting, Reeves explained that once he secured a publisher for Karski, a book could serve as the key to everything else the government wanted him to do. If executed properly, it would open doors among magazine publishers so Jan could write articles about the Polish cause. If it turned out to be successful, there would be at least some chance of arranging a movie deal based on it, whereas Jan's current efforts to interest Hollywood were hopeless, according to Reeves. And in the course of publicizing the book, the author would gain much more media exposure and have many more opportunities to speak about Poland's war effort than would otherwise be available. For his part, Reeves made clear why he considered the deal worthwhile. "He thinks the book will be a sensation," Jan cabled to Professor Kot in London.

At the same time, however, Reeves laid down the law to Karski. If they were to work together, the Pole would have to follow his rules. For starters, they would have a 50–50 financial arrangement. Reeves would siphon off half of everything Karski made from the book. (The standard take for literary agents at the time was 10 percent.) Moreover, Jan would be under a strict writing regimen. The book would be worthless if he did not finish it quickly. Every week, he was to bring a certain number of manuscript pages to Reeves' office. And the content of the book had to meet Reeves' specifications. He wanted the story of Karski's adventures, not some dry treatise on the organization of the underground movement, and certainly not anything that would add fuel to the Polish-Soviet dispute. No American publisher would ever lend its name to a volume of obvious propaganda from a foreign government. Karski needed to understand that at the outset, Reeves told him.

Jan agreed enthusiastically to the terms Reeves set out. He was not as completely hoodwinked about the money involved as Reeves may have imagined. "I accepted financial conditions very onerous to myself," he told the government-in-exile, adding that he did so intentionally. "I want very urgently to interest my agent financially," Karski explained in a letter to London, "so that he will assure the maximum exposure for the book. I operate under the assumption that the propaganda effect is more important than a few hundred of the 'author's' dollars."

From London, Kot gave his assent to the deal, though he still cherished the notion of at least a short-subject documentary on the underground movement and instructed Karski not to give up on the film idea just yet. But by the beginning of April 1944, Jan had forsaken almost all other activities to concentrate on the task at hand. He had the cooperation of the Polish embassy and its New York propaganda office, which retained a bilingual typist for him and set up an office for him in a Manhattan hotel room. There he reported early every morning to dictate his memoirs.

"It was tremendous work," he wrote in a report to the government shortly after finishing the first draft. "I worked literally day and night, from one interval to the next and on to bedtime. . . . I have never in my life been so overworked and tired as I am currently. The last three months of work on the book now seem like a nightmare to me."

How weary the stenographer became may be left to the imagination. In the space of a few weeks, she typed roughly one thousand pages of text—sometimes taking dictation in English, sometimes in Polish, and sometimes simultaneously translating from Polish to English as Jan spoke. Since her English was better than Karski's, she reworded his thoughts when he spoke in that language.

The project moved along smoothly for the first few months. Karski turned in his text to Reeves on schedule, and even pleasantly surprised his agent with the quality of his work. The initial plan had been for Reeves and a freelance editor, William Poster, to fashion the book themselves based on detailed information from Karski. But after seeing the first installments of Jan's work, Reeves and Poster changed plans somewhat. "Upon getting acquainted with my manuscript," Karski proudly reported to his superiors in England, "they considered that it possessed a certain freshness, that it had a good, 'bookish' construction, that it was written with sufficient literary talent, and that after supplemental translation . . . and a little 'adaptation,' it would be suitable for publication."

Before long, however, Jan began to realize that the "adaptation" the Americans had in mind did not necessarily serve his and the Polish government's interests. First came a conflict over a chapter on the nefarious activities of the Soviet-sponsored Communist agents in Poland. Karski's position on his country's relations with the USSR was moderate by Polish standards, but he did want to convey to American readers a sense of the difficulties his underground movement faced as a result of Communist misdeeds. Reeves flatly rejected the chapter. Not only would it be controversial, he said, but it was also a departure from the agreed first-person format of the book, since Karski had not personally encountered the Communist provocateurs.

Jan considered the issue so important that he sent a telegram to Mikołajczyk, seeking his advice on how to respond. The prime minister and others in the government agreed that "if a book such as this is possible for the price of omitting the Eastern question, it is better to do that than not to do it at all." Ultimately, Karski added a very conciliatory postscript to the book, conceding that there were other anti-Nazi elements in Poland carrying on their activities under the direction or influence of Moscow.

Other conflicts arose over similar instances in which Reeves' interests diverged from Karski's. Jan complained that his agent tended to "exaggerate my role and significance and to stress the sensational parts of the story, not the ideological-political." At the same time, though, Reeves apparently was skeptical of some of Karski's sensational claims. "I had the greatest difficulty in convincing my agent that the book set forth authentic information," he later reported. After Jan obtained a letter from Mikołajczyk affirming that the government stood behind his word, Reeves expressed less concern.

Despite these assurances, much of what Karski wrote was far from accurate—even before Reeves and Poster began "adapting" the text. Security concerns, naturally, forced him to alter scores of details. He changed the names of nearly all underground members he mentioned, falsified his own background and family history, and fabricated logistical aspects of his missions. "I had to be careful so that after the war they would not hang me for breaching security," Karski later said, only partly tongue-in-cheek. But he also distorted facts in order to provide more dramatic illustrations of the underground experience. His friend Tadeusz Pilc, for example, became "Tadeusz Kilec," dying not in Buchenwald but on a public gallows in the main square of Lublin, after a heroic attempt to derail a train.

"I never altered the essential reality," Karski wrote, in a report that discussed the manuscript's "adaptations." His assertion is debatable. Jan clearly made every effort to put across a positive image for the resistance movement; such was the entire purpose of his book. He mentioned its endemic political infighting, but conveyed none of his own disgust with the surreal partisan fancies of certain underground publications. He did not discuss the violent opposition of right-wing factions in Poland to any hint of detente with the Soviet Union. His text contained no references to the Polish anti-Semitism Jan witnessed, nor did it mention most of the people he had met after reaching England.

After Reeves succeeded early that summer in persuading Boston-based Houghton Mifflin Company to publish the book, still more "adaptations" ensued. At the end of June, Karski reported to the government about one such enhancement:

> My publishers especially emphasized building up the Jewish part of the book. They want me to write about the struggle in the Warsaw Ghetto [the uprising that took place five months after Jan reached England], despite my opinion that it would not be related to the overall construction of the book. They think that it will be more beneficial for Poland and will also deepen the interest of American public opinion in the book. Maybe I will use their suggestion—not only for the above reasons, but also because the longer I am away from the horrors of the Homeland and further from the front, the more I feel the terrible tragedy of Polish Jewry.

In the final text of the book, the Bund and Zionist leaders in Warsaw tell Karski of plans for the Ghetto uprising. Karski may well have added this detail, which does not conform to what later became known of the origins of the revolt, in response to Houghton Mifflin's suggestions.

The publisher also wanted more of another type of content. Late in the summer, Karski was invited to Boston for dinner with a Mr. Houghton (apparently retired president Edward O. Houghton) of Houghton Mifflin Company. Houghton told Jan he was delighted with the manuscript. But then, leaning conspiratorially toward his guest, he expressed one reservation. "Mr. Karski, we expect that your book will be widely read," said Houghton. "The American public expects to find certain things in a book like this. Our readers will surely notice what my staff and I have noticed about your manuscript. Mr. Karski, you describe here four years of your life. Yet you say little about your personal life. Did you never fall in love during that time? There must have been something!"

Karski shook his head, smiling.

Houghton chuckled slightly. "Surely—and I speak only for my readers—" he continued, "surely you don't want to create the impression that you have something to hide, that perhaps you do not prefer women."

"Mr. Houghton, I give you my word of honor," parried Karski. "There is no such secret. I simply didn't have time for any affairs! You read the manuscript. I was in transit all the time, or in Russia, or in the Gestapo jail, in Kraków, in Warsaw, in London, in Washington. There was nothing!"

Houghton cast his eyes down at the table. "Pity," he said softly.

Jan's protestations of innocence were in vain. Subtle hints of a romance between him and Danuta Sławik (identified as "Danuta Sawa" in the text) were suitably included in the book.

Karski's primary motivation in the book project was bolstering Poland's image in the United States. His agent and publisher were driven by a desire to sell books. It may well be that neither side had any particular commitment to historical accuracy and neither intended the book to be a comprehensive document of Karski's wartime experiences. Neither, apparently, foresaw that scholars decades later would rely on *Story of a Secret State*, as Houghton Mifflin decided to title the book, for important source material on the history of the Final Solution and other wartime topics, unaware of its gaps or "adaptations."

~

On June 6, 1944, as Allied forces stormed the beaches of Normandy, Jan sat in a downstairs room at Blair House, residence of foreign dignitaries visiting Washington. He was waiting for orders from Stanislaw Mikołajczyk. President Roosevelt had finally granted the Polish prime minister an audience, after stalling him for eight months, and Mikołajczyk had arrived in Washington on June 5 for a state visit. He had asked that Karski be made available to him, though Jan had no assigned duties and was not to accompany Mikołajczyk during his official meetings. Embassy officials told him only that he should report to Blair House every morning at 8:30, ready to respond to the premier's needs.

Mikołajczyk's visit came at a crucial moment in Polish-Soviet relations. With the Polish government-in-exile more isolated from all its allies than ever before, the pressure for it to compromise in order to placate Stalin was intense. Mikołajczyk was prepared to offer some concessions, though little short of a de facto renunciation of Poland's sovereignty would truly satisfy Stalin. The Polish leader hoped to impress Roosevelt and other Americans as moderate and reasonable; he hoped that FDR, in return, would intercede with Stalin to bring about some rapprochement between the two quarreling nations.

Jan's role in Mikołajczyk's strategy was to make sure the prime minister did not have bad breath when he met American officials. Mikołajczyk called for him on his first morning at Blair House. "I forgot my toothpaste," he said, in a mild panic. "Can you find me some?"

Karski rushed down the stairs. He asked a guard at the door where the nearest open drugstore was. The guard immediately whistled through his fingers for reinforcements. A police motorcycle roared up. "Wisconsin Avenue at N Street!" the guard yelled to the driver. "Drugstore, open 24 hours—take him there!"

Jan clambered onto the back of the bike and held on for dear life. The policeman sped down the streets of the capital, red light flashing, siren blaring as he forged through busy intersections, with a bareheaded young man in a business suit on the back. At the store, Jan snatched a tube of toothpaste from the shelf, tossed a dollar on the counter, and ran out the door.

"What happened? What happened?" asked the guard back at Blair House.

"The Polish prime minister forgot toothpaste when he left London," said Karski, sprinting up the stairs.

"Jesus Christ," muttered the voice behind him.

Mikołajczyk's talks with Roosevelt seemed to go well. Both parties privately expressed guarded optimism that a breakthrough might be at hand in Poland's prolonged impasse with the Soviet Union. The Polish leader extracted a promise from FDR "that he could count upon the moral support of the United States government in any efforts that the premier might make to reach a mutually satisfactory understanding with the Soviet authorities," as Secretary of State Cordell Hull put it. Hull immediately began to back away, however, when Mikołajczyk pressed him to make that commitment more specific. Diplomatic observers saw little real benefit for Mikołajczyk from the visit. "While he may have done a service to his people by conveying the impression that reasonable Poles exist, and so added to the sadly depleted stock of goodwill for them in Washington," commented a British embassy report to the Foreign Office, "he does not . . . seem to have obtained anything tangible from the president."

After nine days in Washington, Mikołajczyk prepared to return to London. As Jan lined up with other Poles to shake hands with the departing leader, Mikołajczyk took him aside. "The president will defend us," he whispered, putting the best possible face on Roosevelt's vague promise. "One should not talk about it."

Two days after the prime minister left, Roosevelt sent a message to Stalin about the visit. He was clearly eager to allay any fears the Soviet leader may have had that the United States would make common cause with Poland to oppose Stalin's territorial and political ambitions regarding Poland. "I can assure you," wrote the president, "that no specific plan or proposal in any way affecting Polish-Soviet relations was drawn up."

~

Jan apologetically told his bosses in London that there had been little time for him to cultivate a public persona in support of the Polish cause, and that he had also kept a low profile for fear of giving Houghton Mifflin the impression that he was a mere propaganda agent. In fact, though, he did find time to make quite a few public appearances, giving "several large-scale lectures on [his] standard theme" before charitable, business, civic, Jewish, and women's groups in New York City, Utica, Pittsburgh, Detroit, and Washington.

Arranging these engagements and advertising Jan's availability was Clark H. Getts, a prominent booking agent whose other clients included inspirational author Dale Carnegie. Reeves had put Karski in contact with Getts in April 1944, inaugurating a relationship through which Jan would make more than two hundred speeches in a year and a half. He was handsomely paid, usually earning five hundred dollars per lecture. When news came in August that the long-planned general uprising of the underground movement in Warsaw had begun, Jan was stung by guilt over his absence from the action, in which over 160,000 Poles were to die. His contribution to the war effort seemed pitifully inadequate. But at least he could take some small pride in the fact that he was carrying out his propaganda mission at such a low cost to the government.

Yet Karski was actually losing money on his lectures. He had cut a deal with Getts that was almost as unfavorable as his contract with Reeves, and then Reeves demanded a percentage of his lecture fees, since he had set Jan up with Getts. Thus, from every paycheck, Karski lost 40 percent to Getts and 20 percent to Reeves—before deducting his expenses, which came entirely out of his own pocket. As his speaking calendar filled, often with engagements far apart that required extravagant outlays for airline tickets and hotels, his losses mounted. Jan would eventually post a net loss of three thousand dollars on his speaking tours.

Still, Getts and Reeves were delivering as promised. Starting in September, Reeves placed excerpts from the forthcoming book or articles based on Jan's experiences in such major magazines as *The American Mercury, Collier's,* and *Harper's Bazaar.* Jan had also written stories for *Life* and the *Jewish Forum* during the summer. And on balance, he could hardly complain about his financial situation. While still drawing five hundred dollars each month in salary from the government, he began collecting checks for the articles and advances against royalties from Houghton Mifflin. In October, when the Book-of-the-Month Club chose *Story of a Secret State* as its primary selection for January 1945, he collected a large windfall. Altogether, Jan cleared over eight thousand dollars from his writings alone in the autumn of 1944.

Getts too accomplished what Jan hired him to do. As the release date for the book drew near, the booking agent arranged several high-profile lecture dates for Karski. If Jan had any anxiety about speaking in front of large numbers of people in a foreign language (and with a very heavy accent), he got over it quickly at events such as the *New York Herald Tribune*'s annual "Builders of the World Ahead" forum. A huge crowd filled the ballroom of New York's Waldorf-Astoria Hotel for the symposium, held in mid-October. Preceding Karski at the podium was actress Shirley Temple; slated to speak just after him were Arkansas congressman J. William Fulbright and a young Army Air Corps trainee named Harris L. Wofford, each destined to serve in the United States Senate.

Jan gave his standard speech to the *Herald Tribune* forum's audience. "It has been the misfortune of our national history," he began by saying, "that for 150 years, much energy of every Polish generation must be sacrificed not to build roads, railways, factories, but to fight for Polish independence." He went on to outline the structure of the underground movement and the nature of his involvement in it. He told the stories of his capture in Slovakia and subsequent escape, his black-propaganda work at the Sławik estate, and his tour of the Nazi death camp. "I would like nothing better than to purge my mind of these memories," he said of the latter experience, "to obliterate from my mind the thought that such things ever happened."

Haunted by his memories, Jan took every opportunity to raise the subject of the Jewish tragedy in the course of his travels and encounters. During a brief swing through Canada in November 1944, he had dinner at the Montreal home of a Polish family named Brzeziński. A young boy sat quietly at the table, looking on in astonishment as Karski told of the extent of Hitler's genocidal campaign against the Jews.

"Are you saying there are no Jews left in Poland, that the small towns which used to have so many Jews are now, literally, devoid of Jews?" asked the boy's father.

"Yes," Jan said flatly, without elaboration.

Half a century later, former U.S. National Security Adviser Zbigniew Brzeziński would remember the exchange over his family's dinner table as "one of those moments when something is registered in memory, like a scar, and it stays there."

Given the number of accounts that had emerged from Europe of a systematic campaign by Hitler to exterminate the Jews under his control, it may be difficult for a later observer to imagine how any well-informed person could have failed to understand the Jews' fate. Jan was far from a lone voice publicizing the Holocaust; by late 1944, newspapers in Allied and neutral countries had carried news of it regularly for two years. Yet a survey conducted in December 1944 found only 27 percent of the American public willing to acknowledge that Jews in Europe were being subjected to a campaign of genocide. Only 4 percent believed that more than five million Jews had been murdered.

Perhaps alluding to this lack of comprehension, Jan told a reporter from the *New York Post* that he was appalled by the attitudes of many Americans he encountered. "They do not think of the war," he said, "and they do not believe much of what has happened. If those people there lived through those things, the least others can do is only please to believe them."

∼

Jan's increasingly public profile in the last months of 1944 made him vulnerable to criticism from Poles and Polish-Americans who opposed the government-in-exile. His notoriety even extended across the ocean, as he explained in a letter to a government minister:

Two of my friends wrote to me from London, reporting that I have been called a 'pessimist,' and maybe even 'pro-Russian,' with regard to our current political troubles. This opinion, if there is any truth to it, has shaken me very deeply. I could not sleep for several nights. Obviously I cannot defend my loyalty to the legal authorities of the underground movement or to the government, but I should think that I have given enough evidence during this war—to the last, literally to the final minutes, literally unto death—to prove that I am capable of being loyal and faithful to my authorities and government.

Karski had a genuine faith in prime minister Mikołajczyk's ability to effect a negotiated solution to the Soviet deadlock. Although he sensed that the outcome would be painful for Poland, he considered some compromise on the territorial issue necessary in order to preserve his nation's independence. There was little to prevent Stalin, after all, from making Poland another Soviet Socialist Republic. But when Jan publicly expressed his confidence in the London regime, he set himself in opposition to the opinions of a large segment of the Polish exile community.

That opposition led to a bitter exchange between Karski and Henryk Floyar Rajchman, one of Marshal Piłsudski's legionnaires and a prewar cabinet minister. Rajchman, who lived in the United States during the war, was a passionate opponent of the policies of Sikorski and later Mikołajczyk. Jan wrote to the former government official after hearing from a friend that Rajchman had denounced him before a crowd of Poles in Detroit, calling him "a scoundrel, a fake diplomat, living in luxury and acting to the detriment of Poland." Karski expressed his outrage, tried to defend himself (a little disingenuously—he mentioned his frugal living conditions but not the huge amounts of money he was making), and demanded an explanation.

Rajchman responded with a letter elaborating on his allegations. He berated Karski at length for "uttering the code words of capitulation to the Soviets" in his speeches. "You know that the government of Mikołajczyk not only does not represent the will of our country but actually obstructs that will," Rajchman wrote. "This government consciously falsifies information from the Homeland that criticizes its policy toward the Soviet Union. . . . The country demands an uncompromising stand from the government-in-exile. But the government demands capitulation from the country."

A few weeks after receiving this letter, Jan learned that Rajchman's point of view had prevailed in London. On November 24, 1944, just four days before the publication date of *Story of a Secret*

State, Mikołajczyk resigned from the government-in-exile. Stalin had rebuffed an offer from him that would have given the Soviets virtually all the land they wanted in eastern Poland except for the city of Lwów, and three out of the four political parties represented in the cabinet had rejected his last desperate attempts to fashion a compromise acceptable to the Soviets. Other moderates left the government with Mikołajczyk. The successor regime, dominated by hard-line rejectionists opposed to any accommodation with Stalin, lost all influence in Allied councils and became, in essence, the first in a series of powerless, symbolic governments-in-exile that continued to carry the standard of a free Poland until 1989.

Jan still preserved some faint hope that Mikołajczyk might find a way to rescue Poland from the abyss of communist domination. His faith in the deposed premier was so strong that he would have dropped everything he was doing to return to Poland, in the event that Mikołajczyk asked him to serve any government he might be able to form in coalition with the communists. (When Mikołajczyk did eventually return to the country, however, assuming a subordinate position as the token non-communist in a government controlled by Stalin, Karski did not follow him. After threats on his life, Mikołajczyk fled Poland in 1947, escaping in a truck that belonged to the American embassy.)

Developments in London placed Karski in the bizarre position of conducting a propaganda campaign on behalf of beneficiaries who could not be clearly identified. He did not fully represent the new government, whose personalities he either did not know or did not like, although he continued to draw a salary from that government through its embassy in Washington. He retained a personal loyalty to the former prime minister and to Ambassador Ciechanowski, who remained at his post despite his opposition to the new regime. And he continued to speak in the name of the Polish underground movement, or whatever remained of it after the debacle of the Warsaw uprising. (After holding out for sixty-three days despite Stalin's obstruction of Allied attempts to send aid to the besieged city, the fighters in Warsaw had surrendered to the Germans on October 2.)

Just as Jan was attempting to sort out his proper role at a moment when the cause of a free Poland was reeling on all fronts, he realized that with the upcoming publication of his book he had scored his country's greatest propaganda coup of the war. It was a hollow victory indeed.

~

From the moment of its release on November 28, *Story of a Secret State* immediately succeeded beyond the wildest dreams of Karski and his superiors. It became apparent within days that the book would reach a broader audience than the Poles had considered possible when Jan was dispatched to America nine months earlier.

Favorable reviews appeared in *Time, The New Yorker*, the *New York Times Book Review*, the *Washington Post*, the *Los Angeles Times*, and over a hundred other newspapers and magazines. Interviewing the author on his New York radio show, Bennett Cerf praised the book as "one of the most burning and unforgettable narratives I have ever read." In his syndicated column, Ed Sullivan called it a "great story" that would make readers "feel closer to the headlines." The *Saturday Review of Literature* lauded it as "one of the finest books to emerge from World War II."

Only a minority of reviewers seized on any flaws in the text. A writer in Omaha, unknowingly criticizing the rewriting effort of the book's various editors rather than Jan's own work, called it "overwritten" and "monotonous," commenting that "Mr. Karski is so determinedly 'literary' that he blunts a story that needed no frills." Another reviewer found the writing style "pedestrian at times," but still thought that "the content eclipse[d] the defect." Edward Weeks of *Atlantic Monthly* wrote that "the story of Poland's torture and redemption should be one of the epics of our time, but this gray, foggy, fragmentary record leaves me cold."

Spurred on by what *Publisher's Weekly* termed a "big ad campaign," sales of the book took off. Houghton Mifflin's run of fifty thousand copies sold briskly, as did an additional 350,000 printed for the Book-of-the-Month Club. Reeves soon found publishers for foreign editions in Great Britain, France, Norway, and Sweden, and a Popular Library paperback edition appeared later. Although *Story of a Secret State* never appeared on the bestseller lists, it posted enough sales to yield $100,000 in royalties for Reeves and Karski to split in 1945.

A lengthy book tour began on December 1, and Jan stayed almost constantly on the road for the next six months. The cities went by in a blur: Galveston, Topeka, Oklahoma City, New Orleans, Charlotte, Rochester, Hartford, Indianapolis, Toledo, and on and on—speaking to a group of executives one day, a chamber of commerce the next, a church or synagogue the day after, a book club the following week. He had become, as he later liked to say, a "professional hero." It was a lonely grind.

Karski was not as alone as he thought, however. As he attracted more and more public notice, he came to the attention of the Foreign Nationalities Branch (FNB) of the Office of Strategic Services. The OSS was not burdened by the legislative mandate that forbids its successor, the Central Intelligence Agency, from conducting surveillance operations in the United States. The Foreign Nationalities Branch, headed by a right-wing Republican named DeWitt Poole, existed solely to monitor the activities of individuals (regardless of whether they were American citizens) and organizations with ties to certain ethnic backgrounds. A staff of analysts for the branch combed through émigré-oriented and foreign-language publications produced in the United States; a network of informants kept it posted on activities involving foreigners and Americans with "foreign-sounding" names.

The Foreign Nationalities Branch officials who tracked Karski appear to have been unaware that he had been in contact with most of the top officers of the OSS during his secret mission in 1943. The FNB had first taken an interest in the purposes of his trip before he left England in February 1944—although OSS personnel in London told the branch they knew nothing about his intended travels. It caught up with Karski after his book was published and sent agents to report on at least two of his speaking appearances. Their reports include frank appraisals of his rhetorical style and political arguments, shedding light on dimensions of Karski's public efforts that are less evident in newspaper accounts of his lectures.

After Jan spoke before a Polish-American audience in Chicago on January 25, 1945, an agent noted that he had "delivered a lengthy address, which some of the guests found hard to follow because of his inadequate English. They liked his animation nevertheless," the observer added. This agent also included in his surveillance report a letter of protest Jan had written to the *Chicago Sun,* whose article on his appearance had referred to him as the "self-styled authoritative head of the Polish underground." Karski had accused the *Sun* reporter of disloyalty to the Allied war effort.

At Cleveland's Severance Hall two weeks later, about one thousand people turned out for Jan's lecture. The Foreign Nationalities Branch agent monitoring this event felt it relevant to comment that "quite a few negroes were present." He found Karski "a restrained but very effective speaker." Projecting a "restrained" appearance must have required some effort of will for Karski on the evening of February 12—the day Allied leaders announced the results of their conference at the Black Sea resort of Yalta. They had decided that the USSR should have all it wanted of eastern Poland. No Poles had been privy to the talks.

The American observer in Cleveland reported that Karski "devoted quite a bit of his time to the 'Jewish' cause" and seemed eager "to convince everybody that the Polish government-in-exile is not anti-Semitic." The agent went on:

> Karski stated that while the Poles lost quite a few people, the Jews in Poland, out of 3,500,000 people, lost 3,000,000. He told the audience that the Polish Jews deserve all the support they can get from the Americans. That the Americans should believe the Jewish leaders when they tell them about Poland['s] Jewish suffering. That he, Karski, is amazed that some Americans do not feel the Jewish propaganda. In fact he believes the Jewish leaders do not give the full picture of horror in what happened to the Jews in Poland.

~

The "full picture of horror" had not been revealed in detail by the Soviets, who had already liberated such mass-murder sites as Majdanek and Auschwitz. It began to emerge only after British and American troops stumbled upon German camps such as Bergen-Belsen and Dachau in April 1945. At that point, a wave of revulsion swept through England and the United States, dampening the giddy air of impending victory. Newspapers and politicians expressed shock that such things could happen in the twentieth century. Jan was not shocked.

In this time of bitter tidings, he wandered through a strange country and witnessed, in each day's newspapers, the final acts of a black pageant ending in utter and complete disaster for both Poland and the Jewish people. Jan continued his speeches. He knew of nothing else to do. But whenever he came off the road for a few days, he sought escape.

In Manhattan, where he kept an apartment, Karski could immerse himself in myriad diversions. There was always some entertaining way for him to part with a portion of his riches. Jan indulged a passion for music and dance, losing himself for a few hours on a Saturday afternoon at the Metropolitan Opera, or marveling at the spectacle of a Broadway musical. There, at least, one could still find a happy ending.

His favorite show, one he had seen a number of times since it opened in April 1944, was *Fancy Free*, a ballet about three sailors on leave in New York and three girls they meet as they carouse. Jan, tremendously impressed with the production's music, choreography, and dancing, was delighted to discover a little bistro near Carnegie Hall that was a late-night haunt for its cast members. He began frequenting the bohemian bar when he was in town. Soon he had introduced himself to *Fancy Free*'s composer and to the dancer who had choreographed the ballet—both of them young unknowns in the first flush of success.

Karski passed many a raucous evening in their company, well aware that they tolerated him mainly because he was buying the drinks, but nevertheless reveling in their irreverent attitudes and obscene backstage banter. Long after he had lost touch with them, he would retain fond memories of Jerome Robbins and Leonard Bernstein, the drinking buddies who had helped him forget his miseries for a few brief moments.

～

As the war in Europe ended in May 1945, Karski's gravy train began to grind to a halt. Reeves and Getts began to look upon him as a commercial liability as his public profile became more and more transparently anti-Communist. This was an unavoidable transition, after Soviet occupation forces in "liberated" Poland had seized sixteen of the underground's top leaders whom they had invited to a negotiating session. Jan could hardly fail to denounce the treachery of the arrest and subsequent Moscow show trial of the only political leaders in a position to oppose Stalinist rule in Poland. To his agents, however, Karski's comments were just a sour distraction from the euphoria of V–E Day—which Jan had spent in Times Square, marveling at the pandemonium, his own celebration more muted.

A hostile analysis of *Story of a Secret State*, published in the magazine *Soviet Russia Today*, further diminished Jan's star value. A publication sponsored by America's ally did carry some weight in public opinion, even though many Americans already had grave misgivings about that ally. The review denounced Karski as an aristocrat with inadequate feeling for the working man. It echoed Stalinist propaganda aimed at Poland earlier in the war, which had made much of the alleged irresponsibility of the London-directed underground and the suffering of ordinary Poles under the German policy of collective responsibility. It even implied that Karski must have been an anti-Semite, since he had dealings with Polish nationalists. And the article seized upon his statements in the wake of the Yalta agreement, which he had termed "another Munich for Poland." Attacking him as misinformed and naive, it concluded, not inaccurately: "He is now but an instrument of the propaganda apparatus of the London government-in-exile."

Karski's public-speaking engagements dwindled immediately. "It killed me," he later recalled. Ironically, though, the taint of controversy had the immediate effect of making him somewhat more in demand among anti-communist audiences. For a few weeks, he received a steady stream of engraved invitations to elegant dinners for large numbers of guests at the homes of people with names like Dupont and Vanderbilt. But there he was certainly preaching to the converted; the socialites at these events were naturally allied with the Poles against the communists in any case.

One moment from these encounters kept Karski chuckling for the rest of his life. An older woman, her hair dyed blond and elaborately coiffed, her neck, wrists, and fingers dripping pearls and rubies, leaned over toward Jan in the course of an exquisite banquet. "Oh, Mr. Karski, I'm just reading your book," she said. "What a book! I just came to the part where the Gestapo starts to torture you. Oh, what a beautiful, beautiful scene!"

Finally, Karski's paid engagements dried up entirely, leaving him with a puzzling plethora of invitations to high-caste cocktail parties. Only after attending a few of them, at which he generally shook hands with everyone in a receiving line and then was left to mope in a corner, did he learn how the system worked. There was a price on party talent among the rarefied echelons of the East Coast. Any hostess who wanted to attract a good crowd would retain the services of a charming, exiled aristocrat from Europe whose personal credentials were supposed to wow the invited guests. At the end of the evening, the hostess would slip a few large bills into the coat pocket of the hired luminary. But word had gotten around in society: Instead of discreetly hiring a stateless prince or baron to ornament a gathering, the nobility could retain Karski for free. He probably made better conversation, too.

In the midst of these dispiriting (if sometimes amusing) experiences, Karski discovered one meaningful and productive use for his talents. In May 1945, he had been approached by Hugh Wilson, a former American ambassador to Germany who had come out of retirement to spend the war with the Office of Strategic Services. Wilson set out to recruit Karski for a project hatched by the former Republican president of the United States, Herbert Hoover.

It had occurred to Hoover that the nations recently "liberated" by the Red Army might spend a long time under its yoke, and that during that time every effort would be made to falsify their wartime histories. Moreover, many of the documents revealing the true histories of those nations' governments-in-exile and underground movements were in danger of disappearing, either through intentional action or neglect. There was no way to preserve records in the countries themselves, but each had a government-in-exile in London and consulates and embassies throughout the world where copies of key documents would have been held. Hoover wanted to gather those papers in one safe place: the Hoover Institution on War, Revolution, and Peace at Stanford University, in Palo Alto, California.

After meeting with the former president, Karski wholeheartedly endorsed his idea. "Collection of these materials is very important for us, from a historical-political point of view," Jan argued in a June 1945 report to the authorities he still nominally served in London. He urged the government-in-exile to approve his travel and allow him to send to California whatever papers were available at Polish outposts in London, Paris, Rome, and other locales. Anticipating the government's assent, he made plans for a four-month European visit, to begin in July.

It was destined to be a successful hunting expedition. Jan would obtain most of the Polish documents he was after, as well as papers from Estonian and Latvian offices throughout the continent. Only when he approached Lithuanian officials would he come away empty-handed. Cordially, the Lithuanians said they would gladly cooperate with the Hoover venture—but they would not hand over their sensitive papers to a Pole. Polish-Lithuanian tension, which had simmered for centuries over contested borders and the Lithuanians' resentment over Polish domination, was too deep-rooted. From 1918 to 1938 there had been no diplomatic relations, or even mail service, between Poland and Lithuania.

The Hoover mission took on special symbolic importance because of what had happened just before Jan sailed for London. On July 5, 1945, the long death watch over the legitimate government of Poland came to an end. The United States withdrew recognition from the Polish government-in-exile in favor of the Soviet-backed rulers now firmly entrenched in Poland.

Karski, staying in Ciechanowski's home in Washington at the time, accompanied the diplomat to the embassy. The ambassador called the staff together and delivered the news. Although recognition had been withdrawn, he said, all staffers were free to stay at their jobs—if they were willing to work for the new "government of national unity." Ciechanowski announced that he would abandon his post. He polled the staff members. Karski and the other Poles stepped forward, one by one, to announce that they would follow the ambassador's lead. The only two exceptions were employees in nonpolitical roles.

Ciechanowski did not wait around for the representatives of the Soviet-sponsored government to claim their prize. He took the keys to the embassy and rode to the State Department, there demanding to see a representative of the American government. He was received by Elbridge Durbrow, the young Polish-desk officer who had correctly divined Stalin's intentions toward Poland two years earlier. Regardless of his personal sympathies, Durbrow was sworn to uphold United States policy. He made no response as the ambassador first read a statement of protest, then dropped the keys on the desk. "I hereby cede our embassy," Ciechanowski said, "to the people responsible for what has happened to my country."

Even as he set out for newly liberated Europe, on a mission to collect scraps of paper attesting to the sovereignty of the government he had unstintingly served, Jan had become a man without a country.

EPILOGUE

Silence Vowed, Silence Broken

Anonymity came easily. By the time Karski returned to the United States late in 1945, he was out of the public eye entirely. Amid the booming chaos of postwar America, he became just another European refugee, albeit a rather wealthy refugee. The people who had flocked to his speaking appearances a year earlier were now preoccupied with other concerns—finding homes, having babies, restarting interrupted lives.

Jan wanted to be forgotten. Once more enjoying the high life in New York, living in an apartment on Manhattan's Upper West Side, he felt the same urge as the Americans around him to leave the war behind. Beneath his devil-may-care persona, Karski was consumed with bitterness over the futility of his wartime efforts. He coped with his suppressed rage, and with the psychological trauma brought on by the horrors he had experienced, through an act of will: He forced the past out of his mind. Jan promised himself that he would never again speak about the war unless there was a compelling reason to do so, and that he would remain forever silent about his experiences involving the Jewish Holocaust.

"At that time I hated humanity," Karski later remembered. "I broke with the world." He felt that if he had lived in another time and place, he would have cloistered himself in a monastery. "I imposed on myself a pledge never to mention the war to anybody," he said.

Like so many who had survived the conflagration, Jan turned his attention to matters of home and hearth. Not long after his return from Europe, he was introduced to the daughter of a South American diplomat. A relationship quickly developed, and they were soon married. The marriage came to an end, however, after less than two years.

Alone again at the age of thirty-four, Jan began casting about to find a new direction for his life. He called on his old mentor, former ambassador Ciechanowski, for career advice. All three of the options Ciechanowski came up with involved contacts from Jan's war years. Jan's first aspiration was to work for the State Department. After all, he had always wanted to be a diplomat. Perhaps he could achieve that goal in the service of the United States, which he had come to see as the last bulwark against the seemingly unstoppable, demonic force of Soviet Communism.

Charles Bohlen, the senior diplomat who had been one of the first American officials Karski had met on his 1943 trip, told him a job could probably be arranged in the Eastern European division at the State Department. But there was a hitch. As a native of a now-Communist nation, Karski was ineligible under department rules for a high-level security clearance. Since many positions required top-secret clearance, he would reach a plateau early in the foreign service. The prospect of a dead-end job in government bureaucracy did not appeal to him.

Next on Jan's list was a job at the new United Nations. There too he could put his diplomatic training to work. He called on Helen Rogers Reid, vice-president of the *New York Herald Tribune*, who had introduced him to a large audience at the Waldorf-Astoria when he spoke before the newspaper's annual world-affairs forum in 1944. Reid, a key power broker with many friends in high places, confidently assured Karski that she could swing a staff appointment at the United Nations for him. But he would have to make one polite gesture in exchange for the job. Since he, as a Polish national, would technically be nominated by the Polish government, courtesy would require that he go to the Polish embassy and thank the Communist regime's ambassador for his assistance. When Jan flatly refused to have any such contact with the Stalinist regime running his Homeland, Reid withdrew her offer.

Finally, Karski went to see Father Edmund A. Walsh, regent of Georgetown University's School of Foreign Service, one of the most fervently anti-Communist Americans he had met in the course of his 1943 mission. Jan had toyed with pursuing a doctoral degree in political science before the war, and he was ready to reconsider the prospect of an academic career. Walsh gave him the bad news first: Jan's credits from Jan Kazimierz University in Lwów were worthless in the American system. He would have to complete all the course work necessary for a master's degree before he could even begin pursuing his doctorate.

But Walsh knew how the war had victimized Karski. He found a kindred spirit in the young Pole, a devout Catholic (if less so now than before the war) and fervent anti-Communist like Walsh himself. He offered Jan a scholarship covering full tuition at the School of Foreign Service, as well as two hundred dollars per month in financial aid for living expenses. This stipend was so generous that Karski was able to build up his savings from it; ex servicemen on the GI Bill, by contrast, received only sixty-five dollars a month. Jan commenced his studies in the spring of 1949.

Money had become a concern by this point. Years of living the good life had taken their toll on the nest egg he had socked away from *Story of a Secret State*'s profits. In 1949, he spent the last of his savings in a gesture of fraternal duty. Jadwiga and Marian Kozielewski had escaped from Poland in January 1946, apparently with American assistance. (Jan had appealed to his contacts at the State Department to help them get out, since a right-winger like Marian was sure to be a wanted man in Soviet-run Poland. They did receive help in their escape, but the stern and taciturn Marian never revealed precisely how and from whom.) Jan received letter after letter from his brother, who was living in Paris, insisting that the Red Army was sure to sweep across Western Europe soon. Marian was desperate to get across the Atlantic.

With refugee quotas full, the only way a Pole could settle in North America was to take advantage of a loophole in Canadian immigration laws that allowed foreigners to settle in that country if they owned and worked farmland there. Karski bought the farm, a scraggly fifty acres outside Montreal that came with two cows, a swaybacked horse, and a few dozen of what he recalled as "hysterical chickens." In 1949, Warsaw's former police chief and his urbane wife settled into this rustic abode.

The brother whom Jan loved and feared like a strict father, and the sister-in-law to whom he had always felt devoted, eventually settled in Washington. Marian became a night security guard at the Corcoran Gallery of Art. But he never reconciled himself to living in the United States, one of the countries that had, in his view, betrayed Poland to the communists. Bitterness over his nation's fate and his own consumed Marian. In 1964, he took his own life. Jadwiga lived under Karski's care until her death in 1989.

~

Dr. Jan Karski, a newly minted Ph.D., returned home from his graduation ceremony to find a note awaiting him. Father Walsh was inviting him to join the Georgetown University faculty as a lecturer. From that moment in 1953 until his official retirement in 1984, and afterward through several years of limited involvement, Karski would devote his professional life to Georgetown.

He "established himself as one of the really great professors at Georgetown," in the words of Peter F. Krogh, dean of the School of Foreign Service since 1970. Using his natural gift for communication to establish a rapport with his students, Karski became one of the most popular teachers on campus. Like many academics of his era, he put more effort into teaching than into research and scholarly publication. His command of the subject matter and his engaging manner of explaining it made him, according to Krogh, "a virtuoso performer in the classroom."

Karski's courses in comparative government and theory of Communism were nearly always oversubscribed, year in and year out. One School of Foreign Service student he did not teach was 1968 graduate Bill Clinton; thus Karski narrowly avoided becoming acquainted with a third United States president. In his later years on the faculty, Karski did have basketball star Patrick Ewing as a student.

Most of Professor Karski's students probably knew little or nothing about his past. *Story of a Secret State* was out of print, he would not voluntarily bring up his wartime exploits, and even his faculty colleagues generally had only a dim knowledge of what he had done during the war. Sometimes students who came across *Story of a Secret State* in the library would press him to tell war stories, but Karski would only grudgingly oblige.

During the 1950s, Jan mentioned his background only for a specific purpose—to denounce Communism. He portrayed himself to his classes and in occasional speaking engagements as a former prisoner of the Soviets, who had seen his native country stolen away by Stalin. Jan kept certain inconvenient sentiments to himself in this regard: the grudging respect he had felt for some Communists he met during the war, his relatively dovish stance toward Russia during the war, and the personal devotion he still felt toward the prime minister of Communist Poland, Józef Cyrankiewicz, who had helped to save his life.

The professor's fulminations against the Red Peril earned him the nickname "McCarthyski" from his students; Karski wore it with good humor and a little pride. He was actually connected with certain activities on the fringes of the 1950s Red Scare, but nothing he was later ashamed of. A crony of Senator Joseph McCarthy, Representative Charles Kersten (R-Wisc.), seized upon a hostile review Karski wrote in 1954 about a pro-Communist history of Poland, using it to condemn the author and Harvard University Press as Communist dupes. And Karski appeared before Kersten's Red-hunting committee later the same year, acting as translator for Józef Światło, a prominent Polish Communist who had recently defected. In neither case, however, did Karski himself take part in McCarthyite activities.

In 1954, Jan became a citizen of the nation to which he now demonstrated such loyalty. His naturalization involved one touchy aspect: his name. Technically, he had broken the law when he applied for an American visa in 1943 under the assumed name Jan Karski. Nazi war criminals had been (and would continue to be) deported from the United States for the same offense. A little concerned, Karski took up the matter with friends at the State Department, who helped him avoid a bureaucratic entanglement over the falsification. But when he then told the Immigration and Naturalization Service that he wanted to become a citizen under his true name, the agency balked. After all the trouble he had gone to in dealing with the issue of the false name, an agent said, Jan was really asking for too much. And why did he want to take a difficult-to-pronounce name like Kozielewski anyway?

Karski took an assimilationist approach to his immigrant experience. Though he could not shed his thick Polish accent, he worked hard to cultivate the attitude and image of a true-blue American. He did maintain contact with exiled Poles in the United States, Britain, and France, but he remained aloof from the ceaseless political machinations and personal antagonisms of Polish anti-Communist movements. His loyalty now lay with the United States.

Early in his Georgetown career, Jan discovered a way to make money that would have left him scandalized if he had been a professor at a Polish university. He began buying and renovating old houses in Washington, moving from one property to another in a rapidly gentrifying area south of the Capitol building. During summer vacations and the three days a week when he had no classes to teach, Karski took up a hammer. "Other teachers went fishing," he recalled with some satisfaction.

He learned carpentry, wiring, and other skills on the job. He lived in one of the apartments he subdivided (in violation of unenforced local codes) out of each nineteenth-century row house he worked on; Marian and Jadwiga always occupied another. Marian would castigate him for washing windows and painting gutters in broad daylight, condemning such labor as disgraceful behavior for a professor. But Karski's American colleagues, unburdened by old-world concepts of dignity, praised his hard work and can-do attitude—especially when they heard of the profits he was turning each time he sold one house and moved on to another.

~

Karski's missionary fervor against Communism impressed State Department officials, who approached him in 1955 with the idea of using this new citizen as an ambassador of the "American way of life." After wrangling an unscheduled leave from Georgetown, Karski departed in September 1955 on a four-month international lecture tour sponsored by the United States Information Service. His itinerary took him through South Korea, South Vietnam, Thailand, Cambodia, East and West Pakistan, India, Ceylon, Burma, the Philippines, and Turkey.

In 140 speeches, delivered in English before crowds of up to seven thousand people, Karski played his part in the United States struggle to win over hearts and minds in countries susceptible to Communist influence. He presented his successful immigrant experience as evidence of capitalism's superiority, while recounting the Soviet treachery that had deprived Poles and others of freedom. His mission may have struck some listeners as imperialistic, but they listened nonetheless. An American consul in East Pakistan (now Bangladesh) described the effect Karski had on a crowd in a provincial town: "Dr. Karski, leaving the platform at Jagganath, was followed outside by a great swarm of students and stood there discussing further points, completely lost to sight in the crowd."

U.S. authorities considered the mission successful, and they invited Karski to take on an even longer speaking tour eleven years later. Elaborating the same themes—but this time often facing more skeptical audiences full of sharp questions about the Vietnam War—he spent six months traveling throughout Asia, Africa, and the Mediterranean. From September 1966 until February 1967, Karski lectured in English and French in Japan, South Korea, Singapore, South Vietnam, Nepal, East and West Pakistan, India, Lebanon, Turkey, Greece, Tunisia, Algeria, the Congo, Cameroon, and Senegal. Again the State Department judged his efforts as quite successful; embassy officers described Karski's performances as "brilliant," "impressive," and "one of the intellectual events of the year."

This public work was not the only outlet for Karski's patriotic impulses. Given his rightist foreign-policy views, his wartime experience in clandestine operations, and the intertwining of America's academic world with its intelligence establishment, it is perhaps not especially surprising that Karski maintained ties with the Central Intelligence Agency and other secret services in the United States. This involvement dated back to 1945, when the Federal Bureau of Investigation invited him to lecture counterintelligence officers on the subversive methods of underground movements. It continued into his career at Georgetown: The first class he ever taught, on contract through the Pentagon, was a course on psychological warfare.

American propaganda operations burgeoned as the Cold War got under way; between 1948 and 1953, secret congressional appropriations for "information programs" ballooned from $20 million to $133 million. Karski had an opportunity to play a part in this growing business at a certain point in the 1950s, when the Department of Defense offered him a top position in its psychological warfare apparatus. Because the job was a presidential appointment, however, Jan shied away. In his words: "I didn't want to leave Georgetown for this job, then lose this job when the administration changed. Perhaps Georgetown would not take me back, and I would become a carpenter."

This was not the government's only offer, however. In 1956, Karski took on a high-level analysis project commissioned directly or indirectly by the CIA. In October and November 1956, a spirit of defiance had swept through the populations of Hungary and, to a lesser extent, Poland, culminating in a change of Communist leaders in Poland and a full-scale revolt against Soviet domination in Hungary. With a presidential election campaign under way in the United States, rhetoric from some American quarters seemed to suggest that U.S. troops would move to support the Hungarian revolutionaries against the Red Army. But President Dwight D.

Eisenhower, in no mood to start World War III, stood aside as Soviet troops brutally crushed one of the most serious challenges to Russian hegemony in Eastern Europe between 1945 and 1989.

In the immediate aftermath of the Hungarian debacle, some Hungarians and other observers cast blame on Radio Free Europe—a "liberation"-oriented broadcast service, supposedly independent, whose funding by the CIA was the worst-kept secret in Washington. It was alleged that the Hungarian broadcasts of Radio Free Europe had encouraged resistance to the Soviets and furthered the false impression that the United States would fight to defend Hungary from a Soviet clampdown. President Eisenhower took a personal interest in getting to the bottom of these charges, ordering an impartial review of the radio station's possible role in fomenting the Hungarian uprising.

Certain parties—he has never said exactly who—engaged Karski to write a report on this issue, closely analyzing broadcast scripts from the weeks before and during the doomed uprising. The report that Karski later described having written was identical in scope and substance to a document that CIA chief Allen Dulles sent to the White House on November 20, 1956. Whether this is the same report Karski wrote cannot be definitely determined. Its author concluded that Radio Free Europe "did not incite the Hungarian people to revolution," nor did it "offer hope that American military help would be forthcoming to the patriots." It did, however, go beyond its approved bounds on a few isolated occasions "in identifying itself with the Hungarian patriot aims, and in offering certain tactical advice to the patriots."

Always careful to keep secrets and not wanting to appear to brag about cloak-and-dagger exploits, Karski spoke in later life about this assignment only guardedly, and only after learning that documents concerning the matter had been declassified. There are indications that Karski performed other services for American covert-operations authorities, again involving propaganda, but he did not reveal the nature of any other activities he may have undertaken.

~

As middle age encroached on Karski—he turned forty in 1954—his myriad activities in intelligence, real estate, and academia did not occupy all his attention. One evening in the mid-1950s he attended a modern dance performance at a Washington synagogue. He had been attracted by the marquee performer, a dancer he had first seen in London when he was a young diplomatic apprentice in 1938. The dancer was Pola Nirenska.

Born Pola Nirensztajn in 1910, the dancer had made a name for herself at an early age as an avant-garde performer. Her father, a Jewish traditionalist, was horrified at her career path; in his eyes, her barefoot style of dancing was every bit as scandalous as prostitution. But Pola persevered, and by the late 1930s she was performing throughout Europe. When the war came, she took refuge in England. Her parents escaped to Palestine. But most of her brothers and sisters perished in the Holocaust.

Pola had little opportunity to make a living in England during and after the war. In 1949, she left London for New York, arriving with only twenty dollars and a suitcase. She took a job as a dishwasher at an Italian restaurant, where she was allowed to eat all she liked of each day's leftovers. She ate little else for the next two years. Later in life, she would absolutely refuse to do two things: wash dishes and eat Italian food.

Eventually her talents became known in New York, and Pola benefited from the generosity of wealthy arts patrons who pitied her for the dire financial circumstances she was enduring. She began teaching dance in New York, then moved to Washington, where she finally scraped up enough money to open a dance studio. She was struggling along with a loyal cadre of students but little income when she first met Karski.

He found her address and wrote her a note after seeing her dance at the synagogue. Jan told Pola how much he admired her performance. He floated the idea of a date. He heard nothing from her. After a few weeks, he found her telephone number and called to invite her to dinner. She agreed to meet him—but only for lunch.

By 1956 they were often together, notwithstanding the radically opposite views they had of that year's presidential race. Jan was campaigning for Eisenhower in Polish neighborhoods, an "I Like Ike" button constantly on his lapel. Pola was intensely loyal to Democrat Adlai Stevenson. She told Karski that in a fascist-leaning, racist society like the United States, she was willing to go as far to the right as Stevenson—but that anybody more conservative must be a fascist.

They waited until 1965 to wed, and then settled into a comfortable married life. They spoke English around the house, although Pola preferred the Polish "Jan" or "Jasiu" to the form of address most of his colleagues and English-speaking friends adopted, "John" or "Johnny." Karski was a doting husband, very supportive of her increasingly successful career as a dance teacher and choreographer. A few years after their marriage, they moved into a spacious house near the Georgetown campus, decorated with tasteful but progressive artwork (much of it by mutual friends like Felix Topolski) and featuring a basement studio with a heated floor for Pola and her dancers.

By the early 1970s, Karski had become a well-known fixture at Georgetown. Strolling the campus with his omnipresent cigarette, "he struck a very dignified figure," recalled Peter Krogh. He walked or rode the bus to work—a truly urban creature, Jan had never developed any taste for driving cars.

Unbeknownst to all but Pola and his closest faculty associates, Karski had one as-yet-unfulfilled professional ambition. He felt that there was a need for a comprehensive history of Poland's relations with the more powerful states that had always exercised control over its destiny. In 1974, he received a Fulbright scholarship to pursue such a project. His work took him back to Poland for the first time since the war, on a research trip lasting several months. He spent one memorable evening of this visit in the company of Józef Cyrankiewicz, in an encounter that must have left both the anti-Communist American professor and the retired prime minister of Communist Poland with mixed emotions. The men reminisced warmly, if guardedly, until three in the morning.

Karski worked for another decade on his magnum opus, which would finally be published in 1985 as *The Great Powers and Poland: 1919–1945*, earning the author widespread acclaim in academic journals. As he taught his classes, sifted methodically through documents, and churned out drafts of the book, his wife continued to build her reputation in the world of dance. They vacationed throughout the world and quietly enjoyed their modest affluence at home. Jan took pleasure in giving Pola a materially comfortable life, after all that she had endured for her art in the past. There was an air of bourgeois normalcy about their existence, almost as though the war had never touched their lives.

~

But the past did not remain buried. As those who had lived through the Holocaust aged, and as their children grew old enough to seek some understanding of the unfathomable, more and more survivors began breaking the silence. Books analyzing and reminiscing about Jewish life and death under the Nazi terror appeared with increasing frequency in the 1970s and 1980s. Jews and non-Jews alike pondered the meaning, the ultimate impact on humanity, of this most profound crime against humanity.

By the late 1970s, Karski still harbored no more enthusiasm for speaking out about his experiences than he had felt in prior decades. But the persistence of a Jewish filmmaker from France would compel him to cast aside his vow of silence. Claude Lanzmann first approached Karski in 1977 with the idea of including him in a documentary that would tell the story of the Holocaust as it had never been told, relying solely on the testimony of witnesses, victims, and perpetrators. Lanzmann set out his epic aspirations in letters and telephone calls for over a year, refusing to accept Karski's refusal to "go back," as the professor often put it—to confront the cruel past, to bare his psychological wounds before a camera.

In a July 1978 letter, Lanzmann addressed the subject of Polish passivity toward the Final Solution. The tone of the note suggests that the filmmaker, unaware that Karski was not a Polish chauvinist, felt a need to reaffirm his lack of any anti-Polish bias. In English, Lanzmann wrote:

> The official Polish point of view on this issue—and I agree personally very much upon it—is that if there is any guilt of non-assistance to persons in danger, this guilt is to be found much more in the attitude of the Western World than in the Polish one. I was very much impressed during this inquiry in Poland, when I discovered how many Poles endangered their lives in order to help the Jews. As you know, this question of rescue will be one of the major items of my film, and this is the reason why your testimony will be so important.

Lanzmann also promised Karski he would not be drawn into political discussions or assessments of broad issues, which Karski wanted to avoid. These assurances, as well as Lanzmann's insistence that Karski had a historical responsibility to appear in the film, finally persuaded him to cooperate. Lanzmann and his crew spent two days at Karski's home in October 1978. The film they shot depicted Karski in an extreme state of mental agitation even before the interview could get under way. "Now I go back thirty-five years," he said to Lanzmann, his voice distant. "No," he then said, bursting into tears, "I don't go back." Haltingly raising himself from his seat, Karski fled down a hallway.

After he returned, Lanzmann questioned him at exhaustive length—four hours the first day and four hours the next. Pola, unable to bear the tension, left the house.

In 1985, Lanzmann finally released his film, *Shoah*, taking the title from the Hebrew term for the Holocaust. At more than nine hours in length, it was indeed an epic. Portions from the interview sessions with Karski took up about forty minutes of the finished work. Yet the only topic covered during that time was what Karski witnessed in the Warsaw Ghetto. Lanzmann edited out most of Karski's reminiscences about his efforts to alert the world to the Jewish catastrophe. In fact, the entire documentary made almost no mention of efforts by Poles to aid Jews. The "question of rescue" was not, as Lanzmann had promised Karski, "one of the major items" of the film, nor even a minor item. *Shoah* was replete, however, with images of Polish anti-Semitism, including interviews with Polish peasants and others who recalled the extermination of the Jews in their midst without remorse, some even expressing satisfaction with what had happened.

Many Poles and Polish-Americans reacted with outrage. The Polish-American Congress denounced the film for presenting "a narrow, one-sided view of the Polish people as anti-Semites, to a degree which hardly distinguishes them from the German Nazis." Rancorous arguments about *Shoah* appeared in many publications over the course of several months.

The controversy put Karski in a difficult position. However reluctantly and unwittingly, he had played a part in a film that was accused of defaming the Polish people. But he genuinely admired Lanzmann's work nonetheless. At a time when some of his friends and admirers in the Polish exile community were publishing bitter diatribes against Lanzmann, Karski authored an article in which he declared that *Shoah* was "unquestionably the greatest movie about the tragedy of the Jews."

In the article, published in English, French, and Polish in various publications, Karski wrote that he understood why the "rigorous construction" of Lanzmann's film prevented him from dealing with any subject other than the actual process of the extermination of the Jews. He understood the need Lanzmann felt to demonstrate that "the Jewish Holocaust was *unique* and *incomparable*." Karski made clear that he would have preferred to see Lanzmann use the portions of their interview that dealt with his mission to the West, but he refrained from condemning the movie. Instead, he called for the making of an "equally great, equally truthful" film that would present "a second reality of the Holocaust . . . not in order to contradict that which *Shoah* shows but to complement it."

Claude Lanzmann was not the only student of the Holocaust to "discover" Karski. Elie Wiesel, a survivor of Auschwitz, had become one of the foremost interpreters of the Nazi genocide; in 1986, he would be awarded the Nobel Peace Prize for his efforts. In 1980, Wiesel was preparing a Washington conference on the Holocaust when he learned by accident that there was a Jan Karski on the faculty at Georgetown University. His call to the professor set in motion a series of events that would thrust Karski further into the public spotlight in coming years.

In October 1981, the International Liberators' Conference, coordinated by Wiesel and sponsored by the United States Holocaust Memorial Council, brought together former soldiers from the United States, Britain, and the Soviet Union who had taken part in the liberation of Nazi camps. Top officials from several governments were in attendance as well. But the star of the show was Karski, who spoke publicly about his Jewish mission for the first time since 1945.

"There was laughter when he imitated Roosevelt, and there were tears when he described the Warsaw Ghetto and its misery," Wiesel later recalled. "He received an ovation when he spoke of his vow never to forget what he had been allowed to observe." Wiesel summed up his reaction to Karski's reemergence succinctly. "Jan Karski: a brave man?" he wondered. "Better: a just man."

In concluding his remarks, Karski bared emotions he had suppressed for more than three decades. He made it clear that he was now ready to "go back," to commit himself to the cause of remembrance:

> The Lord assigned me a role to speak and write during the war, when—as it seemed to me—it might help. It did not.
>
> Furthermore, when the war came to its end, I learned that the governments, the leaders, the scholars, the writers did not know what had been happening to the Jews. They were taken by surprise. The murder of six million innocents was a secret. . . .
>
> Then I became a Jew. Like the family of my wife—all of them perished in the ghettos, in the concentration camps, in the gas chambers—so all murdered Jews became my family.

But I am a Christian Jew. I am a practicing Catholic. Although I am not a heretic, still my faith tells me the second Original Sin has been committed by humanity: through commission, or omission, or self-imposed ignorance, or insensitivity, or self-interest, or hypocrisy, or heartless rationalization.

This sin will haunt humanity to the end of time.

It does haunt me. And I want it to be so.

After the speech, two Israelis introduced themselves to Karski. One was Gideon Hausner, who had served as state prosecutor of Adolf Eichmann. The other was Yitzhak Arad, director of the Yad Vashem Martyrs' and Heroes' Remembrance Authority, Israel's official agency for commemoration of the Holocaust. "Professor Karski," said Hausner, "you will come to Israel."

~

Jan and Pola traveled to Jerusalem in June 1982, just as Israel's war with Lebanon was erupting, for a three-week visit sponsored by the Israeli government. Along the Avenue of the Righteous, leading to the Yad Vashem memorial, he planted a tree bearing his name. At the memorial, on a hill overlooking the holy city, he spoke of his past efforts and of the brighter future represented by the State of Israel.

He was presented with a medallion recognizing him as one of the "righteous among nations" in honor of his wartime labors on behalf of the Jews. Inscribed on the medal are these words from the Talmud, the book of Sanhedrin: "He who saves one life rescues humanity, just as a murderer destroys the principle of life itself."

In the years following this ceremony, Karski practically made a career of collecting awards. At a pace rivalling that of his exhausting 1945 book tour, he traveled throughout the United States, Canada, Britain, Poland, Sweden, and Denmark, addressing crowds of admirers and receiving honors great and small. He accepted honorary degrees from three American universities, citations from three state legislatures, the Pope Pius XI Award of B'nai B'rith and the Archdiocese of Washington, the Eisenhower Liberation Medal of the U.S. Holocaust Memorial Council, the American Liberties Medallion of the American Jewish Committee, and numerous other awards. Even after he swore off all further engagements in 1991, Jan was lured into accepting more: In 1993, at the age of 79, slowed by painful arthritis, he traveled twice to Poland and once to Australia, the latter representing the last continent he had not previously visited.

Most but not all of the groups inviting Karski to speak or bestowing honors on him were Jewish-oriented. Others were Polish, Catholic, interfaith, or nondenominational. Though he always emphasized the uniqueness of the Jewish tragedy, Karski's message was not sectarian in nature. His new legions of "fans" lauded him and listened to him because of something more universal that he represented. Michael Berenbaum, project director of the United States Holocaust Memorial Museum, told the audience at one award ceremony that "Jan Karski has redeemed the image of humanity precisely at the moment when by his very being, by his heroic deeds, he indicts the image of humanity."

Pola, still traumatized by her family's experience of the Holocaust, was uncomfortable with her husband's newfound fame and could not bear to hear him speak of the past. She did not approve of his departures on the lecture circuit. In her inimitably gruff but affectionate manner, she would tell Jan: "You did what you had to do. Now shut up. You shouldn't blow your own horn. You've turned into an actor, worse even than Reagan."

It was partly in deference to Pola's needs that Karski began withdrawing from the public eye by the end of the 1980s. Despite a lifelong habit of heavy smoking, he had maintained reasonably good health. But she had suffered from heart problems and other painful ailments chronically since the 1970s. She needed his support. Ever the devoted husband, he took her to European spas and made every other effort possible to keep her comfortable. She poured much of her remaining energy into a choreographic project in which she finally grappled, through the medium of dance, with her feelings about the Holocaust. The performances met with enthusiastic reviews.

Pola Nirenska Karski died in July 1992. In her memory and as his legacy, Karski established two permanent annual awards out of his life's savings—one for promising dancers, the other for authors depicting the contributions of Jews to Polish culture and science.

In 1989, after the peaceful, parliamentary collapse of Poland's Communist administration, the Polish government-in-exile surrendered the regalia of the Polish state to President Lech Wałęsa. At last, all Poles in the world could recognize a regime in Poland as the legitimate government of the Polish people.

In 1991, Karski returned to a Poland finally free of conquering powers, receiving an honorary doctorate from Warsaw University and lecturing for the State Department once more. He enjoyed the trip, but was not overly emotional about it: He had long ago become an American. Still, he must have felt a certain satisfaction, if not vindication, at finally having his wartime efforts recognized in the land of his birth.

He himself now took an unorthodox view of those exertions and of the entire underground struggle. "Did we not demand too much from the nation, and from ourselves?" he asked in his speech at Warsaw University. What good had it done, he wondered, for three million ethnic Poles to lay down their lives in adherence to a strict principle of noncollaboration with the enemy? "Hungary, Romania, Slovakia, Croatia—they fought alongside the Third Reich," he noted, and they came out no worse off than Poland. "In every other country occupied by the Germans, there was a government submissive to the occupant, but it was also a government that attempted to salvage whatever was possible," said Karski. He cited the example of the French government's decision not to defend Paris from the Nazi onslaught, for fear of bringing about the revered city's destruction.

The honoree contrasted Paris, which "emerged in all its magnificence," with Warsaw, which "collapsed in hunger and ruins. Glory to the heroes of Warsaw, who fought to liberate it," said Karski. But was ancient Warsaw wholly the property of its population and defenders? "Warsaw was built by ten generations, and those generations also had a right to express their opinions," lectured Karski. "Should Warsaw have been exposed for destruction? Unfortunately, those generations could not speak. But in France they spoke."

The former underground member voiced doubts about his native land's tradition of rebellion. "Every Polish uprising in the nineteenth century was a disaster. Still, every generation takes up a new revolution," he said. "They rose up to keep Poland from being Russified, to keep Poland from being Germanized. Yet the Slovak nation was under Hungarian domination for a thousand years. The Czechs were under Austrian domination four hundred years. In Serbia, Bulgaria, and Romania, Turkey ruled for 450 years. And none of those nations lost its national identity. All of them survived. Why were we so afraid that the Poles would lose their national identity? History proves that to denationalize a nation that lives on its own territory is impossible. But to murder a nation, to destroy its cities, churches, libraries, and schools—this can be done. This," Karski concluded, "was the fate of Poland."

In April 1993, Karski returned to Poland again, traveling to Warsaw with U.S. Vice President Albert Gore to take part in commemorations of the fiftieth anniversary of the Warsaw Ghetto uprising. Karski walked over the area of the former Ghetto, tears welling in his eyes. He sat in a place of honor as a monument was dedicated to Szmul Zygielbojm, who had taken his life in despair over what he had learned about the extermination of Jews in Poland—including the news he had heard from Karski. President Wałęsa singled Karski out for special notice in his speech.

Martin Peretz, publisher of *The New Republic* magazine, was another member of Gore's delegation. As the Polish president spoke, he noted the reaction of the Poles and Jews assembled for the ceremony. "Karski is one of 'the righteous among the nations,' " wrote Peretz, "and when Wałęsa mentioned that he was in our midst, the crowd's sudden hush indicated that the people knew we were in the presence of one of those obsessives whose obsessions make him both brave and good."

∼

On May 12, 1994, in a ceremony at the Israeli Embassy in Washington, Jan Karski was made an honorary citizen of the State of Israel.

Glossary of Names

Angers. French city that served as seat of Polish government-in-exile, October 1939–June 1940. Karski arrived there early in 1940.

Bartoszewski, Władysław. Young underground member introduced by Karski to Zofia Kossak in 1942; became a leading activist in Kossak's "Konrad Żegota Committee," dedicated to saving Jews. After the war, Bartoszewski wrote several historical works concerning Polish responses to the Holocaust. President Lech Wałęsa later appointed him ambassador to Austria.

Beck, Józef. Polish foreign minister in the years leading up to the German invasion of September 1939. Karski worked for the Ministry of Foreign Affairs during this period. Beck's overconfident foreign policy brought him intense criticism after the Blitzkrieg.

Bełżec. Town in eastern Poland that Karski passed through in 1940 and where he later reported witnessing a Nazi death camp in operation. There was a camp at Bełżec where over five hundred thousand Jews perished, but the horrors Karski witnessed actually took place in Izbica Lubelska, a transit camp integral to the operation of Bełżec.

Biddle, Anthony J. Drexel, Jr. American ambassador to Poland until September 1939; ambassador to the Polish government-in-exile in France and later in England; first met Karski in February 1943 in London. Biddle may have played a role in suggesting Karski's 1943 trip to the United States and in arranging his audience with President Roosevelt, who was a close friend of the ambassador.

Bielecki, Tadeusz. Leader of the Polish National Party in exile. Karski carried political messages to and from him in 1940 and 1942 despite personal reservations about their right-wing content.

Bund. Jewish socialist political movement which took an active role in organizing the Warsaw Ghetto's resistance; led during the war by Leon Feiner in underground Poland and by Szmul Zygielbojm in exile.

Ciechanowski, Jan. Polish ambassador to the United States during the war; arranged Karski's meetings with Roosevelt and others during secret visit to Washington in 1943; took a paternal interest in Karski, having just lost one of his own sons in the war.

Cyrankiewicz, Józef. Leader of Polish socialists in Kraków; helped to arrange Karski's escape from Gestapo custody in Nowy Sącz. Karski later collaborated closely with him in Kraków. Arrested in 1942, Cyrankiewicz survived captivity at Auschwitz. He later embraced Communism and served as prime minister of Poland in the 1950s.

Delegate. The top-ranking civilian officer of the Polish underground movement, a position held by Cyryl Ratajski until just before Karski left Poland in the fall of 1942.

Donovan, William J. ("Wild Bill"). Director of the U.S. Office of Strategic Services, forerunner of the Central Intelligence Agency; met with Karski in August 1943.

Durbrow, Elbridge. Official of State Department's Polish desk who took note of Ambassador Biddle's report on meeting with Karski; later met with Karski in Washington.

Easterman, A.L. British official of the World Jewish Congress who pressed the British government to take action after seeing Karski's report on the extermination of the Jews.

Eden, Sir Anthony (later Lord Avon). Foreign secretary of Great Britain during the war years; met with Karski twice in 1943; served as prime minister in the 1950s.

Feiner, Leon. Leader of the underground Jewish Socialist Bund movement in Warsaw; met with Karski in August 1942 and arranged his visits to the Warsaw Ghetto and a Nazi transit camp in Izbica Lubelska.

Frankfurter, Felix. Justice of U.S. Supreme Court; son of an immigrant Jewish family from Austria. When Karski told him, in July 1943, of the atrocities against Jews he had witnessed, Frankfurter responded: "I am unable to believe you."

Getts, Clark H. Booking agent who arranged Karski's American speaking engagements in 1944–1945.

Głód, Karol. Young underground member who took part in the action that freed Karski from Gestapo custody in Nowy Sącz; later captured and imprisoned at Auschwitz, where he died.

Göbbels, Josef. Chief of propaganda for Hitler's Nazi regime; in his diary, mocked the Allied proclamations about war crimes that followed Karski's arrival in England.

Gollancz, Victor. British publisher and Jewish activist; suffered a nervous breakdown after meeting Karski and hearing of the Nazi mass murders in Poland.

Göring, Hermann. Founder of the Luftwaffe and member of Hitler's inner circle. Karski saw him speak at a Nuremburg rally in 1935.

Himmler, Heinrich. Chief of the SS (*Schutzstaffel*, literally, "Defense Unit"); one of the principal architects of the Nazi extermination of Jews.

Home Army (*Armia Krajowa*, or AK). The military force of the Polish underground movement, known until early 1942 as the Union for Armed Struggle.

Hoover, Herbert. Thirty-first president of the United States (1929–1933); enlisted Karski at the end of the war to travel to Europe and gather documents for the Hoover Institution on War, Revolution, and Peace at Stanford University.

Hull, Cordell. American secretary of state until 1944; met Karski briefly in 1943.

Izbica Lubelska. Nazi camp in eastern Poland that Karski visited in August 1942 where he witnessed a horrible scene; functioned as a holding camp and looting station for transports of Jews on their way to Bełżec death camp.

Jenet, Józef. Sixteen-year-old underground member who took part in the action that freed Karski from Gestapo custody in Nowy Sącz; later captured and imprisoned at Auschwitz, where he died.

Jewish Fighting Organization (*Żydowska Organizacja Bojowa,* or ŻOB). Main underground group operating in Warsaw Ghetto; not yet fully active when Karski visited the Ghetto.

Jewish Military Union (*Żydowska Związek Wojskowy,* or ŻZW). Underground faction organized by right-wing Revisionist Jews in Warsaw Ghetto; assisted in logistics of Karski's visits to the Ghetto in August 1942.

Kanicki, Jan. False name adopted by Karski as he traveled in 1940.

Karski, Jan. False name first used by Jan Kozielewski as he traveled in 1940, often further concealing his true identity through other false names; became Kozielewski's "primary" identity after he reached England in November 1942. Because Karski had applied for a diplomatic visa in this name in 1943, he felt obliged to keep using it in the United States after the war, out of a lingering fear that he might be deported for having entered the country under false pretenses. He was unable to revert to his birth name when he was granted American citizenship in 1954.

Kąty. Site of the Sławik family's estate south of Kraków, where Karski spent seven months in security quarantine after his escape from the Gestapo.

Katyń. The most famous of several sites where Polish officers and civilians were massacred by Soviet secret policemen on the orders of Stalin. Over twenty thousand military officers, clergymen, lawyers, doctors, and other "bourgeois enemies" of Communism were put to death in the spring of 1940, including many who had been held with Karski at Kozel'shchina. After advancing German forces discovered the mass graves at Katyń in April 1943 and accused the Soviets of the crime, the Polish government-in-exile asked for an independent investigation by the International Red Cross, prompting Stalin to accuse the Poles of collusion with Hitler and to sever diplomatic relations with the Polish government-in-exile.

Kawałkowski, Aleksander. Leader of the Polish underground movement in France, composed largely of laborers and miners who were working in France on a migrant basis when the war broke out. Kawałkowski helped coordinate Karski's clandestine passage through France in October and November 1942.

Kirschenbaum, Menachem. Jewish underground leader; one of the few members of the General Zionist faction to attain prominence in the Warsaw Ghetto's underground movements. Kirschenbaum was probably the Zionist leader Karski met with Bund leader Leon Feiner.

Koestler, Arthur. German-born Jewish author of numerous well-known novels, including *Darkness at Noon.* Koestler met Karski in 1943 in London, where he scripted a BBC broadcast in Karski's name, arranged for Karski's story of genocide to be printed in a pamphlet together with contributions by Thomas Mann and Alexei Tolstoy, and wrote a novel with a protagonist modeled on Karski.

Komorowski, Tadeusz (pseudonym: "Bór"). General in the underground Home Army who helped to arrange Karski's escape from Gestapo custody in Nowy Sącz; later appointed commandant of the Home Army; led the failed general uprising of the underground in Warsaw, August–October 1944.

Korboński, Stefan. A leader of the Peasant Party within the underground who became chief of the Directorate of Civil Resistance, in charge of the underground justice system, morale operations, and other aspects of the underground struggle. Korboński met with Karski in 1940 and again in 1942 before his missions. He later lived in Washington, where he wrote several works of history concerning the underground movement.

Kossak (Kossak-Szczucka), Zofia. Catholic writer whose works had achieved world renown before the war. Despite her own prewar anti-Semitism and that of her associates, she formed the underground Front for the Rebirth of Poland largely as a pro-Jewish movement, then helped to form the Konrad Żegota Committee to save Jews. She survived imprisonment at Auschwitz. Kossak exercised a profound spiritual influence over Karski, who was a member of the Front for the Rebirth of Poland.

Kot, Professor Stanisław. Interior minister, ambassador to the Soviet Union, and minister of information for the Polish government-in-exile during the war. Kot closely supervised Karski's visit to France in 1940 and, after becoming minister of information in July 1943, oversaw much of Karski's activity in the United States.

Kozielewska, Jadwiga. Sister-in-law of Jan Karski; wife of Marian Kozielewski.

Kozielewska, Laura. Sister of Jan Karski who briefly and reluctantly took him in after he escaped from captivity in 1939. Her husband Aleksander was tortured and executed by the Germans in the early weeks of the war. Laura died just after the end of the war.

Kozielewski, Jan. Birth name of Jan Karski.

Kozielewski, Marian. Brother of Jan Karski, eighteen years his elder. Marian used his influence as a top police official and member of the prewar ruling elite to help Jan launch a diplomatic career. After the war started, he initiated his younger brother into the underground movement. Arrested in 1940, Marian spent several months in Auschwitz but was released and reentered the underground movement. As the war went on, the brothers drifted apart over political differences. After the war, Jan helped Marian escape from Poland and settle first in Canada and later in the United States.

Kozielewski, Stefan and Walentyna. Parents of Jan Karski. Both died before the war.

Krauze, Father Edmund. Priest at Warsaw's Church of the Holy Cross; involved in underground activities. Karski met Marian at this church in 1939. Krauze said a secret mass for Karski before his departure to the West in 1942.

Kucharski, Witold. True name of Karski's friend from Lwów who escaped to France early in the war; false name adopted by Karski as he traveled in 1940. "Witold" became Karski's standard appellation in the underground.

Kwaśniewski, Jan. False name used by Karski in meetings with some British officials in late 1942 and early 1943.

Landau, David John ("Dudek"). Member of Jewish Military Union who escorted Karski through tunnel under Muranowska Street to enter the Warsaw Ghetto.

Langrod, Bronisława. Activist in Kraków wing of socialist underground movement. Karski lived in a room of her apartment briefly in 1941.

Lanzmann, Claude. French filmmaker whose nine-hour 1985 documentary *Shoah* generated controversy about Poles' responsibility in the Holocaust. Karski appears in the movie for approximately forty minutes.

Law, Richard. Parliamentary secretary for foreign affairs in Churchill's government during the war; received Karski's report on atrocities in November 1942 and later met with Karski himself.

Lerski, Jerzy. Friend of Karski from Jan Kazimierz University in Lwów; escaped to France and later became a courier at Karski's suggestion.

Librach, Jan. Senior Polish diplomat who accompanied Karski to some meetings in London early in 1943.

Makowiecki, Jerzy. Karski's immediate superior in the underground's Bureau of Information and Propaganda, 1941–1942; active in movement to shelter Jews. Makowiecki sent Karski on mission to rescue a Jewish couple. Karski was unaware of Makowiecki's Jewish heritage until his murder, apparently by Polish anti-Semites, in 1944.

Mikołajczyk, Stanisław. Interior minister and, from July 1943 until November 1944, prime minister of the Polish government-in-exile. Karski worked closely with Mikołajczyk and continued to believe Mikołajczyk would find a solution to the Polish-Soviet impasse even after his resignation from the government.

Musiał, Franciszek (pseudonym: "Myszka"). Guide who escorted Karski during his ill-fated second mission across Slovakia. Captured with Karski, Musial survived torture in Prešov and almost five years of imprisonment at Auschwitz.

Nirenska, Pola. Second wife of Jan Karski, married to him from 1965 until her death in 1992. Born Pola Nirensztajn, the daughter of middle-class Polish Jews, she took an interest in modern dance from an early age and had become prominent in European artistic circles before the war. Several of her brothers and sisters perished in the Holocaust. After spending the war years in England, she emigrated to the United States in 1949, working at first as a dishwasher in a New York restaurant. Within a decade, she owned her own dance studio in Washington, D.C., where she taught, performed, and choreographed for the rest of her life.

Nowak, Jan (born Ździsław Jeziorański). Courier who carried out missions to and from Poland after Karski arrived in England. After the war, having become an American citizen, he headed the Polish section of Radio Free Europe.

Nowy Sącz. Town in southern Poland; site of Karski's escape from German captivity.

Pilc, Tadcusz. High-school friend of Karski who became a left-wing activist in the underground in Kraków; captured in 1941; perished at Buchenwald the following year.

Piłsudski, Marshal Józef. Polish revolutionary leader whose cult of personality dominated political life in Poland between World War I and World War II; died 1935. Karski was raised to revere "Commandant" Piłsudski as "the father of the country."

Prešov. Town in Slovakia where Karski was held after his capture by Gestapo at village of Demjata.

Raczkiewicz, Władysław. Figurehead president of Polish government-in-exile. Karski carried a message to him from Polish Jews, asking him to press Pope Pius XII to condemn the Nazi extermination campaign.

Raczyński, Count Edward. Polish ambassador to Great Britain and acting foreign minister, 1941–1943; one of the most respected Polish leaders in the eyes of the Allies. Perhaps the longest-living senior statesman of any nation involved in World War II, he died in 1993 at the age of 102.

Retinger, Józef. Mysterious but trusted aide to General Sikorski, assigned to escort Karski to meetings in London.

Riegner telegram. An early account of the Nazi systematic plan to exterminate the Jewish race; sent from Geneva by Gerhart Riegner of the World Jewish Congress in August 1942, but not made public until November 1942.

Roosevelt, Franklin D. Thirty-second president of the United States; received Karski in the living quarters of the White House for a lengthy meeting on July 28, 1943.

Rowecki, Stefan (pseudonyms: "Grot," "Kalina"). Commander of the Home Army, the military wing of the Polish underground movement, from its inception in 1940 under its original name, the Union of Armed Struggle, until his capture on a Warsaw street on June 30, 1943. Held at the Sachsenhausen concentration camp until August 1944, he was then executed in retaliation for the underground movement's general uprising in Warsaw.

Ryś, Zbigniew. Leader of Home Army team that spirited Karski out of the hospital at Nowy Sącz.

Rysiówna, Zofia. Sister of Zbigniew Ryś; carried messages to and from Karski in Nowy Sącz hospital as his escape was being arranged.

Savery, Frank. British diplomat with specialty in Polish affairs; met secretly with Karski in December 1942.

Schwarzbart, Ignacy. Jewish member of the Polish National Council, a quasi-parliamentary body within the government-in-exile; also active on behalf of the World Jewish Congress in England with regard to Polish-Jewish affairs; met with Karski in 1942 and 1943, leaving detailed comments about Karski in his diary.

Selborne, Lord (Roundell Cecil Palmer, Third Earl of Selborne). Head of a British covert-operations division, the Special Operations Executive, under the cover title of Minister for Economic Warfare. Foreign Secretary Anthony Eden introduced Karski to Selborne in 1943.

Sikorski, General Władysław. Prime minister of the Polish government-in-exile and commander-in-chief of Polish armed forces, November 1939–July 1943; died in airplane crash at Gibraltar, July 4, 1943. Karski reported to him during his visits to France in 1940 and to England in 1943.

Siudak, Paweł. Polish interior ministry official who helped to coordinate Karski's activities during his visits to France in 1940 and to England in 1943. Karski lived with him for a while in London.

Sławik, Danuta. Young woman in the underground who hosted Karski at her family's remote estate during his quarantine period in 1940–1941; captured and executed soon after Karski left the estate.

Słowikowski, Jan. Doctor in Nowy Sącz hospital who took part in the conspiracy resulting in Karski's escape. Słowikowski soon fled Nowy Sącz and survived the war, but his brother Teodor was executed in retribution for the escape.

Sosnkowski, General Kazimierz. Polish military leader in exile and right-wing political figure; resigned from government in July 1941 but named commander-in-chief after Sikorski's death in July 1943. Karski reported to him in Paris during his 1940 trip and was tricked into a meeting with him in London in 1943, when Sosnkowski was out of power.

Staniszewski, Msgr. Władysław. Priest of Polish church in London. Karski gave him the consecrated Host he had worn around his neck while crossing Europe in 1942.

Starzyński, Stefan. Mayor of Warsaw at the time of the Blitzkrieg; chose to remain at his post under occupation instead of going into hiding. Starzyński was arrested in October 1939; died in German custody.

Świętochowski, Ryszard ("Pan Ryszard," or "Mr. Richard"). Political leader who attempted to assume command of Polish underground movement in 1940. When Karski failed to return immediately from France with Sikorski's blessing for the proposed command structure, Świętochowski set out for France himself and was captured. He died in captivity.

Świt. Secret radio station broadcasting from England into Poland, although seemingly emanating from within Poland. Karski advised the station's personnel during several visits to its facility outside London.

Szafran, Tadeusz. Young underground member who took part in the action that freed Karski from Gestapo custody in Nowy Sącz; later captured; executed at Biegonice, August 21, 1941.

Union for Armed Struggle (*Związek Walki Zbrojnej*, or ZWZ). Original name of the Polish underground movement's military force, known after early 1942 as the Home Army.

Walsh, Father Edmund. Jesuit regent of Georgetown University's School of Foreign Service (now named in his honor) when Karski began his academic career there.

Weinbergs. Jewish couple escorted by Karski from Warsaw (or possibly Otwock) to a hiding place on an estate near Puławy in eastern Poland. Despite Karski's rescue efforts, they perished after peasants on the estate denounced them to the Germans.

Wiesel, Elie. Survivor of Auschwitz who has written extensively about the meaning of the Holocaust; winner of 1986 Nobel Peace Prize. Wiesel helped to convince Karski to "go public" with his experiences in 1981, after many years of silence.

Wise, Rabbi Stephen. Founder of World Jewish Congress; foremost American Jewish leader during the war; met with Karski in August 1943.

Witold. Pseudonym regularly used by Karski within the Polish underground movement.

Zionism. Movement encompassing a broad spectrum of Jewish political thought, whose adherents were united by the common goal of establishing a Jewish state while often bitterly divided over the means to that end. Those divisions were reflected in differing reactions of Zionist factions to Nazi terror, ranging from accommodationism to unyielding resistance.

Znamirowski. Pseudonym occasionally used by Karski within the Polish underground movement.

Zygielbojm, Szmul. Leader of the Jewish Socialist Bund movement in exile. After meeting with Karski in London, Zygielbojm intensified his efforts to convince the Allies to take action on behalf of the Jews. In despair at the Western governments' failure to do so, he killed himself on May 12, 1943.

Sources and Notes

Abbreviations Used in Notes

AJA: American Jewish Archives, Hebrew Union College, Cincinnati; including:

    /WJCC: World Jewish Congress Collection

    /Waldman: Papers of Morris D. Waldman, chairman of the American Jewish Committee during the war years

AAN: Archiwum Akt Nowych (New Archival Collection), Warsaw

FDRL: Franklin Delano Roosevelt Library, Hyde Park, New York

HIA: Papers of Polish government-in-exile, Hoover Institution Archives, Stanford University, Palo Alto, California; including:

    /Karski: Jan Karski collection—documents related to Karski and compiled by him as he gathered documents under the direction of Herbert Hoover in 1945

    /MSZ: Ministerstwo Spraw Zagranicznych (Ministry of Foreign Affairs)

    /MSW: Ministerstwo Spraw Wewnętrznych (Ministry of Interior)

    /MID: Ministerstwo Informacji i Dokumentacji (Ministry of Information and Documentation)

    /Mikołajczyk: Papers of Stanisław Mikołajczyk, interior minister and later prime minister of the Polish government-in-exile

JPIA: Józef Piłsudski Institute of America, New York

K. Int(s).: Authors' in-person interviews with Jan Karski in Bethesda and Chevy Chase, Maryland, in December 1987, February 1992, June 1992, October 1992, May 1993, and October 1993, as well as numerous telephone interviews

LC: Library of Congress, Washington, D.C.

NA: National Archives, Washington, D.C.

PI: Polish Institute, London

PRO: Public Record Office, London

SPP: Studium Polski Podziemnej (Polish Underground Study Trust), London

Story: Jan Karski, *Story of a Secret State* (Boston: Houghton Mifflin, 1944)

YVA: Yad Vashem Archives, Jerusalem

A note concerning *Story of a Secret State*: Karski's own wartime account of his adventures is a valuable but often unreliable source. For security reasons, Karski was obliged to omit many details, distort some events, and include a substantial amount of misinformation about his own identity and the identities of

268

others in the underground movement. Diplomatic considerations also influenced the book, since Karski was not at liberty to divulge many of his contacts in London and Washington. And in accordance with the propagandistic interests of the Polish government and the commercial interests of his American publisher, Karski employed a certain degree of dramatic license in his writing. The authors have not used any information from this book without independently confirming its accuracy.

Preface

Falconi, Carlo. *The Silence of Pius XII*. New York: Little, Brown and Co., 1970.

Hamilton, Iain. *Koestler: A Biography*. New York: Macmillan, 1982.

Hochhuth, Rolf. *Soldiers*. New York: Grove Press, 1968.

Laqueur, Walter. *The Terrible Secret: Suppression of the Truth about Hitler's "Final Solution."* Boston: Little, Brown and Co., 1980.

   x   **many legends:**   Falconi (pp. 196–197) wrote that Karski met the Pope, Hochhuth that he had an affair with Churchill's secretary, and Hamilton (p. 79) that he committed suicide. Hamilton's book did include a footnote questioning its own assertion.

  xi   **"apologetic literature":**   Laqueur, *The Terrible Secret*, pp. 121–122.

Chapter 1   Autumn of Flight

Much of this account of the Blitzkrieg and its aftermath, and Karski's imprisonment in the USSR and subsequent escape, is derived from the authors' interviews with Jan Karski, supplemented by details gathered from *Story of a Secret State* and confirmed by Jan Karski. As far as can be determined, Karski mentions this period only once in his reports written during the war. A 1940 resumé of his activities discusses his captivity at Kozel'shchina and Kielce very briefly, noting that he spent about six weeks in Soviet captivity and ten days at the camp located between Kielce and Radom (Box 25, HIA/Mikołajczyk).

The Dark Side of the Moon. London: Faber and Faber, 1946.

Gilbert, Martin. *The Holocaust*. New York: Holt, Rinehart, & Winston, 1986.

Kamiński, Jan Bronisław. Unpublished diary. Katyn Institute, Kraków.

Karski, Jan. *The Great Powers and Poland: 1919–1945*. Bethesda: University Press of America, 1985.

Karski, Jan. Interviews with authors, 1987–1993.

Karski, Jan *Story of a Secret State*.

Katyn Institute, Kraków. Soviet leaflets.

Korboński, Stefan. *The Polish Underground State, 1939–1945*. New York: Columbia University Press, 1978.

Paul, Allen. *Katyn: The Untold Story of Stalin's Polish Massacre*. New York: Charles Scribner's Sons, 1991.

Szcześniak, Andrzej Leszek. *Zmowa (Conspiracy)*. Warsaw, 1990.

Tarczyński, Marek, ed. *Zbrodnia katyńska—droga do prawdy (The Crimes of Katyn: The Path toward Truth)*. Warsaw, 1992.

Taylor, James, and Warren Shaw. *The Third Reich Almanac*. New York: World Almanac, 1987.

Zawisza, Jerzy. Interview with Nikita Petrov in *Memorial* (Moscow), April 1993.

Zbrodnia katyńska w świetle dokumentów (The Crimes of Katyn in Light of Documents), vol. 3. London: Gryf Publications Ltd., 1960.

3   "You're not here to be my friend":   K. Int. (October 3, 1993).
4   "You look like a clown":   K. Int. (October 3, 1993).
4   almost half the national budget: This statistic and general information on Beck's overconfidence from Karski. *The Great Powers and Poland: 1919–1945*, pp. 234–235, 319–322.
5   barracks inherited from Austro-Hungarian army: Gilbert, *The Holocaust*, p. 121.
6   "treacherous windows of Oswiecim": *Story*, p. 8.
7   'It's quite valuable":   K. Int. (October 3, 1993).
8   childhood in Łódź; "the father of our country": K. Ints. (February 29, 1992; October 3, 1992; June 2, 1993).
9   reciting long passages of poetry: In interviews with the authors seventy years later, Karski could still recite amazingly long sections of the Mickiewicz epic "Pan Tadeusz."
10   "Please, vote" . . . Adeptus Eloquentissimus: K. Int. (June 16, 1992).
11   Parteitag rally: K. Ints. (February 29, 1992; October 3, 1993); Taylor and Shaw, *The Third Reich Almanac*, p. 242.
12   "Why couldn't I be born German?":   K. Int. (October 3, 1993).
12   "Hey, Kozielewski":   K. Int. (June 16, 1992).
14   "The Soviet Army crossed the frontier": *Story*, p. 13.
14   "brotherly help . . . not as enemies": Leaflets in collection of Katyn Institute, Kraków.
14   murder of Polish general; execution of thirty policemen and 130 schoolboys: *The Crimes of Katyn*, pp. 10–11; Szcześniak, *Conspiracy*, p. 58. The general, Józef Konstanty Olszyna-Wilczyński, was murdered in the village of Sopoćkinie, near Grodno; the policemen were killed near Augustów; the cadets were killed in Grodno.
15   description of boxcar: *Story*, p. 20; *Dark Side of the Moon*, pp. 63–67.
15   Janina Lewandowska: Paul, *Katyn*, p. 137. Karski's recollection that the woman in his car was the daughter of a Polish general and his description of her identify her as Lewandowska.

17 description of Kozel'shchina . . . "In this splendid . . . church": Kamiński diary. The diary was found on Kamiński's corpse in a mass grave at Katyn. Although the original diary was later destroyed, a copy was discovered in 1991 by construction workers in Kraków. The document had been hidden in the roof of a building during the years of Communist rule, when Katyn was an unmentionable subject in Poland.

18 "You are exploiters and bloodsuckers": K. Int. (October 2, 1992).

19 an enterprising doctor; Father Ziółkowski: Paul, *Katyn*, pp. 45–46; biographical information from Katyn Institute.

20 "a house painter from Łódź": K. Int. (June 15, 1992.)

21 details regarding execution of officers: Paul, *Katyn*; Tarczyński, *The Path Toward Truth* , pp. 69–71; Zawisza interview with Petrov. Approximately 150 members of special NKVD execution squads carried out the twenty-two thousand murders. Many members have now been identified. Some are still alive.

22 "You are leaving the camp": *Story*, p. 38.

23 "Citizens of Poland!": *Story*, p. 40; K. Int. (June 16, 1992).

24 "Those fleas are always there": K. Int. (October 3, 1993).

Chapter 2   Apprentice to the Underground

Buyko, Major Bolesław. Testimony to Polish investigators, 1946. Archive of the Ministry of Foreign Affairs, Warsaw.

Eisenbach, Artur. *Hitlerowska polityka zagłady Żydów* (*The Nazi Political Extermination of the Jews*). Warsaw: Książka i Wiedza, 1961.

Engel, David. *In the Shadow of Auschwitz: The Polish Government-in-Exile and the Jews, 1939–1942*. Chapel Hill: University of North Carolina Press, 1987.

Karski, Jan. Interviews with authors, 1987–1993.

Karski, Jan. Long, untitled report dated "second half of February 1940." (Hereinafter: "Karski's 1940 report.") Parts of this report are filed in three separate locations within the Stanisław Mikołajczyk papers at the Hoover Institution Archives. A personal resumé attached to it is at Box 25, HIA/Mikołajczyk. Parts I, II, and III, concerning the logistics of Karski's trip to France, the general conditions of life in Poland and internal political developments, are at Box 9, HIA/Mikołajczyk. Part IV, Karski's report on conditions of life for Jews in Poland, is at Box 12, HIA/Mikołajczyk.

Karski, Jan. *Story of a Secret State*.

Korboński, Stefan. *The Polish Underground State*.

Lerski, Jerzy. *Emisariusz "Jur"* (*Emissary "Jur"*). London: Polish Cultural Foundation, 1984.

27 "What's wrong?": K. Ints. (February 28, 1992; June 15, 1992; June 6, 1993); *Story*, p. 48.

28 "What are you doing still in function?": K. Ints. (June 15, 1992; June 6, 1993).

29 Mayor Starzyński's speech to policemen: Buyko testimony.

30 "POL Insurance Co.": Name cited in Karski's 1940 report—resumé.

30 "Leave me out of it": K. Int. (June 15, 1992).

31 "Raise your right hand": K. Ints. (June 15, 1992; October 3, 1993).

33 whirlwind tour: Cities listed in Karski's 1940 report—resumé.

33 "typical and neat German town": Karski's 1940 report—general conditions.

34 Młyńska Street prison: Korboński, *The Polish Underground State*, p. 2.

34 "virile methods": Karski's 1940 report—general conditions.

34 "As a result of these pressures": Karski's 1940 report—general conditions.

35 anti-Jewish restrictions: Eisenbach, *Nazi Political Extermination of the Jews*, pp. 148–151.

35 "cleansing the lands seized": Karski's 1940 report—Jewish living conditions.

35 "gymnastics and hygiene lesson"; other torments: Karski's 1940 report—Jewish living conditions.

36 anti-Jewish violence: Engel, *In the Shadow of Auschwitz*, pp. 19, 29, 219. Widespread violence against Jews, characterized by some as pogroms, broke out in November 1918 and again between 1935 and 1938. An investigation into the 1918 events found that Jews were killed in nineteen different localities, with seventy-two deaths in Lwów alone.

37 friendships with Jews in early life: K. Ints. (February 28, 1992; October 3, 1992; June 2, 1993).

39 "Those thugs might disfigure . . . did not want to get involved": K. Int. (May 8, 1993).

39 second Borzęcki meeting: K. Ints. (June 15, 1992; October 3, 1993).

41 "You boast and boast": K. Int. (October 3, 1993).

42 Jewish camp at Bełżec: Karski's 1940 report—Jewish living conditions.

42 border crossing at Bełżec: *Story*, pp. 94–98; K. Int. (October 3, 1993).

43 Lerski's escape: Lerski, *Emisariusz "Jur"*. Lerski left Lwów on December 6, 1939, according to his memoirs.

43 encounter with Professor Kucharski: K. Int. (October 3, 1993).

Chapter 3 Off to the Phony War

Engel, David. "An Early Account of Polish Jewry Under Nazi and Soviet Occupation Presented to the Polish Government-in-Exile, February 1940." *Jewish Social Studies* (Winter 1983), pp. 1–16.

Karski, Jan. Interviews with authors, 1987–1993, including Karski's reminiscences of comments made to him by Józef Cyrankiewicz in 1974.

Karski, Jan. Karski's 1940 report.

Karski, Jan. Long untitled report on aspects of the underground movement,

April 1943 (Hereinafter: "Karski's 1943 report on underground elements"). Box 1, HIA/Karski.

Karski, Jan. "Raport z misji Jana Karskiego w r.1940" ("Report on the Mission of Jan Karski in 1940"), February 17, 1944. Box 2, HIA/Karski.

Karski, Jan. *Story of a Secret State.*

Korboński, Stefan. *Bohaterowie polskiego państwa podziemnego jak ich znałem* (*Heroes of the Polish National Underground As I Knew Them*). New York: Bicentennial Publishing Corp., 1987.

Korboński, Stefan. *W imieniu Rzeczypospolitej* (*In the Name of the Republic*). Paris: Instytut Literacki, 1954.

Korboński, Stefan. *The Polish Underground State.*

Kunert, Andrzej Krzystof. *Słownik biograficzny konspiracji warszawskiej 1939–1944* (*Biographical Dictionary of Conspiracy in Warsaw, 1939–1944*), vol. 2. Warsaw: Pax, 1991.

Pużak, Kazimierz. "Wspomnienia 1939–1945" ("Memoirs 1939–1945"), *Zeszyty Historyczne* (*Historical Papers*), 1978.

45 **January 20, 1940; details of train trip:** Karski's 1940 report—"Journey of the Author."
46 **experiences in Kraków and Zakopane:** Karski's 1940 report—"Journey of the Author."
46 **"Unbelievably greedy"; details of ski trip:** Karski's 1940 report—"Journey of the Author"; *Story*, p. 48.
47 **"Are you a Catholic?":** Karski's 1940 report—"Journey of the Author."
48 **"I cannot refrain":** Karski, "Report on the Mission of Jan Karski in 1940."
48 **hospitalization in Budapest:** *Story*, p. 112.
49 **experiences in Budapest:** K. Int. (October 3, 1993); *Story*, p. 112.
49 **"Jan Kanicki":** Karski's 1940 report—Jewish living conditions. A code key attached to this section includes the notation "Kanicki = Jan Karski." Also, the resumé attached to Karski's 1940 report is signed "Jan Kanicki."
49 **"I am a Polish officer"; encounter at Modane:** K. Int. (October 3, 1993).
51 **"like a Parisian banker"; meetings with Kot:** *Story*, p. 118. K. Ints. (October 3, 1993; December 1987).
52 **Karski's report on Jewish situation:** The report itself is a part of Karski's 1940 report, filed at Box 12, HIA/Mikołajczyk. This discussion owes much to the analysis of Engel, "An Early Account."
55 **"Let me explain something":** K. Ints. (October 3, 1992; May 8, 1993).
56 **"Go to Paris":** K. Int. (May 8, 1993).
57 **encounters with Sosnkowski, Garczyńska, Łukasiewicz:** K. Int. (May 8, 1993); *Story*, p. 122.
60 **"I just didn't want to have you on hand":** K. Int. (May 8, 1993).
60 **meetings with Lerski:** K. Int. (May 8, 1993); *Story*, p. 119.
61 **"he does not need to have scruples":** Karski, "Report on the Mission of Jan Karski in 1940."

62 **"an abuse of my services":** Karski, "Report on the Mission of Jan Karski in 1940."

62 **Józef Cyrankiewicz:** K. Ints. (December 1987; May 8, 1993; October 3, 1993).

62 **date of arrival in Warsaw; date of Marian's arrest:** Karski's 1943 report on underground elements, section 20, "Państwowy Korpus Bezpieczeństwa" ("National Security Corps"). The arrest date of May 7, 1940, is given in Kunert, *Biographical Dictionary*, p. 100. Karski confirmed that he arrived in Warsaw on the same day his brother was arrested.

64 **Political Coordinating Committee; fate of members:** Korboński, *The Polish Underground State*, pp. 26–35.

64 **Karski's meeting with committee:** Korboński, *Heroes*, pp. 122–123; Korboński, *The Polish Underground State*, p. 31; Pużak, "Memoirs," p. 28.

66 **"The Socialist Party is well aware":** K. Int. (October 3, 1992).

Chapter 4 Sacrifice

Bieniek, Józef. "Chłopski kurier" ("Peasant Courier"), *Wrocławski tygodnik katolików* (*Wrocław Catholic Weekly*), May 5, 1971. (An account of Karski's capture based on an interview with the guide captured with him, Franciszek Musiał.)

Karski, Jan. Interviews with authors, 1987–1993, including Karski's reminiscences of comments made to him by Józef Cyrankiewicz in 1974.

Karski, Jan. "Notatka dla Rządu polskiego: Dotycząca misji Jana Karskiego w Londynie" ("Note for the Polish Government: Concerning the Mission of Jan Karski to London"), November 30, 1942. Box 2, HIA/Karski.

Karski, Jan. "Report on the Mission of Jan Karski in 1940."

Karski, Jan. Speech given at Waldorf-Astoria Hotel, New York, October 17, 1944. Reprinted in *Builders of the World Ahead*, published by *New York Herald-Tribune*, 1944.

Karski, Jan. *Story of a Secret State.*

Komorowski, Tadeusz ["Bór"]. *The Secret Army*. New York: Macmillan, 1951.

Laskowik, Józef (one of the bribed policemen). Interview with author, January 1987.

Morawski, Jan (member of the rescue team). Interview with author, February 1986.

Ryś, Zbigniew, and Zofia, Ryś (formerly known as Zofia Rysiówna). Interview with author, March 1986.

Ryś, Zofia. Letter to Jan Karski, undated [September 1993]. Personal archive of Jan Karski.

Słowikowski, Jan. Interview with author, March 1986.

Wnuk, Wlodzimierz. *Walka podziemna na szczytach* (*The Underground Struggle at its Peak*), Warsaw, 1965.

70 "It is important that General Sikorski should know": K. Int. (October 3, 1993).
70 "Myszka"; details about Musiał: Bieniek, "Peasant Courier."
71 "Is there something bothering you?": K. Int. (October 3, 1993); *Story*, p. 136.
72 "Isn't there some place?": *Story*, p. 140.
72 village called Demjata: Bieniek, "Peasant Courier."
73 trying to remember Antoni: Bieniek, "Peasant Courier"; *Story*, p. 142.
73 a man of peace: K. Int. (June 15, 1992).
73 details of arrest: Bieniek, "Peasant Courier"; *Story*, p. 143; K. Int. (October 3, 1993). Thirty years would pass before Karski learned the fate of Musiał, his guide. Tortured by the Gestapo in Prešov and then sent back to prison in Poland, Musiał was sentenced to death. According to Musiał, however, his wife heard of the sentence and, with their four children in tow, besieged the office of the Gestapo official responsible for it. Weary of her pleading, the German stayed the execution just to get the woman out of his hair. Sent to Auschwitz, Musiał remained at the camp until it was liberated (Bieniek, "Peasant Courier").
75 details of interrogation and torture: Bieniek, "Peasant Courier"; *Story*, pp. 145–163; K. Ints. (October 3, 1992; October 3, 1993).
81 lapse later noted with consternation: Komorowski, *The Secret Army*, pp. 43–44.
81 suicide attempt: Bieniek, "Peasant Courier"; *Story*, pp. 145–163; K. Ints. (October 3, 1992; October 3, 1993).
82 Slovakian hospital: *Story*, pp. 165–177; Karski, "Report on the Mission of Jan Karski in 1940."
83 "What can I do to help you?": K. Int. (June 15, 1992); *Story*, p. 180.
84 confession: K. Int. (June 15, 1992).
85 "Everybody's crying": K. Ints. (June 15, 1992; October 3, 1993). Karski always maintained that Rysiówna came to him dressed as a nun—a natural and seemingly necessary disguise. Zofia Ryś, however, has specifically denied that she wore such a disguise (Ryś letter).
85 twenty thousand zlotys: Ryś letter.
86 produced a kitchen knife: Ryś interview.
86 sedative-laced water: Laskowik interview.
87 fell into the arms of Ryś: Ryś interview; *Story*, p. 187.
87 hauled Jan back into the boat: Ryś interview; Ryś letter; *Story*, p. 189.
88 "We must leave you here": *Story*, p. 190.
88 "You better cut out all those thanksgivings": Karski speech, October 17, 1944.
90 "Tomorrow, on 21 August": Wnuk, *The Underground Struggle*, p. 135.

Chapter 5   A Routine Existence

Bartoszewski, Władysław, and Zofia Lewin. *Righteous Among Nations*. London: Earlscourt Publications, 1969.

Dobroszycki, Lucjan. "The Jews in the Polish Clandestine Press, 1939–1945," in *The Jews in Poland* (Andrzej K. Paluch, ed.), vol. 1, pp. 289–296. Kraków, 1992.

Falconi, Carlo. *The Silence of Pius XII.*

Karski, Jan. Interviews with authors, 1987–1993.

Karski, Jan. "Notatka dla Prof. Kota" ("Note for Prof. Kot"), April 13, 1943. Box 2, HIA/Karski.

Karski, Jan. "Note for the Polish Government: Concerning the Mission of Jan Karski to London."

Karski, Jan. "Report on the Mission of Jan Karski in 1940."

Karski, Jan. *Story of a Secret State.*

Kossak, Zofia. Manifesto of front for the Rebirth of Poland, reprinted in *Wiadomości polskiej misji katolickiej w Londynie* (*News of the Polish Catholic Mission in London*), June 1943. Personal archive of Jan Karski.

Kossak, Zofia. "Protest" of Front for the Rebirth of Poland, file A.9.III.2a/4, PI.

Lewandowska, Stanisława. "The Authentication Activities of the Polish Resistance Movement During the Second World War," *Acta Poloniae Historica*, 1984, pp. 181–218.

Michalski, Czesław. *Wojna warszawsko–niemiecka* (*The Varsovian-German War*). Warsaw, 1974.

Prot, Janina (niece of Aniela Steinsbergowa). Interview with author, October 1993.

Representation of Polish Jewry. Minutes of meeting in New York attended by Karski, August 9, 1943. Reprinted in *Archives of the Holocaust* (Abraham J. Peck, ed.), vol. 8, pp. 287–294. New York: Garland Publishing, 1990.

Schwarzbart, Ignacy (Jewish official of Polish government-in-exile). Diary. File M2/771, YVA.

Sławik, Lucjan. Letter to Karski, May 27, 1973. Personal archive of Jan Karski.

Szapiro, Paweł. *Wojna żydowsko–niemiecka: Polska prasa konspiracyna 1943–1944 o powstaniu w getcie Warszawy* (*The Jewish-German War: Polish Conspiratorial Press 1943–1944 Concerning the Warsaw Ghetto Uprising*). London: Aneks, 1992.

Tangye, Derek. *The Evening Gull*. London: Sphere Books, 1991.

Załuska, Wanda (socialist activist with whom Karski worked in Kraków). Interview with author, January 1989.

91 **Oblivious to events in Nowy Sącz:** Karski first learned of the executions that followed his escape when one of the authors of this book told him about them in 1986. Shocked, he immediately wrote to the president of the Polish government-in-exile (which continued to function in London

until the fall of the Polish communists in 1989), asking that those who died as a result of their efforts to free him be posthumously awarded the order Virtuti Militari, Poland's highest medal.

92   **quarantine at Sławik estate:**   K. Ints. (February 28, 1992; August 4, 1993; October 3, 1993); Sławik letter; *Story*, pp. 195–218.

92   **black propaganda:**   K. Int. (October 3, 1993); *Story*, pp. 214–217.

93   **"They were against the Germans":**   K. Int. (August 4, 1993).

94   **Karski's stay in Kraków:**   Karski, "Note for the Polish Government"; Karski, "Report on the Mission of Jan Karski in 1940"; K. Ints. (May 8, 1993; June 6, 1993; August 4, 1993).

95   **"Józef, don't go!":**   K. Int. (June 6, 1993).

96   **conditions in Warsaw:**   Michalski, *The Varsovian-German War*.

97   **false documents and other defensive measures:**   Lewandowska, "Authentication Activities."

99   **analyzing underground publications:**   K. Int. (October 3, 1992).

99   **"liaison girls":**   K. Int. (October 3, 1992); *Story*, pp. 280–281.

100   **"You do a great job"; "Did you leave anything?":**   K. Int. (October 3, 1992).

101   **relationship with Renee:**   K. Int. (October 3, 1992).

102   **rescue of Dr. and Mrs. Weinberg:**   In private meetings held after he reached the West in 1942, Karski repeatedly mentioned an episode in which he had tried to help individual Jews escape from the Nazis. These sources create confusion and raise the possibility that Karski was involved in more than one such attempt, but the authors are convinced that the Weinberg effort was his only attempt to save individual Jews.

Both in Tangye (*The Evening Gull*, p. 106) and in the minutes of the Representation of Polish Jewry meeting that Karski attended, he is quoted as saying that he saved an elderly Jew, a retired Polish army colonel, from the ghetto at Otwock near Warsaw. Tangye quotes Karski as specifying that he was ordered to carry out this action by his superior in the Home Army. Schwarzbart (diary, March 15, 1943) reports that Karski claimed to have saved a lawyer named Emil Steinsberg and his wife; in a note added in 1955, Schwarzbart says the Steinsbergs survived the war despite being denounced by Poles. Janina Prot, niece of Emil Steinsberg's wife Aniela, said that Emil Steinsberg was killed in the war. Aniela, a socialist activist who was in contact with Karski during the war, did survive despite denunciations by Poles. But according to Prot, she never spoke of Karski having saved her.

Without prompting, Karski himself recalled the Weinberg incident vividly in an interview with one of the authors, but he had not mentioned it in numerous prior interviews or in any of his public appearances during the 1980s and 1990s. He had apparently forgotten it. He was certain that it was his only effort to save Jews personally. He said Jerzy Makowiecki had asked him to do it. He specifically recalled that Dr. Weinberg had been an army officer, but he did not remember ever being in Otwock. Karski said he had known Aniela Steinsbergowa well, but he did not recall trying to rescue her (K. Ints. October 3, 1992; May 8, 1993).

The authors believe that in all likelihood, Karski told Schwarzbart about the Weinberg episode and also mentioned that he was collaborating with Schwarzbart's friend Emil Steinsberg. Schwarzbart then confused the two stories as he wrote his diary. The references to Otwock are harder to explain; it is possible that Karski rescued the Weinbergs not from Warsaw but from Otwock, or that they had been hiding in Otwock before coming to Warsaw.

105 **Zofia Kossak; Front for the Rebirth of Poland:**   K. Ints. (May 8, 1993; August 4, 1993); *Story*, pp. 287–291; Kossak, manifesto; Bartoszewski and Lewin, *Righteous Among Nations*, pp. xxvi–xxvii; Szapiro, *The Jewish–German War*, p. 218 (quoting an anti-semitic passage in a 1943 FOP publication); Dobroszycki, "The Jews in the Polish Clandestine Press," pp. 293–294. The authors are grateful to Prof. Lucjan Dobroszycki of the Yivo Institute for Jewish Research and Yeshiva University for furnishing information about Zofia Kossak.

106 **"intense battle":**   L. Frassati, *Il Destino passa per Varsavia* (*Destiny Passes Through Warsaw*). Bologna, 1949. Quoted in Falconi, *The Silence of Pius XII*, p. 169.

107 **"her especially rare moral values":**   Karski, "Note for Prof. Kot."

107 **"the inspiration and the finest flame":**   *Story*, p. 291.

107 **"I loved her":**   K. Int. (May 8, 1993).

108 **communist underground activities:**   K. Int. (June 6, 1993).

Chapter 6   Witness

Ainsztein, Reuben. *Jewish Resistance in Nazi-Occupied Eastern Europe*. London: Paul Elek, 1974.

Bartoszewski, Władysław. "Lata wojenne Stanisława Herbsta" ("The War Years of Stanisław Herbst") in *Na drodze do niepodległosci* (*On the Way to Independence*). Paris: Editions Spotkania, 1987.

Bartoszewski, Władysław, and Zofia Lewin. *Righteous Among Nations*.

Bund archives. Yivo Institute, New York, file ME40–11 (hereinafter: "Yivo Bund file"), including the following articles on Leon Feiner that mention Karski: "Dr. Leon Feiner–Berezowski," *Unzer Tsait*, dated "London, March 1945," signed "L.B."; I. Wilner, "Dr. Leon Feiner: The Heroic Leader and Fighter in the Warsaw Ghetto," *Forward* (New York), April 2, 1945; Aniela Steinsbergowa, "Towarzysz Mikołai," *Przegląd Socjalistyczny* (Warsaw), May 1, 1947; article on Feiner with title page missing, *Unzer Shtime* (New York), July 31, 1951; Pinchas Schwartz, "A Stoical Man Broke Down—On the Death of Leon Feiner," *Unzer Tsait*, no date. Also included: anonymous memoir by someone who knew Feiner, written in Polish.

Dawidowicz, Lucy. *The War Against the Jews, 1933–1945*. New York: Seth Press, 1986.

Engel, David. *Facing a Holocaust: The Polish Government-in-Exile and the Jews, 1943–1945*. Chapel Hill: University of North Carolina Press, 1993.

Engel, David. "The Western Allies and the Holocaust: Jan Karski's Mission to the West, 1942–44," *Holocaust and Genocide Studies*, 1990, pp. 363–380.

Feiner, Leon. "Berezowski" letter to Szmul Zygielbojm (Bund leader in London), August 31, 1942. File A.9.III.2a/5, PI.

"The Ghetto Speaks." Newsletter produced by the U.S. branch of the General Jewish Workers Union of Poland (affiliated with the Bund), March 1, 1943. File C186/9, AJA/WJCC.

Grabitz, Oberstaatsanwältin Helga, of State Attorney's Office for Hamburg District Court (Staatsanwaltschaft bei dem Landgericht Hamburg). Letter to author about Izbica Lubelska evidence, August 25, 1993.

Hilberg, Raul. *Perpetrators, Victims, Bystanders*. New York: Aaron Asher Books/HarperCollins, 1992.

Karski, Jan. Interviews with authors, 1987–1993.

Karski, Jan. "Note for the Polish Government: Concerning the Mission of Jan Karski to London."

Karski, Jan. Speech at The Washington Hebrew Congregation, Washington, D.C., March 29, 1987. Personal archive of Jan Karski.

Karski, Jan. *Story of a Secret State*.

Klugman, Aleksander. "Kurier z getta" ("Courier from the Ghetto"), *Nowiny Kurier* (Tel Aviv), June 21, 1974. Personal archive of Jan Karski.

Korboński, Stefan. *Heroes of the Polish National Underground As I Knew Them*.

Kossak, Zofia. "Protest" of Front for the Rebirth of Poland.

Kozlowski, Maciej. "The Mission That Failed" (interview with Karski). *Dissent* (Summer 1987), pp. 326–334.

Landau, David John. Interviews and correspondence with author, October 1993.

Lanzmann, Claude. *Shoah: An Oral History of the Holocaust* (text of the film). New York: Pantheon Books, 1985.

Laqueur, Walter. *The Terrible Secret*.

Marszałek, Józef. Letter to author, October 1993, concerning site of Izbica Lubelska camp.

Neustadt, Meilech. *Khurbn un oyfshtand fun di yidn in varshe* (*Destruction and Rising: The Epic of the Jews in Warsaw*), vol. 2. Tel Aviv: General Federation of Jewish Labor in Palestine, 1948.

Pawlik, Adam (sanitation worker in the Krasnystaw region who often traveled through Izbica between 1940 and 1943). Testimony given March 1, 1946, at Lublin. From Zentrale Stelle der Landesjustizverwaltungen, Ludwigsberg, Aktennummer IV Kps. 144/46, pp. 126–127.

Ratajski, Delegate Cyryl ("Wrzos"). Telegram to "Stem" (Interior Minister Stanisław Mikołajczyk), September 3, 1942. Item 202/I-6, p. 23, depesza 113, AAN.

Representation of Polish Jewry. Minutes of meeting attended by Karski, August 9, 1943.

Smakowski, Jakub. Diary, *Pamiętniki z getta Warszawskiego* (*Diaries from the Warsaw Ghetto*). Warsaw: Panstwowe Wydawnictwo Naukowe, 1988.

112 **"It is not a bad idea":** K. Int. (August 4, 1993).
112 **"How would you feel":** K. Int. (August 4, 1993).
112 **Knoll's nomination as department head:** Karski did carry this request to Gen. Sikorski in London. In 1943, Knoll was granted the position he desired.
113 **"All of the party leaders":** K. Int. (August 4, 1993).
114 **wildly divergent ideas:** K. Int. (March 30, 1993). The Socialist Party, for instance, espoused a planned economy, "abandoning the immoral capitalistic system, which operates only for profit," as Karski was told. "I reported it," he recalled, "but I am not a socialist." The Peasant Party advanced the notion that "all education should be free of charge, from elementary school all the way to postgraduate level." Karski's comment: "Well, at that time as well as today, I considered it stupid. Education cannot be given free of charge to everybody on every level, because then you will have nincompoops in colleges and graduate schools. But I conveyed the message as given."
114 **unanimity against Communist threat:** K. Int. (June 6, 1993).
115 **Bureau of Information and Propaganda:** Bartoszewski, "The War Years of Stanisław Herbst," pp. 101–111; Bartoszewski and Lewin, *Righteous Among Nations*, p. xxxvi. The BIP included a section devoted to Jewish affairs. Two non-Jews in that division, Henryk Wolinski and Stanisław Herbst, joined a Jewish member, Ludwik Widerszal, in preparing written materials on the Jewish tragedy for Jan to carry. Widerszal was murdered by right-wing Polish extremists on the same day as Jerzy Makowiecki, June 13, 1944.
115 **origins of Jewish resistance movement:** Dawidowicz, *The War Against the Jews*; Bartoszewski and Lewin, *Righteous Among Nations*, pp. xxvi–xl.
115 **Jewish Military Union:** Ainsztein, *Jewish Resistance*, pp. 566–569.
115 **Revisionist movement:** Ainsztein, *Jewish Resistance*, p. 566; Engel, *Facing a Holocaust*, pp. 95–100; K. Int. (June 6, 1993).
115 **very few General Zionists:** The General Zionists tended to cooperate with *Judenräte* and other Nazi-established Jewish bodies, taking the position that a nonconfrontational approach offered the best hope of preserving Jewish lives. Menachem Kirschenbaum was an exception who "upheld almost singlehandedly" the General Zionist side in underground circles, according to Dawidowicz (*The War Against the Jews*, p. 263).
116 **"With his distinguished gray hair":** *Story*, p. 321.
117 **identification of Bund and Zionist leaders:** There are several indications that Feiner was the Bund leader. First, the physical description

given by Karski matches Feiner's. Also, numerous accounts of Feiner's life, written shortly after his death in February 1945 (Feiner survived the war but died of cancer), take it for granted that he met Karski (Yivo Bund file). An article by Aniela Steinsbergowa, who knew Karski during the war and probably knew Feiner as well, also speaks of a dramatic meeting between "Witold" and Feiner (*Przegląd Socjalistyczny* article, Yivo Bund file). A letter that Feiner sent to the Bund leadership in London reiterates many of the arguments he made to Karski and includes a postscript mentioning "the contents of the interview given to the messenger bringing the present document" (Feiner letter to Zygielbojm). In the absence of any other messenger coming from Poland after holding an "interview" with Feiner during this period, the note must refer to Karski.

Several historians have speculated about the identity of the Zionist leader at the meetings. Bartoszewski and Lewin assert that the Zionist was "probably" Menachem Kirschenbaum (*Righteous Among Nations*, p. 542). Walter Laqueur suggests the contact may have been Kirschenbaum or Adolf Berman (*The Terrible Secret*, p. 230). Berman survived the war and settled in Israel; in an article on Karski published in a Tel Aviv newspaper, he was quoted as denying that he met Karski (Klugman, "Courier from the Ghetto"). A postwar biographical sketch of Kirschenbaum makes no mention of Karski (Neustadt, *Destruction and Rising*, pp. 634–636). Former Ghetto fighter David John Landau, who knew Kirschenbaum and other Jewish underground leaders, is convinced that Kirschenbaum was the Zionist whom Karski met (Landau interviews and correspondence).

117 **"It was an evening of nightmare"; description of meeting:** *Story*, pp. 320–329; K. Int. (October 2, 1992); Kozłowski, "The Mission That Failed," pp. 327–328; Karski speech.

118 **"the man whose nerves and arteries became wires":** Schwartz, "A Stoical Man Broke Down," Yivo Bund file.

120 **material assistance for Jews:** In interviews, Karski has said that Feiner and the Zionist leader also told him of agitation among younger elements in the Ghetto for a desperate Jewish revolt (which did take place in April 1943). Karski has said that the men requested weapons in addition to the other assistance they sought. He recalled that the Jews complained of having been denied weaponry by the Home Army. Although Karski's recollections on this point seem very precise, they cannot be entirely accurate. At least Karski's first discussion with Feiner, and probably all of his contacts with the Jews, took place before August 31, 1942 (see above). The first recorded attempts by Jewish fighters to obtain weapons from the Home Army came in September 1942. Only one of these inquiries reached the Home Army chief, Gen. Stefan Rowecki, and the controversy over whether the Poles would furnish weapons did not arise until some weeks later (Bartoszewski and Lewin, *Righteous Among Nations*, p. xxxvii). The Jewish Fighting Organization did not conclude an alliance with the Home Army until October. At least one source does credit Feiner as the first Jewish leader to demand weapons and to call for armed resistance in the Ghetto (anonymous memoir by someone who knew Fei-

ner, Yivo Bund file). And Karski clearly had some inkling that the Jews intended to revolt, as suggested in *Story* (p. 328). But he could not have discussed weaponry with the Jews in any detail.

120 **"Let the Jewish people do something":**   Report by an anonymous courier (Karski), in "The Ghetto Speaks."

120 **"Witold, I know the English":**   K. Int. (February 29, 1992).

121 **dates of Karski's visits to Ghetto:**   In the earliest extant report by Karski on the subject ("The Ghetto Speaks"), he gave an August date for the visits. In subsequent reports and statements, Karski suggested he toured the Ghetto in September or October. Former ghetto fighter David John Landau, who escorted Karski during one of the ghetto trips, would not have been available to do so after August (Landau interviews and correspondence).

121 **"Dudek" Landau; details about tunnel:**   Landau interviews and correspondence. Corroborating details about Landau from Smakowski diary, p. 302.

122 **"There was hardly a square yard":**   *Story*, p. 330.

122 **"What does it mean?":**   *Story*, p. 331.

122 **"When a Jew dies":**   *Story*, p. 331; interview with Karski in Lanzmann, *Shoah*, p. 172.

122 **"They are playing, you see":**   *Story*, p. 331; Lanzmann, *Shoah*, p. 174.

122 **"Remember this":**   Lanzmann, *Shoah*, p. 174.

123 **Hitler Youth in Ghetto:**   David John Landau reported another instance in which the Nazis sent children into the Ghetto for indoctrination: "Two SS trucks came over," he recalled. The vehicles were full of young children, five to seven years old, "standing as though in a tram, holding pieces of hanging cloth, not to fall down. . . . A chap of about 15 or 16 jumped out as the leader, and placed boxes next to the truck because they couldn't jump down—they might harm themselves, the little bastards. So he put in boxes like steps. They went into the Ghetto." The leader guided the children, dressed in brown uniforms with black ties, with "little handkerchiefs over their noses," toward the Jewish cemetery. "He showed them how they buried the Jews, how they put a little lime like salt over them, and then stacked the next group of people" (Landau interview, October 5, 1993). The *Hitlerjugend* normally included only boys aged fifteen to eighteen; boys aged ten to fourteen joined a similar organization, *Jungvolk*. Perhaps the children Landau saw were in the *Jungvolk* or some other group.

124 **pushed the bread away:**   Landau letter to Karski, August 20, 1993; Landau interview, October 5, 1993.

124 **Jewish-looking guide; trip to eastern Poland:**   K. Int. (October 2, 1992).

125 **Ukrainian militiaman:**   At various times later in the war, Karski said he had worn Latvian, Lithuanian, and Estonian uniforms. He falsified the nationality for security and perhaps political reasons. "If I wrote Estonian," he explained in an interview, "certainly it couldn't be Estonian. It would be idiotic of me to expose the [underground] Jews' connections with the guards in that way" (K. Int. June 6, 1993). In fact, the camp Karski visited was staffed by Ukrainian troops, mostly former prisoners

of war who had changed allegiances to Germany. Political considerations may also have prevented Jan from mentioning Ukrainian collaborators, since the Polish government-in-exile was keen to maintain good relations with Poland's Ukrainian minority.

125   **"dense, pulsating, throbbing"; description of camp:**   *Story*, pp. 344–351; K. Int. (October 2, 1992).

128   **"sorting point":**   "The Ghetto Speaks."

128   **twelve miles, then twelve kilometers:**   Representation of Polish Jewry minutes.

128   **Scholars of the Holocaust:**   See, for example, Hilberg, *Perpetrators, Victims, Bystanders,* p. 223; Engel, "The Western Allies and the Holocaust," p. 375. The authors are grateful to Professor David Engel of New York University for furnishing them with a copy of this article.

129   **downhill slope:**   The description of the camp's layout that Karski gives in *Story of a Secret State* (p. 344) makes clear that he viewed it from a rise. The elevation of the Izbica Lubelska camp was some forty meters below that of the town itself, according to Professor Józef Marszałek of Curie-Skłodowska University in Lublin, an authority on camps in eastern Poland. Professor Marszałek believes that Izbica Lubelska was the camp Karski saw (letter to author).

129   **sanitation worker's report:**   Pawlik testimony. The authors are grateful to historian Michael Tregenza of Sunbury, England for supplying them with a copy of this document.

129   **Izbica Lubelska as a looting station:**   Karski's account in *Story of a Secret State* displays at least some comprehension of the camp's role as a property collection point. Although he incorrectly states that the victims came from the Warsaw Ghetto, he echoes the sanitation worker's comment about the Jews' having been encouraged to bring along their valuables. Karski writes, "When they had been rounded up, they had been given permission to take about ten pounds of baggage. Most of them took food, clothes, bedding, and, if they had any, money and jewelry" (pp. 345–346).

130   **Izbica Lubelska as a holding camp:**   Confirmed by Grabitz letter.

130   **first notice of planned trip:**   "Wrzos" (Ratajski) telegram to "Stem" (Mikołajczyk).

130   **"The drywall was cracking":**   Korboński, *Heroes*, pp. 123–124.

131   **microfilm:**   The items included on the microfilm are listed in a ledger headed "Materiały otrzymane od Delegata z Kraju," ("Materials sent by the Delegate from the Homeland") p. 4, SPP. Reaction to the news compressed onto the film reached Poland many months later. Bartoszewski and Lewin cite "an official note of the BIP" on a conversation March 24, 1943 with courier Jerzy Lerski, who had recently been sent into Poland by parachute: "The documents brought by W. [Witold] caused a great sensation, the international effects of which are known as the 'Campaign for the Jews' " (*Righteous Among Nations*, p. 541).

131   **protest by FOP:**   Bartoszewski and Lewin give the early September date for its publication (*Righteous Among Nations*, p. xxvi).

Chapter 7   Carrying the Message

Bartoszewski, Władysław, and Zofia Lewin. *Righteous Among Nations* (English adaptation of *Ten jest z ojczyzny mojej*).

Bartoszewski, Władysław, and Zofia Lewin. *Ten jest z ojczyzny mojej: Polacy z pomoca Żydom 1939–1945* (*This is from My Motherland: Poles and Aid to Jews 1939–1945*). Kraków: Wydawnictwo Znak, 1969.

Eden, Anthony. Cable to Viscount Halifax, Washington embassy, December 7, 1942. FO 371/30923, PRO.

Engel, David. *Facing a Holocaust: The Polish Government-in-Exile and the Jews, 1943–1945*.

Engel, David. *In the Shadow of Auschwitz*.

Engel, David. "The Western Allies and the Holocaust: Jan Karski's Mission to the West, 1942–44."

Falconi, Carlo. *The Silence of Pius XII*.

Feiner, Leon. "Berezowski" letter to Szmul Zygielbojm (Bund leader in London), August 31, 1942.

"The Ghetto Speaks." Newsletter produced by the U.S. branch of the General Jewish Workers Union of Poland.

Gilbert, Martin. *Auschwitz and the Allies*. New York: Holt, Rinehart, and Winston, 1981.

The Goebbels Diaries (Louis P. Lochner, ed.). New York: Award Books, 1971.

Henderson, Ian L., of Foreign Office. Note from December 5, 1942. FO 371/32231, PRO.

Hinsley, F.H., and C.A.G. Simkins. *British Intelligence in the Second World War*, vol. 4. New York: Cambridge University Press, 1990.

Karski, Jan. Interviews with authors, 1987–1993.

Karski, Jan. "Note for the Polish Government: Concerning the Mission of Jan Karski to London."

Karski, Jan. "Note for Prof. Kot."

Karski, Jan. *Story of a Secret State*.

Laqueur, Walter. *The Terrible Secret*.

Law, Richard (parliamentary undersecretary for foreign affairs). Memorandum, November 26, 1942. FO 371/30923, PRO.

Office of Strategic Services. "The Franco-Spanish Frontier" (undated, but apparently early 1943). Record group 226, Entry 161, Box 5, Folder 62, NA.

Office of Strategic Services. "Progress Report: Spain," July 28, 1942. Record group 226, Entry 92, Box 78, Folder 22, NA.

Penkower, Monty Noam. *The Jews Were Expendable: Free World Diplomacy and the Holocaust*. Detroit: Wayne State University Press, 1988.

Perlzweig, Maurice. Letter to A.L. Easterman, May 17, 1943. File A14/5, AJA/WJCC.

Perlzweig, Maurice. Note to A.L. Easterman, December 17, 1942. File A14/5, AJA/WJCC.

Raczkiewicz, President Władysław. Diary, Raczkiewicz collection, JPIA.

Raczyński, Edward. *In Allied London*. London: Weidenfeld and Nicolson, 1962.

Ravel, Aviva. *Faithful unto Death*. Montreal: Workmen's Circle, 1980.

Roberts, Sir Frank. Interview with author, August 1993.

Roberts, Frank (Foreign Office). Memoranda, December 1 and December 5, 1942. FO 371/30923, PRO.

Roberts, Frank (Foreign Office). Memorandum, December 14, 1942. FO 371/30924, PRO.

Schwarzbart diary.

Schwarzbart, Ignacy. 1942 engagement book. File H261, AJA/WJCC.

Schwarzbart, Ignacy. Telegram to World Jewish Congress, December 1, 1942. File A14/12, AJA/WJCC.

Sikorski, Gen. Władysław. Letter to Lord Selborne (Special Operations Executive), August 26, 1942. File A.9.VI.1./2, PI.

Siudak, Paweł (Polish Interior Ministry). Memorandum, November 25, 1942. File A.9.VI.1./21, PI.

Studium Polski Podziemnej (Polish Underground Study Trust), London (SPP). Clandestine dispatches between Polish underground movement in Warsaw, Polish underground movement in France, and Polish government-in-exile in London.

Wasserstein, Bernard. *Britain and the Jews of Europe, 1939–1945*. Oxford: Clarendon Press, 1979.

Wilkinson, Col. Peter (Special Operations Executive). Letter to Frank Roberts (Foreign Office), January 5, 1943. FO 371/34552, PRO.

Wise, Stephen. *Challenging Years: The Autobiography of Stephen Wise*. New York: G.P. Putnam's Sons, 1949.

Younger, Maj. K.G., of MI5. Letter to J.G. Ward (Foreign Office), December 22, 1942. FO 371/32231, PRO.

Zabiełło, Stanisław. Telegram to Stanisław Mikołajczyk, October 23, 1942, with Polish Intelligence (II Division) memorandum, November 6, 1942. Box 74, HIA/MSZ.

135 **October 1:** In the absence of any source giving the exact date of Karski's departure from Warsaw, this date is extrapolated from several clues. Just after arriving in London, Karski reported that he left in October ("Note for the Polish Government"). The Polish Foreign Minister, Count Edward Raczyński, writes in his memoirs that Karski was "still in Warsaw" at "the beginning of October." When Karski indicated on several other occasions that he left in late October, he was clearly in error; he may have been giving a false date in order to make his reports seem more fresh. A number of telegrams from Polish officials in London to military and civilian leaders in Warsaw (and vice versa) discuss his journey, and these leave the impression that plans changed continually both before and during the trip. Karski's departure was originally set for September 11 (Rowecki dispatch to London HQ, September 9, 1942, File 2.3.4.3.1.2, SPP), but London requested a delay of two or three days to finalize arrangements (Protasewicz dispatch to Rowecki, September 9, 1942, File 2.3.4.3.1.2, SPP). The delay must have lasted longer, however, since Rowecki was still discussing plans for the journey in a September 19 dispatch (File 3.8.3.1.1, SPP). On October 2, Rowecki notified London that "Witold" had left "with a group of French workers on a document that was purchased from one of them" (File 3.8.3.1.1, SPP). An October 6 cable from Mikołajczyk to the government delegate (Teka 10/szafa 12, SPP) confirms Karski's arrival in Paris.

135 **"You will wear Christ's Body"; other details of mass:** *Story*, p. 354; K. Int. (June 6, 1993).

137 ***"Jestem Witold od Waci":*** Password given in telegram from "Rawa" (Protasewicz, coordinator of couriers in London) to "Kalina" (Rowecki), September 9, 1942. File 2.3.4.3.1.2, SPP.

138 **five thousand Polish "agents":** Sikorski letter to Lord Selborne.

138 **fears for Jan's safety:** Zabiełło telegram to Mikołajczyk, October 23, 1942; Polish Intelligence memorandum, November 6, 1942.

138 **"Why didn't you provide":** Mikołajczyk telegram to delegate, (October 6, 1942). Teka 10/ szafa 12, SPP.

138 **thirty-seven thousand złoty:** Karski, "Note for the Polish Government."

138 **Karski's stay in Paris:** K. Ints. (October 2, 1992; May 5, 1993); *Story*, pp. 362–363.

139 **At the nightclubs:** K. Int. (October 2, 1992).

139 **"You are about to become a Communist":** K. Int. (October 2, 1992).

139 **ten to twenty-five thousand francs:** OSS report, "The Franco-Spanish Frontier."

139 **"He is fanatically, stupidly Communist . . . a noble, noble man":** K. Int. (October 2, 1992).

140 **English-speaking man:** OSS, "Progress Report: Spain." At least six OSS agents were operating in Spain at the time. The one who picked up Karski may have been the agent stationed "between Barcelona and the French Frontier."

140 **German agents posing as couriers:** Telegram from Polish Intelligence (II Division) to "Makbol" (contact in France), October 11, 1942; telegram

from Protasewicz to Bern Military Attaché, October 12, 1942. File 3.8.3.1.1, SPP.

140 **"There is no conspiracy":** Warning note from Rowecki to London, dated October 22, 1942, sent by courier. File 2.3.4.3.1.2, SPP.

140 **sealing off Franco-Spanish border:** OSS report, "The Franco-Spanish Frontier."

140 **Bern advised of Karski's possible arrival:** Telegram from Protasewicz to Bern Military Attaché, October 12, 1942. File 3.8.3.1.1, SPP.

141 **"May I have some instructions":** K. Int. (October 2, 1992).

141 **"Gee whiz":** K. Int. (June 15, 1992).

141 **"My boys!":** K. Int. (February 28, 1992).

142 **"Mr. K. was brought out under our auspices":** Wilkinson letter.

142 **SOE notifying Poles:** Siudak memorandum.

142 **at least ten Nazi spies:** Hinsley and Simkins, *British Intelligence*, pp. 335–338, 343–345. Like Karski, most of these agents were citizens of conquered nations, and several claimed to be returning to their exiled governments after carrying out missions in their home countries, just as Karski claimed. In each of these cases, counterintelligence work revealed that the returning agent had been captured by the Germans and had become a double agent. At least four "escapee" spies were hanged.

143 **"I will tell you absolutely nothing":** K. Int. (October 2, 1992).

143 **formal protest:** The Foreign Office file on the diplomatic row occasioned by Karski's detention is FO 371/32231, PRO. The actual transcript of Karski's interrogation is probably in the War Office file WO 208/3689 ("Royal Patriotic Schools, November 1942"), but this file is closed until 2018.

143 **"the Poles are more concerned":** Henderson note.

143 **arrival of microfilm in London:** Confirmed in telegram from "Rawa" (Protasewicz) to "Kalina" (Rowecki), November 17, 1942 ("Witold's mail is at headquarters") (File 3.8.3.1.1, SPP).

143 **"News is reaching the Polish Government":** Two-page report filed in FO 371/30923, PRO. The Poles also prepared a more comprehensive account from the microfilmed materials. A November 27 telegram from A.L. Easterman to World Jewish Congress headquarters in New York mentions a "special twenty-page report received Polish government giving terrible details mass massacres" (File A14/12, AJA/WJCC).

144 **emergence of news about Holocaust:** Many historians have addressed this topic. In addition to primary source material, this account draws on several Holocaust histories, notably: Gilbert, *Auschwitz and the Allies*; Engel, *In the Shadow of Auschwitz*; Laqueur, *The Terrible Secret*; and Penkower, *The Jews Were Expendable*.

144 **"It seemed to me so devilish":** Quoted in Engel, *In the Shadow of Auschwitz*, p. 176.

145 **skepticism of Jewish observers:** Laqueur, *The Terrible Secret*, pp. 184–185.

146 **Riegner telegram:** Laqueur, *The Terrible Secret*, pp. 77–82; Wise, *Challenging Years*, pp. 274–279.

146 **Palestinian exchangees:** Laqueur, *The Terrible Secret*, pp. 190–194; Engel, *In the Shadow of Auschwitz*, p. 198.

146 **"already destroyed":** Quoted in Penkower, *The Jews Were Expendable*, p. 80.

146 **release of Polish report:** An Associated Press article on the report appeared in American newspapers on November 24. The Poles' decision to release Karski's information may not have been entirely independent of events in Palestine. On November 23, Foreign Minister Raczyński had responded to an urgent query from the Representation of Polish Jewry in Palestine by cabling that the government could not confirm the evacuation of the Warsaw Ghetto (Engel, *In the Shadow of Auschwitz*, p. 197). It is most unlikely that Raczyński was unaware of the information Karski had sent. Possibly he was stalling for time in the hope of obtaining more details from Karski when he arrived. Whatever the Poles' motives were for withholding the information, they may have been forced to release it by the publicity given to the Palestinian exchangees' reports beginning on November 23. Of Karski's arrival, Raczyński later commented: "There is no doubt that his visit prompted us to act" (letter to Martin Gilbert, September 19, 1980, cited in *Auschwitz and the Allies*, p. 93).

146 **meeting with Richard Law:** Law memorandum. Gilbert, *Auschwitz and the Allies*, offers a more extensive account of this meeting and of the emergence in London of news about the exterminations (pp. 92–97).

147 **"He told a very lengthy story":** Younger letter.

148 **"Drink":** K. Int. (October 2, 1992).

148 **"The Jewish leaders in Warsaw":** K. Ints. (December 1987; October 2, 1992).

149 **"You were crazy":** K. Int. (October 2, 1992).

149 **"I will hang it on the church's portrait":** K. Int. (June 6, 1993).

149 **"to explain officially":** Karski, "Note for the Polish Government."

150 **"Have read today all reports":** Schwarzbart telegram.

150 **meeting with Zygielbojm and Schwarzbart:** At least one historian has asserted that Karski did not meet these Jewish leaders until months after his arrival in England, suggesting that he and the government did not view his Jewish mission with great urgency (Engel, "The Western Allies and the Holocaust," pp. 365, 376). But several sources confirm that Karski met with both men on December 2, 1942. Bartoszewski and Levin give this date for the meeting (*This Is from My Motherland*, pp. 31–32; not in the English version, published as *Righteous Among Nations*). "The Ghetto Speaks" gives this date as well. The newsletter includes a detailed account of Karski's oral presentation. Some of the quotes attributed to Karski (who is not named) appear to have been embellished for propaganda purposes or distorted for security reasons, but most of the report is confirmed by other sources. In his engagement book for 1942, Schwarzbart penciled in "Siudak" on the page for December 2; interior ministry official Paweł Siudak escorted Karski to his meetings. And on December 3, at a meeting of Jewish organizations in London, Schwarzbart and Zygielbojm reported on the briefing they had received the previous day from a Polish underground member newly arrived in London (Penkower, *The Jews Were Expendable*, p. 84).

151 "We are only too well aware": "The Ghetto Speaks," March 1, 1943, p. 1; *Story*, p. 328.
151 "It is impossible": *Story*, p. 336.
152 "It will actually be a shame": Zygielbojm broadcast, December 13, 1942, quoted in Ravel, *Faithful unto Death*, p. 170.
152 One official . . . "the most complete": Roberts memoranda, December 1 and December 5, 1942.
152 "little doubt": Eden cable to Halifax.
153 ten-page diplomatic note: The version sent to the British government is filed at FO 371/30924, PRO.
153 Churchill's interest: Roberts memorandum, December 14, 1942.
153 Eden in Commons: The fullest account of Eden's December 17 appearance is in Wasserstein, *Britain and the Jews of Europe*, pp. 172–175.
153 "decisions taken to punish": Feiner ("Berezowski") letter to Zygielbojm.
153 Karski denounced the Allied policy: Comment by Karski quoted in Schwarzbart diary, March 15, 1943.
154 "Many of us believe here": Perlzweig letter to Easterman, May 17, 1943.
154 "We must forget about reprisals": Perlzweig letter to Easterman, December 17, 1942.
154 "His voice vibrating with emotion": *Chips: The Diaries of Sir Henry Channon* (R. Rhodes James, ed., London, 1970), pp. 423–424, quoted in Wasserstein, *Britain and the Jews of Europe*, p. 173.
154 "At the Wailing Wall": *The Goebbels Diaries*, pp. 283–284.
154 "His tales of heroism": Raczyński, *In Allied London*, p. 127.
155 "Bon appétit, et bonne chance!" K. Int. (July 26, 1993).
155 courier project: Karski, "Note for the Polish Government."
155 telegrams from Karski: Teka 10/szafa 12, SPP.
156 candidates for escape: Karski, "Note for Prof. Kot."
156 meeting with Raczkiewicz: Raczkiewicz diary. After a December 15 meeting with Schwarzbart, Raczkiewicz left notes that suggest he reacted somewhat defensively to questions about a Jewish issue.
156 "Poland is a Catholic nation": K. Int. (October 2, 1992).
156 "The laws of God trampled under foot": Raczkiewicz to Pope Pius XII, January 2, 1943; reply, February 16, 1943; in Falconi, *The Silence of Pius XII*, pp. 218–219.

Chapter 8 In Official Circles

Bartoszewski, Władysław, and Zofia Lewin. *Righteous Among Nations*.

Joseph Conrad: Life and Letters (G. Jean–Aubry, ed.), vol. 2. New York: Doubleday, Page & Co., 1927.

Eden, Anthony. Report to War Cabinet on conversations with Karski, February 17, 1943. CAB 66/34, PRO.

Edwards, Ruth Dudley. *Victor Gollancz: A Biography*. London: Victor Gollancz Ltd., 1987.

Engel, David. *Facing a Holocaust: The Polish Government-in-Exile and the Jews, 1943–1945.*

Engel, David. *In the Shadow of Auschwitz: The Polish Government-in-Exile and the Jews, 1939–1942.*

Engel, David. "The Western Allies and the Holocaust: Jan Karski's Mission to the West, 1942–44."

Foreign Relations of the United States, 1943. Washington: Government Printing Office, 1963.

Garliński, Józef. *Poland, S.O.E. and the Allies*. London: Allen and Unwin, 1969.

Gutman, Yisrael. *The Jews of Warsaw 1939–1943: Ghetto, Underground, Revolt.* Bloomington: Indiana University Press, 1982.

Karski, Jan. Interviews with the authors, 1987–1993.

Karski, Jan. "Notatka o rozmowach Jana Karskiego z politykami i publicystami angielskimi" ("Note on the conversations of Jan Karski with English politicians and publicists"), not dated (May 1943) (Hereinafter: "May 1943 report"). Box 1, HIA/Karski.

[Karski, Jan], "Notatka w sprawie rozmów odbytych przez J. Kwaśniewskiego z osobistościami angielskimi i amerykańskimi w Londynie" ("Note on conversations carried out by J. Kwaśniewski with English and American personages in London"), March 25, 1943. Box 1, HIA/Karski.

Karski, Jan. "The Polish Question, 1940–1945: The Secret Diplomacy of Churchill and Roosevelt," *Polish Affairs*, 1987, pp. 1–12.

Karski, Jan. *Story of a Secret State*.

Karski, Jan. Telegram to government delegate in Poland, December 4, 1942, Teka 10/szafa 12, SPP.

Koestler, Arthur. *Arrival and Departure*. New York: Macmillan, 1943.

Koestler, Arthur. Letter to Karski, October 12, 1943. Personal archive of Jan Karski.

Laqueur, Walter. *The Terrible Secret*.

Lerski, Jerzy. *Emisariusz "Jur."*

Lerski, George [Jerzy]. *Poland's Secret Envoy, 1939–1945*. New York: Bicentennial Publishing Corp., 1988.

Librach, Jan. "Notatka dla Pana Prezesa" ("Note for the Prime Minister"), February 10, 1943 (account of Karski's meeting with Richard Law, to which Librach escorted him). Archiwum Jana Libracha I, JPIA.

Osborne, Harold. Letter to Mikołajczyk, January 10, 1943. Box 10, HIA/Mikołajczyk.

Raczyński, Count Edward. *In Allied London*. London: Weidenfeld and Nicolson, 1962.

Savery, Frank. Minutes of conversation with Karski, sent by Savery to Frank Roberts (Foreign Office), December 30, 1942. FO 371/34552, PRO.

Schwarzbart diary.

Selborne, Lord (Roundell Cecil Palmer), Fragmentary Memoir, Selborne Papers, Bodleian Library, Oxford University.

Sikorski, Gen. Władysław. Diary (appointment calendar). Kol. 1/43, PI.

Tangye, Derek. *The Evening Gull*.

Tangye, Derek. *The Way to Minack*. London: Sphere Books, 1975.

Topolski, Feliks. *Fourteen Letters*. London: Faber and Faber, 1988.

157 **Christmas Eve dinner:** Lerski, *Emisariusz "Jur,"* p. 65; Raczyński, *In Allied London*, p. 128.
158 **man in front of bombed-out building:** K. Int. (May 8, 1993).
158 **informed the underground that he would return:** Karski telegram.
159 **"He has infused new life":** Osborne letter to Mikołajczyk.
160 **"Kwaśniewski":** British and Polish archives both include reports by and about an envoy from the underground named "Kwaśniewski," who arrived in England at the same time, met all the same people, and left the same general impression on the British as Karski. There can be no doubt that "Karski" and "Kwaśniewski" are the same person. In an interview (May 1, 1993), Karski said that while he did not specifically remember the name "Kwaśniewski", he did recall occasionally using a name other than Karski while in London. An August 25, 1943 telegram from Witold Babiński of the Polish Foreign Ministry to the Polish embassy in Washington appears conclusive on the issue: It refers to the envoy then in Washington as "Karski/Kwaśniewski" (Telegram file, HIA/MSZ).
160 **"He is an active member":** Savery minutes.
162 **"It is very possible":** K. Int. (May 8, 1993).
162 **"attitude of society toward the Government":** Karski, "Note on Conversations."
162 **grave misgivings:** Lerski, *Poland's Secret Envoy*, p.66: "Karski expressed some surprise at the Sikorski Government's bungling of the last Polish-Soviet agreement. At lunch in one of the restaurants near Piccadilly, he reproached in my presence the high-ranking diplomat, Dr. Jan Librach, for not securing the recognition of the prewar 'Riga Frontier'. . . . From Karski's reactions I became aware of the unbending attitude of Poland's genuine underground leaders regarding any sort of compromise with Russia on territorial or political issues."
163 **Savery's note:** Note given verbatim and Karski's reaction recorded in "Note on Conversations," which also mentions that Savery burned the note.
164 **"The Polish position":** Karski, "The Polish Question," p. 7.

164   "Young man, you have worked hard"; Virtuti Militari: *Story*, pp. 381–382; K. Int. (October 2, 1992); Sikorski diary, February 3, 1943.

164   "What happened to your mouth?":   K. Int. (June 15, 1992).

166   Józef Retinger: The purported intelligence dossier, an eight-page typescript with notes in Polish, dated March 1942, is filed in the Retinger collection, JPIA. A undated report that seems to have been prepared by Retinger's enemies among the Polish exiles is in the Tomasz Arciszewski collection, PI (Kol. 97/25).

166   accusations against Retinger by Jews: Rumors that Retinger would be assigned to the Polish embassy in Washington in 1943 prompted World Jewish Congress leader Arieh Tartakower to notify the State Department that such an appointment would be "harmful to our interests." (File H260, AJA/WJCC).

166   "unofficial intermediary":   Conrad to Richard Curle, August 20, 1916, in Jean–Aubry, *Joseph Conrad*, p. 174.

166   "closely connected with the fighting":   Garliński, *Poland, S.O.E. and the Allies*, p. 162.

166   "In American records":   Retinger report in Arciszewski collection, Kol. 97/25, PI.

167   "Don't try to be Rejtan":   K. Int. (March 30, 1993).

167   "Will I be able to see Churchill?":   K. Ints. (June 15, 1992; December 1987).

167   "No time for tennis":   K. Int. (June 15, 1992).

167   Eden reviewed Savery's report: Eden initialed the note from Frank Roberts transmitting Savery's minutes.

168   "He didn't show any reaction":   Karski, "Note on Conversations."

168   "The Polish report on the atrocities":   K. Ints. (June 15, 1992; December 1987).

168   Polish advocacy of retaliation: In December 1942, the Germans had begun clearing an area in eastern Poland of all traces of Polish habitation; it was to become a purely German settlement. Since the murders and deportations in the area bore a resemblance to the Einsatzgruppen activities that had eliminated the Jewish population from the same area in 1941, underground leaders speculated that Hitler was proceeding from a policy of mere terror against ethnic Poles to a plan of mass extermination along the lines of the Final Solution of the Jewish question. The Polish government had already taken the lead among the Allies in pressing for some sort of aid to the suffering Jews; whether it began working any more earnestly when non-Jewish Poles were imperiled cannot be definitely determined (cf. Engel, *Facing a Holocaust*, pp. 42–45). The Polish government's appeals for leaflets and retaliation are filed at Box 76, HIA/MSZ. The German "ethnic cleansing" operation in eastern Poland ran into concerted resistance from the underground; because of this and German losses on the eastern front, it never reached its projected scale.

168   "Step over to the window":   K. Int. (June 15, 1992); *Story*, p. 383.

169   "Sir, will I have the honor":   K. Int. (June 15, 1992).

169   Eden's report to War Cabinet: Filed at CAB 66/34, PRO.

169 **"You've made a good impression on us":** K. Ints. (June 15, 1992; May 8, 1993).
170 **"This is Lord Selborne":** K. Ints. (June 15, 1992; May 8, 1993).
171 **"When I arrived at Chequers":** Selborne memoir.
171 **"Polish underground authorities":** Karski, "Note on Conversations."
171 **World War I atrocity propaganda:** Cf. Associated Press dispatch from Brussels, March 29, 1915, quoting General von Bissing, German military governor of Belgium: "Because smallpox vaccine has been introduced into Germany, some evil joker spreads the report that the Germans intend to inoculate the Belgian children with poison."
172 **"What happened?":** K. Ints. (June 15, 1992; May 8, 1993).
173 **Curzon Line:** Librach, "Note for the Prime Minister."
173 **"the most dispiriting impression":** Karski, "Note on Conversations."
174 **"I remember you very well":** K. Ints. (January 31, 1993; December 1987).
174 **"Most clearly of all":** Karski, "Note on Conversations."
174 **"strictly confidential" memorandum:** Anthony J. Drexel Biddle report to Secretary of State Cordell Hull, March 3, 1943, in *Foreign Relations of the United States, 1943*, vol. 3, pp. 338–342.
175 **"it is no longer certain":** Eden report to War Cabinet.
176 **duty to convey the unvarnished facts:** Comment by Karski quoted in Schwarzbart diary, March 15, 1943.
176 **"I understand that you have been in London":** K. Int. (June 15, 1992).
177 **"As a Pole and as a human being":** Schwarzbart diary, March 15, 1943.
178 **"a rare phenomenon":** Schwarzbart diary, date unknown, File M2/587, YVA. Quoted in Gutman, *The Jews of Warsaw*, p. 362.
178 **"in none of them, even in Karski":** Schwarzbart, "Rozmowa z p. Markiem Celtem" ("Conversation with Marek Celt"), February 6, 1945. File M2/141, YVA. Quoted in Engel, *Facing a Holocaust*, p. 171.
178 **MI5 agent under orders:** Tangye, *The Evening Gull*, p. 105. The authors are grateful to Derek Tangye for furnishing them with copies of his books.
178 **encounter with Tangye:** Tangye, *The Way to Minack*, p. 148.
178 **"I arranged lunch":** Tangye, *The Evening Gull*, p. 106.
178 **"He was then a modern warrior":** Topolski, *Fourteen Letters*, no page number.
178 **Topolski party:** Karski, May 1943 report.
179 **script written by Koestler in Karski's name:** Copies of the script are filed at the Koestler Archive (University of Edinburgh Library), and at File F1, AJA/WJCC. The latter version includes a note to the effect that the broadcast was presented on July 8, 1943, with the script read by Duncan Grinnell Milne. BBC records show that the broadcast took place on the BBC European Service on July 7 (J. Kavanagh of BBC Written Archives Centre, letter to author, March 24, 1993). In at least one of these broadcasts, the speaker introduced himself as "Karski," breaching the secrecy of Karski's mission and infuriating Polish intelligence officials. Karski was in the United States at the time, but upon his return he was forced to write an angry letter to Koestler, denouncing him for carelessness (a draft, erroneously addressed to "Mr. Kestner," is at Box 2, HIA/

Karski). Apparently before the letter could be sent, Koestler wrote to Karski: "I hear from Feliks Topolski that some fools are trying to be disagreeable to you in connection with a broadcast of mine. Here is the story of that broadcast. . . ." Koestler goes on to shift blame for the lapse (not very convincingly) to the BBC (Koestler letter, October 12, 1943). The authors are grateful to Professor Michael Scammell of Cornell University, author of a forthcoming biography of Koestler, for his assistance in interpreting Koestler's relationship with Karski.

179   **Koestler's novel about Karski:**   The protagonist of *Arrival and Departure* is introduced as a refugee from Nazi-style oppression, crossing enemy lines to reach "Neutralia" much as Karski transited occupied Europe to reach Spain and later England; there are two mentions of his teeth having been knocked out, as Karski's were by Gestapo truncheons; and the book presents details of the mass-murder operations then under way that resemble Karski's revelations.

179   **"a state of near-hysteria":**   Ruth Dudley Edwards, *Victor Gollancz: A Biography*, p. 372.

179   **"Soviet Government may desire to cause a break":**   Durbrow memorandum, April 9, 1943, in *Foreign Relations of the United States, 1943*, vol. 3, p. 373.

Chapter 9   Defeat in Victory

Adelman, Ken. "Seeing Too Much" (interview with Karski), *Washingtonian*, July 1988, pp. 61–67.

Berle, Adolf. Diary. Box 215, Berle papers, FDRL.

Biddle, Anthony J. Drexel. Report to President Franklin D. Roosevelt, June 2, 1943. President's Secretary's File/Biddle, FDRL.

Brownell, Will, and Richard N. Billings. *So Close to Greatness: A Biography of William C. Bullitt*. New York: Macmillan, 1987.

Ciechanowski, Jan. *Defeat in Victory*. New York: Doubleday & Co., 1947.

Ciechanowski, Jan. Letter to Adolf Berle, July 3, 1943. Berle correspondence, Box 30, FDRL.

Ciechanowski, Jan. Report to Ministry of Foreign Affairs, "Wykorzystanie pobytu w USA p. Jana Karskiego" ("Utilization of Jan Karski's visit to USA"), August 5, 1943. Box 49, HIA/MSZ.

Cox, Oscar. Letter to Walter Lippmann, July 6, 1943. Cox papers, FDRL.

Cox, Oscar. Memorandum to Harry Hopkins, July 6, 1943. Cox papers, FDRL.

Durbrow, Elbridge. Interview with author, July 8, 1992.

Foreign Relations of the United States, 1943. Washington: Government Printing Office, 1963.

Frankfurter, Felix. Diary. Reel 1, Frankfurter papers, LC.

Frankfurter, Felix. Personal file on anti-Semitism. Reel 77, Frankfurter papers, LC.

Goldmann, Nahum. Memorandum, October 6, 1942. Box D92, Folder 1, AJA/WJCC.

"Holocaust Still Haunts Messenger Who Failed." Associated Press dispatch, October 29, 1981.

Karski, Jan. Diplomatic passport. Personal archive of Jan Karski.

Karski, Jan. Interviews with authors, 1987–1993.

Karski, Jan. "Notatka z rozmowy z Prezydentem F.D. Roosevelt'em w środc, 28/VII.1943r." ("Notes from a conversation with President F.D. Roosevelt on Wednesday, July 28, 1943"). Box 1, HIA/Karski.

Karski, Jan. "The Polish Question, 1940–1945: The Secret Diplomacy of Churchill and Roosevelt."

Karski, Jan. "I Raport p. Karskiego z pobytu w U.S.A." ("Report #1 of Mr. Karski on his visit to U.S.A."), July 24, 1943. Box 1, HIA/Karski.

Karski, Jan. "II Raport Jana Karskiego z pobytu w U.S.A." ("Report #2 of Jan Karski on his visit to U.S.A."), August 1943. Box 1, HIA/Karski.

Karski, Jan. "Raport Znamirowskiego-Karskiego z jego podróży do Stanów Zjednoczonych." ("Report of Znamirowski-Karski on his trip to the United States"), October 5, 1943. Folder "Poczta od Rządu" ("Mail from the Government") No. 17, Item 202/I-19, pp. 105–109, AAN.

Karski, Jan. Story of a Secret State.

Mikołajczyk, Stanisław. Letter to Ciechanowski, June 8, 1943. Personal archive of Jan Karski.

Mikołajczyk, Stanisław. Telegram to government delegate in Poland, June 22, 1943. Teka 11, Szafa 12, SPP.

Mitkiewicz, Leon. Unpublished memoirs (New York, 1967). Kol. 50/15B, PI.

Office of Strategic Services/Foreign Nationalities Branch. Memorandum from "Major Morris" (OSS) to Philip Horton, October 8, 1943. OSS/FNB microfiche, INT-21PO-589, NA.

Office of Strategic Services/Foreign Nationalities Branch. Report on interview with Ciechanowski, June 17, 1943. OSS/FNB microfiche, INT-21PO-464, NA.

Raczyński, Edward. Letter to Ciechanowski, June 9, 1943. Personal archive of Jan Karski.

Raczyński, Edward. Telegram to Ciechanowski, May 5, 1943 (requesting visa for Karski). Alphabetical file on passports and visas, HIA/MSZ.

Representation of Polish Jewry. Minutes of meeting attended by Karski, August 9, 1943.

Rogers, James Grafton. *Wartime Washington: The Secret OSS Journal of James Grafton Rogers*. Frederick, Maryland: University Publications of America, 1987.

Scaife, Maj. Alan M. (OSS). Memorandum to DeWitt Poole (chief of OSS Foreign Nationalities Branch), December 29, 1943. OSS/FNB microfiche, INT-21PO-632, NA.

Waldman, Morris (American Jewish Committee). Minutes of meeting with Karski, August 10, 1943. Box 4, Folder 6, AJA/Waldman.

Wilson, Hugh (OSS). Memorandum, May 12, 1943 (mentioning visa request for Karski). Record group 226, Entry 92, Box 299, Folder 4, NA.

Wise, Stephen. *Challenging Years: The Autobiography of Stephen Wise*.

181 **"news about Soviet partisans":** Raczyński telegram to Ciechanowski.
182 **Biddle denounced Kot:** Biddle report to Roosevelt.
182 **State Department telegram:** Cited in Wilson memorandum.
182 **"his splendid memory":** Raczyński letter to Ciechanowski.
182 **"extraordinary intelligence":** Mikołajczyk letter to Ciechanowski.
182 **"Karski departed for three months:** Telegram dated June 22, 1943. Teka 11/szafa 12, SPP.
182 **June 10, June 16:** Karski diplomatic passport.
183 **Władysław Ciechanowski:** Obituaries of the ambassador's son appeared in the *New York Herald Tribune*, December 6, 1942, and the *New York Journal American*, December 9, 1942.
183 **"most undiplomatic blasts":** OSS report on Ciechanowski.
183 **"tall, dark young man":** Ciechanowski, *Defeat in Victory*, p. 179.
183 **dermatological treatment:** Ciechanowski, "Utilization of Jan Karski's visit to U.S.A."
184 **"The whole town sleeps naked":** Rogers, *Wartime Washington*, p. 106.
184 **"Avoid the Poles":** K. Int. (February 28, 1992).
184 **Ciechanowski's strategy:** Ciechanowski, "Utilization of Jan Karski's visit to U.S.A."
185 **"1. Don't exaggerate":** Karski, "Report #1."
185 **false arrival dates:** See, for example, Cox memo to Hopkins, Representation of Polish Jewry minutes, and Waldman minutes, each citing February 1943 as arrival date. Karski told Roosevelt that he had left at the beginning of March 1943 ("Notes from a conversation with President F.D. Roosevelt").
185 **"small informal men's dinner":** Ciechanowski letter to Berle.
186 **telegram on 4th of July:** Sikorski to Roosevelt, July 4, 1943, in *Foreign Relations of the United States, 1943*, vol. 3, p. 437.
186 **news of Sikorski's death:** Biddle to Hull and Roosevelt, July 5, 1943, in *Foreign Relations of the United States, 1943*, vol. 3, pp. 437–438.
187 **"bloodcurdling":** Cox letter to Lippmann.
187 **Frankfurter took Bullitt aside:** Frankfurter diary, June 9, 1943. Frankfurter also once interceded with the Army Medical Corps on behalf of a Jewish doctor who felt his career had been stymied by anti-Semitism (Anti-Semitism file).

187 **"very badly impressed by Frankfurter":** Goldmann memorandum.

187 **"make your hair stand on end":** Cox memorandum to Hopkins.

188 **Karski's encounter with Frankfurter:** K. Ints. (February 28, 1992; December 1987). Frankfurter left no record of the meeting. There is a gap in Frankfurter's diaries beginning in late June 1943; he is known to have edited the journals before releasing them to the Library of Congress.

189 **"We are endeavoring to work out":** Berle diary, July 10, 1943.

190 **"The government sends us money":** Karski, "Report #1."

190 **"Karski is polished . . . a little irritating":** Mitkiewicz memoirs, p. 19.

191 **"I have never met a man":** Ciechanowski, *Defeat in Victory*, p. 179.

191 **"an amazing day . . . The Poles have a whole government":** Rogers, *Wartime Washington*, pp. 117–118. Present at the July 9 OSS meeting were John C. Wiley, a career diplomat who headed two OSS departments during the war; Hugh Wilson, a former ambassador to Germany who had come out of retirement to help launch OSS (and who would later arrange Karski's postwar missions on behalf of Herbert Hoover); James Murphy, chief of counterintelligence; Col. G. Edward Buxton, Donovan's top assistant; Brig. Gen. John Magruder, deputy director for intelligence; Whitney H. Shepardson, chief of secret intelligence; three academics brought into the agency as political analysts; and James G. Rogers.

192 **"propaganda against the Soviet":** Scaife memorandum to Poole.

193 **March 1943 meeting with Eden:** Karski, "The Polish Question," p. 7.

194 **"He was a guy we were counting on":** Durbrow interview.

195 **background regarding Bullitt, Welles; Kennan and Shirer quotations:** Brownell and Billings, *So Close to Greatness*, pp. 294–297, 331; President's Secretary's File/Bullitt, FDRL.

195 **Karski's conversation with Bullitt:** Karski, "Report #2."

196 **"told the President":** Karski, "Report #1."

196 **"The invitation came suddenly":** Karski, "Notes from a conversation with President F.D. Roosevelt."

197 **"He really projected majesty":** K. Int. (June 16, 1992).

197 **Karski's discussion with Roosevelt:** The main source for this account of the meeting is Karski's contemporary report ("Notes from a conversation with President F.D. Roosevelt"). Ciechanowski left a lengthy account in *Defeat in Victory* that differs from Karski's official report in small but sometimes significant ways, as when the ambassador claims that Karski had visited Treblinka as well as Bełżec (he had not) and that he told Roosevelt about these visits.

199 **Rabbi Wise and Roosevelt:** Wise had approached the president on July 22 to ask permission to undertake a special initiative to save some Jews by paying a ransom. Roosevelt gave his assent to the scheme (Wise, *Challenging Years*, p. 277). Wise, who was close to Roosevelt, had evidently discussed the extermination of the Jews with FDR before: Early in 1943 he wrote that Roosevelt "feels as strongly about the whole wretched Jewish situation as we do [and] has expressed himself personally to me in the strongest terms." (Wise letter to A.L. Easterman, January 25, 1943. File A14/5, AJC/WJCC.)

200 **Karski denied mentioning Bełżec and Ghetto:** K. Int. (June 16, 1992).

201   walking backwards: Adelman, "Seeing Too Much," p. 66.
201   "Overnight, the Karski mission":   Associated Press, "Holocaust Still Haunts Messenger Who Failed."
201   "Having so many times had the opportunity":   Ciechanowski, "Utilization of Jan Karski's visit to U.S.A."
202   "The Poles are obviously highly pleased":   "Major Morris" memorandum.
202   report sent to Poland: "Report of Znamirowski-Karski." In this report, Karski erroneously gives his arrival date in the United States as July 15, 1943; his diplomatic passport confirms that he reached New York on June 16.
202   "The President seems so thrilled":   Ciechanowski, "Utilization of Jan Karski's visit to U.S.A."

Chapter 10   Unmasked

Allen, D. (Foreign Office). Note from December 31, 1943. FO 371/34551, PRO.

Babinski, Witold. Telegram to Karski, August 25, 1943. Telegram file, HIA/ MSZ.

Ciechanowski, Jan. Report to Ministry of Foreign Affairs, "Rozmowa z Sekretarzem Stanu Cordell Hull dnia 21/VII.43" ("Conversation with Secretary of State Hull on July 21, 1943"). Box 49, HIA/MSZ.

Ciechanowski, Jan. Report, "Utilization of Jan Karski's visit to U.S.A."

Ciechanowski, Jan. Telegram to Ministry of Foreign Affairs, October 18, 1943. Box 176, HIA/MSZ.

Ciechanowski, Jan. Telegram to Stanisław Mikołajczyk, August 5, 1943. Box 49, HIA/MSZ.

The Second World War Diary of Hugh Dalton (Ben Pimlott, ed.). London: Jonathan Cape, 1981.

Engel, David. *Facing a Holocaust: The Polish Government-in-Exile and the Jews, 1943–1945.*

[Hemingway], Martha Gellhorn. "Three Poles," *Collier's*, March 18, 1944, p. 17.

Karski, Jan. "Czwarty raport J. Karskiego z pobytu w U.S.A." ("Fourth report of J. Karski on his trip to U.S.A."), no date (September 1943). Box 1, HIA/ Karski.

Karski, Jan. Diplomatic passport.

Karski, Jan. Interviews with authors, 1987–1993.

Karski, Jan. May 1943 report.

Karski, Jan. "Notatka dla Pana Premiera" ("Note for the Prime Minister"), erroneously dated September 11, 1943. (The correct date is probably October 11. Karski did not arrive in England until September 19, according to his diplomatic passport. The topic on which this memorandum follows up was first raised in another note on October 5.) Box 2, HIA/Karski.

Karski, Jan. "Notes from a conversation with President F.D. Roosevelt on Wednesday, July 28, 1943."

Karski, Jan. "The Polish Question, 1940–1945: The Secret Diplomacy of Churchill and Roosevelt."

Karski, Jan. "Raport p. Karskiego: Spostrzeżenia i wnioski" ("Report of Mr. Karski: Observations and conclusions"), August 22, 1943. Box 2, HIA/Karski.

Karski, Jan. "Report #2 of Jan Karski on his visit to U.S.A."

Karski, Jan. "Raport Nr. 3 J. Karskiego z pobytu w U.S.A.: Sprawy żydowskie" ("Report #3 of J. Karski on his visit to U.S.A.: Jewish affairs"), not dated (August 1943). Box 1, HIA/Karski.

Karski, Jan. "Report of Znamirowski-Karski on his trip to the United States."

Karski, Jan. "Sprawozdanie z działalności propagandowej Jana Karskiego o sprawach krajowych w okresie 10.43r-1.II.44r." ("Report on propaganda activities of Jan Karski regarding Home affairs, October 1943-February 1, 1944"), February 17, 1944. Box 2, HIA/Karski.

Karski, Jan. Story of a Secret State.

Kochanowicz, Tadeusz. Na wojennej emigracji (Into Fighting Exile). Warsaw: Wyd. Książka i Wiedza, 1975.

Kot, Prof. Stanisław. Telegram to Karski, August 17, 1943. Box 222, HIA/MID.

McLaren, Moray (Foreign Office Political Intelligence Department). Letter to Mikołajczyk, October 7, 1943. Box 10, HIA/Mikołajczyk.

Mikołajczyk, Stanisław. Letter to Ciechanowski, February 20, 1944. Personal archive of Jan Karski.

Nowak, Jan. Kurier z Warszawy (Courier from Warsaw). London: Odnowa, 1978.

Representation of Polish Jewry. Minutes of meeting attended by Karski, August 9, 1943.

Representation of Polish Jewry. Protocol of plenary session, September 16, 1943 (discussion of Karski visit). File M2/558, YVA.

Ripa, Karol (Chicago Consul General). Report to Ministry of Foreign Affairs, August 20, 1943. Box 49, HIA/MSZ.

Rogers, James Grafton. Wartime Washington: The Secret OSS Journal of James Grafton Rogers.

Rollyson, Carl. Nothing Ever Happens to the Brave: The Story of Martha Gellhorn. New York: St. Martin's Press, 1990.

Romer, Tadeusz. Telegram to Jan Ciechanowski, August 7, 1943. Box 49, HIA/MSZ.

Scaife, Maj. Alan M. Memorandum to DeWitt Poole (OSS Foreign Nationalities Branch), December 29, 1943.

Schwarzbart, Ignacy. Letter to Stephen Wise, August 12, 1941. File A14/8, AJA/WJCC.

Strakacz, Sylwin (New York Counsel General). Letter to Ministry of Foreign Affairs, September 21, 1943. Box 177, HIA/MSZ.

Strakacz, Sylwin. Report to Ministry of Foreign Affairs, August 12, 1943. File M2/62, YVA.

Tartakower, Arieh (World Jewish Congress). Memorandum to Stephen Wise et al., July 21, 1943 (concerning Karski's impending visit). File D97/3, AJA/WJCC.

Waldman, Morris (American Jewish Committee). Minutes of meeting with Karski, August 10, 1943.

Waldman, Morris. Partial manuscript of memoirs. Box 4, Folder 6, AJA/Waldman.

Wise, Stephen. *Challenging Years: The Autobiography of Stephen Wise.*

Wise, Stephen. Memorandum, October 8, 1943. File D97/3, AJA/WJCC.

Wise, Stephen. Memorandum to Arieh Tartakower, undated. File D92/1, AJA/WJCC.

Yolles, Piotr P., and K. Kołodziejczyk (Polish Publishers' and Newspapermen's Association). Letter to Ciechanowski, August 19, 1943. Box 49, HIA/MSZ.

205   **list sent by Roosevelt:**   K. Int. (June 16, 1992). The list itself has not been found in any archive. Karski later recalled that it included Felix Frankfurter, Ben Cohen, Oscar Cox, Nahum Goldmann of the World Jewish Congress, Stephen Wise, and William Donovan, among others.

205   **meetings scheduled:**   The agenda for the remainder of Karski's stay in the United States was largely set before he met Roosevelt. By the third week of July, Polish officials were making arrangements for him to meet Jewish leaders in New York. In late July, the Polish consulate in New York alerted World Jewish Congress leaders about a "special representative of the Polish government who came from Poland a few months ago after having spent two years there and who is expected in New York next week" (Tartakower memorandum). In one of his own reports, Karski mentioned his planned meetings with Wise and others, as well as upcoming trips to Chicago and Detroit ("Report #1").

205   **officials Karski met in Washington:**   Karski, "Report #1"; "Report #2."

206   **twelve million dollar credit:**   Ciechanowski, "Conversation with Secretary of State Hull" and "Utilization of Jan Karski's visit to U.S.A."

206   **"second part of my stay":**   Karski, "Report #2."

206   **cabled London for permission:**   Ciechanowski telegram to Mikołajczyk; Romer telegram to Ciechanowski.

206   **"after fulfilling orders":**   Karski, "Report #2."

206   **meetings with labor leaders:**   Attendance lists, HIA/Karski, Box 2.

207 antagonisms among Jewish groups: Easterman to Schwarzbart, September 10, 1943. File F1, AJA/WJCC. The friction was evident in London as well. Even though Polish National Council member Ignacy Schwarzbart was affiliated with the World Jewish Congress, he got along poorly with A.L. Easterman, its British representative. After receiving a copy of the minutes of Karski's meeting with the Representation of Polish Jewry, Easterman wrote an accusatory letter to Schwarzbart demanding to know who Karski was. Although Easterman had received the Polish report distilled from Karski's information in November 1942, he had evidently never been informed of the envoy's presence in London.

208 "swinishness":   Wise memorandum to Tartakower.

208 Schwarzbart warning about Ciechanowski: Schwarzbart letter to Wise.

208 "The ambassador's face":   Waldman memoir fragment, pp. 92–93.

209 Karski's tales of atrocities: In his last report before leaving England, Karski noted that the stories were part of his standard presentation in his second round of meetings with Britons (May 1943 report).

209 accounts of meetings: Representation of Polish Jewry minutes; Representation of Polish Jewry protocol; Waldman minutes; Karski, "Report #3"; Karski, "Fourth report."

209 "Because of the real impression":   Karski, "Report #3."

210 "all Poles have changed":   Representation of Polish Jewry minutes.

210 "almost everybody kept diligently asking":   Karski, "Report #3."

210 "Poland will rise again!":   Karski, "Report #3."

210 transfer of funds to Poland: Karski, "Report #3"; Karski, "Fourth report"; Strakacz letter, September 21, 1943; Engel, Facing a Holocaust, pp. 92–93.

210 "young, strong, athletic Jews":   Karski, "Fourth report."

211 escape of Bronisława Langrod: Babiński telegram.

211 list of potential escapees: Strakacz letter, September 21, 1943.

211 "the damage that the anti-Semitic press is doing":   Representation of Polish Jewry protocol.

211 "my role consisted solely and exclusively":   Karski, "Fourth report." Emphasis in original.

212 Waldman's minutes: Waldman's records include both a summary of Karski's presentation and a separate document conveying the points Waldman wished to make. The latter document is undated and does not mention Karski by name, but since it was prepared in advance of a discussion with a Pole who had recently arrived in the United States from Poland, and since events mentioned in it confirm that it was written in the latter half of 1943, it clearly was intended for the meeting with Karski.

212 "Later he wrote a book":   Waldman memoir fragment, p. 95.

212 "I still believe":   Wise memorandum.

213 "told again the drama":   Rogers, Wartime Washington, p. 106.

213 "the hecatombs of sacrifice":   Resolution attached to Ripa report.

213 "the socialists and Jews":   "Report of Mr. Karski: Observations and conclusions."

214 **letter from Polish-American journalists:** Yolles and Kołodziejczyk letter.

214 **"The ambassador was afraid":** Karski, "Fourth report."

215 **"Upon your return":** Kot telegram.

215 **September 19, 1943:** Karski diplomatic passport.

215 **"Mr. Prime Minister":** K. Int. (February 28, 1992).

215 **"A certain Jan Karski":** K. Ints. (December 1987; February 28, 1992). No written record of the broadcast has been found.

216 **no evidence that the broadcast took place:** There is evidence, however, confirming that the government did claim that Karski had been "deconspired." Telegram from Foreign Minister Tadeusz Romer to Ciechanowski, November 11, 1943, Telegram file, HIA/MSZ; Romer letter to Ciechanowski, January 25, 1944, personal archive of Jan Karski; Mikołajczyk letter to Ciechanowski, February 20, 1944, personal archive of Jan Karski.

216 **plans to send Karski back to United States:** First mentioned in Romer telegram to Ciechanowski, November 11, 1943. Telegram file, HIA/MSZ.

217 **"lend his assistance . . .";"very much respected":** McLaren letter to Mikołajczyk. An account by a Polish employee of the radio station also attests to the high esteem in which Karski was held (Kochanowicz, *Into Fighting Exile*, pp. 110–115).

217 **Karski's personal attitude toward Soviets:** Karski, "Note for the Prime Minister"; K. Int. (June 6, 1993).

217 **articles in English and Scottish newspapers:** Examples: "Pole Here from the Underground," *Sunday Express*, September 26, 1943; "Nazi Rule in Poland: Attempt to Demoralise Youth," *Glasgow Herald*, November 23, 1943; " 'Official' Underground," *Edinburgh Scotsman*, November 24, 1943 (clippings in the personal archive of Jan Karski)

217 **"attacking Russia":** *Daily Worker*, January 24, 1944 (clipping in the personal archive of Jan Karski).

217 **"He was a little man"; Wells meeting:** K. Int. (October 3, 1992); "Report on propaganda activities of Jan Karski."

218 **"of a radical persuasion":** Ciechanowski telegram to Ministry of Foreign Affairs.

218 **"He was tall and dark":** Gellhorn [Hemingway], "Three Poles."

218 **trying to convince her husband:** Rollyson, *Nothing Ever Happens to the Brave*, pp. 189–190.

218 **"One thing it tends to skate over":** Allen note. Karski's article had appeared in the *Polish Fortnightly Review*, December 15, 1943.

219 **Roosevelt feigned sleep:** *The Second World War Diary of Hugh Dalton*, p. 687.

220 **"coldly, almost cynically":** Nowak, *Courier from Warsaw*, pp. 251–252.

221 **February 21:** Karski diplomatic passport.

221 **"he needs to be presented":** Mikołajczyk letter to Ciechanowski, February 20, 1944.

221 **"Piorun, I will tell you":** K. Ints. (May 8, 1993; June 16, 1992).

Chapter 11   Fame in Vain

Banaczyk, Władysław (Interior Minister). Note to Ciechanowski, February 19, 1944. Personal archive of Jan Karski.

Brzeziński, Zbigniew. Letter to author, October 13, 1993.

Burton, Humphrey (biographer to Leonard Bernstein). Interview with author, October 1993.

Drohojowski, Jan. Telegram to Polish Information Center/New York regarding Karski's impending arrival, February 21, 1944. Box 160, HIA/MSZ.

Foreign Relations of the United States, 1944. Washington: Government Printing Office, 1964.

Grot, Eve. "Not the Whole Story" (article attacking Karski), *Soviet Russia Today,* March 1945.

Naomi, Jolles, interview with Karski, *New York Post,* January 4, 1945.

Karski, Jan. Diplomatic passport.

Karski, Jan. Exemption statement filed with U.S. Department of Justice under Foreign Agents Registration Act, January 22, 1945. File 800.01B11/2–2245, State Department central files, NA.

Karski, Jan. Interviews with authors, 1987–1993.

Karski, Jan. Letter to Henryk Floyar Rajchman, August 16, 1944. Karski personal file, JPIA.

Karski, Jan. Letter to "Mr. Minister" (unnamed, probably Prof. Stanisław Kot) on initial film and book contacts, March 17, 1944. Box 160, HIA/MSZ.

Karski, Jan. Letter to "Mr. Minister" (unnamed, probably Kot), on progress of book and abandonment of film idea, June 30, 1944. Box 160, HIA/MSZ.

Karski, Jan. Letter to "Mr. Minister" (unnamed, probably Kot), on progress of book and other work; defense of "pessimistic" attitude, August 24, 1944. Box 160, HIA/MSZ.

Karski, Jan. "Raport o książce" ("Report on the Book"), January 15, 1945. File A.11.474/2/275, PI.

Karski, Jan. "Report of Mr. Karski: Observations and Conclusions."

Karski, Jan. Scrapbook of reviews and other press mentions. Personal archive of Jan Karski.

Karski, Jan. "Sprawozdanie z działalności" ("Report on Activities"), June 6, 1945. Karski personal file, JPIA.

Karski, Jan. Telegram to Professor Kot, March 23, 1944. Box 160, HIA/MSZ.

Karski, Jan. Waldorf-Astoria speech, October 17, 1944.

Kot, Prof. Stanisław. Telegram to Karski, April 5, 1944. Box 160, HIA/MSZ.

Kot, Prof. Stainsław. Telegram to Polish Information Center/New York, granting Karski permission to drop other projects and focus on book, April 6, 1944. Box 160, HIA/MSZ.

Laughlin, Henry A. *An Informal Sketch of the History of Houghton Mifflin Company.* Cambridge, Mass.: Riverside Press, 1957.

Mikołajczyk letter to Ciechanowski, February 20, 1944.

Office of Strategic Services/Foreign Nationalities Branch. Report on Karski's Chicago visit, January 30, 1945. OSS/FNB microfiche, INT-21PO-1097, NA.

Office of Strategic Services/Foreign Nationalities Branch. Report on Karski's Cleveland visit, February 20, 1945. OSS/FNB microfiche, INT-21PO-1123, NA.

Polish Consulate/New York. Telegram to Ministry of Information, December 1, 1944. Box 160, HIA/MSZ.

Polish Ministry of Information. Telegram to Polish Consulate/New York, December 11, 1944. Box 160, HIA/MSZ.

"Pre-Reviews of *Story of a Secret State.*" Book-of-the-Month Club (undated compilation, late 1944). Personal archive of Jan Karski.

Rajchman, Henryk Floyar. Letter to Karski, October 26, 1944. Karski personal file, JPIA.

Romer, Tadeusz (Polish Foreign minister). Letter to Ciechanowski, January 25, 1944. Personal archive of Jan Karski.

Washington Despatches 1941–1945: Weekly Political Reports from the British Embassy (H.G. Nicholas, ed.). London: Weidenfeld and Nicolson, 1981.

Yahil, Leni. *The Holocaust: The Fate of European Jewry, 1932–1945*. Oxford: Oxford University Press, 1990.

223 **February 27, 1944, arrival date:**   Karski diplomatic passport.
223 **first suggested during his prior visit:**   "Report of Mr. Karski: Observations and Conclusions."
223 **"It is warm"; sleeping in theaters:**   Jolles interview; K. Int. (October 3, 1993).
224 **plans for Karski's mission:**   Romer letter to Ciechanowski, January 25, 1944; Banaczyk letter to Ciechanowski, February 19, 1944; Mikołajczyk letter to Ciechanowski, February 20, 1944.
224 **"established communication":**   Karski letter, March 17, 1944.
224 **other propaganda efforts:**   Karski letter, March 17, 1944; Paul Winkler, "Polish Underground: Its Many-Sided Operations," *Washington Post*, March 27, 1944.
224 **Emery Reeves:**   K. Ints. (February 28, 1992; October 3, 1993).
225 **"He thinks the book will be a sensation":**   Karski telegram to Kot, March 23, 1944.
225 **"I accepted financial conditions":**   Karski letter, June 30, 1944.
226 **Kot gave his assent:**   Kot telegram to Polish Information Center/New York, April 6, 1944.
226 **"It was tremendous work":**   Karski letter, June 30, 1944.
226 **"Upon getting acquainted with my manuscript":**   Karski letter, June 30, 1944.
226 **conflict over chapter on Communists:**   Karski, "Report on the Book," January 15, 1945.

227 "if a book such as this is possible":   Karski, "Report on the Book," January 15, 1945.

227 "exaggerate my role" . . .; "the greatest difficulty":   Karski, "Report on the Book," January 15, 1945.

227 "I had to be careful":   K. Int. (June 15, 1992).

227 "I never altered the essential reality":   Karski, "Report on the Book," January 15, 1945. Cf. Karski letter, June 30, 1944: "Names, places and a whole series of situations in the underground movement are faked."

228 "My publishers especially emphasized":   Karski letter, June 30, 1944.

228 meeting with Mr. Houghton: K. Ints. (February 28, 1992; October 3, 1993). Laughlin, *An Informal Sketch*, pp. 8, 13. Edward O. Houghton retired from his family's publishing house in 1939 but remained involved in its operations. The only other Houghton then active at the firm was Henry O. Houghton, clerk of the corporation.

230 motorcycle adventure: K. Int. (May 8, 1993).

230 "he could count upon the moral support":   Secretary of State Cordell Hull cable to Ambassador Averell Harriman, June 17, 1944, *Foreign Relations of the United States, 1944*, vol. 3, pp. 1285–1289.

230 "While he may have done a service":   *Washington Despatches*, p. 371.

231 "The President will defend us":   K. Int. (May 8, 1993).

231 "I can assure you that no specific plan":   Roosevelt letter to Stalin, June 17, 1944, *Foreign Relations of the United States, 1944*, vol. 3, p. 1284.

232 cleared over eight thousand dollars from his writings: Karski exemption statement.

232 "It has been the misfortune":   Karski speech, October 17, 1944.

233 dinner with Brzeziński family: Brzeziński letter; November 1944 date from Karski diplomatic passport.

233 only 27 percent of the American public: Yahil, *The Holocaust*, p. 606.

233 "They do not think of the war":   Jolles interview.

233 "Two of my friends wrote to me":   Karski letter, August 24, 1944.

234 "a scoundrel, a fake diplomat":   Quoted in Karski letter to Rajchman, August 16, 1944.

234 "uttering the code words of capitulation":   Rajchman letter to Karski, October 26, 1944.

236 reviews of book: Book-of-the-Month Club, "Pre-Reviews of *Story of a Secret State*"; Karski scrapbook.

236 "big ad campaign":   Alice Hackett, "P.W. Forecast for Buyers," *Publisher's Weekly*, November 18, 1944, p. 2009. Karski reported to London that Houghton Mifflin had spent "some tens of thousands of dollars" on advertisements for the book.

236 foreign editions: *Mon témoinage devant le monde* (Paris: Editions Self, 1948); *Den hemmelige stat* (Oslo: Aas & Wahls, 1946); *Den hemliga staten* (Stockholm: Natur och Kultur, 1945). In addition, reviews of the book appeared in Australia and South Africa, though it is unclear whether separate editions were published in those countries. Karski also signed contracts for Italian, Danish, Spanish, Portugese, Hebrew, and Arabic translations to be published in Europe, South America, and the Middle East. For unknown reasons, however, none of these editions was actually pub-

lished. Karski received at the time (and has received again in recent years) offers from Polish-language presses to publish translations of the book. Both during the war and later in life, he strenuously opposed the issuance of a Polish edition. The book's dramatizations and intentional oversim-plifications—however necessary they may have been to put across the Polish message to an American audience—would be immediately appar-ent to a Polish reader, Karski argued, and would thus harm his reputa-tion.

237 **Karski in Chicago:** OSS Foreign Nationalities Branch report dated Jan-uary 30, 1945. OSS/FNB microfiche, INT-21PO-1097, NA.

237 **Karski in Cleveland:** OSS Foreign Nationalities Branch report dated February 20, 1945. OSS/FNB microfiche, INT-21PO-1123, NA.

239 **Fancy Free; drinking with Bernstein and Robbins:** K. Int. (October 3, 1993); Burton interview. Karski recalled that dancer John Kriza was also often present. Karski insisted that the bistro where he met Bernstein and Robbins was not the Russian Tea Room but another establishment close to Carnegie Hall. Bernstein biographer Humphrey Burton says the com-poser and his friends favored the Russian Tea Room as a hangout, but that in other respects, Karski's story is consistent with what is known of Bernstein's lifestyle at the time.

239 **hostile analysis:** Grot article.

240 **"It killed me":** K. Int. (February 29, 1992).

240 **"Oh, Mr. Karski, I'm just reading":** K. Int. (October 3, 1993).

241 **"Collection of these materials"; mission for Hoover:** "Report on Activ-ities," June 6, 1945; K. Int. (October 3, 1993).

242 **"I hereby cede our embassy":** K. Int. (October 2, 1992).

Epliogue: Silence Vowed, Silence Broken

Berenbaum, Michael. Address at *Perspective* Awards Dinner, June 11, 1983. Reprinted in *Perspectives* (Polish-American periodical), September/October 1983.

Central Intelligence Agency. Memorandum on Radio Free Europe, November 20, 1956, transmitted by CIA Director Allen Dulles to White House Staff Sec-retary Col. A.J. Goodpaster. From Dwight D. Eisenhower Library; furnished to authors by National Security Archive, Washington, D.C.

Foreign Relations of the United States, 1952–54. Washington: Government Print-ing Office, 1984.

Howland, Harold E. (State Department). Letter to Father Brian A. McGrath of Georgetown University (regarding Karski's Asian lecture tour), October 25, 1955. Personal archive of Jan Karski.

Karski, Jan. Interviews with authors, 1987–1993.

Kersten, Hon. Charles J. "Professor Sharp's Book Aids the Enemy," *Congres-sional Record*, April 14, 1954.

Korboński, Stefan. *The Jews and the Poles in World War II*. New York: Hippo-crene Books, 1989.

Krogh, Peter F. (Dean of the Edmund A. Walsh School of Foreign Service, Georgetown University). Interview with author, November 1993.

Lanzmann, Claude. Letter to Karski, July 7, 1978. Personal archive of Jan Karski.

Lanzmann, Claude. *Shoah: An Oral History of the Holocaust* (text of the film).

O'Brien, William P. (State Department). Letter to Father Gerard J. Campbell of Georgetown University (regarding Karski's Asian Mediterranean-African lecture tour), June 1, 1967. Personal archive of Jan Karski.

Peretz, Martin. "Warsaw Diarist," *The New Republic*, May 10, 1993.

"Polish Ex-Spy Tells of Red Doublecross," *Milwaukee Sentinel*, October 22, 1954.

Trump, Christopher. "Far East Journey," *The Foreign Service Courier* (George-town magazine), May 31, 1956.

Wiesel, Elie. "A Survivor Remembers Other Survivors of *Shoah*," *New York Times*, November 3, 1985, Sec. 2, pp. 1, 20.

243 "At that time I hated humanity": K. Int. (October 2, 1992).
246 "established himself": Krogh interview.
247 "McCarthyski": K. Int. (October 2, 1992).
247 Karski and Red-baiting congressman: Kersten, "Professor Sharp's Book Aids the Enemy"; "Polish Ex-Spy Tells of Red Doublecross."
248 "Other teachers went fishing": K. Int. (October 2, 1992).
248 State Department lecture tours: Howland letter; Trump, "Far East Journey"; O'Brien letter; K. Int. (October 2, 1992).
249 appropriations for "information programs": *Foreign Relations of the United States, 1952–54*, vol. 2, part 2, pp. 1601, 1644.
249 "I didn't want to leave Georgetown": K. Int. (October 3, 1993).
250 Radio Free Europe analysis project: CIA memorandum; K. Int. (October 3, 1993).
250 indications of other intelligence activities: In interviews, Karski has repeatedly commented about having been "up to [his] neck in the psychological warfare" during the 1950s and 1960s. He has not elaborated.
251 Pola Nireńska: K. Int. (October 2, 1992).
253 "The official Polish point of view": Lanzmann letter, July 7, 1978.
253 "Now I go back thirty-five years": Lanzmann, *Shoah*, p. 167.
254 "a narrow, one-sided view": Statement issued by Polish-American Con-gress, 1985. Reprinted in Korboński, *The Jews and the Poles in World War II*, p. 108.
254 "unquestionably the greatest movie": The English text of Karski's ar-ticle appeared in *Together*, the newsletter of the American Gathering/ Fed-eration of Jewish Holocaust Survivors, July 2, 1986; the French text in

Esprit (Paris), February 1986; and the Polish text in *Kultura* (Paris), November 1985.

255 **"There was laughter":**   Wiesel, "A Survivor Remembers Other Survivors."

255 **"The Lord assigned me a role":**   Reprinted in Korboński, *The Jews and the Poles in World War II*, p. 103.

256 **"You will come to Israel":**   K. Int. (October 2, 1992).

257 **"Jan Karski has redeemed the image":**   Berenbaum address.

257 **"You did what you had to do":**   K. Int. (October 2, 1992).

258 **"Did we not demand too much?":**   K. Int. (June 16, 1992).

259 **"Karski is one of 'the righteous' ":**   Peretz, "Warsaw Diarist."

Index

Algeciras, Spain, 142
Algeria, 249
Allied forces
  attitude toward Poland, 53, 114
  desire to aid Polish Jews, 118–20, 132,
    152–53
  failure to aid Jews, 145–46, 177, 189,
    199, 208
  and Poland/Soviet Union settlement,
    161–68, 192–93, 196, 218–19, 235,
    238
Amalgamated Clothing Workers Union
  (ACWU), 207
American Federation of Labor (AFL), 207
American Federation of Polish Jews, 207
American Jewish Committee, 207–9, 211,
  256
American Jewish Congress, 207, 210
American Jewish Joint Distribution Com-
  mittee, 207–8, 210–11
The American Mercury, 191, 232
Angers, France, 31, 48–52, 56, 59–61, 63,
  69, 113, 260
Arad, Yitzhak, 256
Asquith, H. H., 166
Atlantic Monthly, 236
Auschwitz, 6, 56, 63, 89, 96, 108, 176,
  198, 238, 255
  See also Concentration/Extermination
    camps, Oświęcim
Australia, 256–57

Balkans, 138
Barcelona, Spain, 140
Bartoszewski, Władysław, 107, 260
BBC, 31, 100, 152, 179
Beck, Józef, 4, 174, 260
Begin, Menachem, 116
Belgium, 11, 69, 146
Bełżec, 41–42, 52, 104, 128–31, 150–51,
  198, 260
  See also Concentration/Extermination
    camps
Berenbaum, Michael, 257
Bereza Kartuska, 39
Bergen-Belsen, 238
  See also Concentration/Extermination
    camps
Berle, Adolf, 189–90

Berlin, 137, 219
Berman, Adolf, 116–17, 211
Bernstein, Leonard, 239, 306n
Biddle, Anthony J. Drexel, Jr. (Tony),
  174–75, 179, 181–82, 194, 260
Biddle, Francis, 174, 205
Bielecki, Tadeusz, 148, 176–77, 260
Bieńkowski, Witold, 135
Blitzkrieg, 6, 27, 51, 69, 94, 146, 174
B'nai B'rith, 166, 256
Bohlen, Charles, 189, 244
Borzęcki, Marian, 32, 39–40, 56, 63–64
Brussels, 137
Brzeziński, Zbigniew, 233
Buchenwald, 96, 227
  See also Concentration/Extermination
    camps
Budapest, Hungary, 48–49, 51, 62, 71
Bullitt, William C., 187, 194–96, 200
Bund (Jewish Socialist), 115–18, 120–21,
  123, 144, 150–52, 156, 161, 206–7,
  228, 260
Burma, 248

Cambodia, 248
Cameroon, 249
Canada, 233, 256
Central Intelligence Agency (CIA), 249–50
  See also Office of Strategic Services
Cerf, Bennett, 236
Ceylon, 248
Charlotte, N.C., 236
Chełmno, 104, 144
  See also Concentration/Extermination
    camps
Chicago, IL, 213, 215, 216
Chicago Sun, 237
Chicago Tribune, 213
Churchill, Winston, 148, 151, 153, 162,
  167, 171, 184, 218–22, 224
Church of the Holy Cross (Warsaw), 28,
  62, 135
Ciechanowski, Jan, 206, 214, 221, 235,
  242, 260, 297–98n
  antagonistic nature of, 208
  and training of Karski, 183–93, 218,
    244
  visits White House, 197, 200–202
Cieszyn, Poland, 34

Cleveland, OH, 237–38
Clinton, Bill, 246, 259
Cohen, Ben, 186
Collier's, 191, 218, 224, 232
Communists
  Polish government-in-exile and activities of in Poland, 108–9, 114, 226
  See also José
Concentration/Extermination camps, 22,
  129, 189
  Auschwitz, 6, 56, 63, 89, 96, 108, 176,
    198, 238, 255
  Bełżec, 41–42, 52, 104, 128–31, 150–51,
    198, 260
  Bergen-Belsen, 238
  Buchenwald, 96, 227
  Chełmno, 104, 144
  Dachau, 199, 238
  Izbica Lubelska, 128–29, 148, 209, 262,
    283n
  Majdanek, 198, 238
  Mauthausen, 199
  Oranienburg, 199
  Ravensbrück, 89, 199
  Sobibor, 104, 150
  Stanisławów, 198–99
  Treblinka, 104–5, 143, 150, 198
Congo, 249
Congress of Industrial Organizations
  (CIO), 207
Conrad, Joseph, 166
Cox, Oscar, 186–87, 190
Cranborne, Lord, 175
Croatia, 258
Curzon Line, 173, 193, 219
Cyrankiewicz, Józef, 62, 85, 94–96, 108,
  246, 252, 260
Czarnek, Zbigniew, 19
Czechoslovakia, 4, 129
Czerniakow, Adam, 143
Częstochowa, Poland, 45, 149

Dachau, 199, 238
  See also Concentration/Extermination
  camps
Daily Worker, 217
Dalton, Hugh, 175
Danzig Corridor, 4, 200
Dębski, Aleksander, 64
Delegate of the Government (Poland), 69,
  99, 113–14, 117, 130, 138, 155, 199,
  260–61
Denmark, 256
Department of State
  See United States, Department of State
de Rothschild, James, 154
Detroit, MI, 214, 231

Donovan, William J. (Wild Bill), 141, 184,
  191, 213, 261
Drymmer, Tomir, 3–5
Dubinsky, David, 207
Dulles, Allen, 250
Durbrow, Elbridge, 179, 189, 194, 242,
  261

Early, Steve, 195
Easterman, A. L., 146, 154, 261, 301n
Eden, Sir Anthony (Lord Avon), 152–54,
  167–69, 171–73, 175, 193, 219–10,
  224, 261
Ehrlich, Ludwik, 38
Eichmann, Adolf, 256
Eisenhower, Dwight D., 249–51
Ejbuszyc, Lejba, 37
Engel, Kurt, 129–30
England, 251, 256
  See also Great Britain
Ewing, Patrick, 246

Federal Bureau of Investigation (FBI),
  249
Feiner, Leon, 116–24, 128, 131, 151–53,
  206, 261, 281–82n
Feis, Herbert, 205–6
"Final Solution," 124, 145, 154, 188, 199,
  208–9, 229, 253
Foreign Office, U.K., 146–47, 152–53,
  159–60, 173, 177, 218, 230
France, 4, 44, 69, 82, 137–38
  Lyon, 139
  Modane, 49–50
  Normandy, 229
  Paris, 31, 49–50, 55–60, 137–39, 194,
    198, 258
  Perpignan, 139
  Vichy Regime, 138
Franco, Francisco, 139, 141
Frankfurter, Felix, 186–91, 209, 261
From the Abyss (Kossak), 108
Front Odrodzenia Polski (FOP; Front for
  the Rebirth of Poland), 105–7, 131–
  32, 135, 144, 156
Fuchs, Izio, 37–38
Fuchs, Salus, 37–38
Fulbright, J. William, 232

Galveston, TX, 236
Garczyńska, Maria (Marysia), 58–59
General Gouvernement, 33, 53
Geneva, Switzerland, 74, 76, 94, 145, 168
Georgetown University, 205, 221, 246–49,
  252, 255
Germany, 3–4, 11, 44, 54, 97, 109, 111,
  162, 191
  Berlin, 137, 219

and nonaggression pact with Soviet
Union, 14
and partition of Poland, 22
and prisoner swap, 19–20
See also Nazi Party
Gestapo, 98, 108–9, 115, 136–39, 190, 210
Karski's escape from, 87–89
Karski's imprisonment by, 74–80, 82–
83, 229
techniques of, 34, 36, 45, 71, 103,
150–51
underground leaders captured by, 56,
63, 94–96, 186
Getts, Clark H., 231–32, 239, 261
Gilbraltar, 142, 181, 186
Głód, Karol, 86–87, 89, 261
Göbbels, Jósef, 93, 154, 261
Goldberg, Sasha, 37
Goldmann, Nahum, 187, 208
Gollancz, Victor, 179, 261
Gore, Albert, Jr., 259
Göring, Hermann, 11–12, 93, 154, 261
Great Britain
Foreign Office, 146–47, 152–53, 159–60,
173, 177, 218, 230
and Holocaust, 238
and relations with Poland, 4, 44, 180
and relations with Soviet Union, 163,
195–96
and Royal Air Force (RAF), 120, 183
and Special Operations Executive, 110,
141–42, 171, 173
See also England; London
The Great Powers and Poland, 252
Greece, 249
Greenwood, Arthur, 175

Hamann, Heinrich, 89
Harper's Bazaar, 232
Hartford, CT, 236
Hashomer Hatzair, 116
Hausner, Gideon, 256
Hemingway, Ernest, 218
Hemingway, Martha Gellhorn, 218
Henderson, Loy, 189
Herbst, Stanisław, 280n
Heydrich, Reinhard, 104
Hillman, Sidney, 207
Himmler, Heinrich, 143, 154, 261
Hitler, Adolf, 47–49, 141
Allies' reaction to, 144–45, 171, 219
Poland's reaction to, 4, 96–97, 118–20,
156, 224
propaganda against, 92–93
Hitlerjugend (Hitler Youth), 11–12, 123,
150, 282n
Holocaust, 35, 179, 233, 243, 251–55, 257
Allied reaction to, 143–156, 177

Jewish reaction to, 131, 144, 146, 187,
207
Home Army (Armia Krajowa; AK)
See Union for Armed Struggle
Hoover, Herbert, 191, 241, 261–62
Hoover Institute on War, Revolution, and
Peace, 241
Hopkins, Harry, 187, 206
Houghton, Edward O., 228–29, 305n
Houghton Mifflin Company, 228, 231, 236
Hull, Cordell, 175, 202, 206, 230, 262
Hungary, 47–48, 70–73, 109, 210, 249, 258
Budapest, 48–49, 51, 62, 71
Košice, 71–72

Iłłakowicz, Jerzy, 135
India, 248–49
Indianapolis, IN, 236
International Ladies' Garment Workers
Union (ILGWU), 207
Israel, 256, 259
See also Jerusalem; Palestine; Zionism
Italy, 21, 49, 192
Izbica Lubelska, 128–29, 148, 209, 262,
283n
See also Concentration/Extermination
camps

Jagiellonian University, 50
Japan, 249
Jenet, Józef, 86–87, 89, 262
Jerusalem, 145–46, 256
Jewish Agency, 146
Jewish Fighting Organization (Żydowska
Organizacja Bojowa; ŻOB), 116, 121,
262
Jewish Forum, 232
Jewish Military Union (Żydowska Zwią-
zek Wojskowy; ŻZW), 115–16, 121,
262
José (Spanish Communist), 139–40
Józef Piłsudski Gimnazjum, 37

Kalinin, U.S.S.R., 21
Karski, Jan (Jan Kozielewski, Jan Kanicki, Kwaśniewski, Znamirowski,
Witold)
and American mission (1943), 181–215
and American mission (1944), 223–42
capture and imprisonment of (1939),
14–23
capture of in Slovakia (1940), 73–75
childhood of, 8–10
and Christianity, 9, 135–6, 149, 214
diplomatic career of, 11–13
attitudes about education, 280n
escape from prison, 23–25
and FOP activity, 105–8

Karski, Jan *(Continued)*
  travels to France (1940), 44–61
  and Georgetown University, 245–48
  and *The Great Powers and Poland*, 252
  witnesses Holocaust, 117–28
  honors of, 255–59
  hospitalization and escape of (1940),
    82–88
  identity of deciphered, 215–16, 302n
  and Jan Kazimierz University, 10–11,
    38–39
  Jewish friends of, 37–39
  hides in Kąty, 91–94
  and lecture circuit, 231–29
  meets with U.S. labor and Jewish
    groups, 205–13
  prepares for London, 113–14
  London activities of (1942–43), 157–79
  travels to London (1942), 135–43, 286–
    87n
  marriages of, 243–44, 251–52
  carries microfilm, 132, 138, 284n
  and mobilization, 3–5
  returns to Poland (1940), 61–62
  meets with Roosevelt, 196–202
  and *Shoah*, 253–55, 308n
  and social tolerance, 9
  and *Story of a Secret State*, 224–29, 306n
  suicide attempt of (1940), 80–82
  torture of (1940), 74–80
  joins underground, 30–33
  and relations with the underground,
    63–66
  works for U.S. government, 241–42,
    248–50, 308n
  returns to Warsaw (1939), 26–30
  works in Warsaw (1941), 98–104
  attempts rescue of Weinbergs, 102–4,
    209, 267, 277–78n
Karsten, Charles, 247
Kąty, 88, 91, 262
Katyń, 21, 179, 181, 262
Kawałkowski, Aleksander, 137–39, 262
Kharkov, U.S.S.R., 21
Kielce, Poland, 22, 24, 27, 45
Kiev, U.S.S.R., 16
Kirschenbaum, Menachem, 116–17, 262–
    63, 281n
Knoll, Roman, 111–13
Koestler, Arthur, 179, 263, 294n
Komorowski, Tadeusz (Bór), 85, 94–96,
    263
Konopka, Józef, 17–18
Konrad Żegota Committee, 107
Korbońska, Zofia, 130
Korboński, Stefan, 64–65, 69–70, 130,
    159, 263
Kossak (Kossak-Szczucka), Zofia, 105–8,

117, 131–32, 135, 155–56, 164, 263,
    278n
Kot, Professor Stanisław, 50–53, 55–61,
    65, 182, 185, 214–16, 225–26, 263
Kozel'shchina, 16–20
Kozielewska, Jadwiga, 5, 44, 63, 245–48, 263
Kozielewski, Jan
  See Karski, Jan
Kozielewski, Marian, 164, 245, 248, 263
  as chief of Warsaw security, 26–33, 61
  capture of, 63, 81, 176
  as Jan's patron, 4, 8, 10, 12, 44
  as Piłsudskite, 39–41, 51, 55–58, 111
Kozielewski, Stefan and Walentyna, 8, 37,
    264
Kraczkiewicz, Karol, 155
Krajewski, Alfred, 48
Kraków, Poland, 5–6, 45–46, 62, 70, 91,
    93–96, 98, 100, 166, 212–23, 229
Krauze, Father Edmund, 135, 264
Kriza, John, 306n
Krogh, Peter, 246, 252
Kucharski, Eugeniusz, 43
Kucharski, Witold (friend of Karski), 43,
    264
"Kucharski, Witold" (assumed name of
    Karski), 74, 84, 90, 264
  See also Witold
Kuh, Frederick, 178
Kuśniarz, Tomasz, 185
"Kwaśniewski," 160–61, 264, 291n
  See also Karski, Jan

Landau, David John (Dudek), 121, 123,
    264, 282–83n
Lane, Allen, 179
Langrodowa, Bronisława, 94–95, 211, 264
Lanzmann, Claude, 253–55, 264
  See also Shoah
Laura, (sister of Karski), 27–28, 263
Law, Richard, 146–47, 173, 264
Lebanon, 249
Lerski, Jerzy, 38, 42, 60–61, 73, 157–58,
    175, 264
Lewandowska, Janina, 15, 21
"Liaison girls," 99
Librach, Jan, 264, 292n
Lidice, Czechoslovakia, 104
Life, 224, 232
Lippman, Walter, 187, 190–91
Lisbon, Portugal, 191
Lithuania, 241
Łódź, Poland, 8–10, 32–33, 62, 96, 104,
    207
London, 12, 97, 112–13, 145, 158, 214–16
Los Angeles Times, 236
Lublin, Poland, 52, 124, 128, 227
Luftwaffe, 6, 11

Łukasiewicz, Juliusz, 59–60
Lwów, Poland, 10, 33, 38, 41–43, 44, 58, 74, 76, 192, 235, 244
Lyon, France, 139

McCarthy, Joseph, 247
McCloy, John, 205–6
McCormick, Col. Robert, 213
MacFarlane, Mason, 142
Madrid, Spain, 140–41
Maginot Line, 69
Majdanek, 198, 238
  See also Concentration/Extermination camps
Maisky, Ivan, 193
Makowiecki, Jerzy, 98–102, 115, 135, 264, 280n
Mann, Thomas, 179
Mauthausen, 199
  See also Concentration/Extermination camps
Mexico, 149, 158, 166
Miklaszewski, Tadeusz, 111–12
Mikołajczyk, Stanisław, 142, 165, 177, 182, 234–35, 264
  as interior minister, 138, 148, 158–60, 185
  as prime minister, 192, 208, 215–17, 221, 227
  visits Roosevelt, 229–31
Mission to Moscow, 223
Modane, France, 49–50
Molotov, V. M., 173, 219
Morgenthau, Henry, 189, 201, 206
Mościcki, Ignacy, 3
Musiał, Franciszek (Myszka), 70–74, 78, 264, 275n
Mussolini, Benito, 49

Nazi party
  Einsatzgruppen, 104, 144
  and Final Solution, 124, 145, 154, 188, 199, 208–9, 229, 253
  Hitlerjugend (Hitler Youth), 11–12, 123, 150
  Jewish Council (German), 131
  and Nuremberg Laws, 11
  Parteitag, 11
  Schutzstaffel (SS), 78–80, 129, 144
  Third Reich, 34, 69, 79, 97, 123, 137, 223, 258
  treatment of Jews, 35–36, 52–54, 121–30, 146
  Wehrmacht, 69, 95, 97, 139
  See also Blitzkrieg; Germany; Gestapo; Göbbels, Jósef; Göring, Hermann; Himmler, Heinrich; Hitler, Adolf
Nepal, 249

Netherlands, 69, 146
New Orleans, LA, 236
The New Republic, 259
New York City, 145, 152, 206–7, 214, 223–24, 231, 236, 243, 251
New York Herald Tribune, 244
New York Post, 233
New York Times, 152, 236
Nireńska, Pola, 251–52, 254, 256–57, 264–65
NKVD, 17–21
Normandy, France, 229
North Africa, 21
Norway, 236
Nowak, Jan (Zdzisław Jeziorański), 220, 265
Nowy Sącz, Poland, 70–71, 83, 85–86, 88–89, 91, 93, 136, 265
Nuremberg trials, 153

Office of Strategic Services (OSS)
  See Central Intelligence Agency; United States, Office of Strategic Services
Oklahoma City, 236
Omaha, NB, 236
O'Malley, Owen, 173
Oranienburg, 199
  See also Concentration/Extermination camps
Oświęcim, Poland, 5–6
  See also Auschwitz

Paderewski, Ignacy, 40
Pakistan, 248–49
Palestine, 115–16, 145–46, 152–53, 251
  See also Jerusalem
Paris, 31, 49–50, 55–60, 137–39, 194, 198, 258
Pawiak prison (Warsaw), 63
Pehle, John, 201
Peretz, Martin, 259
Perpignan, France, 139
Phillipines, 248
Pilc, Tadeusz, 62, 85, 94, 96, 227, 265
Piłsudski, Marshal Józef, 8, 29, 31–32, 50–52, 64, 102, 106, 161, 265
  followers of, 39, 41, 55–60, 111, 177, 234
Pittsburgh, PA, 231
Pius XII, 119, 156
Plaskov, Commander, 14
Poland, 3, 4, 238, 256, 258–59
  air force of, 15
  anti-Semitism in, 36, 38, 45–46, 106, 115, 144, 176, 272n
  army of, 3, 5, 41
  Biegonice, 90
  Cieszyn, 34

Poland *(Continued)*
  Częstochowa, 45, 149
  division of, 32–33
  Kraków, 5–6, 45–6, 62, 70, 91, 93–96,
    98, 100, 166, 212–23, 229
  Legionnaires of, 57, 234
  Łódź, 8–10, 32–33, 62, 96, 104, 207
  Lublin, 52, 124, 128, 227
  Lwów, 10, 33, 38, 41–43, 44, 58, 74, 76,
    192, 235, 244
  Ministry of Foreign Affairs of, 3, 10,
    160, 215
  National Council of, 150, 208
  Nowy Sącz, 70–71, 83, 85–86, 88–89,
    91, 93, 136, 265
  Oświęcim, 5–6
  Piwniczna, 70
  Poznań, 32–34, 64
  Puławy, 101, 103
  Przemyśl, 22
  Radom, 22
  Rawa Russka, 42
  and Red Cross, 25
  revolts against Russia, 13, 29
  Tarnopol, 13, 15–16
  Wacława, (code name for Warsaw), 137
  Warsaw, 12, 26–27, 98, 231, 235, 258
  Wilno, 33
  Zakopane, 46
  Zduńska Wola, 34
Polish government-in-exile, 53–54, 61,
  112, 114, 159–61, 165–66, 216, 223,
  225
  and Action N, 92, 94
  in Angers, 31, 34, 49–50, 56, 59, 69
  Bureau of Information and Propaganda
    (BIP), 98, 112, 114–17, 130–31
  and Christian Labor Party, 65
  and Communist activities in Poland,
    108–9, 114, 226
  fall of, 214, 220, 229, 233–35, 240–42
  and Gwardia Ludowa, 108
  reaction of to Holocaust, 143–44, 152,
    211–12, 238, 287–90n, 292–93n
  in London, 97, 99, 107–10, 130, 138
  and National Party, 64, 66, 70, 80
  and Peasant Party, 64, 96, 130
  and Polish underground, 27, 29–30, 51,
    63–66
  and Political Coordinating Committee,
    64–65
  and Socialist Party, 64, 66, 94, 108,
    206
  and Soviet relations, 179–81, 189,
    192–93
  and Union for Armed Struggle (Home
    Army), 64, 107–9, 140, 171, 185, 199
Poltava, U.S.S.R., 16

Poole, DeWitt, 237
Portugal, 109, 191
Poster, William, 226
Poznań, Poland, 32–34, 64
Prawda, 107
Prešov, Slovakia, 74–75, 82, 84, 265
Przemyśl, Poland, 22
Przytycki, Kuba, 37
Publisher's Weekly, 236
Pużak, Kazimierz, 64–65

Raczkiewicz, Władysław, 119, 156, 265,
  289n
Raczyński, Count Edward, 144, 154, 157–
  77, 265
Radio Free Europe, 220, 250
Radom, Poland, 22
Rajchman, Henryk Floyar, 234
Rankowicz, Captain, 12
Ratajski, Cyryl, 113, 117
Rathbone, Eleanor, 179
Ravensbrück, 89, 199
  See also Concentration/Extermination
    camps
Rawa Russka, Poland, 42
Red Cross
  International, 180, 262
  Polish, 25
Reeves, Emery, 224–28, 231–32, 236, 239
Renee (wartime girlfriend of Karski),
  101–2, 135, 155, 164
Representation of Polish Jewry, 207, 219,
  211
Retinger, Józef, 166–69, 172, 177, 184–85,
  208, 221–22, 265, 292n
Rejtan, Tadeusz, 167
Revisionists, 115
Riegner telegram, 145, 187, 265
Ringelblum, Emanuel, 211
Robbins, Jerome, 239, 306n
Roberts, Frank, 173
Rochester, NY, 236
Rogers, James, 184, 191
Romania, 4, 10, 13, 31, 258
Roosevelt, Eleanor, 194
Roosevelt, Franklin D. (FDR), 163, 181–
  82, 184–88, 216, 218–19, 265
  Karski meets with, 196–202
  Stanisław Mikołajczyk meets with,
    229–31
Rowecki, Stefan (Grot, Kalina), 64, 140,
  186, 265
Royal Victoria Patriotic Schools (RVPS),
  142, 147, 149
Russia
  See Soviet Union
Ryś, Zbigniew, 85–88, 265
Rysiówna, Zofia, 70, 84–86, 89, 266

Sambórski, Bogdan, 101, 139
Savery, Frank, 160–62, 165, 168, 170, 172–73, 266
San River, 22
Saturday Review of Literature, 236
Schutzstaffel (SS), 78–80, 129, 144
  See also Himmler, Heinrich
Schwarzbart, Ignacy, 150–51, 177–78, 199, 208–9, 266, 288–89n
Scott, Malcolm, 142–43
Selborne, Lord (Roundell Cecil Palmer, Earl of Selborne), 170–72, 266
Senegal, 249
Shirer, William L., 195
Shoah, 254
  See also Lanzmann, Claude
Siemiątkowska, Madame, 101–3
Sikorski, General Władysław, 31, 40, 44, 50, 55–59, 61, 234, 266
  supports Jews, 119, 147–49, 153, 212
  and Soviet relations, 172–74, 179, 181–82, 184–86
  Poles support, 97, 190
  visits U.S., 161–67
Silverman, Sydney, 146–47, 153
Singapore, 249
Siudak, Paweł, 50, 147–49, 160, 266
Sławik, Danuta, 91–94, 229, 232, 266
Sławik, Lucjan, 92–94
Słonimski, Antoni, 217
Slovakia, 46–47, 56, 62, 71, 81, 96, 101, 232, 258
  Demjata, 72
  Dobšina, 48
  Kapušany, 74
  Prešov, 74–75, 82, 84, 265
  Stara Lubovna, 70–71
  See also Czechoslovakia
Słowikowski, Jan, 86, 89, 266
Słowikowski, Teodor, 89
Sobibor, 104, 150
  See also Concentration/Extermination camps
Sodalicja Mariańska, 9, 32
Sosnkowski, General Kazimierz, 41, 51, 57–59, 61, 176, 266
South Korea, 248–49
South Vietnam, 248–49
Soviet Russia Today, 239
Soviet Union, 13, 76, 97, 108, 162–63, 173, 194, 217, 220, 228–30, 238
  Bolsheviks, 53, 193, 198
  and treatment of Jews, 41
  Kalinin, 21
  KGB, 17
  Kharkov, 21
  Kiev, 16
  NKVD, 17–21

and nonaggression pact with Germany, 14
and partition of Poland, 22
Politburo, 21
Poltava, 16
and prisoner swap, 19–20
Red Army, 13, 33, 53, 109–10, 165, 196, 241, 245, 249
secret police, 109
Stalingrad, 165
Spain, 109, 138–39
  Algeciras, 142
  Barcelona, 140
  Gilbraltar, 142, 181, 186
  Madrid, 140–41
Special Operations Executive, U.K., 110, 141–42, 171, 173
Stalin, Joseph, 214, 224, 246
  and Allies, 173, 196, 200–201
  and border with Poland, 108, 192–94, 217–20
  and relations with Poland, 97, 114, 161–63, 165, 179–82, 208, 229–31, 234–35
Stalingrad, 165
Stanisławów, 198–99
  See also Concentration/Extermination camps
Staniszewski, Msgr. Władysław, 149, 157, 266
Starzyński, Stefan, 28–29, 32, 266
State Department, U.S.
  See Department of State, U.S.
Stevenson, Adlai, 251
Stimson, Henry, 205
Story of a Secret State, 212, 229, 232, 234–26, 239, 245–46
Strich, Archbishop Samuel A., 213–14
Sullivan, Ed, 236
Surzycki, Tadeusz, 70, 75, 80
Sweden, 109, 236, 256
Światło, Józef, 247
Świętochowski, Ryszard (Pan Ryszard; Mr. Richard), 40, 55–56, 63, 266
"Świt," 158–59, 216, 267
Switzerland, 4, 12, 74, 140, 211
  Bern, 140
  Geneva, 74, 76, 94, 145, 168
Szafran, Tadeusz, 87, 89, 267

Tangye, Derek, 178
Tarnopol, Poland, 13, 15–16
Tatra Mountains, 46–47, 70
Teheran, 181, 193, 218, 220
Temple, Shirley, 232
Thailand, 248
Time, 224, 236
Toledo, OH, 236

Tolstoy, Alexei, 179
Topeka, KN, 236
Topolski, Feliks, 178, 252
Treblinka, 104–5, 143, 150, 198
    See also Concentration/Extermination
    camps
Tunisia, 249
Turkey, 248–49

Ukraine, 16, 20, 42
Union for Armed Struggle (Home Army;
    Związek Walki Zbrojnej; ZWZ), 27,
    29–30, 51, 63–66, 107–9, 140, 171,
    185, 199, 261, 267
United States, 238, 242, 246, 256
    Department of State, 146, 153, 182,
    190, 194, 242, 244–45, 247–49, 258
    Foreign Nationalities Branch, 237
    Office of Strategic Services (OSS), 141,
    181–84, 191–92, 194, 202, 213, 237,
    241, 297n
    See also Central Intelligence Agency;
    Department of State, U.S.; Federal
    Bureau of Investigation; Office of
    Strategic Services; War Refugee
    Board
USSR
    See Soviet Union
Utica, NY, 231

Vatican, 106
Versailles Treaties, 11
Vichy Regime (France), 138
Vigilance Gazette, 89
Virtuti Militari, 164
Volksdeutsche, 6, 24
von Ribbentrop, Joachim, 173

Wałęsa, Lech, 257, 259
Waldman, Morris, 208–9, 211–12, 214,
    302n
Wallace, Henry, 195
Walsh, Father Edmund, 205, 244–46, 267
War Refugee Board, U.S., 201

Warsaw, Poland, 12, 26–27, 98, 231, 235,
    258
Warsaw Ghetto, 102, 104–5, 148, 200,
    209, 211, 259
    conditions in, 121–25, 127, 132, 143,
    150–52, 188–89, 254–55
    resistance in, 115–16, 228, 281–82n
Washington, D.C., 163, 179, 181–85, 192–
    93, 209, 213–15, 218, 224, 229, 231,
    245, 247, 251
Washington Post, 224, 236
Weeks, Edward, 236
Weinberg, Dr. and Mrs., 102–4, 209, 267,
    277–78n
Wells, H. G., 217–18
Welles, Sumner, 195
Widerszal, Ludwik, 280n
Wiesel, Elie, 255, 267
Wilkinson, Peter, 173
Wilner, Arie, 116–17
Wilno, Poland, 33
Wilson, Hugh, 241
Wise, Rabbi Stephen, 146, 199, 207–8,
    210, 212, 267
Witold, 65–66, 102, 106, 113, 120, 124,
    137, 139, 264, 267
    See also Karski, Jan
Woburn Abbey, 159
Wofford, Harris, 232
Woliński, Henryk, 280n
World Jewish Congress, 145–46, 150, 154,
    187, 207–8

Yalta, 193, 238, 240
Youth Legion (Polish), 10, 51, 57
Yugoslavia, 49

Zakopane, Poland, 46
Zduńska Wola, Poland, 34
Zionism, 115–21, 156, 228, 267
Ziółkowski, Jan Leon, 19
"Znamirowski," 267
    See also Karski, Jan
Zygielbojm, Szmul, 150–53, 259, 267